DISASTERS AND THE LAW
KATRINA AND BEYOND

DISASTERS AND THE LAW
KATRINA AND BEYOND

Daniel A. Farber
University of California, Berkeley

Jim Chen
University of Minnesota

PUBLISHERS

76 Ninth Avenue, New York, NY 10011
http://lawschool.aspenpublishers.com

Printed in the United States of America.

1 2 3 4 5 6 7 8 9 0

ISBN 0-7355-6228-8

Library of Congress Cataloging-in-Publication Data

Farber, Daniel A., 1950-
    Disasters and the law : Katrina and beyond / Daniel A. Farber, Jim Chen.
        p. cm. -- (Aspen elective series)
    Includes index.
    ISBN 0-7355-6228-8
1. Disaster relief--Law and legislation--United States. 2. Emergency management--Law and legislation--United States. 3. Natural disasters--Law and legislation--United States. 4. Insurance, Disaster--Law and legislation--United States. 5. Hazard mitigation--Law and legislation--United States. 6. Assistance in emergencies--United States. 7. Hurricane protection--Government policy--United States. 8. Disasters--Social aspects. 9. Hurricane Katrina, 2005. I. Chen, Jim, 1966- II. Title.

    KF3750.F37 2006
    344.7305'348--dc22

                                                                2006022487

About Aspen Publishers

Aspen Publishers, headquartered in New York City, is a leading information provider for attorneys, business professionals, and law students. Written by preeminent authorities, our products consist of analytical and practical information covering both U.S. and international topics. We publish in the full range of formats, including updated manuals, books, periodicals, CDs, and online products.

Our proprietary content is complemented by 2,500 legal databases, containing over 11 million documents, available through our Loislaw division. Aspen Publishers also offers a wide range of topical legal and business databases linked to Loislaw's primary material. Our mission is to provide accurate, timely, and authoritative content in easily accessible formats, supported by unmatched customer care.

To order any Aspen Publishers title, go to *http://lawschool.aspenpublishers.com* or call 1-800-638-8437.

To reinstate your manual update service, call 1-800-638-8437.

For more information on Loislaw products, go to *www.loislaw.com* or call 1-800-364-2512.

For Customer Care issues, e-mail *CustomerCare@aspenpublishers.com*; call 1-800-234-1660; or fax 1-800-901-9075.

Aspen Publishers
a Wolters Kluwer business

To my mother, Annette Farber Holland,
who taught me always to expect the worst.

D.A.F.

To Kathleen, with love.

J.C.

SUMMARY OF CONTENTS

CONTENTS

PREFACE

Why a book on disaster law? The reason is simple: It is hard to think of anything equally important that has received such little sustained attention from lawyers and law professors. Hurricane Katrina alone will involve at least a hundred billion dollars in compensation, insurance, and rebuilding efforts, and lawyers will be heavily involved for at least the remainder of the decade in disputes over these funds. Yet, legal thinkers have done little to think through in advance the issues posed by major disasters. Nor have law schools done much to prepare law students to deal with these issues in their later careers.

Part of the reason is that we are all stunned by each new disaster, but rapidly come to view it as exceptional and never to be repeated. Thus, we fail to prepare for the next one. Unfortunately, there is no reason at all to think that Katrina is the last word in disasters. Indeed, current projections regarding global warming indicate an increasing number of major weather disasters, which is consistent with the record of Katrina, Rita, and other major storms of the 2005 hurricane season.

Apart from its practical significance, disaster law also deserves more attention because of its intellectual challenges. At first glance, disaster law seems to be nothing but a collection of legal rules of various kinds that happen to come into play when communities have suffered severe physical damage. But at a deeper level, disaster law is about assembling the best portfolio of legal rules to deal with catastrophic risks—a portfolio that includes prevention, emergency response, compensation and insurance, and rebuilding strategies. Because of this unifying theme, we think that the topic is deserving of serious law school attention even beyond its newsworthy qualities.

The first half of the book is about the Katrina disaster itself. In the introductory chapter, we provide an overview of the issues raised by Katrina and of the evolution of modern disaster law. Chapter 2 explores federalism issues. Beginning with the great Mississippi flood in the 1920s, the federal government has played an ever-increasing role in disaster prevention and relief. As Katrina illustrated, however, the lines between federal and state authority remain unclear, which can sometimes impede responses. Chapter 3 turns to the topic of social vulnerabilities and disaster law. Whole communities feel the impact of disasters, but not everyone feels the impact equally. All too often, the most heavily impacted are those who are most socially vulnerable to begin with. Chapter 4 considers the emergency response to Katrina, a topic that has already given rise to extensive reports by committees in both Houses of Congress and by the White House. Obviously, this phase went very badly in New Orleans, and we ask what went wrong and how the system could be improved.

The second half of the book looks beyond Katrina and its immediate aftermath toward the future. There are limits to how successfully we can prevent harm from disasters. When the harm occurs, the next question is compensation, which is the subject of Chapter 5. Should we use private insurance, government programs, or the tort system to provide a safety net for victims? Chapter 6 turns to the question of disaster mitigation. Disasters usually take place in areas that are already known to be at risk. Beyond the question of immediate response is a long-term issue: how to mitigate the potential impacts of natural disasters or terrorist acts, so as to limit the damage. While less dramatic than emergency response, mitigation may be far more valuable in the long run. Chapter 7 returns to Katrina to discuss the looming question of how to rebuild the city and the flood control system. In Chapter 8, we consider future disasters. Unfortunately, Hurricane Katrina is unlikely to be the last disaster to confront our society. Future hurricanes, earthquakes, floods, pandemics, and terrorist acts may well lie in wait for us. This chapter considers some of the challenges posed by these risks.

We are indebted to a number of individuals for their help in preparing this book on a very abbreviated schedule. We learned a great deal from the students who took our hastily assembled seminars on Katrina at Minnesota and Berkeley. Steve Errick suggested the idea of publishing the materials that we had already assembled for the seminars. Jessica Yarnall, Monami Chakrabarti, Kevin Wells, Nicole Harris, Tony Jones, Liz Kiechle, and especially Jenna Musselman provided important research assistance. The Boalt library staff worked tirelessly to help assemble our website, www.law.berkeley.edu/library/disasters.html. We owe particular thanks there to Michael Lindsey, Linda Kawaguchi McLane, Jenna Musselman, Dean Rowan, Kathleen Vanden Heuvel, and Alice Youman. We received useful comments from Ann Carlson, Oliver Houck, Andrea Peterson, Bob Rabin, Steve Sugarman, and Rob Verchick. We learned a great deal from Bob Bea and Ray Seed about levees and their flaws. Mary Elliott and Laurie Newbauer worked ably on preparing the book for publication. Finally, the usual thanks to family for their patience apply to an even greater degree here. Both of us had full schedules when Hurricane Katrina struck, and our families bore the brunt of this additional demand on our time and energy.

Dan Farber
Jim Chen

August 2006

ACKNOWLEDGMENTS

We are grateful to the following sources for their permission to reprint excerpts of their scholarship:

Association of State Floodplain Managers, Inc., *Hurricanes Katrina & Rita: Using Mitigation to Rebuild a Safer Gulf Coast*, (2005). Used by permission.

Brian Kamoie, *The National Response Plan: A New Framework for Homeland Security, Public Health, and Bioterrorism Response*, 38 J. Health L. 287 (2005). Reprinted with permission from American Health Lawyers Association.

CPR's *Unnatural Disaster: The Aftermath of Hurricane Katrina*, by Member Scholars of the Center for Progressive Reform, White Paper 512, September 2005, or the executive summary to the piece, entitled, *Unnatural Disaster*. Reprinted with permission.

David R. Hodas, *State Law Responses to Global Warming: Is it Constitutional to Think Globally and Act Locally?*, 21 Pace Environmental Law Review 53 (2003). Reprinted with permission.

Donald A. Brown, *The U.S. Performance in Achieving its 1992 Earth Summit Global Warming Commitments*, 32 Environmental Law Reporter 10, 741 (2002). © 2002 Environmental Law Institute. Reprinted with permission from the Environmental Law Reporter. All rights reserved.

Donna E. Arzt, *Sound and Fury: Katrina and the "Refugees" Debate*. available at Jurist Legal News & Research, http://jurist.law.pitt.edu/forumy/2005/10/sound-and-fury-katrina-and-refugees.php (Oct. 3, 2005). Reprinted with permission.

Edward L. Glaeser, *Should the Government Rebuild New Orleans, or Just Give Residents Checks?* In the Economist's Voice, Vol. 2, No. 4, Article 4 (2005), 1-6. available at http://www.bepress.com/ev/vol2/iss4/art4i. Reprinted with permission.

Elaine Enarson, *Women and Girls Last? Averting the Second Post-Katrina Disaster*. available at http://understandingkatrina.ssrc.org/Enarson (Nov. 15, 2005). Reprinted with permission.

Ernest B. Abbott, Otto J. Hetzel & Alan D. Cohn, *State, Local, and First Responder Issues*. Hurricane Katrina Task Force Subcommittee Report (February 2006), a publication by the ABA Standing Committee on Law & National Security, the ABA Section of State & Local Government Law, and the ABA Section of Administrative and Regulatory Law, published online at www.abanet.org/natsecurity/scolns_hurricane_katrina_report_feb_2006_2.pdf. © 2006 by the American Bar Association. Reprinted with permission.

Human Rights Center, University of California, Berkeley, *After the Tsunami: Human Rights of Vulnerable Populations* (October 2005). Reprinted with permission.

John A. McCarthy, Randall Jackson & Maeve Dion, Posse Comitatus *and the Military's Role in Disaster Relief.* Hurricane Katrina Task Force Subcommittee Report (February 2006), a publication by the ABA Standing Committee on Law & National Security, the ABA Section of State & Local Government Law, and the ABA Section of Administrative and Regulatory Law, published online at www.abanet.org/natsecurity/scolns_hurricane_katrina_report_feb_2006_2.pdf. © 2006 by the American Bar Association. Reprinted with permission.

Martha Thompson & Izaskun Gaviria, OxfamAmerica, *Weathering the Storm: Lessons in Risk Reduction From Cuba*, (Apr. 2004), 6-26. Used by permission.

Oliver A. Houck, *Can We Save New Orleans?*, originally published in 19 Tul. Envtl. L.J. 1 (2006). Reprinted with the permission of the Tulane Environmental Law Journal, which holds the copyright.

Oliver A. Houck, *Rising Water: The National Flood Insurance Program and Louisiana*, originally published in 60 Tul. L. Rev. 61-164 (1985). Reprinted with the permission of the Tulane Law Review Association, which holds the copyright.

Robert Hahn, *The Economics of Rebuilding Cities: Reflections*, in the Economist's Voice, Vol. 2, No. 4, Article 1 (2005), 1-4. available at http://www.bepress.com/ev/vol2/iss4/artl. Reprinted with permission.

Robert L. Rabin & Suzanne A. Bratis, *Financial Compensation for Catastrophic Loss in the United States,* in Financial Compensation for Victims after Catastrophe, ED. M. Faure, T. Honlief, Springer Verlag 2005. available at http://ssrn.com.

Roberta Cohen, *Time for the United States to Honor International Standards in Emergencies,* The Brookings-Bern Project on Internal Displacement. available at http://www.brookings.edu/views/op-ed/cohenr/20050909.htm (Sept. 9, 2005). Reprinted with permission.

Roberts and Todd Wallace, *Action Plan for New Orleans: The New American City—Urban Planning Final Report,* dated Jan. 11, 2006, posted on Bring New Orleans Back website on 6/14/06. Published by Bring New Orleans Back Commission, Urban Planning Committee.

Stephen M. Griffin, *Did the Constitution Fail New Orleans? available at* http://balkin.blogspot.com/2005/10/did-constitution-fail-new-orleans-part.html, (posted October 12, 2005). Reprinted with permission.

Susan L. Cutter, *The Geography of Social Vulnerability: Race, Class, and Catastrophe.* available at http://understandingkatrina.ssrc.org/Cutter/ (Sept. 23, 2005). Reprinted with permission.

DISASTERS AND THE LAW
KATRINA AND BEYOND

INTRODUCTION

Sometime that night the winds came back. Everything in the world had a strong rattle, sharp and short * * * * [Janie] saw the drifting mists gathered in the west—that cloud field of the sky—to arm themselves with thunders and march forth against the world. Louder and higher and lower and wider the sound and motion spread, mounting, sinking, darking.

It woke up old Okechobee and the monster began to roll in his bed. Began to roll and complain like a peevish world on a grumble. The folks in the quarters and the people in the big houses further around the shore heard the big lake and wondered. The people felt uncomfortable but safe because there were the seawalls to chain the senseless monster in his bed. The folks let the people do the thinking. If the castles thought themselves secure, the cabins needn't worry. Their decision was already made as always. Chink up your cracks, shiver in your wet beds and wait on the mercy of the Lord. The bossman might have the thing stopped before morning anyway. It is so easy to be hopeful in the day time when you can see the things you wish on. But it was night, it stayed night. Night was striding across nothingness with the whole round world in his hands. * * *

They huddled closer and stared at the door. They just didn't use another part of their bodies, and they didn't look at anything but the door. The time was past for asking the white folks what to look for through that door. Six eyes were questioning God.

– Zora Neale Hurston[1]

Hurricane Katrina broke America's heart. No previous natural disaster in the nation's history exacted a grimmer toll. More than a thousand Americans died; another million evacuated the Gulf Coast. The legendary city of New Orleans all but sank when its levees failed and the resulting storm surge

---

1. ZORA NEALE HURSTON, THEIR EYES WERE WATCHING GOD 158-159 (Harper Perennial 2006; 1st ed. 1937).

drowned many of the city's feeblest, most vulnerable residents. The flood waters consumed the forlorn hope that the United States could rescue its citizens during their darkest and neediest hour.

The story of Katrina, in its often gruesome detail, forms the backdrop against which we have written this book. We recount this story as it has been told at the highest levels of the United States government—first as a sober factual account by the White House, then as the Senate's gripping narrative of personal survival, suffering, and heroism. The time will come when "the needles thick on the ground" Katrina covered "will deaden the footfall so that we shall move among trees as soundlessly as smoke." ROBERT PENN WARREN, ALL THE KING'S MEN 438 (Harvest 1996; 1st ed. 1946). "But that will be a long time from now, and soon now we shall go . . . into the convulsion of the world, out of history into history and the awful responsibility of Time." *Id.*

THE WHITE HOUSE

The Federal Response to Hurricane Katrina: Lessons Learned 5-9 (2006)

Hurricane Katrina was the most destructive natural disaster in U.S. history. The overall destruction wrought by Hurricane Katrina * * * vastly exceeded that of * * * the Chicago Fire of 1871, the San Francisco Earthquake and Fire of 1906, and Hurricane Andrew in 1992.

Seventy-five hurricanes of Katrina's strength at landfall—a Category 3— have hit the mainland United States since 1851, roughly once every two years. Yet Katrina was anything but a "normal" hurricane. First, Katrina was larger than most. Hurricane Camille, a Category 5 storm that devastated the Gulf Coast in 1969, had top wind speeds that exceeded those of Katrina upon landfall, but Camille's hurricane force winds only extended seventy-five miles from its center, whereas Katrina's extended 103 miles from its center. As a result, Hurricane Katrina's storm surge affected a larger area than did Hurricane Camille's. In all, Hurricane Katrina impacted nearly 93,000 square miles across 138 parishes and counties. The extreme intensity that Hurricane Katrina reached before landfall on the Gulf Coast, as well as its size, meant that its storm surge was consistent with a more powerful storm. In fact, * * * the height of Hurricane Katrina and Camille's respective storm surges were comparable to each other.

Hurricane Katrina's winds and a storm surge that crested up to twenty-seven feet high dealt a ferocious blow to homes, businesses, and property on the coast and for many miles inland. This storm surge overwhelmed levees all along the lowest reaches of the Mississippi River and the edges of Lake Pontchartrain. The consequences for New Orleans, which sits mostly below sea level, were dire. Significant levee failures occurred on the 17th Street Canal, the Industrial Canal, and the London Avenue Canal. Approximately 80 percent of the city was flooded.

The flooding destroyed New Orleans, the Nation's thirty-fifth largest city. Much as the fire that burned Chicago in 1871 and the earthquake and fire that leveled San Francisco in 1906 destroyed the economic and cultural centers of an entire region, so too did Hurricane Katrina destroy what many considered to be the heart of the Gulf Coast. The destruction also called to mind the Galveston Hurricane of 1900, which thoroughly devastated the town of Galveston, Texas. At the time, Galveston was an economic and cultural center of Texas and was the State's fourth largest city.

Even beyond New Orleans, Katrina's span of destruction was widespread. Indeed, one of the gravest challenges presented by this particular disaster was the vast geographic distribution of the damage. Towns and cities, small and large, were destroyed or heavily damaged up and down the Gulf Coast and miles inland. From Morgan City, Louisiana, to Biloxi, Mississippi, to Mobile, Alabama, Hurricane Katrina's wind, rain, and storm surge demolished homes and businesses. * * *

Hurricane Katrina contradicts one side of an important two-part trend. For at least a century, America's most severe natural disasters have become steadily less deadly and more destructive of property (adjusted for inflation). * * * Yet, Hurricane Katrina not only damaged far more property than any previous natural disaster, it was also the deadliest natural disaster in the United States since Hurricane San Felipe in 1928. * * *

Measuring Hurricane Katrina: The Path of Destruction

Estimating disaster damage is not an exact science * * * . Estimates vary but, considering property damage alone, Hurricane Katrina is America's first disaster—natural or man-made—to approach the $100 billion mark.

Housing	$67 billion
Consumer durable goods	$ 7 billion
Business property	$20 billion
Government property	$ 3 billion
Total	**$96 billion**

Table 1.1.   Estimated damage from Hurricane Katrina and the New Orleans flood

Hurricane Katrina devastated far more residential property than had any other recent hurricane, completely destroying or making uninhabitable an estimated 300,000 homes.

This far surpasses the residential damage of Hurricane Andrew, which destroyed or damaged approximately 80,000 homes in 1992. It even exceeds the combined damage of the four major 2004 hurricanes, Charley, Frances, Ivan, and Jeanne, which together destroyed or damaged approximately 85,000 homes. * * *

Hurricane Katrina's damage was extensive. The storm destroyed so many homes, buildings, forests, and green spaces that an extraordinary amount of debris was left behind—118 million cubic yards all told. In comparison, Hurricane Andrew created 20 million cubic yards of debris. The debris from Katrina, if stacked onto the space of a football field, would reach over ten and a half miles high.

Hurricane Katrina's effects on the economy have yet to be fully reckoned. The worst consequences were local: between August and September, the unemployment rate doubled from 6 to 12 percent in the most affected areas of Louisiana and Mississippi. In Louisiana, Mississippi, and Alabama, salaries and wages fell by an estimated $1.2 billion in the third quarter of 2005. But short-term, economic ripples reached the entire country through the rising cost of gasoline. The approach of the storm forced the temporary shutdown of most crude oil and natural gas production in the Gulf of Mexico. In the immediate wake of Hurricane Katrina, gasoline prices rose sharply nationwide. The combined effects of Hurricane Katrina and Hurricane Rita, which made landfall on the border between Texas and Louisiana early on September 24, 2005, were such that, between August 26, 2005, and January 11, 2006, 114 million barrels of oil production capacity were left unused, equivalent to over one-fifth of yearly output in the Gulf of Mexico.

The storm devastated the regional power infrastructure. In Louisiana, Mississippi, and Alabama, approximately 2.5 million power customers reported outages. * * *

Communications suffered as well. The storm crippled thirty-eight 911 call centers, disrupting local emergency services, and knocked out more than 3 million customer phone lines in Louisiana, Mississippi, and Alabama. Broadcast communications were likewise severely affected, as 50 percent of area radio stations and 44 percent of area television stations went off the air.

Much more than any other hurricane, Katrina's wrath went far beyond wind and water damage. In fact, Hurricane Katrina caused at least ten oil spills, releasing the same quantity of oil as some of the worst oil spills in U.S. history. Louisiana reported at least six major spills of over 100,000 gallons and four medium spills of over 10,000 gallons. All told, more than 7.4 million gallons poured into the Gulf Coast region's waterways, over two-thirds of the amount that spilled out during America's worst oil disaster, the rupturing of the *Exxon Valdez* tanker off the Alaskan coast in 1989.

The wave of destruction created environmental and health hazards across the affected region, including standing water, oil pollution, sewage, household and industrial chemicals, and both human and animal remains. The storm surge struck 466 facilities that handle large amounts of dangerous chemicals, thirty-one hazardous waste sites, and sixteen Superfund toxic waste sites, three of which flooded. The surge also destroyed or compromised 170 drinking water facilities and dozens of wastewater treatment facilities.

Most terrible of all and most difficult to measure, however, were Hurricane Katrina's human effects.

Measuring the Immeasurable: The Human Toll

When the winds and floods of Hurricane Katrina subsided, an estimated 1,330 people were dead as a result of the storm. The vast majority of the fatalities—an estimated 80 percent—came from the New Orleans metropolitan area; Mississippi suffered greatly as well, with 231 fatalities. Many of the dead were elderly or infirm. In Louisiana, approximately 71 percent of the victims were older than sixty, and 47 percent of those were over seventy-five. At least sixty-eight were found in nursing homes, some of whom were allegedly abandoned by their caretakers. Of the total known fatalities, there are almost two hundred unclaimed bodies remaining at the Victim Identification Center in Carville, Louisiana. As awful as these horrifying statistics are, unfortunately they are not the end of the story. As of February 17, 2006, there were still 2,096 people from the Gulf Coast area reported missing.

For the survivors, the aftermath of Hurricane Katrina has been characterized by a mixture of grief, anxiety, and frustration. Around 770,000 people were displaced—the largest since the Dust Bowl migration from the southern Great Plains region in the 1930s. After Hurricane Katrina, housing options often arrived slowly to those who could not return to their ruined homes; by the end of October, there were still more than 4,500 people staying in shelters. * * *

Moreover, many victims found it difficult to reconstruct their shattered lives. In many cases, they had either lost or forgotten basic documents, such as insurance information, birth certificates, and marriage licenses, which would later prove essential to rebuilding their lives. Most of the evacuees did not have access to their medical records, which increased the risk of complications when receiving medical treatment. For those who returned to their homes in the Gulf region, basic services were still wanting. By January, 85 percent of public schools in Orleans parish had still not reopened; in the metropolitan area, approximately two-thirds of the retail food establishments, half of the bus routes, and half of the major hospitals remained closed. For Katrina's victims, a sense of "back to normal" still seems far away.

Of the 1.1 million people over the age of sixteen who evacuated in August 2005, approximately 500,000 of those evacuees had not returned home by late December. For the evacuees who have not returned to their homes, jobs have been scarce. Their unemployment rate was just below 28 percent in November and over 20 percent in December. The former evacuees who did return to their homes in the Gulf region had better access to work with an unemployment rate of 12.5 percent in November, which fell to 5.6 percent in December. In July, before Katrina hit, the unemployment rate in the most affected areas of Louisiana and Mississippi had been 6 percent.

By any measure, Hurricane Katrina was a national catastrophe. Similar to the images of grief and destruction on September 11, 2001, the images of suffering and despair from Hurricane Katrina are forever seared into the hearts and memories of all Americans.

UNITED STATES SENATE COMMITTEE ON HOMELAND SECURITY AND GOVERNMENTAL AFFAIRS

Hurricane Katrina: A Nation Still Unprepared 1-1 to 1-14, 2-1 to 2-2 (2006)

In the early morning of Monday, August 29, 2005, Hurricane Katrina came ashore in southern Louisiana, changing American history. Since September 11, 2001, when two American cities suffered devastating attacks, the

United States had been working to better protect itself. Almost four years and billions of dollars later, Katrina destroyed an entire region, killing more than 1,500, leaving hundreds of thousands homeless, and ravaging one of America's most storied cities.

Katrina revealed that this country remains ill-prepared to respond to a catastrophe. More should have been done to prepare before the storm and to mitigate the suffering that followed: More to save lives; more to evacuate the most vulnerable citizens; more to move the victims to safety earlier; more to get aid to affected areas sooner. Before the storm, government planning was incomplete and preparation was often ineffective, inadequate, or both. Afterward, government responses were often tentative, bureaucratic, or inert. These failures resulted in unnecessary suffering. * * *

Hurricane Katrina laid waste to 90,000 square miles of land, an area the size of the United Kingdom. At its fiercest, the storm extended for 460 miles, nearly the distance from Kansas City to Dallas. As the Mississippi Gulf Coast's Sun-Herald pointed out, "the world's fastest river rapids move at about 10 to 12 feet per second," challenging even experienced athletes protected by kayaks and life jackets. At about only a third of its strength, Katrina's storm surge—the swell of water snowballed by a storm approaching shore—"could have been moving as fast as 16 feet per second."

Though Katrina made landfall as a Category 3 storm * * *, it had begun driving storm surge in the Gulf of Mexico, when it had been a Category 5. As a result, Katrina brought ashore surge that reached as high as 27 feet above normal sea levels in Mississippi and between 18 and 25 feet in Louisiana. By contrast, New Orleans had no levees or flood walls higher than 17 feet. Though levees had begun to breach as early as landfall, overtopping of the levees may have caused an equal amount of damage.

Citizens and government officials alike knew that it was only a matter of time before a hurricane inundated the Gulf Coast—especially New Orleans, which lies as much as 10 feet below sea level, and continues to sink an inch every three years. (Meanwhile, wave-slowing marshlands and barrier islands in coastal Louisiana erode by 10 square miles a year—losing the area of a football field every 30 minutes—due to flood-control constraints on the Mississippi River, which prevent it from depositing sediments to replenish the subsiding soils.)

For years, meteorologists and emergency-management and government officials had referred to it, simply, as the "New Orleans scenario." In 1965, Hurricane Betsy, also a Category 3, had provided a preview of Katrina when, in the memorable words of Louisiana's then-U.S. Senator Russell Long, it "picked up the lake [Pontchartrain] . . . and put it inside New Orleans and Jefferson Parish." When Hurricane Andrew leveled parts of south Florida in 1992, Dr. Robert Sheets, then the head of the National Weather Service, reminded Congressional investigators that the country had actually been lucky —for a while afterward, the storm looked like it was making way for New Orleans. * * *

Andrew had come "within a gnat's eyelash of being our nightmare and the big one," he [told the Committee on Governmental Affairs]. Dr. Sheets displayed a computer projection of what Andrew's storm surge would have done had the hurricane's track shifted slightly and hit New Orleans directly. It showed the hurricane whipping the waters of Lake Borgne, on the eastern side of the city, and Lake Pontchartrain, on the northern edge of the city, over the city's levees.

Katrina would follow this very pattern 12 years later. "The city will be under 20 feet of water," Dr. Sheets predicted.

In 1998, Hurricane Georges narrowly missed New Orleans, striking Mississippi and Alabama instead. Roused by the close call, local emergency-management planners began to seek federal funding for a massive exercise to consider the potential impact of a direct strike on New Orleans by a slow-moving—and, therefore, more damaging, by virtue of its longer duration—Category 3 hurricane. That funding did not arrive for five years. The effort, known as the Hurricane Pam exercise, finally began in 2004, and tried to address the consequences of a Katrina-like hurricane as developed by government scientists and emergency-management officials and contractors: Widespread flooding; 67,000 dead; 200,000 to 300,000 in need of evacuation after landfall, and hundreds of thousands displaced in need of shelter, exceeding state and local capabilities; hospitals and nursing homes overcrowded and short on critical resources; and incapacitated first responders. Sadly, Katrina proved many of these predictions true.

Katrina formed on August 23, 2005, 200 miles southeast of the Bahamas. Within 24 hours, it had been designated Tropical Storm Katrina by the National Hurricane Center. Two days later, it became a Category 1 hurricane, just two hours before striking the Florida coast between Fort Lauderdale and Miami. By early afternoon on Friday, August 26, Max Mayfield, the director of the National Hurricane Center, and fellow forecasters in the Miami headquarters and regional offices throughout the Gulf Coast believed Katrina might be heading toward New Orleans.

Dr. Mayfield called his friend Dr. Walter Maestri, the emergency-preparedness director of Jefferson Parish, on the western edge of New Orleans. " 'This is it,'" Maestri recalled Mayfield saying. "'This is what we've been talking about all of these years. It's a 30-90 storm.'" * * * "That's the [latitude] and [longitude] of the city of New Orleans," Maestri explained. Beginning with that phone call, Dr. Mayfield and other forecasters embarked on a round of urgent communications * * *.

Ordinary citizens, as well as their leaders in local, state, and federal government knew that Katrina was coming. But few could imagine the impact. By the time Katrina subsided, it had taken with it the Gulf Coast as its 9.5 million residents knew it. * * *

Katrina carried away not only police cruisers and homes, but also the instruments of daily life. "All our medical records, all the legal documents," Lynn Christiansen, a housewife in St. Bernard Parish, recounted. "My safety deposit was under water for three weeks." * * *

Katrina turned first responders—police, medical personnel, etc.—into some of the storm's first victims. As the storm pummeled New Orleans, some 80 police officers—5 percent of the city's force—were stranded at home * * * *

"Almost every dispatcher and 911 operator [in the New Orleans police department's emergency operations center] was crying, [said superintendent Warren Riley]. "I did not know that only moments earlier, the Industrial Street Canal levee breached and had an almost 200-yard opening and water was now pouring into the Lower Ninth Ward. . . . It went from nothing to as high as 14 feet within 23 minutes. We had 600 911 calls within the first 23 minutes. . . . But [the 911 dispatchers and operators] were powerless to assist. . . . We still had sustained winds in excess of 100 miles per hour." * * *

Most of the people in the area, civilians and officials alike, could talk to no one at all. Telephone lines were down. Switching stations were flooded. Radio and cell-phone towers had been knocked out. Some emergency personnel had to rely on runners to relay messages. As Mississippi Governor Haley Barbour described it, "My head of the National Guard might as well [have] been a Civil War general for the first two or three days, because he could only find out what was going on by sending somebody."

On Saturday, a day before New Orleans Mayor Ray Nagin would order the first mandatory evacuation of New Orleans in the city's history, city residents had begun to evacuate using a system known as contraflow, which converts incoming highway lanes to outbound to expedite evacuation. More than a million residents of southeastern Louisiana left the area in just over 24 hours, a marked improvement over the 12-15 hour bottlenecks that stalled the evacuation before Hurricane Ivan in 2004.

Those delays, coupled with the fact that Ivan—initially a Category 5 storm that came within 135 miles of New Orleans—banked eastward at the last moment, persuaded some to remain behind this time.

Gulf Coast residents call it "hurricane roulette." Some who had endured 1969's Category 5 Hurricane Camille, the region's benchmark for catastrophic storms, thought that no other storm could come close. But Katrina ended lifetimes of successful storm-dodging. * * * As Biloxi city spokesman Vincent Creel said of Camille survivors lulled into a false sense of security, Hurricane Camille killed more people in 2005 than it did in 1969.

In many cases, however, hubris or miscalculation had nothing to do with why some stayed behind. Katrina struck in the very last days of August, when those living check-to-check were running out of their bi-weekly or monthly allotments. Tens of thousands didn't have cars. Even many who did may not have been able to shoulder the costs of evacuation; the average cost for three days for a family of four, including lodging, food, and transportation, could easily exceed a thousand dollars * * *. For the poor of neighborhoods like the Lower Ninth Ward, one of the city's lowest-lying areas, this was an impossible sum, though they had an alternative in the Superdome, the city's "refuge of last resort."

Nearly 100,000 New Orleanians either couldn't or didn't comply with Mayor Nagin's evacuation order. The city had no plan for evacuating them, and the Louisiana Department of Transportation and Development * * * had done nothing by the time of landfall. New Orleans' enterprising health department director, Dr. Kevin Stephens, had begun negotiating agreements with several transportation agencies, but they remained incomplete at the time of landfall. Federal officials, who had participated in the Pam exercise and knew that state and local authorities would need evacuation help, had no plans in place, either.

Bobbie Moreau, a legal secretary in Nairn, a small town in Plaquemines Parish, stayed at home because she didn't have the means to evacuate. She was with her daughter Tasha and Tasha's four-month-old daughter, who was born prematurely and required a heart monitor. Moreau woke up at 4 a.m. on Monday, just as the wind and storm surge preceding Katrina's eye were reaching shore. "The pressure was so bad in the house, I opened a crack in the living room window," she recalled. When she walked into the den, she saw water pouring through the grout in the marble tile that lined a part of the wall. By the time she had climbed to the second floor, the water had risen halfway up the stairs. Moreau could see her living-room furniture floating.

"I shut the door upstairs, I guess thinking I could shut the water out," she said. "From then it was a nightmare. I held the baby at the foot of the bed fanning her. The pressure was awful; we thought the windows were going to pop. We got on our knees and prayed and begged God to save us.

"Then I felt the water under me on the second floor. . . . I got up and walked to the window and the water was right under the window. My legs felt like Jell-O, I staggered. My daughter screamed, 'Mama, what's wrong?' I knew at that moment we were going to die."

But "in an instant, survival kicked in." Moreau tore the canopy from the bed and tied knots so that she and Tasha could hold on to each other. She used a belt to create a makeshift life jacket for the baby. With the water halfway up the bed, they climbed out onto the roof, managing to take along Moreau's three dogs. "The eye of the hurricane was on us," Moreau recalled. "I told my daughter, you will have to swim and get a boat, I am too weak. She said, 'Mama, I'm scared.' There was dead animals floating by, snakes, debris, oil. I told her, 'We will die if you don't.' She handed me the baby and slipped into the water. . . . Then I lost sight of her and called and called because the wind was picking up.

"And then I knew it was the eye. Nothing but silence. I thought she had drowned. I was crying and praying. And then I heard an outboard motor start up. And I knew she was alive.

"Where she pulled [up] the boat, the power lines to the house was between us," Moreau continued. "I had to drop the baby through the power lines to her and the dogs and then myself. By then, the wind was so hard, we could not control the boat with the motors. . . . We came to a stop in the top of some little trees. We huddled under the steering wheel with the baby because a window was broke out of the cabin. We stayed there for about 6-7 hours. The wind would almost turn the boat over and we sang and prayed. . . . It was so weird. Felt like we were the only people left in the world, everything covered by water."

Around the same time, at Hancock Medical Center in Bay St. Louis, Mississippi, the first floor was beginning to flood. Patients would have to be moved upstairs. Staffers managed to use the elevator to move a 600-pound, non-ambulatory patient to safety before flood waters damaged the hospital generators. Physicians and service staff carried the remaining patients up-stairs on their backs. The first floor quickly filled with three feet of water, disabling and washing away equipment.

The Hancock staff had considered evacuating its 34 patients, but eventu-ally decided to "shelter in place." In the past, patients had deteriorated and even died while languishing in evacuation gridlock, some of it in response to storm warnings that turned out to be false alarms. But few hospitals had the resources to withstand the assault of a storm like Katrina, and, as the Hurri-cane Pam exercise predicted, became victims themselves. State governments had failed to address the problem prior to the storm. In Louisiana, the De-partment of Health and Hospitals required nursing homes to have evacuation plans, but did not require the institutions to actually follow them.

On the second floor of Hancock, patients were treated in the hall, as wind and rain prevented the use of patient rooms. Because the water pumps failed, staff had to use buckets of water to flush toilets. Maintenance staff hung multi-colored emergency glowlights to mark the way down corridors and stairwells. Because communications were down, no one knew whether their loved ones had made it.

Forty miles away, at Ocean Springs Hospital, physicians struggled with dwindling supplies and an increasing number of patients. "We couldn't ster-ilize anything because there was no power," said Dr. Bill Passarelli, a cardi-ologist who was on duty as Katrina came ashore. "There were only like two surgical packets left. So unless somebody was absolutely going to die, you weren't going to surgery." * * *

The first fatalities arrived at around 5 p.m., before the wind had died down. [Dr. Jeff Bass, an emergency-room doctor, said:] "A friend who was a police officer told me that every bayou and every waterway had bodies in them, and that they were pulling bodies from the trees. . . . Our morgue only holds two people. We had living people to worry about. At about 6 o'clock I wrote * * * 'DON'T BRING US ANY MORE DEAD BODIES. WE DON'T HAVE ENOUGH ROOM FOR THE LIVING PEOPLE.'"

"I had always dreamed of working for Doctors Without Borders and going to a Third World country right after a disaster," Dr. Bass said. "Never in my wildest dreams did I think I would experience that without leaving my home."

At Hancock, survivors who had injured themselves clinging to trees or breaking out of their attics were also beginning to trickle in, many after walking for miles, others on makeshift stretchers, as ambulances had been washed away. Staff treated 850 new patients during the next 48 hours. Though a Hancock medical specialist had e-mailed the director of the Na-tional Disaster Medical System less than 24 hours after landfall that county authorities were "pulling bodies from trees," a federal Disaster Medical Assis-tance Team did not arrive until Wednesday evening. * * *

The Coast Guard performed heroically during Katrina, rescuing more than half of the 60,000 survivors who were stranded by the storm. (The Lou-isiana Department of Wildlife & Fisheries, the state's lead agency for search-and-rescue, similarly distinguished itself, rescuing much of the rest.) * * *

[T]he Coast Guard's first Katrina rescue, at 2:50 p.m. on the day of land-fall, came in response to "a Mayday from a frantic woman saying that her and her daughter . . . and her grandchild were stuck on a small boat in the middle of the city of Port Sulphur." It was Bobbie Moreau, who had managed to use the radio in the boat her daughter had found to summon the Coast Guard. * * *

As for many survivors of Katrina, the rescue hardly brought Moreau's ordeal to a close. The Coast Guard crew dropped off her and her family at West Jefferson Hospital in Jefferson Parish. "Barefoot, no purse, no money, no shoes," Moreau recalled. "My daughter went in with the baby. I sat on the curb crying." Soon, they were moved to a shelter. "There was over 100 people in one room. The heat was incredible, could not go outside with the baby for mosquitoes. We fanned her all night." Moreau appealed to a National Guardsman, but she said he told her they would be at the shelter for another week. "My daughter said, 'I am not going to let my baby die. We are going to walk out of here and get help.'"

According to Moreau, Jefferson Police tried to prevent her from leaving, presumably for her safety, but "I said, 'Do what you want to do, I have nothing left anyway.'" Moreau and her family snuck out when the police were distracted by a scuffle and hitched a ride to Westwego, on the west bank of the Mississippi River, where a friend lived. He had evacuated.

"I broke into his house, cooled the baby off, we took a shower and ate can food," Moreau said. "He had left his truck in the driveway. . . . [It] had no gas in it, and there was nowhere to buy gas, so I siphoned gas out of his boat, two gallons at a time, and put [it] into his truck. I left him a letter with my nephew's phone number [in Arkansas]. The only clothes he had that would fit us was boxer shorts and t-shirt, so that is what we left in. . . . We went across the Sunshine Bridge [across the Mississippi River], got to Prairieville, and my nephew picked us up. We had a hard time since then, but we made it."

In the Lower Ninth Ward, Reverend Leonard Lucas of Light City Church was trying to persuade dazed survivors to leave their homes. Parts of the neighborhood had flooded to the rooftops after weak levees on its west side gave way in two spots to water from Lake Borgne rushing down the Mississippi River Gulf Outlet. "We went house to house telling people they had to leave," Reverend Lucas recalled. "They kept coming and coming and coming. People were leaving everything and only taking a packed bag and their kids.

"Some people had pets and wouldn't leave them. I don't know how many people told me that their pet 'was all they had.' We kept telling everyone to go to Stallings Park in the Upper Ninth * * *. It was a steady flow of people marching like zombies to the park." The less fortunate who were stranded on rooftops sometimes remained there for days awaiting rescue.

Some of the rescues were performed by volunteers who came to help in the wake of the storm. The assistance was unorganized and frustrated authorities trying to streamline response. Groups of volunteers in civilian clothes converged, frequently armed and without coordination, on the same areas of a sometimes lawless city, adding to the tension.

But they also performed an invaluable service. Among them was Jeohn Favors, an emergency management technician (EMT) from Franklin, an hour west of New Orleans, who joined a group of fellow firefighters and police heading to the city. * * * Favors's crew hotwired empty boats, rescuing 350 people from rooftops by the end of the day. By his account, they were the first rescuers in Lakeview, a neighborhood in western New Orleans. They traveled through water riddled with six-foot plumes of flames rising from what must have been gas leaks. Power lines—some still active—hung above the water; beneath, submerged obstructions threatened to puncture the boats. * * *

Someone like Favors helped Kemberly Samuels, a teacher who sheltered from the storm with her husband at a housing development in St. Bernard Parish, where he worked. The building flooded. "You know, everyone heard about all the young gang bangers in New Orleans, but you didn't hear about the young men who came and found us," she said. * * * "They came . . . on Tuesday night with boats. "They brought us food and drinks. I asked them where they got it from, they said, 'Don't worry about that, just eat it.' They also said the boats were 'borrowed.'"

The rescuers took Samuels and her husband to Interstate 610, a highway overpass in downtown New Orleans where rescuers had begun depositing survivors. (Local authorities had identified only one official drop-off point, at an intersection of Interstate 10 and the Lake Pontchartrain Causeway known as the Cloverleaf, about two miles away. It was also the only rescue point where they had positioned food, water, and medicine.) "There were people lined up as far as I could see," Samuels recalled. "I saw one 9-year-old boy try to drag his grandmother up the interstate on a blanket. She was too weak to make it on her own. I tried to get them help, but none of the officials would help them. It was so hot you wouldn't believe. . . . We went for a while without water and when it finally did get there they just started throwing it at the crowd. People were fighting over it and I did not want to get in the middle of that. They did the same thing with the MREs [Meals Ready to Eat]," the military-style rations.

Though the Federal Emergency Management Agency (FEMA) positioned resources in the area before the start of the hurricane season, the food and water—critical supplies when a disaster has disrupted local services—were insufficient. Mississippi received only a fifth of the water and ice that state officials estimated was necessary; shipments didn't meet demand in Mississippi until September 9, 12 days after landfall.

FEMA, the federal government's primary disaster-response agency, had no effective supply-tracking system, so replenishing provisions turned out to be complicated. Planning and coordination were so poor that truck drivers didn't know where to go, and emergency-management officials didn't know what was en route, or when it might show up. Phone lines were down, so it was hard to clarify. * * *

The situation called for occasionally morbid forms of improvisation. In Bay St. Louis, Mississippi, Bill Carwile, FEMA's lead representative in Mississippi, and Robert Latham, the head of the state's emergency-management agency, encountered a funeral home director "in tears. And he says, you know, I have no more room for bodies. . . . My funeral home is full and I'm fixing to have to start putting people in the parking lot and on the sidewalk," Latham recalled. FEMA had ordered several refrigerator, or reefer, trucks as temporary morgues, but they hadn't arrived.

Just then, a tractor-trailer pulled up. "I said, What are you hauling?" Latham continued. "[The driver] said, Well, I'm hauling ice. . . . I said, Well, can I rent your truck? . . . We need to use it as a morgue. And he said, No, this is the way I make my living. If I give you that, I won't ever be able to use that trailer again for hauling ice or anything else refrigerated. I says, can we buy your truck? I'll buy it. I looked at Bill and I said, Bill, can I do this? He said, Yeah, we're going to do what we have do." Carwile and Latham negotiated a price ($25,000) and started loading bodies. The reefer trucks finally showed up five days later.

Supplies also were stretched at the New Orleans Superdome, the "refuge of last resort" for city residents who did not evacuate. It saved many lives during the hurricane, but at a dismaying cost. Lighting and plumbing failed. As 25,000 evacuees waited in heat and humidity for evacuation buses that wouldn't arrive for days, the Superdome deteriorated into nightmarish squalor. * * * [T]he Superdome became a center of the crisis, a symbol of the ways in which America failed New Orleans.

Dorothy Stukes rode out the hurricane at * * * her home in Gentilly. She didn't evacuate because her sister, who had recently undergone surgery, was at Charity Hospital, in the Central Business District. After the storm had passed, she went outside and walked for several miles until city police officers picked her up and drove her to the Superdome.

"A female officer searched us before we went inside," she recalled. "She took some medicine I had, but she also took some insulin from an elderly woman behind me because it was not in its proper box. I don't know how they expected her to make it without her insulin. When we got in, we found a chair and just sat there. All I could think about was my daughter. The last time I talked to her, water was coming through the walls and roof of her house. I didn't know if she was dead or alive.

"The Dome was horrible; it was like jail or something," she went on. "One guy jumped from a balcony and committed suicide. We saw some people having sex under a blanket. There were kids all around. Some kids found where they were hiding the ice and stole some of it and started selling it. Most of the supplies were going to the people [special-needs patients] up in the suites. Some folks found a newborn baby in a trashcan; they ended up taking care of it. People were sleeping in the halls on cardboard boxes in the middle of all that waste. And it stank; it was past stink due to all the urine and feces all over the floor. We just sat there and put our shirts over our face to mask the smell. We used an empty MRE bag and a box to go in. We would try to hide ourselves but you couldn't really get away. They wouldn't open any extra doors to let us get fresh air."

Among Stukes' fellow refugees was Patricia Morris, a home-care nurse who had passed up the chance to evacuate to Mississippi with her daughter because she wanted to help at the Superdome. "I kept telling [the] National Guard that I'm a registered nurse, and disaster-certified," she said. "Finally they got angry with me, and told me, Look, woman, Red Cross didn't even show," referring to the Red Cross' refusal to certify and staff the Superdome because it was in the flood zone. Morris says she offered her help to FEMA medics, as well as representatives of the state health department. "I could not understand with all the need they had how they could refuse help," she said. (Generally, medical personnel turned away volunteers because there was no way to evaluate their skills.)

Meanwhile, Morris had to find ways around the same indignities as Dorothy Stukes. "After the second day I decided that if I didn't eat, I wouldn't have to go to the bathroom," she said.

As conditions at the Superdome deteriorated, officials scrambled to find a way to evacuate the population. Prior to landfall, city authorities had failed to position buses outside the flood zone. The Regional Transit Authority, the city's transit system, prepositioned two fleets of buses on high ground within New Orleans, but no level of government attempted to send drivers until three days after landfall.

On Monday, the day of landfall, Louisiana Governor Kathleen Blanco had turned to FEMA Director Michael Brown with a request for 500 buses. He promised they would come. For reasons that have never been explained, those buses did not begin to arrive at the Superdome until Wednesday evening. By Katrina's impossible clock, two and a half days was a lifetime. Waiting, even if because the facts on the ground weren't clear, was an unconscionable luxury. If ever there was a time to overreact, this was it.

"We kept being told that the buses were coming," Dorothy Stukes said. "They promised they were coming on Monday, and then Tuesday, and then Wednesday. Thursday they finally got us to line up to load on the buses. At first they said [to] make a single-file line, and then someone said women and children first. Some of the men started snatching kids away from women so they could get on the bus."

"After we got on the bus they wouldn't tell us where they were taking us, and they said they forgot to load water for us," Kemberly Samuels recalled. "Once we got settled we started reading signs and realized we were going to Houston. We found out that there were kids on the bus that had been separated from their parents. There were at least four. I was asked to take care of one of them. Once we got to Houston, I took the kid to a Red Cross official and let them know that the kid had gotten lost. By that time, a lot of people had gotten sick. People were bathing in the sinks. We hadn't had a bath since Sunday. It was now Friday."

The Louisiana National Guard troops who developed the Superdome evacuation plan were assisted by members of a 50,000-strong Guard deployment from all 50 states, as well as the District of Columbia, Puerto Rico, the Virgin Islands, and Guam. After initiating the Superdome evacuation on Thursday, they moved on to the Ernest N. Morial Convention Center.

Tuesday evening, Mayor Nagin had opened the Convention Center as an alternate refuge. Before landfall, the city had not intended to use the Convention Center for this purpose, so no food or water had been positioned, and few law enforcement, medical or government personnel were present. Over the next two days, 19,000 people converged on the facility, but all levels of government were slow to grasp the gravity of the unfolding crisis. The first supplies may not have arrived until Thursday. The first media reports of the crowds at the Convention Center appeared Wednesday evening; by the next day there was video of thousands of stranded, desperate victims chanting "We want help."

The National Guard moved in on Friday, restoring order, distributing provisions, and evacuating the entire population in just over a day. Louisiana National Guard Colonel Jacques Thibodeaux recalled his first encounter with the people inside: "[T]he first time I went into the building . . . groups of people just lying there immobile, and when I say immobile, they assume that several were deceased because they actually kicked a couple to see if they were, 'Hey, are you okay?' just to see, to get an assessment, and they didn't move." The people Thibodeaux saw were alive, but so malnourished that they did not respond to physical stimuli.

"They're hot, they're tired, they're hungry," Wendell Shingler, the head of the Federal Protective Service, * * * recalled. "They had no place to go to the bathroom. They—some of these folks could not walk, so they were relieving themselves in their pants, and they had just lost their sense of humanity, they had lost their sense of dignity, and that was something that you could just see, they were just so distraught. They had now gone from a retired person with a home and probably some income to a homeless person sitting on a sidewalk, owning everything they had in the bag."

Though initial reports like Colonel Thibodeaux's suggested that as many as a hundred had died at the Convention Center, the actual toll was far lower. But this was cold comfort. One of Katrina's most enduring images was that of 91-year-old Ethel Freeman, whose lifeless body, partially covered by a poncho, sat in a wheelchair at the Convention Center for days.

The evacuation of most of the city was complete by Saturday, when 8,800 active-duty ground troops began to arrive. It's unclear why President Bush waited until Saturday to deploy federal ground troops—whether because of delay in settling command issues with state officials, because of the Defense Department's doctrine of relying on National Guard units first, because of federal units' inability to take on law-enforcement duties, or other reasons. The National Response Plan, the document meant to guide federal response to a disaster like Katrina, assigns a supporting role to the Department of Defense, to be called on by FEMA as necessary. On Thursday evening, three and a half days after landfall, FEMA asked the Department of Defense to take over its logistics operation. By that time, the Department had already begun to mobilize * * * ships, aircraft, and medical support. Some commanders had seized the initiative to mobilize assets so that they would be ready to deploy when the orders finally came.

Perhaps the most visible among them was Lieutenant General Russel Honoré, Commander of U.S. First Army, based in Atlanta, Georgia. Military commanders have limited authority to deploy their troops without orders from above as part of an "exercise." A native Louisianan who had assisted FEMA during the 2004 hurricane season, Honoré decided to stage an "exercise" that took his command element to Camp Shelby, Mississippi. Once Katrina subsided, Honoré was ideally positioned to take charge, and was named head of Joint Task Force Katrina by U.S. Northern Command, the headquarters for domestic military operations.

"When you landed here, with everybody walking with these red berets, in 45 minutes everybody's attitude changed," said Colonel Terry Ebbert, a former Marine who was New Orleans' head of Homeland Security when Katrina struck. "Nothing really changed but their attitude. Everybody, instantaneously, when they saw these guys walking down the street, you know, they're all good-looking, slim, tough guys that walk with a swagger, and it was over. Everybody felt good. Had that response come in on Tuesday," Colonel Ebbert said, the situation may have improved sooner.

* * * * *

The Gulf Coast has been trying to find its way back to normalcy. In the days after the storm "the weather was beautiful, . . . but you'd smell rotting flesh in the air," Dr. Bill Passarelli, the cardiologist from Ocean Springs, Mississippi, recalled. "Whether it was animal or human you didn't know, but it was everywhere. The closer you got to water the more intense it was.

"Just the devastation that was seen, it causes extreme—sudden and extreme duress," Passarelli continued. "And we saw people who had heart attacks just from seeing their houses. One lady in particular, my daughter's Spanish teacher, died that way. She was away for the storm, she survived the storm, and two days after the storm came back and died on her property."

"Every little detail of life as I knew it here on the Gulf Coast before the storm has changed," Dr. Jeff Bass, Passarelli's colleague, wrote in an e-mail to friends in late September. "The schools are damaged, most of the local businesses are closed, and almost all of the police cars are from out of state because virtually all of the local cruisers were washed away. On the street, instead of greeting people with, 'Hi, how are you?' the greeting is 'Hi, do you have a home, and is it livable?'"

Some 17,000 people lost jobs when the storm wiped out the local off-shore casinos, Bass continued. The destruction of Keesler Air Force Base in Biloxi unemployed 50,000 more, he wrote. "Almost all of the nice local restaurants have been destroyed . . . along with many of the small Mom and Pop businesses. I doubt that they carried adequate insurance."

Katrina destroyed or made uninhabitable 300,000 homes and caused as much as $150 billion in damage. In three Mississippi coastal counties alone, it left behind more debris than the 9/11 attacks and Hurricane Andrew, the most destructive recent hurricane, combined. * * * In some cases, the survivors have chosen to rebuild elsewhere. As of late January, half of New Orleans' population had not returned.

Hurricane Katrina: Indicators of Impact

Deaths caused by Hurricane Katrina, as of March 20, 2006	1,527
Deaths caused by 20th century's previous most lethal hurricane, 1935's "Labor Day Hurricane" in Florida	400+
Land area damaged by Hurricane Katrina	90,000 sq. miles
Ratio of area damaged by Katrina to area of United Kingdom	1:1
Homes destroyed or made unlivable by Hurricane Katrina	300,000
Ratio of homes damaged or made unlivable by Katrina to the number similarly affected by 1992's Hurricane Andrew, the most destructive recent hurricane	10:1
Estimated economic loss related to Hurricane Katrina	$125 - $150 billion
Estimated economic loss related to 20th century's previous most destructive hurricane (Andrew, FL, 1992)	$48.4 billion (2005 dollars)
Economic losses from 9/11 terror attacks, 2001	$87 billion (2005 dollars)
Louisiana unemployment rate, August 2005	5.6 percent
Louisiana unemployment rate, September 2005	12.1 percent
Extent of Katrina's tropical-storm force winds the day before landfall	460 miles
Approximate ratio to distance from Kansas City to Dallas	1:1
Sustained-wind speed at landfall, August 29, near Buras, LA	125 miles per hour
Rainfall accumulation along Golf Coast from Katrina	8 to 10 inches
Storm surges above normal ocean levels, various locations	20 to 30 feet
Electric customers, all types, left without power by storm	1.7 million
Gulf of Mexico daily oil output shut down by Katrina	95 percent
Number of oil spills caused by Katrina	142
Gallons of oil spilled	8 million
Gallons of oil recovered by Coast Guard as of Dec. 7, 2005	3.8 million
Estimated debris created by Hurricane Katrina	111 million cubic yards
Ratio to debris created by Hurricane Andrew	6:1
Number of children reported displaced/missing	5,088
Number reunited with families or guardians	5,088
Last date at which bodies have been found in New Orleans	April 17, 2006
Number of bodies unclaimed or unidentified	200
Approximate ratio of New Orleans population in 2000 to January 2006	3:1
Ratio of tons of debris created by Katrina in the three coastal Mississippi counties, as compared to the combined debris of the 9/11 attacks and Hurricane Andrew	1:1

CHAPTER 2

FEDERALISM: THE CONSTITUTIONAL AND STATUTORY FRAMEWORK

Katrina damaged not only the physical and social fabric of its immediate victims. The storm also undermined public confidence in the ability of government at all levels—federal, state, and local—to respond effectively to natural disasters, terrorist attacks, and other emergencies. Confusion over the precise allocation of governmental responsibility arguably crippled the crucial first stages of the response to Katrina as the storm approached and then struck the Gulf Coast. Worse still, perhaps, the public came to believe that a divided, disorganized official response aggravated the impact of the storm and deepened the injury suffered by Katrina's most vulnerable victims.

This chapter analyzes the divided authority of federal and state governments to respond to emergencies. The federal structure of the United States underlies the basic statutory framework that allocates authority between federal, state, and local officials. The Stafford Act and the Posse Comitatus Act figured prominently during Katrina and in the storm's political aftermath. This chapter also explores a range of exceptions to the Posse Comitatus Act, especially the Insurrection Act.

A. FEDERALISM AS FRIEND OR FOE?

Ours is a federal system of government. The federal government is regarded as a government of enumerated powers. As the Supreme Court has often observed, the federal government enjoys no powers except those that are set out in the Constitution. The Tenth Amendment specifically provides that "[t]he powers not delegated to the United States by the Constitution, nor prohibited by it to the States, are reserved to the States respectively, or to the people." Given this limitation, federal authority to respond to emergencies must be derived from Congress's constitutional "Power[s] To lay and collect Taxes, Duties, Imposts and Excises, to pay the Debts and provide for the common Defence and general Welfare"; "[t]o regulate Commerce with foreign Nations, and among the several States"; and "[t]o provide for calling forth the Militia to execute the Laws of the Union, suppress Insurrections and repel Invasions." U.S. Const. art. I, § 8, cl. 1, 3, 15. Congress's power to enforce the Thirteenth, Fourteenth, and Fifteenth Amendments further enables the federal government to protect civil rights and civil liberties during turmoil.

In times of emergency, fidelity to federalism may blur the boundaries between the federal, state, and local governments. What is arguably the "national neurosis" of federalism in times of peace and stability, *see* Edward L. Rubin & Malcolm Feeley, *Federalism: Some Notes on a National Neurosis*, 41 UCLA L. REV. 903 (1994), can turn lethal if competing levels of government misunderstand how authority is allocated by the Constitution and by federal statutes. The following excerpt provocatively asks whether the Constitution's treatment of the federal government as one of enumerated powers failed New Orleans during Katrina:

STEPHEN GRIFFIN, DID THE CONSTITUTION FAIL NEW ORLEANS?

http://balkin.blogspot.com/2005/10/did-constitution-fail-new-orleans-part.html
(Oct. 12, 2005)

In the immediate aftermath of Hurricane Katrina, journalists and the public began asking why the effort to aid the citizens of New Orleans floundered so badly. A number of news stories * * * laid part of the blame on a defective system of governance.

[A Newhouse News Service] story stated that the muddled response to Hurricane Katrina exposes something known by Washington insiders: "For reasons that run deep and probably can't be fixed, Washington has difficulty making long-range plans, coordinating its actions and tackling the tough political decisions required for swift disaster response and other critical responsibilities." Washington veterans cited these factors: (1) power and authority are fragmented as the framers intended; (2) election cycles mean attention spans are short; (3) bureaucracy stifles initiative; and (4) intense partisan conflict. The story quoted Paul Light, professor of public service at New York University: "'Chief among the federal government's structure problems is its division of responsibility.' 'It's built into the Constitution that we have a federal system where states and localities have a lot of responsibility.' 'Part of this is embedded in the system that we don't want a strong federal presence. . . . The founders were clear in wanting to protect citizens from the national government.'"

Could the Constitution have something to do with Katrina? The important theme in the Newhouse story is the persistence of the eighteenth-century federal order. In this system, there are separate governments that do not share power. If coordinated action is required, everyone has a veto before the bargaining starts. *Washington Post* columnist David Broder recently wrote of Hurricane Katrina that "The failure to respond to that disaster exposed one of the few real structural weaknesses in our Constitution: a mechanism to coordinate the work of local, state and national governments." News reports show that a week after Katrina made landfall, local, state and federal officials were still arguing over who was in charge.

A long article in the [*New York Times*] on September 11 analyzed the breakdown in the government's response. It stated: "As the city bec[ame] paralyzed both by water and by lawlessness, so did the response by government. The fractured division of responsibility—Gov. Blanco controlled state agencies and the National Guard, Mayor Nagin directed city workers and Mr. Brown, the head of FEMA, served as the point man for the federal government—meant no one person was in charge. Americans watching on television saw the often-haggard governor, the voluble mayor and the usually upbeat FEMA chief appear at competing daily press briefings and interviews." And: "The power-sharing arrangement was by design, and as the days wore on, it would prove disastrous. Under the Bush administration, FEMA redefined its role, offering assistance but remaining subordinate to state and local governments. 'Our typical role is to work with the state in support of local and state agencies,' said David Passey, a FEMA spokesman."

As I write this post, the arguments continue, now over who will lead the effort to reconstruct the city and southern Louisiana * * * . But if more intergovernmental coordination is required * * * , the framers of the Constitution and constitutional scholars might well reply that coordination of government was not the point of the original constitutional plan. In eighteenth-century terms, a "coordinated" response by all levels of government to a policy problem poses a great risk of tyranny.

What of natural disasters, events that are nearly by definition beyond the capability of local and state governments? * * * [I]t took many decades and repeated disasters to convince national officials, including the President, that the federal government had a role to play in alleviating the effects of natural disasters. For much of American history, victims of natural disasters were pretty much on their own. As a matter of policy at least, the federal government was not concerned with whether U.S. citizens starved or died from lack of medical care after a natural disaster. It was certainly not concerned with providing financial assistance to ensure that they had food and shelter. That was a matter for private relief efforts and whatever local officials were on hand.

Part of the point of [JOHN M. BARRY, RISING TIDE: THE GREAT MISSISSIPPI FLOOD OF 1927 AND HOW IT CHANGED AMERICA (1998)] is that the provision of federal assistance after the 1927 flood and the assumption of federal responsibility for flood control along the Mississippi river represented a great change in the American system of governance. * * * [T]he twentieth century saw a major change in the constitutional order, one involving greater federal involvement in matters previously jealously guarded by state governments. The change is usually attributed to the Great Depression, although works such as Barry's show that change was in the air even in the 1920s.

Most of us have grown up in a world in which federal assistance in time of disaster is taken for granted. So why did the government stumble so badly after Hurricane Katrina? The answer provides an instructive lesson in how constitutional change occurs and, in many respects, the continued role of the eighteenth-century federal structure. After the Great Depression, the constitutional order changed in a somewhat helter-skelter unplanned fashion. Certainly no constitutional amendment was approved that might have provided firm legitimacy and guidance to the federal government's new power. The formal structure of American federalism remained intact. And so it is still the case that when natural disasters strike, the divided power of the federal structure presents a coordination problem. The kind of coordination that had to occur to avoid the Katrina disaster requires long-term planning before the event. The American constitutional system makes taking intergovernmental action difficult and complex. The process of coordinating governments can thus take years. In many ways, the government was just at the beginning of that process at the time of Katrina, although we are now four years distant from the terrorist attacks of September 11 that set the latest round of disaster coordination in motion.

Suppose, however, that we don't have the luxury of taking the time to satisfy every official with a veto. This is the key point of tension between what contemporary governance demands and what the Constitution permits. Informal constitutional change such as the kind that occurred in 1927 can take us only so far. What Hurricane Katrina shows is that even after decades of experience with natural disasters, federal and state governments are still uncoordinated and unprepared. The reasons they are unprepared go to the heart of the constitutional order. We can do better in the future only by directly confronting the difficult task of adapting an eighteenth-century constitutional order to contemporary circumstances.

NOTES AND QUESTIONS

1. The American constitutional tradition has long suspected that "emergency powers . . . tend to kindle emergencies." Youngstown Sheet & Tube Co. v. Sawyer, 343 U.S. 579, 650 (1952) (Jackson, J., concurring). What circumstances would justify a federal decision to displace state and local officials from their presumptive leadership of emergency responses?

   a. The federal government intervenes upon a state's request.

   b. The federal government preemptively responds to an emergency before state officials can decide whether to request federal assistance.

   c. The federal government directly countermands a governor's request that the task of emergency response be left to state and local officials.

Compare these possibilities to the "over-simplified grouping of practical situations in which" the President's assertion of emergency powers might upset the separation of powers within the federal government. *Id.* at 635.

2. Article IV, section 4 of the Constitution pledges that "[t]he United States shall guarantee to every State in this Union a Republican Form of Government, and shall protect each of them against Invasion; and on Application of the Legislature, or of the Executive (when the Legislature cannot be convened) against domestic Violence." In Luther v. Borden, 48 U.S. (7 How.) 1 (1849), the Supreme Court declined to decide which of two competing factions represented the lawful government of Rhode Island, reasoning that the responsibility "rests with congress to decide what government is the established one in a State." *Id.* at 42 ("Congress must necessarily decide what government is established in the State before it can determine whether it is republican or not."); *see also* Pacific Tel. Co. v. Oregon, 223 U.S. 118 (1912). Although *Luther* is regarded as foreclosing judicial enforcement of the republican guaranty clause, *see* Baker v. Carr, 369 U.S. 186, 218-224 (1962), does this provision of the Constitution empower the political branches of the federal government to "guarantee to every State . . . a Republican Form of Government" or to "protect [the states] against Invasion" or "domestic Violence"? Reconsider this question in connection with the Insurrection Act, 10 U.S.C. §§ 331-334. *See infra* pp. 43-47.

3. Other provisions of the Constitution explicitly contemplate emergency situations that warrant special rules. Article I, section 10, clause 3 provides: "No State shall, without the Consent of Congress, lay any Duty of Tonnage, keep Troops, or Ships of War in time of Peace . . . or engage in War, *unless actually invaded, or in such imminent Danger as will not admit of delay*" (emphasis added). Article I pledges that "[t]he privilege of the Writ of Habeas Corpus shall not be suspended, *unless when in Cases of Rebellion or Invasion the public Safety may require it*." *Id.* art. I, § 9, cl. 2 (emphasis added). The Third Amendment promises that "[n]o Soldier shall, *in time of peace* be quartered in any house, without the consent of the Owner," but allows quartering soldiers "*in time of war*" according to "a manner to be prescribed by law" (emphases added). Finally, the Fifth Amendment's promise of "presentment or indictment of a Grand Jury" applies neither to "cases arising in the land or naval forces" nor to cases "in the Militia, *when in actual service in time of War or public danger*" (emphasis added). These provisions evidently contemplate a pair of contrasting conditions: "War" versus "Peace," and "public Safety" versus "Danger" or "public danger." What circumstances give rise to "War" within the meaning of the Constitution? "Peace"? "Safety"? "Danger"?

4. Printz v. United States, 521 U.S. 898 (1997) established the proposition that the Tenth Amendment bars the federal government from "commandeering" state executive officers for the purpose of implementing federal law. "The power of the Federal Government would be augmented immeasurably if it were able to impress into its service—and at no cost to itself—the police officers of the 50 States." *Id.* at 922. "[N]o comparative

assessment of the various interests" at stake "can overcome [the] fundamental defect" of allowing the federal commandeering of state executive officers to "offend[]" the "very principle of separate state sovereignty." *Id.* at 935.

5.   Although the Supreme Court of late has found limits to Congress's power to regulate commerce, the Justices concede that "Congress' commerce authority includes the power to regulate those activities having a substantial relation to interstate commerce." United States v. Lopez, 514 U.S. 549, 558-559 (1995). The "proper test" of Congress's commerce powers "requires an analysis of whether the regulated activity 'substantially affects' interstate commerce." *Id.* at 559.

a. Given the interdependence of local activities and the national (or, indeed, global) economy, is there any disaster that would not "substantially affect" interstate commerce? May Congress invoke its commerce power to enact a general emergency response statute authorizing the federal government to respond whenever a natural disaster, terrorist attack, or other emergency has the potential to "substantially affect" interstate commerce?

b. *Lopez* arguably represents an anomaly within a constitutional tradition that has tolerated an ever larger degree of federal involvement in local affairs since the New Deal. The scope of federal involvement transcends the strictly "commercial" and readily embraces matters, such as civil rights, that nonlawyers might regard as "moral" rather than economic. Has the public understanding of the constitutionally mediated balance of power between the federal government and the states shifted so dramatically since the New Deal that the presumptive leadership of state and local governments in emergency response has actually reversed? In other words, do ordinary Americans expect the federal government, rather than state or local governments, to take the lead role in responding to natural disasters and other emergencies? If so, does such an expectation justify wholesale reconsideration of federalism during disasters?

c. In answering these questions, consider the actual scope of federal involvement in natural disasters and other emergencies over the last three decades: "Since 1974, an average of thirty-eight major disasters have been declared annually. In 2004, a near record disaster season, the President issued sixty-eight major disaster declarations and seven emergency declarations." THE WHITE HOUSE, THE FEDERAL RESPONSE TO HURRICANE KATRINA: LESSONS LEARNED 12 (2006).

B.   THE FEDERAL STATUTORY FRAMEWORK

The Constitution and Supreme Court opinions on federalism represent only the first step in understanding the relationship between federal, state, and local authorities during disasters. Far greater practical significance resides in the statutes that define the federal role in emergency response, law enforcement, and disaster relief. Chief among these laws are the Robert T. Stafford Disaster Relief and Emergency Assistance Act, 42 U.S.C. §§ 5121-5206, which authorizes the deployment of federal military resources for disaster relief operations upon the request of the governor of an affected state, and the Posse Comitatus Act, 18 U.S.C. § 1835, which generally prohibits the use of the military to perform law enforcement functions.

1. STAFFORD ACT

As an initial exercise in applying the Stafford Act, consider this investigation into "whether or not the necessary steps were taken to give the Federal Government in general, and the Federal Emergency Management Agency (FEMA) in particular, the legal authority needed to act to save lives and mitigate the damage stemming from Hurricane Katrina":

CONGRESSIONAL RESEARCH SERVICE MEMORANDUM

HURRICANE KATRINA—STAFFORD ACT AUTHORITIES AND ACTIONS BY
GOVERNOR BLANCO AND PRESIDENT BUSH TO TRIGGER THEM

---

http://fpc.state.gov/documents/organization/53576.pdf (Sept. 12, 2005)

The Stafford Act is designed to provide a means by which the federal government may supplement state and local resources in major disasters or emergencies where those state and local resources have been overwhelmed. The Act provides separate but similar mechanisms for declaration of a major disaster and for declaration of an emergency. Except to the extent that an emergency involves primarily federal interests, both declarations of major disaster and declarations of emergency must be triggered by a request to the President from the Governor of the affected state.

[Section 401 of the Stafford Act, 42 U.S.C. § 5170, governs major disaster declarations. Section 501, *id.* § 5191, governs emergency declarations.]

§ 5170. Procedure for declaration.

All requests for a declaration by the President that a major disaster exists shall be made by the Governor of the affected State. Such a request shall be based on a finding that the disaster is of such severity and magnitude that effective response is beyond the capabilities of the State and the affected local governments and that Federal assistance is necessary. As part of such request, and as a prerequisite to major disaster assistance under this chapter, the Governor shall take appropriate response action under State law and direct execution of the State's emergency plan. The Governor shall furnish information on the nature and amount of State and local resources which have been or will be committed to alleviating the results of the disaster, and shall certify that, for the current disaster, State and local government obligations and expenditures (of which State commitments must be a significant proportion) will comply with all applicable cost-sharing requirements of this chapter. Based on the request of a Governor under this section, the President may declare under this chapter that a major disaster or emergency exists.

§ 5191.   Procedure for declaration.

(a)   Request and declaration

All requests for a declaration by the President that an emergency exists shall be made by the Governor of the affected State. Such a request shall be based on a finding that the situation is of such severity and magnitude that effective response is beyond the capabilities of the State and the affected local governments and that Federal assistance is necessary. As a part of such request, and as a prerequisite to emergency assistance under this chapter, the Governor shall take appropriate action under State law and direct execution of the State's emergency plan. The Governor shall furnish information describing the State and local efforts and resources which have been or will be used to alleviate the emergency, and will define the type and extent of Federal aid required. Based upon such Governor's request, the President may declare that an emergency exists.

(b) Certain emergencies involving Federal primary responsibility

The President may exercise any authority vested in him by section 5192 of this title or section 5193 of this title with respect to an emergency when he determines that an emergency exists for which the primary responsibility for response rests with the United States because the emergency involves a subject area for which, under the Constitution or laws of the United States, the United States exercises exclusive or preeminent responsibility and authority. In determining whether or not such an emergency exists, the President shall consult the Governor of any affected State, if practicable. The President's determination may be made without regard to subsection (a) of this section.

A major disaster declaration by the President opens the door to two types of federal disaster assistance: general federal assistance under Section 402(a) of the Stafford Act, 42 U.S.C. § 5170a, and essential federal assistance under Section 403 of the Stafford Act, 42 U.S.C. § 5170b. These provide:

§ 5170a.   General Federal assistance.

In any major disaster, the President may —

(1) direct any Federal agency, with or without reimbursement, to utilize its authorities and the resources granted to it under Federal law (including personnel, equipment, supplies, facilities, and managerial, technical, and advisory services) in support of State and local assistance efforts;

(2) coordinate all disaster relief assistance (including voluntary assistance) provided by Federal agencies, private organizations, and State and local governments;

(3) provide technical and advisory assistance to affected State and local governments for —

(A) the performance of essential community services;

(B) issuance of warnings of risks and hazards;

(C) public health and safety information, including dissemination of such information;

(D) provision of health and safety measures; and

(E) management, control, and reduction of immediate threats to public health and safety; and

(4) assist State and local governments in the distribution of medicine, food, and other consumable supplies, and emergency assistance.

§ 5170b. Essential assistance

(a) In general

Federal agencies may on the direction of the President, provide assistance essential to meeting immediate threats to life and property resulting from a major disaster, as follows:

(1) Federal resources, generally

Utilizing, lending, or donating to State and local governments Federal equipment, supplies, facilities, personnel, and other resources, other than the extension of credit, for use or distribution by such governments in accordance with the purposes of this chapter.

(2) Medicine, food, and other consumables

Distributing or rendering through State and local governments, the American National Red Cross, the Salvation Army, the Mennonite Disaster Service, and other relief and disaster assistance organizations medicine, food, and other consumable supplies, and other services and assistance to disaster victims.

(3) Work and services to save lives and protect property

Performing on public or private lands or waters any work or services essential to saving lives and protecting and preserving property or public health and safety, including –

(A) debris removal;

(B) search and rescue, emergency medical care, emergency mass care, emergency shelter, and provision of food, water, medicine, and other essential needs, including movement of supplies or persons;

(C) clearance of roads and construction of temporary bridges necessary to the performance of emergency tasks and essential community services;

(D) provision of temporary facilities for schools and other essential community services;

(E) demolition of unsafe structures which endanger the public;

(F) warning of further risks and hazards;

(G) dissemination of public information and assistance regarding health and safety measures;

(H) provision of technical advice to State and local governments on disaster management and control; and

(I) reduction of immediate threats to life, property, and public health and safety.

(4) Contributions

Making contributions to State or local governments or owners or operators of private nonprofit facilities for the purpose of carrying out the provisions of this subsection.

(b) Federal share

The Federal share of assistance under this section shall be not less than 75 percent of the eligible cost of such assistance.

(c) Utilization of DOD resources

(1) General rule

During the immediate aftermath of an incident which may ultimately qualify for assistance under this subchapter or subchapter IV-A of this chapter, the Governor of the State in which such incident occurred may request the President to direct the Secretary of Defense to utilize the resources of the Department of Defense for the purpose of performing on public and private lands any emergency work which is made necessary by such incident and which is essential for the preservation of life and property. If the President determines that such work is essential for the preservation of life and property, the President shall grant such request to the extent the President determines practicable. Such emergency work may only be carried out for a period not to exceed 10 days.

(2) Rules applicable to debris removal

Any removal of debris and wreckage carried out under this subsection shall be subject to section 5173(b) of this title, relating to unconditional authorization and indemnification for debris removal.

(3) Expenditures out of disaster relief funds

The cost of any assistance provided pursuant to this subsection shall be reimbursed out of funds made available to carry out this chapter.

(4) Federal share

The Federal share of assistance under this subsection shall be not less than 75 percent.

(5) Guidelines

Not later than 180 days after November 23, 1988, the President shall issue guidelines for carrying out this subsection. Such guidelines shall consider any likely effect assistance under this subsection will have on the availability of other forms of assistance under this chapter.

(6) Definitions

For purposes of this section –
    (A) Department of Defense
        The term "Department of Defense" has the meaning the term "department" has under section 101 of Title 10.
    (B) Emergency work
        The term "emergency work" includes clearance and removal of debris and wreckage and temporary restoration of essential public facilities and services.

The declaration of an emergency by the President makes federal emergency assistance available [under] Section 502 of the Stafford Act, 42 U.S.C. § 5192:

§ 5192. Federal emergency assistance.

(a) Specified

In any emergency, the President may –
    (1) direct any Federal agency, with or without reimbursement, to utilize its authorities and the resources granted to it under Federal law (including personnel, equipment, supplies, facilities, and managerial, technical and advisory services) in support of State and local emergency assistance efforts to save lives, protect property and public health and safety, and lessen or avert the threat of a catastrophe;
    (2) coordinate all disaster relief assistance (including voluntary assistance) provided by Federal agencies, private organizations, and State and local governments;
    (3) provide technical and advisory assistance to affected State and local governments for –
        (A) the performance of essential community services;
        (B) issuance of warnings of risks or hazards;
        (C) public health and safety information, including dissemination of such information;
        (D) provision of health and safety measures; and
        (E) management, control, and reduction of immediate threats to public health and safety;
    (4) provide emergency assistance through Federal agencies;
    (5) remove debris in accordance with the terms and conditions of section 5173 of this title;
    (6) provide assistance in accordance with section 5174 of this title; and
    (7) assist State and local governments in the distribution of medicine, food, and other consumable supplies, and emergency assistance.

(b) General

Whenever the Federal assistance provided under subsection (a) of this section with respect to an emergency is inadequate, the President may also provide assistance with respect to efforts to save lives, protect property and public health and safety, and lessen or avert the threat of a catastrophe.

* * * Governor Kathleen Babineaux Blanco requested, by letter dated August 27, 2005, addressed to the President of the United States, through the Regional Director of FEMA Region VI, that the President declare an emergency for the State of Louisiana due to Hurricane Katrina for the time period from August 26, 2005, and continuing, pursuant to Section 501(a) [of the Stafford Act, 42 U.S.C. § 5191]. The Governor's letter indicated that the affected areas were "all the southeastern parishes including the New Orleans Metropolitan area and the mid state Interstate I-49 corridor and northern parishes along the I-2 corridor that are accepting the thousands of citizens evacuating from the areas expecting to be flooded as a result of Hurricane Katrina." The letter also indicated that Governor Blanco, "[i]n response to the situation [had] taken appropriate action under State law and directed the execution of the State Emergency Plan on August 26, 2005 in accordance with Section 501(a) of the Stafford Act." * * *

Governor Blanco's August 27, 2005, request for an emergency declaration also included her determination, pursuant to 44 C.F.R. § 206.35, that "the incident is of such severity and magnitude that effective response is beyond the capabilities of the State and affected local governments, and that supplementary Federal assistance is necessary to save lives, protect property, public health, and safety, or to lessen or avert the threat of disaster." She specifically requested "emergency protective measures, direct Federal Assistance, Individual and Household Program (IHP) assistance, Special Needs Program assistance, and debris removal." She provided preliminary estimates of the type and amount of emergency assistance needed under the Stafford Act and * * * other statutory authorities, indicated the nature and amount of state and local resources being or to be used to alleviate the conditions of the emergency, and certified that the State of Louisiana and local governments would assume all non-federal share of costs required by the Stafford Act.

[On August 27, 2005,] President Bush "declared an emergency exists in the State of Louisiana and ordered Federal aid to supplement state and local response efforts in the parishes located in the path of Hurricane Katrina beginning on August 26, 2005, and continuing." [A White House press release dated August 27 provided "[s]pecifically" that] "FEMA is authorized to identify, mobilize, and provide at its discretion, equipment and resources necessary to alleviate the impacts of the emergency. Debris removal and emergency protective measures, including direct Federal assistance, will be provided at 75 percent Federal Funding." * * *

By a letter dated August 28, 2005, to the President through the Regional Director, FEMA Region VI, Governor Blanco requested that President Bush "declare an expedited major disaster for the State of Louisiana as Hurricane Katrina, a Category V Hurricane, approaches our south coast of New Orleans, beginning on August 28, 2005, and continuing. * * *" Her letter identified the parishes expected to receive major damage from the hurricane, those parishes anticipated to receive significant damage from tropical storm force wind and heavy rain after Hurricane Katrina's landfall, and those parishes affected by the evacuation of persons from the southeastern parishes in implementation of the Louisiana Shelter Operations Plan. The letter further indicated that the Governor had taken appropriate action under state law, had directed execution of the State Emergency Plan on August 26, 2005, and had declared a state of emergency for the state to support the State Evacuation and Sheltering Plan. In her letter, the Governor indicated that a preliminary damage assessment would be conducted as soon after landfall as possible and stated the Governor's determination that the incident would be of such severity and magnitude that effective response would be beyond the state and local governments' capabilities and would require supplementary federal assistance. She outlined the nature and amount of state and local resources that had been or would be used to alleviate the conditions resulting from the disaster. * * *

Noting that the State Hazard Mitigation Plan had been approved by FEMA on April 15, 2005, Governor Blanco requested hazard mitigation for eligible applicants having a FEMA approved Local Hazard Mitigation Plan and for those parishes approved within the application period for this disaster. In light of the extraordinary nature of the hurricane and anticipated damage to impacted areas including the New Orleans Metropolitan Area, the Governor requested an increase of the federal cost share to 100% for Individual Assistance, all categories of Public Assistance, and Direct Federal Assistance, while certifying that the state and local governments would assume the applicable non-federal share of costs required by the Stafford Act. She requested direct federal assistance for work and services to save lives and property, including a direct debris removal mission, and agreed to indemnify and hold the United States harmless for any claims arising from removal of debris or wreckage from the disaster.

On August 29, 2005, President Bush declared a major disaster for the State of Louisiana, beginning on August 29, 2005, and continuing. This major disaster declaration was amended on September 1, 2005, and again on September 4, 2005. * * * The original declaration of a major disaster [70 Fed. Reg. 53,803 (Sept. 12, 2005)] provided:

> Notice is hereby given that, in a letter dated August 29, 2005, the President declared a major disaster under the authority of the Robert T. Stafford Disaster Relief and Emergency Assistance Act, 42 U.S.C. 5121-5206 (the Stafford Act), as follows:
>
> I have determined that the damage in certain areas of the State of Louisiana, resulting from Hurricane Katrina beginning on August 29, 2005, and continuing, is of sufficient severity and magnitude to warrant a major disaster declaration under the Robert T. Stafford Disaster Relief and Emergency Assistance Act, 42 U.S.C. 5121-5206 (the Stafford Act). Therefore, I declare that such a major disaster exists in the State of Louisiana.
>
> In order to provide Federal assistance, you are hereby authorized to allocate from funds available for these purposes such amounts as you find necessary for Federal disaster assistance and administrative expenses.
>
> You are authorized to provide Individual Assistance and assistance for debris removal and emergency protective measures (Categories A and B) under the Public Assistance program, and Hazard Mitigation in the designated

areas; and any other forms of assistance under the Stafford Act you may deem appropriate subject to completion of Preliminary Damage Assessments (PDAs), unless you determine the incident is of such unusual severity and magnitude that PDAs are not required to determine the need for supplemental Federal assistance pursuant to 44 CFR 206.33(d). Direct Federal assistance is authorized.

Consistent with the requirement that Federal assistance be supplemental, any Federal funds provided under the Stafford Act for Public Assistance, Hazard Mitigation and the Other Needs Assistance under Section 408 of the Stafford Act will be limited to 75 percent of the total eligible costs. For a period of up to 72 hours, you are authorized to fund assistance for debris removal and emergency protective measures, including direct Federal assistance, at 100 percent of the total eligible costs. Federal funding for debris removal will remain at 75 percent.

Further, you are authorized to make changes to this declaration to the extent allowable under the Stafford Act.

The time period prescribed for the implementation of section 310(a), Priority to Certain Applications for Public Facility and Public Housing Assistance, 42 U.S.C. 5153, shall be for a period not to exceed six months after the date of this declaration.

The Federal Emergency Management Agency (FEMA) hereby gives notice that pursuant to the authority vested in the Under Secretary for Emergency Preparedness and Response, Department of Homeland Security, under Executive Order 12148, as amended, William Lokey, of FEMA is appointed to act as the Federal Coordinating Officer for this declared disaster. * * *

[On September 1, 2005, in light of the severity and magnitude of the disaster, the President amended the original disaster declaration's cost sharing arrangements "to authorize Federal funds for debris removal and emergency protective measures (Categories A and B), including direct federal assistance under the Public Assistance program at 100 percent of total eligible costs, for a 60-day period retroactive to the date of the major disaster declaration." On September 4, the President again amended his major disaster declaration to make affected Louisiana parishes eligible for public assistance for purposes identified in 42 U.S.C. § 5170b(a)(3)(C)-(G), such as the clearance of roads, construction of temporary bridges, provision of temporary school facilities, and demolition of unsafe structures, in addition to debris removal and emergency protective measures under § 5170b(a)(3)(A) and (B), which the original declaration had extended to those parishes.]

NOTES

1. This report concluded, on the basis of its "review of the statutory authorities under the Stafford Act, the letters of Governor Blanco to President Bush requesting first a declaration of emergency and then a major disaster declaration . . . , as well as the President's responses to those requests," that "the Governor [apparently] did take the steps necessary to

request emergency and major disaster declarations." The report likewise concluded "that the President [apparently] did take the steps necessary to trigger the availability of Stafford Act emergency assistance and disaster assistance."

2. It is essential to distinguish between the Stafford Act's definitions of "major disaster" and "emergency." The Act defines "major disaster" as

> any natural catastrophe (including any hurricane, tornado, storm, high water, wind driven water, tidal wave, tsunami, earthquake, volcanic eruption, landslide, mudslide, snowstorm, or drought), or, regardless of cause, any fire, flood, or explosion, in any part of the United States, which in the determination of the President causes damage of sufficient severity and magnitude to warrant major disaster assistance under this chapter to supplement the efforts and available resources of states, local governments, and disaster relief organizations in alleviating the damage, loss, hardship, or suffering caused thereby.

42 U.S.C. § 5122(2). An "emergency," by contrast, is defined as

> any occasion or instance for which, in the determination of the President, federal assistance is needed to supplement state and local efforts and capabilities to save lives and to protect property and public health and safety, or to lessen or avert the threat of a catastrophe in any part of the United States.

Id. § 5122(1).

　　a. Observe the presence of the word *catastrophe* in both definitions. A "major disaster" is, in the first instance, a "natural catastrophe." An "emergency" presents an "occasion or instance" in which "federal assistance is needed . . . to lessen or avert *the threat of a catastrophe*."

　　b. Does the definition of "major disaster" cover a non-natural event, such as an electronic attack on the Internet, not attributable to fire, flood, or explosion? How about the deliberate release of a biological agent such as smallpox or anthrax? *See* Ernest B. Abbott, *Representing Local Governments in Catastrophic Events: DHS/FEMA Response and Recovery Issues*, 37 URB. LAW. 467, 471 (2005) (suggesting a negative answer to both questions).

3. Section 501(b) of the Stafford Act, 42 U.S.C. § 5191(b), authorizes the President to declare an "emergency" (but not a "major disaster") if "[p]rimary responsibility rests with the United States because the emergency involves a subject area for which . . . the United States exercises exclusive or preeminent authority." Although the Stafford Act directs the President to "consult the Governor of any affected State, if practicable," when "determining whether or not such an emergency exists," the power to declare an emergency on account of the federal government's "primary responsibility" does not require a governor's consent. Presumably this

authority enables the President to declare an emergency in the event of disasters or attacks affecting military installations and other federal properties.

4. The Stafford Act immunizes the federal government against "any claim based upon the exercise or performance of or the failure to exercise or perform a discretionary function or duty on the part of a federal agency or an employee of the federal government in carrying out the provisions of this chapter." 42 U.S.C. § 5148. This language is almost identical to the Federal Tort Claims Act's exception for "[a]ny claim . . . based upon the exercise or performance or the failure to exercise or perform a discretionary function or duty" by a federal employee. 28 U.S.C. § 2680(a). The Stafford Act's immunity provision is interpreted *in pari materia* with the FTCA's frequently litigated "discretionary function" exception. *See* Graham v. FEMA, 149 F.3d 997, 1006 (9th Cir. 1998).

5. The Stafford Act is merely one source of federal emergency authority. The National Emergency Act, 50 U.S.C. §§ 1601-1651, and the Emergency Economic Powers Act, *id.* §§ 1701-1707, grant the President a wide range of powers in the event of a national security, foreign policy, or economic emergency. The Secretary of Health and Human Services is empowered to declare a public health emergency under 42 U.S.C. § 247d. Federal law also grants emergency powers confined to specific industries. *See, e.g.,* 7 U.S.C. § 7715 (authorizing the Secretary of Agriculture to declare an "extraordinary emergency" attributable to "the presence of a plant pest or noxious weed"); 15 U.S.C. §§ 3361-3364 (empowering the President to respond to a natural gas supply emergency); 16 U.S.C. § 824a(c) (enabling the Department of Energy to order interconnection and the generation and transmission of electricity during emergencies).

2. POSSE COMITATUS ACT

The Stafford Act appears to contemplate three distinct circumstances under which the President may deploy federal troops:

> *Essential Assistance (10-Day Authority).* Upon the request of the governor, the President may task the Department of Defense to provide any emergency work the President deems essential for the preservation of life and property in the immediate aftermath of an incident that may ultimately qualify for assistance under a declaration. Such assistance is available for up to ten days before a presidential declaration of an emergency or a major disaster is issued, 42 U.S.C. § 5170b(c). Emergency work can include the clearance and removal of debris and wreckage and the restoration of essential public facilities and services, 42 U.S.C. § 5170(c)(6)(B). The provision is designed to be utilized in instances where communications problems impede the ability to meet the prerequisites for declaring an emergency or major disaster or the ability to coordinate the work through FEMA.
>
> *Emergency.* Unless the President determines that a disaster implicates preeminently federal interests, the declaration of an emergency under the Stafford Act requires that the governor of the affected state first make a de-

termination that the situation is of such severity and magnitude that the state is unable to respond effectively without federal assistance, which determination must include a detailed definition of the type and amount of federal aid required, 42 U.S.C. § 5191. The governor must also implement the state's emergency response plan, for example, by activating the state's National Guard units under state control (in which case the Posse Comitatus Act does not apply to them), and provide information regarding the resources that have been committed.

Major Disaster. The prerequisites for a major disaster declaration are similar to those for an emergency, 42 U.S.C. § 5170. The governor must first execute the state's emergency plan and make a determination that state capabilities are insufficient to deal with the circumstances. However, the governor need not specify which forms of assistance are needed. The governor must provide information regarding the resources that have been committed and certify that the state will comply with cost sharing provisions under the Stafford Act. There is no provision for the declaration of a major disaster without the governor's request. If the governor activates Guard units and keeps them under state control, those units are not restricted by the Posse Comitatus Act. If the state's National Guard units are called into federal service to respond to an emergency or a major disaster, their role is statutorily restricted to the disaster relief operations authorized under the Stafford Act.

Jennifer K. Elsea, *The Use of Federal Troops for Disaster Assistance: Legal Issues* 5 (CRS Report for Congress, Order Code RS22266, Sept. 16, 2005).

Observe the prominence of the Posse Comitatus Act, 18 U.S.C. § 1835: "Whoever, except in cases and under circumstances expressly authorized by the Constitution or Act of Congress, willfully uses any part of the Army or the Air Force as a posse comitatus or otherwise to execute the laws shall be fined under this title or imprisoned not more than two years, or both." This statute, rooted in objections to the purported abuse of federal military power during Reconstruction, presents the most significant obstacle to the deployment of federal troops in response to natural disasters and other emergencies.

UNITED STATES V. RED FEATHER

392 F. Supp. 916, 921-924 (D.S.D. 1975),
aff'd sub nom. United States v. Casper, 541 F.2d 1275 (8th Cir. 1976)

BOGUE, District Judge. * * *

Upon careful examination of the legislative history of 18 U.S.C. § 1385, this Court has reached several conclusions of law. First, the clause contained in 18 U.S.C. § 1385 "uses any part of the Army or the Air Force as a posse comitatus or otherwise" means the direct active use of Army or Air Force personnel and does not mean the use of Army or Air Force equipment or materiel. 18 U.S.C. § 1385 was intended by Congress * * * to eliminate the direct active use of federal troops by civil law enforcement officers. The prevention of the use of military supplies and equipment was never mentioned in the debates, nor can it reasonably be read into the words of the Act. Only the direct active use of federal [troops is] forbidden, unless expressly authorized by the Constitution or by Act of Congress. An Act of Congress, 10 U.S.C. § 331, has authorized the President of the United States to order use of the militia and armed forces, but no such order was issued by the President as to the Wounded Knee occupation. The Congressional debates clearly reveal that * * * Congress intended to prohibit the direct active use of any unit of federal military troops of whatever size or designation to include one single soldier or large units such as a platoon or squadron, to execute the laws. * * * [W]hen 18 U.S.C. § 1385 was enacted, many Southerners resented the use of federal troops in places in which government had been reestablished, especially since such use was often directed, in their view, toward altering the outcome of elections in Southern states. For example, in the disputed Tilden-Hayes election of 1876, Rutherford B. Hayes obtained the necessary electoral votes only because the disputed votes of South Carolina, Louisiana, and Florida were all awarded to him. In each of these states the elections were accomplished by the use of federal troops, ostensibly to preserve the peace, and in each state when elections were contested, the troops supported the reconstruction candidates. Of primary concern was the prospect of United States marshals, on their own initiative, calling upon troops to form a posse or to otherwise perform direct law enforcement functions to execute the law. Thus, * * * the act was intended to stop army troops, whether one or many, from answering the call of any marshal or deputy marshal to perform direct law enforcement duties to aid in execution of the law. * * *

[T]he intent of Congress in enacting this statute and by using the clause "uses any part of the Army or the Air Force as a posse comitatus or otherwise," was to prevent the direct active use of federal troops, one soldier or many, to execute the laws. Congress did not intend to prevent the use of Army or Air Force materiel or equipment in aid of execution of the laws. Moreover, through enactment of the Economy Act of 1932, 31 U.S.C. § 686, Congress has provided extremely broad authorization for any executive department or independent establishment to place orders with any other willing department for materials, supplies, equipment, work, or service. As far back as 1915 Congress established procedures for the War and Navy Departments to procure or perform services for each other. In 1920 these procedures were extended to any government department which procured by purchase or manufacture stores or materials, or performed services for any other department. * * *

[T]his Court concludes that 18 U.S.C. § 1385 may be violated only through the direct active use of troops for the purpose of executing the laws and 18 U.S.C. § 1385 is not violated by the use of Army or Air Force materiel, supplies, or equipment of any type or kind in execution of the law. As applied to the instant motion, this conclusion of law means that evidence of the direct active use of Army or Air Force troops, one soldier or many, by the United States marshals or agents of the Federal Bureau of Investigation during the occupation of Wounded Knee, is unlawful conduct under 18 U.S.C. § 1385 and is relevant and material to disprove the third element of the charge against the defendants under 18 U.S.C. § 231(a)(3), that "law enforcement officer[s]" were "in the lawful performance of (their) official duties." This conclusion of law also means, and this Court hereby holds, that any evidence of the use of Army or Air Force materiel, supplies, or equipment of any type or character by United States marshals or agents of the Federal Bureau of Investigation to execute the laws during the occupation of Wounded Knee is not unlawful conduct under 18 U.S.C. § 1385 and therefore is irrelevant, immaterial, and inadmissible * * * *

[T]his holding is not only dictated by the statute and its legislative history, but from a practical economic standpoint, this holding is supported by common sense. During and after any natural disaster in this country whether due to flood, heavy snowstorms, earthquake, tornado or otherwise, there is always the possibility of looting and other acts of civil disorder. Most of this nation's smaller governmental units simply cannot maintain an inventory of emergency vehicles and other equipment adequate to meet such a crisis. If the affected municipality or county requests and receives, and law enforcement officers are using Department of Defense equipment or supplies to aid in enforcing the laws, * * * it would violate common sense and do violence to the intent of Congress in passing 18 U.S.C. § 1385 to hold that those arrested for criminal acts must be released because law enforcement officers were using military equipment to aid in executing the law.

NOTES AND QUESTIONS

1. "The phrase 'posse comitatus' is literally translated from Latin as the 'power of the county' and is defined at common law to refer to all those over the age of 15 upon whom a sheriff could call for assistance in preventing any type of civil disorder." United States v. Hartley, 796 F.2d 112, 114 n.3 (5th Cir. 1986); *accord* United States v. Yunis, 681 F. Supp. 891, 891 n.1 (D.D.C. 1988); *see also* H.R. REP. No. 97-71, Part II, 97th Cong., 1st Sess. 4 (1981) (citing 1 WILLIAM BLACKSTONE, COMMENTARIES *343-344), *reprinted in* 1981 U.S.C.C.A.N. 1781, 1786.

2. In addition to barring what *Red Feather* describes as the "direct active use" of military resources in law enforcement, the Posse Comitatus Act has been interpreted by the Department of Defense as generally prohibiting "direct" military involvement in civilian law enforcement but permitting "indirect" assistance such as the transfer of information obtained during normal military operations and other actions that "do not subject civilians to [the] use [of] military power that is regulatory, prescriptive, or compulsory." DoD Directive 5525.5 § E4.1.7.2; *accord* U.S. v. Hitchcock, 286 F.3d 1064, 1069, *amended on other grounds*, 298 F.3d 1021 (9th Cir. 2002). Federal courts typically classify potential violations of the Act according to three tests used to determine when military involvement in law enforcement transcends the presumptively permissible zone of "indirect" assistance: (1) whether civilian law enforcement officials have made "direct active use" of military personnel, (2) whether military involvement

has "pervaded the activities" of civilian authorities, and (3) whether the military has become so entangled in civilian law enforcement as to subject citizens to the "exercise of military power that is regulatory, proscriptive, or compulsory in nature." *See, e.g.*, United States v. Kahn, 35 F.3d 426, 431 (9th Cir. 1994); *Yunis*, 924 F.2d at 1094; *Hartley*, 678 F.2d at 978 n.24.

3. Another way (albeit vague) of stating the permissible scope of military involvement in civilian law enforcement is that the military may play a "passive" role, such as providing logistical support. *See, e.g.*, State v. Nelson, 298 N.C. 573, 260 S.E.2d 629, *cert. denied*, 446 U.S. 929 (1980).

4. Courts typically take a benign view of the origins and purposes of the Posse Comitatus Act: "The purpose of this statute is to prevent use of the federal army to aid civil authorities in the enforcement of civilian laws. Congress adopted the Act's precursor in 1878 in response to abuses resulting from such use in former Confederate States after the Civil War. The Act reflects a concern, which antedates the Revolution, about the dangers to individual freedom and liberty posed by use of a standing army to keep civil peace." Gilbert v. United States, 165 F.3d 470, 472 (6th Cir. 1999). During the fiercely contested presidential election of 1876, President Ulysses S. Grant sent federal troops as a posse comitatus at polling places in Florida, Louisiana, and South Carolina, whose electoral votes were the subject of partisan disputes over the popular vote. An electoral commission, controlled by the Republican Congress that appointed it, awarded all of the contested electoral votes to Republican candidate Rutherford B. Hayes, who prevailed by a single electoral vote over Democrat Samuel J. Tilden. *See, e.g.*, Matthew C. Hammond, Note, *The Posse Comitatus Act: A Principle in Need of Renewal*, 75 WASH. U. L.Q. 953, 954 (1997); H.W.C. Furman, *Restrictions upon Use of the Army Imposed by the Posse Comitatus Act*, 27 MIL. L. REV. 85, 94-95 (1960). *See generally* David E. Engdahl, *Soldiers, Riots and Revolution: The Law and History of Military Troops in Civil Disorders*, 57 IOWA L. REV. 1 (1971).

5. By contrast, other authors vehemently condemn what they consider the whitewashing of the Posse Comitatus Act's odious origins:

> This nineteenth century remnant from the Reconstruction period has been mischaracterized from its very beginnings, at times deliberately. One initial deception was to hide the Act's racist origins by linking the Act with the principles surrounding the founding of the United States, without accounting for the passage of the Constitution or the Civil War. To compound matters, the Act's most vocal nineteenth century supporters incorporated by reference the controversial, yet somewhat contrived, arguments against a standing U.S. army from the revolutionary period. The Act's supporters also hid their unsavory agenda behind patriotic phrases and ideas of the Anti-Federalists that the founders themselves had not put into practice. In short, the Act was carefully disguised in two levels of deliberate misinformation.

The effort to disguise the Act's true origins in Reconstruction bitterness and racial hatred was overwhelmingly successful. The language of misdirection grew over the years by frequent repetition that eventually transformed a hate law into the respected shorthand for the general principle that Americans do not want a military national police force. Additionally, just about everyone examining the law focused on the false historical arguments instead of carefully analyzing the law's actual text and historical context. * * *

Many of the courts analyzing the Act also wrote about the law as if it was the only law or principle that limited the use of the armed forces in a law enforcement role. Some, therefore, have claimed to discern a broader policy or "spirit" behind the Act that is not supported by the historical record or the statute's text. While these wider policies are sound, they are embodied in federalism, the law concerning federal arrest authority, election law, and especially fiscal law. The portion of the Posse Comitatus Act that survived the nineteenth century doesn't have to do all the work, a view that even the Act's original proponents appeared to recognize. Trying to force-fit all these other principles into the surviving part of the Act has only created a need to "discover" a number of implied exceptions and has sowed a great deal of confusion.

Further muddying the waters, much of the commentary about this topic has been infected with a now thoroughly discredited, and racist, historical analysis of the Reconstruction period. Other commentators, and courts, have simply avoided or minimized the Act's brutal racist origins. * * *

Gary Felicetti & John Luce, *The Posse Comitatus Act: Setting the Record Straight on 124 Years of Mischief and Misunderstanding Before Any More Damage Is Done*, 175 MIL. L. REV. 86, 88-92 (2003).

6. Consider another critique, rooted in the belief that the military is neither "the tool of oppression feared by liberal legal scholars and pundits" nor "the 'always successful' organization that those on the right think it is":

The real issue * * * is not whether the military's involvement in law enforcement can be reconciled under both the PCA and our concept of civil liberties; that is likely possible. The real concern with widening the military's participation in law enforcement (as well as other nontraditional military missions) is not an erosion of civil liberties, but an erosion of military capabilities. * * * [Is] the use of military forces in counter-drug operations, or law enforcement in general, * * * a good or bad thing[?] In the end, the use of the military in law enforcement is somewhere in the middle. On the one hand, there are good points. For example, the military's logistical and power projection capabilities increase the reach of American law enforcement. On the other hand, there are bad points. The military tends to think in terms of "complete victory" over an opponent through the use of overwhelming force, which may not be a useful mindset in law enforcement operations. Additionally, using military units for direct or indirect law enforcement degrades those units' readiness for combat operations. * * * The real threat posed by increasing military participation in law enforcement is that use of the military in law enforcement operations will dull the critical war-fighting skills the military services need. Fundamentally, the nation must think and choose wisely, using the military in law enforcement judiciously, when its capabilities can be of most use, of greatest success, and complementary to the skills the military needs to be effective in a modern combat environment.

Michael T. Cunningham, *The Military's Involvement in Law Enforcement: The Threat Is Not What You Think*, 26 SEATTLE U. L. REV. 699, 701-702 (2003). Many of the troops sent to relieve conditions in the wake of Hurricane Katrina had returned from or were en route to foreign tours of duty (particularly in Iraq and Afghanistan). Does the liberal use of military personnel and materiel during disasters effectively open an additional front for these troops at the very moment when American forces are stretched to their limits by active military engagements across the globe?

7. What personnel are covered by the Posse Comitatus Act?

a. Does the Posse Comitatus Act apply to the Navy (including the Marine Corps)? The statute does not name those branches. Courts have divided on the question of whether this omission, by operation of the interpretive canon *expressio unius est exclusio alterius*, confines the Act to the Army and the Air Force, the branches that *are* named in 18 U.S.C. § 1385. Decisions concluding that the statute's plain language excludes the Navy include United States v. Kahn, 35 F.3d 426, 431 (9th Cir. 1994); United States v. Yunis, 924 F.2d 1086, 1093 (D.C. Cir. 1991); United States v. Roberts, 779 F.2d 565 (9th Cir.), *cert. denied*, 479 U.S. 1839 (1986); State v. Short, 113 Wash. 2d 35, 775 P.2d 458 (1989). Decisions holding that the exclusion of the Army and the Air Force from civilian law enforcement evinces a broader legislative desire to exclude the Navy include United States v. Ahumedo-Avendano, 872 F.2d 367, 372 n.6 (11th Cir.), *cert. denied*, 493 U.S. 830 (1989); United States v. Walden, 490 F.2d 372 (4th Cir.), *cert. denied*, 416 U.S. 983 (1974[JC1]).

This theoretical interpretive question has no practical significance. The Department of Defense has applied the proscriptions of the Posse Comitatus Act to the Navy as well as the Army and the Air Force. Congress has directed the Secretary of Defense to "prescribe such regulations as may be necessary to ensure that any activity (including the provision of any equipment or facility or the assignment or detail of any personnel) under this chapter does not include or permit direct participation by a member of the Army, Navy, Air Force, or Marine Corps in a search, seizure, arrest, or other similar activity unless participation in such activity by such member is otherwise authorized by law." 10 U.S.C. § 375. In response to this directive, the Department of Defense has subjected the Navy to the same restrictions on direct participation in law enforcement by Army and Air Force personnel. *See* U.S. Dept. of Defense, Directive No. 5525.5, DoD Cooperation with Civilian Law Enforcement Officials encl. 4, at 4.3 (Jan. 15, 1986), available at http://www.dtic.mil/whs/directives/corres/html/55255.htm and http://www.fas.org/irp/doddir/dod/d5525_5.pdf.

b. "The PCA applies to Reserve members of the Army, Navy, Air Force, and Marine Corps who are on active duty, active duty for training, or inactive duty training *in a Title 10 duty status*. Members of the National Guard performing active duty for training or inactive duty training *in a Title 32 duty status* are subject to the PCA only when the are *in a Title 10 duty status (federal status)*. Members of the National Guard also perform additional duties in a State Active Duty (SAD) status and are not subject to PCA in that capacity. Civilian employees of the Department of Defense are only subject to the prohibitions of the PCA if they are under the direct command and control of a military officer." 1 CENTER FOR LAW & MILITARY OPERATIONS, DOMESTIC OPERATIONAL LAW (DOPLAW) HANDBOOK FOR JUDGE ADVOCATES 15 (2005) (emphases in original; footnotes omitted) (citing 10 U.S.C. §§ 10142, 10143; DoD Cooperation with Civilian Law Enforcement Officials, Department of Defense Directive 5525.5, ¶ E4.2).

8. Does the Posse Comitatus Act restrict the use of armed forces in law enforcement outside the United States? Most courts, finding no congressional intent to restrict uses of American troops abroad, have given the Act no extraterritorial effect. *E.g.*, D'Aquino v. United States, 192 F.2d 338, 351 (9th Cir. 1951), *cert. denied*, 343 U.S. 935 (1952); Chandler v. United States, 171 F.2d 921, 936 (1st Cir. 1948), *cert. denied*, 336 U.S. 918 (1949). The Ninth Circuit, however, has suggested that the extraterritorial applicability of the Posse Comitatus Act remains an open question, citing other statutory restrictions on the use of American troops abroad. *Kahn*, 35 F.3d at 431 n.6 (citing 10 U.S.C. §§ 371-381).

9. As a matter of policy, just how desirable—or execrable—is the Posse Comitatus Act? Does your answer depend on whether military involvement in law enforcement is considered in the abstract, or in the specific context of disasters and other emergencies that overwhelm state and local officials?

10. No person appears ever to have been successfully prosecuted for a violation of the Posse Comitatus Act. *See, e.g.*, Matthew Carlton Hammond, Note, *The Posse Comitatus Act: A Principle in Need of Renewal*, 75 WASH. U. L.Q. 953, 961 (1997). Two Army officers were indicted in 1879, a year after the Act's passage, for sending troops to a U.S. marshal for the purpose of enforcing revenue laws. It is not known whether these officers

were prosecuted. *See id.* at 961 n.53. That said, violations of the Act may yield "[o]ther adverse consequences":

> In many criminal cases, defendants have argued that a violation renders their arrest unlawful; therefore, evidence seized incident to the arrest must be suppressed under the Exclusionary Rule. A review of the cases, however, reveals no federal cases and only one state case in which the Exclusionary Rule was actually applied. In egregious cases, a violation may warrant a civil claim against the military department or the individual service member. A review of these cases, however, reveals only one federal case in which a court supported a tort claim.

Matthew J. Gilligan, *Opening the Gate? An Analysis of Military Law Enforcement Authority over Civilian Lawbreakers on and off the Federal Installation*, 161 MIL. L. REV. 1, 11 (1999). In addition, the Posse Comitatus Act remains "available in criminal or administrative proceedings to punish a lower-level commander who uses military forces to pursue a common felon or to conduct sobriety checkpoints off of a federal military post," and military officers accused of "misusing federal military assets to support a purely civilian criminal matter" have seen "their careers abruptly brought to a close." Craig T. Trebilcock, *The Myth of Posse Comitatus*, J. HOMELAND SECURITY (October 2000) (available at http://www. homelandsecurity.org/journal/articles/Trebilcock.htm).

3. STATUTORY EXCEPTIONS TO THE POSSE COMITATUS ACT

The Posse Comitatus Act does *not* apply "in cases and under circumstances expressly authorized by the Constitution or Act of Congress." 18 U.S.C. § 1385. The Stafford Act is one of the most important statutory exceptions to the Posse Comitatus Act. Other exceptions abound. Congress has authorized the armed forces to share information and materiel with civilian law enforcement agencies. *See* 10 U.S.C. §§ 371-382. These statutory exceptions enable the Secretary of Defense, "in accordance with other applicable law, [to] make available any equipment (including associated supplies or spare parts), base facility, or research facility of the Department of Defense to any Federal, State, or local civilian law enforcement official for law enforcement purposes." *Id.* § 372(a). The Uniform Code of Military Justice, 10 U.S.C. § 801-940, represents perhaps the most extensive exception to the Posse Comitatus Act, insofar as it enables the military to enforce military and civilian laws against members of the armed services by conducting courts-martial and adopting other disciplinary measures.

Of particular interest in the context of terrorism is the Secretary's authority to provide facilities, sensors, protective clothing, or antidotes to "a Federal, State, or local law enforcement or emergency response agency to prepare for or respond to an emergency involving chemical or biological agents if the Secretary determines that the item is not reasonably available from another source." *Id.* § 372(b)(1). Moreover, the Secretary, "upon the request of the Attorney General, may provide assistance in support of Department of Justice activities . . . during an emergency situation involving a biological or chemical weapon of mass destruction." *Id.* § 382(a). The Attorney General may likewise seek military assistance in enforcing federal restrictions on the handling of nuclear materials. *See* 18 U.S.C. § 831(e).

Drug trafficking has earned its own provisions regarding military involvement in law enforcement. Congress has directed the Secretary of Defense to "establish procedures . . . under which States and units of local government may purchase law enforcement equipment suitable for counterdrug activities through the Department of Defense." 10 U.S.C. § 381(a)(1); *see also id.* § 371(c) ("The Secretary of Defense shall ensure, to the extent consistent with national security, that intelligence information held by the Department of Defense and relevant to drug interdiction or other civilian law enforcement matters is provided promptly to appropriate civilian law enforcement officials."). The legal handbook used by Judge Advocates General devotes an entire chapter to military involvement in counterdrug operations. *See* 1 CENTER FOR LAW & MILITARY OPERATIONS, DOMESTIC OPERATIONAL LAW (DOPLAW) HANDBOOK FOR JUDGE ADVOCATES 37-56 (2005).

None of these exceptions relieves the military from the Posse Comitatus Act insofar as civilian law enforcement officers must perform actual arrests. *See* Craig T. Trebilcock, *The Myth of Posse Comitatus*, J. HOMELAND SECURITY (October 2000) (available at http://www.homelandsecurity.org/journal/articles/Trebilcock.htm). The Insurrection Act, 10 U.S.C. § 331-335, however, is a different matter. Originally enacted during the Civil War, *see* Act of July 29, 1861, ch. 25, 12 Stat. 281, the Insurrection Act clearly delegates Congress's power "[t]o provide for calling forth the Militia to execute the Laws of the Union, suppress Insurrections and repel Invasions," U.S. CONST. art. I, § 8, cl. 15, and to enforce the Fourteenth Amendment:

INSURRECTION ACT

10 U.S.C. §§ 331-334

§ 331.   Federal aid for State governments.

Whenever there is an insurrection in any State against its government, the President may, upon the request of its legislature or of its governor if the legislature cannot be convened, call into Federal service such of the militia of the other States, in the number requested by that State, and use such of the armed forces, as he considers necessary to suppress the insurrection.

§ 332.   Use of militia and armed forces to enforce Federal authority.

Whenever the President considers that unlawful obstructions, combinations, or assemblages, or rebellion against the authority of the United States, make it impracticable to enforce the laws of the United States in any State by the ordinary course of judicial proceedings, he may call into Federal service such of the militia of any State, and use such of the armed forces, as he considers necessary to enforce those laws or to suppress the rebellion.

§ 333.   Interference with State and Federal law.

The President, by using the militia or the armed forces, or both, or by any other means, shall take such measures as he considers necessary to suppress, in a State, any insurrection, domestic violence, unlawful combination, or conspiracy, if it —

(1) so hinders the execution of the laws of that State, and of the United States within the State, that any part or class of its people is deprived of a right, privilege, immunity, or protection named in the Constitution and secured by law, and the constituted authorities of that State are unable, fail, or refuse to protect that right, privilege, or immunity, or to give that protection; or

(2) opposes or obstructs the execution of the laws of the United States or impedes the course of justice under those laws.

In any situation covered by clause (1), the State shall be considered to have denied the equal protection of the laws secured by the Constitution.

§ 334.   Proclamation to disperse.

Whenever the President considers it necessary to use the militia or the armed forces under this chapter, he shall, by proclamation, immediately order the insurgents to disperse and retire peaceably to their abodes within a limited time.

NOTES AND QUESTIONS

1. What constitutes an "insurrection"? Consider the following jury charge, issued by the federal district court that tried members of the American Railway Union for their role in the legendary Pullman Strike of 1894:

> Insurrection is a rising against civil or political authority, the open and active opposition of a number of persons to the execution of law in a city or state. Now, the laws of the United States forbid, under penalty, any person from obstructing or retarding the passage of the mail, and make it the duty of the officers to arrest such offenders, and bring them before the court. If, therefore, it shall appear to you that any person or persons have willfully obstructed or retarded the mails, and that their attempted arrest for such offense has been opposed by such a number of persons as would constitute a general uprising in that particular locality, then the fact of an insurrection, within the meaning of the law, has been established; and he who by speech, writing, or other in-

ducement assists in setting it on foot, or carrying it along, or gives it aid or comfort, is guilty of a violation of law. It is not necessary that there should be bloodshed; it is not necessary that its dimensions should be so portentous as to insure probable success, to constitute an insurrection. It is necessary, however, that the rising should be in opposition to the execution of the laws of the United States, and should be so formidable as for the time being to defy the authority of the United States. When men gather to resist the civil or political power of the United States, or to oppose the execution of its laws, and are in such force that the civil authorities are inadequate to put them down, and a considerable military force is needed to accomplish that result, they become insurgents; and every person who knowingly incites, aids, or abets them, no matter what his motives may be, is likewise an insurgent. The penalty for the offense is severe, and, as I have said, is designed to protect the government and its authority against direct attack.

In re Charge to Grand Jury, 62 F. 828, 830 (N.D. Ill. 1894). *See generally* WILLIAM CAWARDINE, THE PULLMAN STRIKE (1973).

2. Those who wage insurrection are well advised, for their own sake and that of their supporters, to succeed. Failed insurrections secure no legal rights or privileges under the surviving regime:

> Viewed from the standpoint of the constitution, the confederate government was nothing more than the military representative of the insurrection against the authority of the United States. The belligerent rights conceded to it in the interest of humanity, to prevent the cruelties which would have followed mutual reprisals and retaliations, were, from their nature, such only as existed during the war. * * * Those who engage in rebellion must consider the consequences. If they succeed, rebellion becomes revolution, and the new government will justify its founders. If they fail, all their hostile acts to the rightful government are violations of law, and originate no rights which can be recognized by the courts of the nation whose authority and existence have been alike assailed.

Stevens v. Griffith, 11 U.S. 48, 51, 52-53 (1884).

3. Much of the Fourteenth Amendment was aimed at imposing special disabilities on the losers of the Civil War. Sections 2, 3, and 4 of that amendment continue to serve notice that those who engage in insurrection or rebellion against the United States do so at their peril. For purposes of apportioning representatives, section 2 prohibits the disenfranchisement of a state's otherwise eligible voters, "except for participation in rebellion, or other crime." Section 3 disqualifies from federal office any person "who, having previously taken an oath, as a member of Congress, or as an officer of the United States, or as a member of any State

legislature, or as an executive or judicial officer of any State, to support the Constitution of the United States, shall have engaged in insurrection or rebellion against the same, or given aid or comfort to the enemies thereof." Section 4 at once secures "[t]he validity of the public debt of the United States, authorized by law, including debts incurred for payment of pensions and bounties for services in suppressing insurrection or rebellion" and bars the United States and its constituent states from "assum[ing] or pay[ing] any debt or obligation incurred in aid of insurrection or rebellion against the United States, or any claim for the loss or emancipation of any slave." Indeed, section 4 provides that "all such debts, obligations and claims shall be held illegal and void."

Does the stigma of the word *insurrection*, as reflected in the punitive provisions of the Fourteenth Amendment and decisions by courts familiar with the Civil War (such as *Stevens* and the Pullman Strike case), impede the contemporary use of the Insurrection Act?

4. Recall Article IV, section 4 of the Constitution: "The United States shall guarantee to every State in this Union a Republican Form of Government, and shall protect each of them against Invasion; and on Application of the Legislature, or of the Executive (when the Legislature cannot be convened), against domestic Violence." *See supra* pp. 22-23.

a. Does this provision represent an affirmative power vested in Congress and the President? A responsibility that the United States must discharge *vis-à-vis* its constituent states? Both?

b. Consider the term *domestic violence*. How does this term compare to the term *insurrection*, as it is used (1) within the Insurrection Act and (2) within Article I, section 8 of the Constitution?

5. The National Guard may be called into the service of the United States "[w]henever—(1) the United States, or any of the Commonwealths or possessions, is invaded or is in danger of invasion by a foreign nation; (2) there is a rebellion or danger of a rebellion against the authority of the Government of the United States; or (3) the President is unable with the regular forces to execute the laws of the United States." 10 U.S.C. § 12406. The Insurrection Act has been used to deploy National Guard units in support of desegregation orders that met "massive resistance" during the 1950s and 1960s. Perhaps the most prominent use of this power took place in September 1957, when President Eisenhower ordered the National Guard and Air National Guard of Arkansas to remove "obstructions to justice in respect to enrollment and attendance at public schools in the Little Rock School District." Exec. Order No. 10,730, 22 Fed. Reg. 7628 (Sept. 24, 1957); *see also* Exec. Order No. 11,053, 27 Fed. Reg. 9681 (Sept. 30, 1962) (Mississippi public schools); Exec. Order No. 11,111, 28 Fed. Reg. 5709 (June 11, 1963) (University of Alabama); Exec. Order No. 11,118, 28 F.R. 9863 (Sept. 10, 1963) (Alabama public schools). These executive orders were preceded by presidential proclamations, issued under 10 U.S.C. § 334, commanding private citizens engaged in an insurgency to disperse and retire peaceably to their homes. *See* Proc. No. 3204, 22 Fed. Reg. 7628 (Sept. 23, 1957) (Little Rock public schools, par-

ticularly Central Little Rock High School); Proc. No. 3497, 27 Fed. Reg. 9681 (Sept. 30, 1962) (Mississippi public schools); Proc. No. 3542, 28 Fed. Reg. 5707 (June 11, 1963) (University of Alabama); Proc. No. 3554, 28 Fed. Reg. 9861 (Sept. 10, 1963) (Alabama public schools). Similar proclamations have been issued in connection with Martin Luther King, Jr.'s, peace march from Selma to Montgomery, *see* Proc. No. 3645, 30 Fed. Reg. 3739 (March 23, 1965), and urban riots throughout 1967 and 1968. *See, e.g.*, Proc. No. 3795, 32 Fed. Reg. 10,905 (July 26, 1967) (Detroit). A dispersal proclamation under section 334 precedes the deployment of National Guard and armed services troops.

6. The Insurrection Act enabled the first President Bush in 1989 to send troops to quell civic unrest in the Virgin Islands after Hurricane Hugo. *See* Proc. No. 6023, 54 Fed. Reg. 39,151 (Sept. 20, 1989); Exec. Order No. 12,690, 54 Fed. Reg. 39, 153 (Sept. 20, 1989). Three years later, President Bush again invoked the Insurrection Act in response to the Rodney King riots in Los Angeles. *See* Proc. No. 6427, 57 Fed. Reg. 19,359 (May 1, 1992); Exec. Order No. 12,804, 57 Fed. Reg. 19,361 (May 1, 1992).

7. Disease often accompanies natural disaster. States typically respond by developing strategies for managing public health crises. *See, e.g.*, THE CENTER FOR LAW AND THE PUBLIC'S HEALTH, THE MODEL STATE EMERGENCY HEALTH POWERS ACT (2001); Elisabeth Belmont et al., *Emergency Preparedness, Response, and Recovery Checklist: Beyond the Emergency Management Plan*, 37 J. HEALTH L. 503 (2004). These plans, however, could fail if disease (whether or not connected to a natural disaster) caused public panic. If a pandemic were to overwhelm the ability of civilian authorities to enforce law and order, could the Insurrection Act authorize military officials to impose quarantines and to adopt other public health measures? *See* Jennifer Elsea & Kathleen Swendiman, *Federal and State Quarantine and Isolation Authority* 22-23 (CRS Report for Congress, Dec. 12, 2005) (yes). Even in the absence of the Insurrection Act, federal law directs military officers to observe "[t]he quarantines and other restraints established by the health laws of any state, respecting any vessels arriving in, or bound to, any port or district thereof." 42 U.S.C. § 97. Federal law also provides that "all such officers of the United States shall faithfully aid in the execution of such quarantines and health laws, according to their respective powers and within their respective precincts, and as they shall be directed, from time to time, by the Secretary of Health and Human Services." *Id.*

4. NONSTATUTORY EXCEPTIONS TO THE POSSE COMITATUS ACT

In addition to exceptions "expressly authorized by . . . Act of Congress," the Posse Comitatus Act is also suspended "in cases and under circumstances expressly authorized *by the Constitution*." 18 U.S.C. § 1385 (emphasis added). In apparent vindication of its constitutional mandate, the Department of

Defense has historically asserted two nonstatutory sources of authority beyond the Stafford Act, the Insurrection Act, or any other statutory exception to the Posse Comitatus Act. *See generally* Jennifer K. Elsea, *The Use of Federal Troops for Disaster Assistance: Legal Issues* 3-6 (CRS Order Code RS22266, Sept. 16, 2005).

First, Department of Defense regulations recognize an inherent emergency power that authorize "[a]ctions that are taken under the inherent right of the U.S. Government, a sovereign national entity under the U.S. Constitution, to ensure the preservation of public order and to carry out governmental operations within its territorial limits, or otherwise in accordance with applicable law, by force, if necessary." DoD Cooperation with Civilian Law Enforcement Officials, DoD Directive 5525.5 (Encl. 4) § E4.1.2.3. This inherent emergency power authorizes

> prompt and vigorous Federal action, including use of military forces, to prevent loss of life or wanton destruction of property and to restore governmental functioning and public order when sudden and unexpected civil disturbances, disaster, or calamities seriously endanger life and property and disrupt normal governmental functions to such an extent that duly constituted local authorities are unable to control the situation.

Operations conducted under this authority ordinarily proceed under an executive order, but Department of Defense regulations authorize military commanders to take emergency action on a unilateral basis whenever "sudden and unexpected civic disturbances (including civic disturbances incident to earthquake, fire, flood or other such calamity endangering life) occur." Military Assistance for Civil Disturbances, DoD Directive 3025.12 § 4.2.2. Two further conditions apply. First, "duly constituted local authorities" must be "unable to control the situation." Second, "circumstances preclude obtaining prior authorization by the President." *Id.*

Second, the Department of Defense allows commanders to provide resources and assistance to civilian authorities when a disaster exceeds the capacity of local authorities and demands immediate action "to prevent human suffering, save lives, or mitigate great property damage." Military Support to Civil Authorities, DoD Directive 3025.1 § 4.5. This "immediate response" authority permits the military to provide the types of assistance otherwise authorized by the Stafford Act, such as rescue, evacuation, and emergency medical services; debris removal; restoration of essential services, including emergency communications; and the delivery of food and other supplies. *See id.* § 4.5.1. Although the immediate response authority does not require a request for assistance from state or local officials, the military is directed *not* to "perform any function of civil government unless absolutely necessary on a temporary basis." *Id.* § 4.4.10. Any military commander who is directed to perform or does undertake to perform "such functions shall facilitate the reestablishment of civil responsibility at the earliest time possible." *Id.* The immediate response authority, derived from no statutes, appears to stem from the historical practice of the armed forces. During the 1906 San Francisco earthquake and fire, for instance, the commander of the Pacific

Division unilaterally directed all troops under his command to help civilian law enforcement officers in their effort to stop looting, fight fires, and protect federal buildings. *See* Jim Winthrop, *The Oklahoma City Bombing: Immediate Response Authority and Other Military Assistance to Civil Authority (MAC)*, ARMY LAW., July 1997, at 3.

Does the Department of Defense's assertion of inherent emergency authority and immediate response authority upset the balance of powers established through the Posse Comitatus Act, Stafford Act, Insurrection Act, and other statutes governing the deployment of federal troops and resources in civilian law enforcement? Consider this overview of restrictions on the use of military personnel and resources in law enforcement:

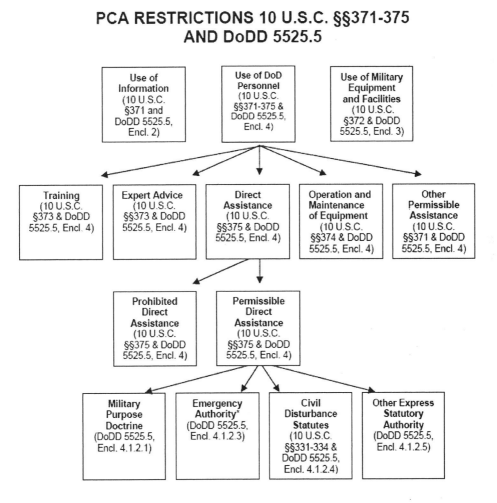

PCA RESTRICTIONS 10 U.S.C. §§371-375 AND DoDD 5525.5

*See DoDD 3025.12 to distinguish Emergency MACDIS Authority from Immediate Response Authority.

1 CENTER FOR LAW & MILITARY OPERATIONS, DOMESTIC OPERATIONAL LAW (DOPLAW) HANDBOOK FOR JUDGE ADVOCATES 18 (2005).

5. REFORMING THE INSURRECTION ACT?

Does the Insurrection Act strike the right balance with the Posse Comitatus Act? Which of the following alternative approaches, if any, would you adopt?

John A. McCarthy, Randall Jackson & Maeve Dion, Posse Comitatus and the Military's Role in Disaster Relief

American Bar Association, Hurricane Katrina Task Force
Subcommittee Report 23, 28-31 (Feb. 2006)

It would seem that rather than enacting new legal structures or eliminating the concept inherent in *posse comitatus*, it would make more sense to more fully and efficiently make use of the legal authorities that are already in place. Establishing clear lines of communication and confirming that leadership understands the roles and limitations of key players can ensure that resources are best applied in disaster situations. * * *

Should the Insurrection Act be revisited? Because it is the most prominent true exception to *posse comitatus*, consideration could be given to broaden its application. Three possibilities regarding such a proposal include:

a. Rename the Insurrection Act, but leave it unchanged

This possibility assumes that the current language of the Insurrection Act sufficiently empowers the military to enforce domestic law in a fairly broad set of circumstances (whenever "the President considers that unlawful obstructions, combinations, or assemblages, or rebellion against the authority of the United States, make it impracticable to enforce the laws of the United States in any State or Territory by the ordinary course of judicial proceedings"), but that the political implications of declaring the loss of civil order an "insurrection" creates an artificial impediment to the exercise of these authorities. Because this word conjures up specific images of attempts to overthrow the government, it may drive leaders to be overly cautious in invoking it, for fear of being accused of overreaching. The reports suggest that this may have been the case with the Administration during Katrina.

This potential problem could be addressed by simply renaming the provision. Perhaps the Insurrection Act could be renamed as the Domestic Disaster Relief Act or Major Disaster Assistance Act, for example. Alternatively, perhaps the proposed title could be combined with its current one. "Insurrection" could remain within the title: *e.g.*, the Domestic Disaster Relief and Insurrection Act. The idea is to limit any political stigma from the name and thus empower leadership to look solely to the circumstances of the disaster for guidance as to whether or not to turn to this authority.

b. Change the language of the statute and rename

Perhaps it is appropriate to more explicitly state the circumstances [under which] "unlawful obstructions, combinations, or assemblages, or rebellion against the authority of the United States, make it impracticable to enforce the laws of the United States in any State or Territory by the ordinary course of judicial proceedings." Instances of looting and other lawless behavior in the aftermath of a major catastrophe perhaps should be explicitly cited as grounds for invoking this Act in order to empower the military to temporarily enforce domestic law until civilian authorities can recover. Perhaps a clause could be added pointing to a situation in which an extreme disaster may have eliminated local and state authority. Adding language regarding a possible role for the military in enforcing a quarantine might also help to clarify its current authority and make clear its authority in this regard.

There is precedent for this in the Immediate Response Authority, a DoD doctrine which allows commanders to provide resources and assistance to civil authorities without or prior to a declaration under the Stafford Act when a disaster overwhelms the capabilities of local authorities and necessitates immediate action. The immediate response authority may also include law enforcement activities that would ordinarily be prohibited by *posse comitatus*. The controlling directive does not require a request from state or local officials, but rather states that DoD Components shall not perform any function of civil government unless absolutely necessary on a temporary basis under conditions of Immediate Response. Any commander who is directed, or undertakes, to perform such functions shall facilitate the reestablishment of civil responsibility at the earliest time possible.

The immediate response authority is not provided for in any statute, but is said to have deep historical roots. The 1906 San Francisco earthquake and fire are noted examples. There, the commanding general of the Pacific Division, on his own initiative, deployed all troops at his disposal to assist civil authorities to stop looting, protect federal buildings, and to assist firefighters.

c. Leave the Insurrection Act as is

There is adequate language in the statute as is and only needs to be better understood and utilized when needed. * * *

How can local authorities, first responders, and local/state police best communicate with the military on the ground? * * * [I]f the military is to play a supporting role as outlined in the Stafford Act, what kinds of communication structures are needed to assure that the resources are applied as contemplated by existing authorities? * * *

How do we balance the needs of the military for international response with respect to the global war on terrorism with the desire to use the military and its resources during national incidents? While the National Guard responded during Hurricane Katrina, many of the troops had either recently returned from Iraq/Afghanistan or were about to leave. * * * Congressional guidance is needed to reexamine, and perhaps reconfigure, the delicate balance struck in law between the military's foreign and domestic roles.

3

EMERGENCY RESPONSE

None of this had to happen.

— U.S. House of Representatives[1][JC2]

In times of disaster, even the soundest legal structure is only as effective as its implementation. "The System did not perform as a system," the Army Corps of Engineers has confessed; "the hurricane protection in New Orleans and Southeast Louisiana was a system in name only." 1 ARMY CORPS OF ENGINEERS, FINAL REPORT OF THE INTERAGENCY PERFORMANCE EVALUATION TASKFORCE (IPET) 3 (June 1, 2006). As it was with infrastructure, so, too, with personnel: By most accounts, the federal and state agencies charged with coordinating the response to Hurricane Katrina performed abysmally. The federal framework, for its part, had been developed in response to the terrorist attacks of September 11, 2001. The four-year cycle from September 11 to Hurricane Katrina, from the worst mass crime to the worst natural disaster in American history, severely tested the law of emergency response. Unfortunately, the United States failed.

This chapter begins by exploring the creation of the Department of Homeland Security and the implementation of Homeland Security Presidential Directive 5 (HSPD-5). It focuses on HSPD-5's two most important components: the National Response Plan and the National Incident Management System. The chapter then turns to the coordination of the federal emergency response system with its state-level and regional counterparts. In addition to reviewing Louisiana's emergency response plan, this chapter explores the

---

1. U.S. HOUSE OF REPRESENTATIVES, A FAILURE OF INITIATIVE: FINAL REPORT OF THE SELECT BIPARTISAN COMMITTEE TO INVESTIGATE THE PREPARATION FOR AND RESPONSE TO HURRICANE KATRINA 123 (2006).

Emergency Management Assistance Compact, a cooperative mechanism for mutual emergency assistance among the states. The chapter concludes by examining two possible avenues for reform. After reconsidering the "disaster czar" role that Herbert Hoover played after the Mississippi River flood of 1927, this chapter scrutinizes the Senate's proposal for restructuring the federal emergency response system.

A. FEDERAL EMERGENCY RESPONSE PLANS

1. THE KATRINA RESPONSE AS A LEGACY OF SEPTEMBER 11, 2001

The Homeland Security Act of 2002, Pub. L. No. 107-296, 116 Stat. 2135 (codified at 6 U.S.C. §§ 101-557), created the Department of Homeland Security (DHS). The Department's "primary mission" is described principally in terms of terrorism; DHS's first three responsibilities are to "prevent terrorist attacks within the United States," to "reduce the vulnerability of the United States to terrorism," and to "minimize the damage, and assist in the recovery, from terrorist attacks that do occur within the United States." 6 U.S.C. § 111(b)(1). Only then does the Homeland Security Act direct DHS to "act[] as a focal point regarding natural and man-made crises and emergency planning." *Id.* § 111(b)(1)(D).

The Homeland Security Act consolidates the functions of the Federal Emergency Management Agency (FEMA) within DHS. *See id.* §§ 313(1), 317(a). The Act represents the most comprehensive reorganization of federal emergency authority since President Carter created FEMA as an independent agency. *See* Reorganization Plan No. 3, 43 Fed. Reg. 41,943 (June 19, 1978); Exec. Order No. 12,127, 44 Fed. Reg. 19,369 (March 31, 1979); Exec. Order No. 12,148, 44 Fed. Reg. 43,239 (July 20, 1979). FEMA assumed, among other functions, the mission of the Federal Disaster Assistance Administration of the Department of Housing and Urban Development and civil defense responsibilities previously assigned to the Department of Defense.

The reorganized FEMA retains "[a]ll functions and authorities prescribed by" the Robert T. Stafford Disaster Relief and Emergency Assistance Act, 42 U.S.C. §§ 5121-5206. *See* 6 U.S.C. § 317(a)(1). FEMA performs multiple additional tasks as part of "its mission to reduce the loss of life and property and protect the Nation from all hazards by leading and supporting the Nation in a comprehensive, risk-based emergency management program." *Id.* § 317(a)(2). This mission comprises five distinct components:

- "mitigation, by taking sustained actions to reduce or eliminate long-term risk to people and property from hazards and their effects"
- "planning for building the emergency management profession to prepare effectively for, mitigate against, respond to, and recover from any hazard"

- "response, by conducting emergency operations to save lives and property through positioning emergency equipment and supplies, through evacuating potential victims, through providing food, water, shelter, and medical care to those in need, and through restoring critical public services"
- "recovery, by rebuilding communities so individuals, businesses, and governments can function on their own, return to normal life, and protect against future hazards"
- "increased efficiencies, by coordinating efforts relating to mitigation, planning, response, and recovery"

Id. § 317(a)(2)(A)-(E). The third component, "response," figured prominently in what is regarded in retrospect as FEMA's greatest failure. During Katrina, FEMA did not distinguish itself in performing any of the specific tasks within the notion of "response"—the positioning of emergency equipment and supplies; evacuation; the provision of food, water, shelter, and medical care; and the restoration of critical public services. *Id.* § 317(a)(2)(C).

The Homeland Security Act assigns the Secretary of Homeland Security a wide range of responsibilities for emergency preparedness and response. In addition to "helping to ensure the effectiveness of emergency response providers to terrorist attacks, major disasters, and other emergencies," the Secretary must manage "the Federal Government's response to terrorist attacks and major disasters" and "coordinating . . . Federal response resources . . . in the event of a terrorist attack or major disaster." *Id.* § 312(1), (3). The Secretary is also directed to "aid[] the recovery from terrorist attacks and major disaster." *Id.* § 312(4).

The Act assigns two further tasks that bear special significance for Homeland Security Presidential Directive 5. First, the Act directs the Secretary of Homeland Security to "build[] a comprehensive *national incident management system* with Federal, State, and local government personnel, agencies, and authorities, to respond to such attacks and disasters." *Id.* § 312(5) (emphasis added). Second, the Act requires the Secretary to "consolidat[e] existing Federal Government emergency response plans into a single, coordinated *national response plan.*" *Id.* § 312(6) (emphasis added).

In 2003, President Bush issued Homeland Security Presidential Directive 5 (HSPD-5), a blueprint for the "management of domestic incidents":

HOMELAND SECURITY PRESIDENTIAL DIRECTIVE/HSPD-5

39 Weekly Comp. Pres. Doc. 263 (March 7, 2003)

Purpose

(1) To enhance the ability of the United States to manage domestic incidents by establishing a single, comprehensive national incident management system. * * *

Policy

(3) To prevent, prepare for, respond to, and recover from terrorist attacks, major disasters, and other emergencies, the United States Government shall establish a single, comprehensive approach to domestic incident management. The objective of the United States Government is to ensure that all levels of government across the Nation have the capability to work efficiently and effectively together, using a national approach to domestic incident management. In these efforts, with regard to domestic incidents, the United States Government treats crisis management and consequence management as a single, integrated function, rather than as two separate functions.

(4) The Secretary of Homeland Security is the principal Federal official for domestic incident management. Pursuant to the Homeland Security Act of 2002, the Secretary is responsible for coordinating Federal operations within the United States to prepare for, respond to, and recover from terrorist attacks, major disasters, and other emergencies. The Secretary shall coordinate the Federal Government's resources utilized in response to or recovery from terrorist attacks, major disasters, or other emergencies if and when any one of the following four conditions applies: (1) a Federal department or agency acting under its own authority has requested the assistance of the Secretary; (2) the resources of State and local authorities are overwhelmed and Federal assistance has been requested by the appropriate State and local authorities; (3) more than one Federal department or agency has become substantially involved in responding to the incident; or (4) the Secretary has been directed to assume responsibility for managing the domestic incident by the President.

(5) Nothing in this directive alters, or impedes the ability to carry out, the authorities of Federal departments and agencies to perform their responsibilities under law. All Federal departments and agencies shall cooperate with the Secretary in the Secretary's domestic incident management role.

(6) The Federal Government recognizes the roles and responsibilities of State and local authorities in domestic incident management. Initial responsibility for managing domestic incidents generally falls on State and local authorities. The Federal Government will assist State and local authorities when their resources are overwhelmed, or when Federal interests are involved. The Secretary will coordinate with State and local governments to ensure adequate planning, equipment, training, and exercise activities. The Secretary will also provide assistance to State and local governments to develop all-hazards plans and capabilities, including those of greatest importance to the security of the United States, and will ensure that State, local, and Federal plans are compatible.

(7) The Federal Government recognizes the role that the private and nongovernmental sectors play in preventing, preparing for, responding to, and recovering from terrorist attacks, major disasters, and other emergencies. The Secretary will coordinate with the private and nongovernmental sectors to ensure adequate planning, equipment, training, and exercise activities and to promote partnerships to address incident management capabilities. * * *

Tasking

(12) The Secretary shall ensure that, as appropriate, information related to domestic incidents is gathered and provided to the public, the private sector, State and local authorities, Federal departments and agencies, and, generally through the Assistant to the President for Homeland Security, to the President. The Secretary shall provide standardized, quantitative reports to the Assistant to the President for Homeland Security on the readiness and preparedness of the Nation—at all levels of government—to prevent, prepare for, respond to, and recover from domestic incidents. * * *

(15) The Secretary shall develop, submit for review to the Homeland Security Council, and administer a National Incident Management System (NIMS). This system will provide a consistent nationwide approach for Federal, State, and local governments to work effectively and efficiently together to prepare for, respond to, and recover from domestic incidents, regardless of cause, size, or complexity. To provide for interoperability and compatibility among Federal, State, and local capabilities, the NIMS will include a core set of concepts, principles, terminology, and technologies covering the incident command system; multi-agency coordination systems; unified command; training; identification and management of resources (including systems for classifying types of resources); qualifications and certification; and the collection, tracking, and reporting of incident information and incident resources.

(16) The Secretary shall develop, submit for review to the Homeland Security Council, and administer a National Response Plan (NRP). The Secretary shall consult with appropriate Assistants to the President (including the Assistant to the President for Economic Policy) and the Director of the Office of Science and Technology Policy, and other such Federal officials as may be appropriate, in developing and implementing the NRP. This plan shall integrate Federal Government domestic prevention, preparedness, response, and recovery plans into one all-discipline, all-hazards plan. The NRP shall be unclassified. If certain operational aspects require classification, they shall be included in classified annexes to the NRP.

(a) The NRP, using the NIMS, shall, with regard to response to domestic incidents, provide the structure and mechanisms for national level policy and operational direction for Federal support to State and local incident managers and for exercising direct Federal authorities and responsibilities, as appropriate.

(b) The NRP will include protocols for operating under different threats or threat levels; incorporation of existing Federal emergency and incident management plans (with appropriate modifications and revisions) as either integrated components of the NRP or as supporting operational plans; and additional operational plans or annexes, as appropriate, including public affairs and intergovernmental communications.

(c) The NRP will include a consistent approach to reporting incidents, providing assessments, and making recommendations to the President, the Secretary, and the Homeland Security Council.

(d) The NRP will include rigorous requirements for continuous improvements from testing, exercising, experience with incidents, and new information and technologies.

(17) The Secretary shall:

(a) By April 1, 2003, (1) develop and publish an initial version of the NRP, in consultation with other Federal departments and agencies; and (2) provide the Assistant to the President for Homeland Security with a plan for full development and implementation of the NRP.

(b) By June 1, 2003, (1) in consultation with Federal departments and agencies and with State and local governments, develop a national system of standards, guidelines, and protocols to implement the NIMS; and (2) establish a mechanism for ensuring ongoing management and maintenance of the NIMS, including regular consultation with other Federal departments and agencies and with State and local governments.

(c) By September 1, 2003, in consultation with Federal departments and agencies and the Assistant to the President for Homeland Security, review existing authorities and regulations and prepare recommendations for the President on revisions necessary to implement fully the NRP.

(18) The heads of Federal departments and agencies shall adopt the NIMS within their departments and agencies and shall provide support and assistance to the Secretary in the development and maintenance of the NIMS. All Federal departments and agencies will use the NIMS in their domestic incident management and emergency prevention, preparedness, response, recovery, and mitigation activities, as well as those actions taken in support of State or local entities. The heads of Federal departments and agencies shall participate in the NRP, shall assist and support the Secretary in the development and maintenance of the NRP, and shall participate in and use domestic incident reporting systems and protocols established by the Secretary. * * *

(20) Beginning in Fiscal Year 2005, Federal departments and agencies shall make adoption of the NIMS a requirement, to the extent permitted by law, for providing Federal preparedness assistance through grants, contracts, or other activities. The Secretary shall develop standards and guidelines for determining whether a State or local entity has adopted the NIMS.

NOTE

HSPD-5 implemented 6 U.S.C. § 312(5) and (6) by establishing two complementary components of a plan for managing "domestic incidents": a National Incident Management System (NIMS) and a National Response Plan (NRP). Together, the NIMS and the NRP comprise the heart of the post–September 11 framework for federal emergency response:

THE WHITE HOUSE

The Federal Response to Hurricane Katrina: Lessons Learned 13-15 (2006)

The National Incident Management System

The National Incident Management System (NIMS) establishes standardized incident management protocols and procedures that all responders —Federal, State, and local—should use to conduct and coordinate response actions. It sets forth a "core set of doctrine, concepts, principles, terminology and organizational processes to enable effective, efficient, and collaborative incident management at all levels" of government. The NIMS provides a common, flexible framework within which government and private entities at all levels can work together to manage domestic incidents of any magnitude. * * *

The central component of the NIMS is the Incident Command System (ICS). The ICS was developed and refined over many years by incident commanders at the Federal, State, and local levels and was being successfully implemented throughout the country prior to being included in the NIMS. The ICS provides a means to coordinate the efforts of individual responders and agencies as they respond to and help manage an incident. The ICS organization, the structure and size of which can be tailored to the complexity and size of any given incident, comprises five major functional areas—Command, Planning, Operations, Logistics, and Finance/Administration. This system grew out of the challenges of interagency coordination experienced when fighting wildfires in western states.

ICS requires that a command system be established from the onset of incident operations, thereby ensuring a unified command and the efficient coordination of multi-agency and multi-jurisdictional efforts. Recognizing that most incidents are managed locally, the command function under ICS is set up at the lowest level of the response, and grows to encompass other agencies and jurisdictions as they arrive. Some incidents that begin with a single response discipline (e.g., fire or police department) within a single jurisdiction may rapidly expand to multi-discipline, multi-jurisdictional incidents requiring significant additional resources and operational support. The concept of unified command is both more important and more complicated when local, State, and Federal commanders are required to coordinate their efforts. ICS clarifies reporting relationships and eliminates confusion caused by multiple, and potentially conflicting, directions and actions. The National Response Plan requires senior officials from multiple levels of government to come together at a single location to establish a common set of objectives and a single incident plan. This group, referred to as the "Unified Command," provides for and enables joint decisions on objectives, strategies, plans, priorities, and public communications.

The National Response Plan

Adopted by the Federal government in December 2004, the NRP is an all-hazards plan that establishes a single, comprehensive framework for managing domestic incidents across all levels of government and across a spectrum of activities that includes prevention, preparedness, response, and recovery. It provides the structure and mechanisms for coordinating Federal support to State and local incident managers and for exercising Federal authorities and responsibilities incorporating the NIMS structure.

The NRP is based on a number of fundamental precepts. Consistent with the traditions and customs that have developed under American federalism, the NRP is built on the premise that incidents are generally handled at the lowest jurisdictional level possible. Local authorities provide the initial response capabilities to every incident, including man-made and natural disasters, and when overwhelmed, request assistance from neighboring jurisdictions. When incidents are of such a magnitude that these resources are overwhelmed, resources are requested from the State, which draws on its own internal emergency response capabilities or requests assistance from neighboring States through mutual-aid agreements. Many large and devastating events are handled this way without any Federal assistance. When Federal response assistance is required, the NRP employs a systematic and coordinated approach to incident management at the field, regional, and Federal agency headquarters levels, establishing protocols for such activities as reporting incidents, issuing alerts and notification, coordinating response actions, and mobilizing resources. Though the NRP generally seeks to preserve the primary role of State and local bodies as first responders, it does recognize some events will be so catastrophic that they will require a greater proactive Federal government response * * *. However, while the NRP recognized the need for a proactive Federal response in a catastrophe, no final plan has been put in place to make this operational.

What Triggers the NRP

The NRP "covers the full range of complex and constantly changing requirements in anticipation of or in response to threats or acts of terrorism, major disasters, and other emergencies." It applies to "all Federal departments and agencies that may be requested to provide assistance or conduct operations in the context of actual or potential Incidents of National Significance." The NRP is also designed to be flexible and scalable: "Consistent with the model provided in the NIMS, the NRP can be partially or fully implemented in the context of a threat, anticipation of a significant event, or the response to a significant event." The NRP can be used to selectively implement specific components in unique situations or can be fully implemented to bring to bear the full efforts and resources of the Federal government.

However, the specific triggers for the National Response Plan and its various components are unclear. In HSPD-5, the President instructed the

Secretary of Homeland Security to coordinate the Federal government's resources utilized in response to or recovery from terrorist attacks, major disasters, or other emergencies if and when any one of the following four conditions applies:

(1) A Federal department or agency acting under its own authority has requested the assistance of the Secretary;
(2) The resources of State and local authorities are overwhelmed and Federal assistance has been requested by the appropriate State and local authorities;
(3) More than one Federal department or agency has become substantially involved in responding to the incident; or
(4) The Secretary has been directed to assume responsibility for managing the domestic incident by the President.

The NRP bases the definition of Incidents of National Significance (INS) "on situations related to" these HSPD-5 criteria. However, the NRP lacks sufficient clarity regarding when and how an event becomes an INS. There are two dimensions to this issue. First, it is unclear whether satisfaction of one or more of the stated criteria is sufficient for an INS to exist, or whether additional considerations must apply. Second, the NRP is unclear as to whether the Secretary must formally declare an INS or, alternatively, whether an INS is triggered automatically when one or more of these criteria are satisfied, including when the President declares a disaster or emergency under the Stafford Act. With respect to Hurricane Katrina, when the Secretary of Homeland Security formally declared the event to be an INS on Tuesday, August 30, 2005, arguably an INS already existed, because two of the four HSPD-5 criteria noted above had already been satisfied.

The lack of clarity on the second issue is illustrated by two seemingly inconsistent NRP provisions; the Scope and Applicability section states that the Secretary is responsible for declaring an INS, which supports an interpretation that an INS cannot be in effect without a declaration by the Secretary, while the Planning Assumptions section states that "all Presidentially declared disasters and emergencies under the Stafford Act are considered Incidents of National Significance," which supports a conclusion that the President's issuance of an emergency declaration for Louisiana on August 27, 2005, put an INS into effect.

Most importantly, however, regardless of how an INS is defined or whether an INS must be formally declared by the Secretary or not, the NRP fails to articulate clearly which specific actions should be taken and what components should be utilized under the NRP as a result of an INS coming into effect. As a practical matter, many of the NRP's functions and structures were already being utilized at the time that the Secretary declared an INS.

Since the NRP was adopted in December 2004, many parts of the Plan had been used to various degrees and magnitudes for thirty declared Stafford Act events to coordinate Federal assistance. Yet, an INS had never formally been declared prior to Tuesday, August 30, 2005—during the Hurricane

Katrina response. The lack of clarity discussed above caused confusion. The process and the operational consequences of declaring an INS should be further defined and clarified.

NRP Concept of Operations

When applied together, the components of the NRP should provide for a unified command structure to serve as the local, multi-agency coordination center for the effective and efficient coordination of Federal, State, local, tribal, nongovernmental, and private-sector organizations with primary responsibility for incident-related prevention, response and recovery actions. In many cases, this takes place at a Joint Field Office (JFO). The JFO co-locates the Principal Federal Official (PFO) and Federal Coordinating Officer in situations not involving multiple FCOs. In HSPD-5, the President designated the Secretary of Homeland Security as the "principal Federal official for domestic incident management." The NRP allows the Secretary to delegate his [JC3]responsibility, defining a PFO "as the Federal official designated by the Secretary of Homeland Security to act as his/her representative locally to oversee, coordinate, and execute the Secretary's incident management responsibilities under HSPD-5 for Incidents of National Significance." The FCO, a position created by the Stafford Act, manages Federal resource support activities and is responsible for coordinating the timely delivery of Federal disaster assistance resources to affected State and local governments, individual victims, and the private sector. At the regional level, a Regional Response Coordination Center (RRCC) coordinates disaster response activities until a JFO can be established.

At DHS headquarters, the Homeland Security Operations Center (HSOC) coordinates "incident information-sharing, operational planning, and deployment of Federal resources" together with its component element at the Federal Emergency Management Agency (FEMA) headquarters, the National Response Coordination Center (NRCC), a "multiagency center that provides overall Federal response coordination for Incidents of National Significance and emergency management program implementation." Strategic-level coordination and resolution of resource conflicts unresolved by the NRCC occurs at the Interagency Incident Management Group (IIMG), an interagency body housed at DHS headquarters.

The coordination of the Federal response—to include capabilities and resources—occurs at the field, regional, and Federal agency headquarters levels through the Emergency Support Function (ESF) framework. ESFs are organized groups of government and private sector entities that provide support, resources, and services. An ESF is staffed by specialists from multiple Federal departments, agencies, and the private sector. The purpose of the ESFs is to integrate skills and capabilities that reside in disparate organizations to coordinate support to State and local response agencies, including both physical resources and staff. The ESFs are structured so that resources and capabilities that are required to assist State and local officials in response and recovery operations can be handled by the appropriate Federal agency.

NOTES AND QUESTIONS

1. The terrorist attacks of September 11 shook public confidence in the federal government's ability to anticipate and intercept terrorist attacks. In this light, the creation of the Department of Homeland Security is understandable: the national trauma of September 11 demanded some sort of legislative response. How compatible are the tasks of combating terror and responding to other emergencies, especially natural disasters? How much prestige and, more importantly, how many financial resources could the new DHS be expected to devote to FEMA's traditional mission? Should there be a separate Cabinet-level department dedicated to emergencies that are *not* tied to military or terrorist attacks?

2. The NIMS and the NRP proceed on the principle that "[i]ncidents are typically managed at the lowest possible geographic, organizational, and jurisdictional level." The NRP takes pains to highlight the "extraordinary powers" of state and local officers "to suspend local laws and ordinances, * * * to establish a curfew, direct evacuations, and, in coordination with the local health authority, to order a quarantine." DEPARTMENT OF HOMELAND SECURITY, NATIONAL RESPONSE PLAN 8 (2004).

3. Even defenders of federalism concede a need to adapt conventional American political theory to the realities of emergency response:

   > Disaster response in America traditionally has been handled by State and local governments, with the Federal government playing a supporting role. Limits on the Federal government's role in disaster response are deeply rooted in American tradition. State and local governments—who know the unique requirements of their citizens and geography and are best positioned to respond to incidents in their own jurisdictions—will always play a large role in disaster response. The Federal government's supporting role respects these practical points and the sovereignty of the States as well as the power of governors to direct activities and coordinate efforts within their States. While we remain faithful to basic constitutional doctrine and time tested principles, we must likewise accept that events such as Hurricane Katrina and the terrorist attacks of September 11, 2001, require us to tailor the application of these principles to the threats we confront in the 21st Century.

   THE WHITE HOUSE, THE FEDERAL RESPONSE TO HURRICANE KATRINA: LESSONS LEARNED 11 (2006).

4. Compare "unity of command" with "unified command":

   > Unity of command: The concept by which each person within an organization reports to one and only one designated person. The

purpose of unity of command is to ensure unity of effort under one responsible commander for every objective.

Unified command: An application of the Incident Command System used when there is more than one agency with incident jurisdiction or when incidents cross political jurisdictions. Agencies work together through the designated members of the Unified Command, often the senior person from agencies and/or disciplines participating in the Unified Command, to establish a common set of objectives and strategies and a single incident action plan.

Id. at 13. The ICS and the rest of the HSPD-5 framework apparently aspire to unified command, but not unity of command. Can unity of command be achieved in a program for emergency response? Should it?

5. The following table classifies Emergency Support Functions according to ESF number, function, and primary implementing department or agency:

ESF #	Emergency Support Function	Primary Department or Agency
ESF #1	Transportation	DOT
ESF #2	Communications	DHS (IAIP/NCS)
ESF #3	Public Works and Engineering	DOD (USACE) and DHS (FEMA)
ESF #4	Firefighting	USDA (Forest Service)
ESF #5	Emergency Management	DHS (FEMA)
ESF #6	Mass Care, Housing, and Human Services	DHS (FEMA) and American Red Cross
ESF #7	Resource Support	GSA
ESF #8	Public Health and Medical Services	HHS
ESF #9	Urban Search and Rescue	DHS (FEMA)
ESF #10	Oil and Hazardous Materials Response	EPA and DHS (U.S. Coast Guard)
ESF #11	Agriculture and Natural Resources	USDA and DOI
ESF #12	Energy	DOE
ESF #13	Public Safety and Security	DHS and DOJ
ESF #14	Long-Term Community Recovery and Mitigation	USDA, DOC, DHS (FEMA), HUD, Treasury, and SBA
ESF #15	External Affairs	DHS (FEMA)

Id. at 16.

6. Among the functions laid out in the NRP, ESF #8, Public Health and Medical Services, figures very prominently. Because natural disasters often destroy hospitals and strain infrastructure in every respect, disease looms large as a source of secondary casualties after a catastrophe:

BRIAN KAMOIE, THE NATIONAL RESPONSE PLAN:
A NEW FRAMEWORK FOR HOMELAND SECURITY,
PUBLIC HEALTH, AND BIOTERRORISM RESPONSE

38 J. HEALTH L. 287, 300-304 (2005)

ESF #8 (Public Health and Medical Services) and the Biological Incident Annex

Two key components of the NRP provide the framework for the response to a biological incident, including bioterrorism. The ESF #8 Annex (ESF #8) provides the general "mechanism for coordinated Federal assistance to supplement State, local, and tribal resources in response to public health and medical care needs." The Biological Incident Annex builds upon ESF #8 and provides additional details regarding a "response to a disease outbreak of known or unknown origin requiring Federal assistance."

A. ESF #8 (Public Health and Medical Services)

ESF #8 brings together fifteen federal departments and agencies and the American Red Cross to coordinate the provision of public health and medical support for federal-to-federal assistance and federal assistance to state, local, and tribal jurisdictions.

Through the ESF #8 structure, the partners bring to bear significant public health and medical resources. HHS is the primary agency for ESF #8 coordination. The Secretary of HHS coordinates the ESF #8 preparedness, response, and recovery actions through the Assistant Secretary for Public Health Emergency Preparedness (ASPHEP).

ESF #8 resources can be activated through the Stafford Act, the Public Health Service Act, or in accordance with the memorandum for federal-to-federal support included in the NRP Financial Management Support Annex. ESF #8 support focuses on the following core functional areas:

- Assessment of public health/medical needs (including behavioral health);
- Public health surveillance;
- Medical care personnel; and
- Medical equipment and supplies. * * *

Throughout operations, ESF #8 coordinates and communicates with federal (at the headquarters and regional levels), state, local, and tribal partners to determine the ongoing public health and medical needs. The ESF #8 structure also allows for consultation with public health and medical subject matter experts as necessary.

B. Biological Incident Annex

The Biological Incident Annex builds upon the processes in the NRP Base Plan and ESF #8 and details more specific actions, roles, and responsibilities associated with the "response to a disease outbreak of known or unknown origin requiring Federal assistance." The Annex specifies "biological incident response actions including threat assessment notification procedures, laboratory testing, joint investigative/response procedures, and activities related to recovery."

The broad objectives of the Federal Government's response to a biological terrorism event, pandemic influenza, emerging infectious disease, or novel pathogen outbreak are to:

- Detect the event through disease surveillance and environmental monitoring;
- Identify and protect the population(s) at risk;
- Determine the source of the outbreak;
- Quickly frame the public health and law enforcement implications;
- Control and contain any possible epidemic (including providing guidance to State and local public health authorities);
- Augment and surge public health and medical services;
- Track and defeat any potential resurgence or additional outbreaks; and
- Assess the extent of residual biological contamination and decontaminate as necessary.

Unlike many types of incidents covered by the NRP, a biological terrorist attack may be covert and not immediately detected, in which case "the first evidence of dissemination of an agent may be the presentation of disease in humans or animals."

A terrorist-induced infectious disease outbreak initially may be indistinguishable from a naturally occurring outbreak; moreover, depending upon the particular agent and associated symptoms, several days could pass before public health and medical authorities even suspect that terrorism may be the cause. In such a case, criminal intent may not be apparent until some time after illnesses are recognized.

"HHS serves as the Federal Government's primary agency for the public health and medical preparation and planning for and response to a biological terrorism attack or naturally occurring outbreak." Consistent with the NRP and NIMS, however, the Biological Incident Annex explicitly acknowledges that "State, local, and tribal governments are primarily responsible for detecting and responding to disease outbreaks and implementing measures to minimize the health, social, and economic consequences * * * ."

NOTES

Independent of the NRP, the Department of Health and Human Services exercises substantial authority to implement a wide range of emergency preparedness and response activities. Surveyed in greater detail by Kamoie, *supra*, at 306-317, these powers are worth noting:

1. *Public health emergency declaration.* The Public Health Service Act, 42 U.S.C. §§ 201-300hh-11, gives the Secretary of Health and Human Services broad emergency authority, including the power to deploy the U.S. Public Health Service Commissioned Corps and other instruments of the Department of HHS, such as the Centers for Disease Control, the Food and Drug Administration, and the National Institutes of Health. Under 42 U.S.C. § 247d, the Secretary can declare a public health emergency and take appropriate steps to respond to such an emergency. The Secretary must find (after consulting with public health authorities "as may be necessary") that: "(1) a disease or disorder presents a public health emergency; or (2) a public health emergency, including significant outbreaks of infectious diseases or bioterrorist attacks, otherwise exists."

2. *Isolation and quarantine.* Although the primary authority of the states over public health includes the power to isolate and quarantine infectious individuals, the federal government regulates individuals who are entering the United States or crossing state boundaries. Under 42 U.S.C. § 264, the Secretary of HHS has the power "to prevent the introduction, transmission, or spread of communicable diseases from foreign countries into the States or possessions, or from one State or possession into any other State or possession." The Secretary may apprehend and examine "any individual reasonably believed to be infected with a communicable disease" who is moving or about to move from one state to another or who poses a probable cause of infection to individuals who will be moving from one state to another. The Secretary may also inspect, disinfect, or destroy infected animals or articles that pose a danger to humans.

3. *Strategic National Stockpile (SNS).* The Public Health Service Act directs the Secretary of HHS to coordinate with the Department of Homeland Security in maintaining a stockpile of "drugs, vaccines and other biological products, medical devices and other supplies" needed to protect the nation during a bioterrorist attack or other public health emergency. 42 U.S.C. § 247d-6b(a)(1). A "stockpile" may consist of either a physical accumulation of supplies or a contractual agreement with vendors to deliver the needed supplies. *See id.* § 247d-6b(e).

4. *Credentialing of health professionals.* The Public Health Service Act directs the Secretary of HHS to establish and maintain a system for advance registration of health professionals to verify credentials, licenses, accreditations, and hospital privileges for professionals who provide services during emergencies. 42 U.S.C. § 247d-7b. The Secretary may also "encourage each State to provide legal authority during a public health emergency for health professionals authorized in another State to provide . . . such health services in the State." *Id.*

5. *Waiver of regulatory requirements.* Federal law waives a wide variety of regulatory requirements in cases of public health emergency. For instance, the Food, Drug, and Cosmetics Act permits the emergency use of

an unapproved new drug, an unlicensed biological product, or a medical device that has not been approved or cleared for commercial distribution in the event of an emergency involving a biological, chemical, radiological, or nuclear agent, *see* 21 U.S.C. § 360bbb-3(a), or after the Secretary of HHS has declared a public health emergency pursuant to 42 U.S.C. § 247d, *see* 21 U.S.C. § 360bbb-3(b)(1). In 2004, a federal district court enjoined the Department of Defense's mandatory anthrax vaccination program on the grounds that the FDA had failed to solicit additional public comments before certifying the safety and efficacy of the anthrax vaccine. *See* Doe v. Rumsfeld, 341 F. Supp. 2d 1, 16 (D.D.C. 2004). HHS responded by issuing its first authorization for emergency use so that the Defense Department could continue anthrax vaccinations. *See* Determination and Declaration Regarding Emergency Use of Anthrax Vaccine Absorbed for Prevention of Inhalation Anthrax, 70 Fed. Reg. 5450 (Feb. 2, 2005).

6. *Shielding emergency health care workers from liability.* The federal government has two tools for shielding health care professionals from liability when they volunteer services during emergencies. First, the Volunteer Protection Act, 42 U.S.C. §§ 14501-14505, immunizes individuals providing volunteer services to nonprofit or governmental organizations. The institutions themselves, however, are not immunized. *See id.* § 14503(c). Second, by hiring health care providers directly, the federal government may protect these professionals. *See* Public Health Security and Bioterrorism Preparedness and Response Act of 2002, Pub. L. No. 107-188, § 102, 116 Stat. 594, 599-603 (amending 42 U.S.C. § 300hh-11(d) to authorize the Secretary of Homeland Security to appoint intermittent employees "in accordance with applicable civil service laws and regulations"); 42 U.S.C. § 5149(b)(1) (enabling federal agencies, for purposes of carrying out the Stafford Act, to appoint temporary personnel without regard to federal civil service requirements); 42 U.S.C. § 209(f) (authorizing the Secretary of HHS to hire public health consultants without regard to civil service rules).

2. THE POST–SEPTEMBER 11 FRAMEWORK IN ACTION

Hurricane Katrina posed the first serious test of HSPD-5 and the twin cornerstones of this approach to managing catastrophic events, the NIMS and the NPR. The post–September 11 framework for emergency response failed many aspects of this initial challenge. As you read the following congressional report on the failure of crucial aspects of the HSPD-5 system, consider what alternatives to the NIMS and the NPR might perform better in catastrophic circumstances such as those presented by Katrina:

U.S. HOUSE OF REPRESENTATIVES, A FAILURE OF INITIATIVE

Final Report of the Select Bipartisan Committee to Investigate the
Preparation for and Response to Hurricane Katrina 131-132 (2006)

With the creation of the Department of Homeland Security (DHS) and the development of the National Response Plan (NRP), an additional layer of management and response authority was placed between the President and FEMA, and additional response coordinating structures were established. The Secretary of Homeland Security became the President's principal disaster advisor responsible for enabling the President to effectively utilize his authority under the Stafford Act to direct all federal agencies, particularly the Department of Defense (DOD), to respond in a coordinated and expeditious fashion. As part of these changes, critical response decision points were assigned to the Secretary of Homeland Security. Secretary [Michael] Chertoff executed these responsibilities late, ineffectively, or not at all. These secretarial authorities include:

- The designation of an incident of national significance (INS);
- The authority to convene the Interagency Incident Management Group (IIMG);
- The designation of the principal federal official (PFO); and
- The invocation of the national response plan's catastrophic incident annex (NRP-CIA).

There was plenty of advance warning by the National Weather Service, and the consequences of a category 4 hurricane striking New Orleans were well-documented. Fifty-six hours prior to landfall, Hurricane Katrina presented an extremely high probability threat that 75 percent of New Orleans would be flooded, tens of thousands of residents may be killed, hundreds of thousands trapped in flood waters up to 20 feet, hundreds of thousands of homes and other structures destroyed, a million people evacuated from their homes, and the greater New Orleans area would be rendered uninhabitable for several months or years. An August 28 report by the department's National Infrastructure Simulation and Analysis Center concluded: "Any storm rated Category 4 or greater . . . will likely lead to severe flooding and/or levee breaching, leaving the New Orleans metro area submerged for weeks or months."

Under these conditions it seems reasonable to expect the criteria for designating an INS would have been met, the appointment of a PFO would be necessary to coordinate an unprecedented federal response, the IIMG would be convened to provide strategic guidance and recommendations to the Secretary and the President, and the NRP-CIA would be invoked to shift the federal response posture from a reactive to proactive mode in order to save lives and accelerate assistance to overwhelmed state and local systems. According to a recent letter submitted by DHS * * * in response to the preliminary observations of the Comptroller General * * *, DHS viewed the NRP-CIA as applicable only to no-notice or short-notice events. And the Select Committee acknowledges that the State of Louisiana expressed its satisfaction with the supplies and that former FEMA Director Michael Brown directed that commodities be "jammed up" the supply chain.

While the NRP-CIA may be particularly applicable to a no-notice event, the Annex itself reflects only that a catastrophic incident may occur with little or no warning. And the pre-positioning of supplies to the satisfaction of state and local authorities, while an appropriate measure for a disaster without catastrophic consequences, was clearly not sufficient for the catastrophic consequences of Hurricane Katrina.

Instead, absent a catastrophic disaster designation from Chertoff, federal response officials in the field eventually made the difficult decisions to bypass established procedures and provide assistance without waiting for appropriate requests from the states or for clear direction from Washington. These decisions to switch from a "pull" to a "push" system were made individually, over several days, and in an uncoordinated fashion as circumstances required. The federal government stumbled into a proactive response during the first several days after Hurricane Katrina made landfall, as opposed to the Secretary making a clear and decisive choice to respond proactively at the beginning of the disaster. The White House Homeland Security Council (HSC), situated at the apex of the policy coordination framework for DHS issues, itself failed to proactively de-conflict varying damage assessments. One example included an eyewitness account of a levee breach supplied by a FEMA official at 7:00 p.m. on August 29. The White House did not consider this assessment confirmed for 11 more hours, when, after 6:00 a.m. the next morning, it received a Homeland Security Operations Center (HSOC) Situation Report confirming the breach.

The catastrophic nature of Katrina confirmed once again that the standard "reactive" nature of federal assistance, while appropriate for most disasters, does not work during disasters of this scale. When local and state governments are functionally overwhelmed or incapacitated, the federal government must be prepared to respond proactively. It will need to anticipate state and local requirements, move commodities and assets into the area on its own initiative, and shore up or even help reconstitute critical state and local emergency management and response structures.

The need for assistance is extreme during the initial period of a catastrophic hurricane, yet the ability of state and local responders to meet that need is limited. That is why it is so important for the federal government, particularly DOD resources, to respond proactively and fill that gap as quickly as possible. Because it takes several days to mobilize federal resources, critical decisions must be made as early as possible so that massive assistance can surge into the area during the first two days, not several days or weeks later. The NRP-CIA was drafted to meet this specific and well known requirement, yet Chertoff never invoked it for Katrina.

NOTES AND QUESTIONS

1. "The Catastrophic Incident Annex of the NRP includes the assumption that large-scale evacuations, whether spontaneous or directed pursuant to authorities, may be more likely to occur after attacks than natural disasters, and that the maintenance of public health will 'aggravate attempts to implement a coordinated evacuation management strategy.'" Keith Bea, *Disaster Evacuation and Displacement Policy: Issues for Congress* 5 (Sept. 2, 2005) (CRS Order Code RS22235). Did this assumption demonstrate that the NRP was "skewed toward . . . terrorist attacks" and therefore less well suited for "address[ing] the complications evident in the evacuation of New Orleans"? *Id.* Nearly four years after September 11, 2001, Katrina posed the question as coarsely as possible: did the United States fundamentally err in assigning responsibility for all emergency response, including relief and rebuilding efforts in connection with natural disasters, to an agency whose principal mission is directed toward detecting and preventing terrorist attacks?

2. Cognitive psychology suggests that human beings exhibit a systematic bias to attribute conduct and causation to living agents, such as humans, animals, or anthropomorphic deities, rather than to inanimate objects or to "nature" in the abstract. *See, e.g.*, JUSTIN L. BARRETT, WHY WOULD ANYONE BELIEVE IN GOD? 31-44 (2004); Martie G. Haselton & David M. Buss, *Error Management Theory: A New Perspective on Biases in Cross-Sex Mind Reading*, 78 J. PERSONALITY & SOC. PSYCH. 81 (2000). This insight may explain the evident bias of the Homeland Security Act, HSPD-5, and the NRP in favor of preparedness against terrorism, which invariably arises from human conduct, and against preparedness against natural disasters, whose causes appear to lie beyond human control. Does awareness of this systematic bias counsel more, not less, attention to natural disasters relative to terrorism or war?

3. More generally, cognitive psychology predicts that humans tend to fear low-probability events that carry grave consequences and lie beyond human control, at least relative to more commonplace or chronic risks. *See, e.g.*, Paul Slovic, *Perception of Risk*, 236 SCIENCE 280 (1987). In addition, humans instinctively calculate—and consequently *miscalculate*—risk according to the "availability heuristic," the ease with which the mind can conjure an example. *See, e.g.*, Timur Kuran & Cass Sunstein, *Availability Cascades and Risk Regulation*, 51 STAN. L. REV. 683, 685 (1999). Finally, because humans react to risk with their emotions, even when they evaluate risk as rationally as they can, the vividness of an event intensifies the response to that event and its consequences. *See* George F. Loewenstein et al., *Risk As Feelings*, 127 PSYCH. BULL. 267, 275-276 (2001). These cognitive biases can lead to "probability neglect," whereby humans focus entirely on perceived emotional impact, without rational consideration of actuarial probability. *See* Cass Sunstein, *Terrorism and Probability Neglect*, 26 J. RISK & UNCERTAINTY 121 (2003). *See generally* Jonathan H.

Marks, *9/11 + 3/11 + 7/7 = ? What Counts in Counterterrorism*, 37 COLUM. HUM. RTS. L. REV. 559, 566-571 (2006).

4. Cognitive bias can seriously distort individual and collective decisionmaking. For instance, millions of Americans substituted driving for air travel in the months after September 11, 2001. This mistaken evaluation of risk caused an estimated 353 deaths in the final months of 2001. *See* Rerd Gigerenzer, *Dread Risk, September 11, and Fatal Traffic Accidents*, 15 PSYCH. SCI. 286 (2004). To what extent does the entire system of emergency response, especially insofar as this body of law was developed in the immediate aftermath of September 11, reflect a collective exercise in the mistaken evaluation of risk?

5. Tort law distinguishes sharply between design defects and manufacturing defects. *Compare* RESTATEMENT (THIRD) OF TORTS: PRODUCTS LIABILITY § 2(b) *with* RESTATEMENT (SECOND) OF TORTS § 402A. *See generally* Frank J. Vandall & Joshua F. Vandall, *A Call for an Accurate Restatement (Third) of Torts: Design Defect*, 33 U. MEM. L. REV. 909 (2003). Linguists distinguish between competence and performance, between the innate capacity to speak and speech as it actually occurs. *See, e.g.*, NOAM CHOMSKY, LANGUAGE AND MIND 4 (enlarged ed. 1972). Was the failure of the NRP during Katrina one of design and capacity, or was it one of execution and performance? The former suggests that the proper remedy lies in legislative reform, perhaps to the point of overhauling the entire law of emergency response. The latter suggests that fault is more appropriately assigned to individual actors: FEMA Director Michael Brown, Secretary of Homeland Security Michael Chertoff, or perhaps even President George W. Bush.

6. The Senate assigned blame at all levels, describing Katrina's relief effort as one plagued by "failures in design, implementation, and execution of the National Response Plan." UNITED STATES SENATE, COMMITTEE ON HOMELAND SECURITY AND GOVERNMENTAL AFFAIRS, HURRICANE KATRINA: A NATION STILL UNPREPARED 27-1 (2006). The Senate's report, *see generally id.* at 27-1 to 27-17, identified failures in all aspects of design, implementation, and execution:

   a. *Insufficient training and exercises.* The NRP "is a complex, ambitious, 400-plus-page high-level plan," a "very detailed, acronym-heavy document that is not easily accessible to the first-time user." Beyond an initial wave of training for headquarters staff of component agencies, DHS evidently made no further efforts to "ensur[e] that the NRP would be well implemented."

   b. *The roles of the principal federal official and the federal coordinating officer.* The NRP's failure to "define the role of the PFO or distinguish it from that of the FCO" posed "an obstacle to an effective, coordinated response to Katrina." The FCO position arises from the Stafford Act's command that the President appoint a federal coordinating officer immediately upon declaring a major disaster or emergency. *See* 42 U.S.C. § 5143. Under the Stafford Act, the FCO appraises the most urgent needs, establishes field offices, coordinates relief efforts, and takes other appropriate action to guide citizens and public officials. *See id.* By contrast, the NRP created the new position of principal federal officer, "personally designated" by the Secretary of Homeland Security as his or her representative as "the lead federal official." DEPARTMENT OF HOMELAND SECURITY, NATIONAL RESPONSE PLAN 33 (2004). The PFO, a nonstatutory post, holds no "directive authority" over the FCO or other officials and does not replace the incident command structure. *Id.*

c. *Potentially overlapping agency roles.* The NRP "fail[ed] to delineate areas of potentially overlapping responsibility among federal agencies." For instance, the NRP assigned responsibility for Emergency Support Function 8, public health and medical services, to the Department of Health and Human Services, even though one of the response mechanisms, the National Disaster Medical System, answers to FEMA and DHS. Consequently, "[i]n the response to Katrina, FEMA and HHS engaged in minimal coordination on pre-positioning and deploying Disaster Medical Assistance Teams."

d. *Contingency and catastrophic planning.* As "a high-level plan, with a core set of principles meant to apply to a wide range of possible events," the NRP "was not designed to address specific scenarios or geographic areas, or to provide operational details." The plan simply failed to "'contemplate' an event on the massive scale of Katrina."

e. *Mistakes in declaring an Incident of National Significance.* According to the NRP, "every event that provokes a Presidential declaration under the Stafford Act automatically becomes an Incident of National Significance." President Bush's August 27, 2005, emergency declaration for portions of Louisiana automatically transformed Hurricane Katrina into an INS. Nevertheless, three days later, Secretary of Homeland Security Chertoff issued another "declaration" designating Katrina an INS. "At minimum, the Secretary's redundant declaration of an Incident of National Significance confused an already difficult situation and suggested a lack of familiarity with core concepts of the NRP within the Secretary's Office."

f. *The appointment of Michael Brown as Principal Federal Official.* Apart from the wisdom of appointing a principal federal officer "who had no experience as an emergency manager," Secretary Chertoff's appointment of FEMA Director Michael Brown as PFO for Katrina "violated the literal requirements of the NRP." The NRP prohibits the PFO "from occupying another position or having another set of conflicting or distracting obligations at the same time."

g. *Non-implementation of the Catastrophic Incident Annex.* "In failing to implement the National Response Plan's Catastrophic Incident Annex (NRP-CIA), Secretary Chertoff ignored a potentially powerful tool that might have alleviated difficulties in the federal response to Katrina." Though not accompanied by changes in the Stafford Act or other legislation (and therefore unable to provide new emergency response authority to federal officials), the NRP-CIA does "set a policy and tone for an urgent and proactive response that moves beyond the usual procedures in responding to an 'ordinary' disaster." In contrast with the standard response to "a 'typical' disaster," which directs the federal government to wait until a state requests aid, the activation of the NRP-CIA during a catastrophe "prompts the government to help without waiting for requests." The NRP-CIA streamlines or expedites the normal procedures for certain Emergency Support Functions on the understanding that "[t]he response capabilities and resources of the local jurisdiction ... may be insufficient and quickly overwhelmed," especially when "[l]ocal emergency personnel who normally respond to incidents may be among those affected and unable to perform their duties." U.S. DEPARTMENT OF HOMELAND SECURITY, NATIONAL RESPONSE PLAN, at CAT-1 (2004).

7. "[T]he NRP-CIA turns what is traditionally a 'pull' system, in which the federal government waits to receive requests from state and local officials, or from other federal agencies, into a 'push' system, where federal authorities proactively deploy resources to mobilization centers close to the disaster or, in certain circumstances, directly to the incident scene to assist in responding to the incident." UNITED STATES SENATE, COMMITTEE ON HOMELAND SECURITY AND GOVERNMENTAL AFFAIRS, HURRICANE KATRINA: A NATION STILL UNPREPARED 27-9 (2006).

The question of pull versus push systems of emergency response commanded further attention in the House of Representatives:

U.S. HOUSE OF REPRESENTATIVES, A FAILURE OF INITIATIVE

Final Report of the Select Bipartisan Committee to Investigate the Preparation for and Response to Hurricane Katrina 136-139 (2006)

Finding: A proactive federal response, or push system, is not a new concept, but it is rarely utilized

What is a push system? In response to most disasters, the federal government provides assistance in response to state requests. This reactive approach is often referred to as a "pull" system in that it relies on states knowing what they need and being able to request it from the federal government. States may make these requests either before disasters strike because of the near certainty that federal assistance will be necessary after such an event, e.g., with hurricanes, or afterwards, once they have conducted preliminary damage assessments and determined their response capabilities are overwhelmed.

Unlike the bulk of the disasters requiring FEMA's response, catastrophic disasters require the federal response to be more proactive. This proactive response is referred to as a "push" system, in which federal assistance is provided and moved into the affected area prior to a disaster or without waiting for specific requests from the state or local governments.

Implementing a push system—a proactive federal response—does not require federalization of the disaster or the usurping of state authority. Although a push system is a proactive response by the federal government, it still requires notification and full coordination with the state. The coordination process, however, should not delay or impede the rapid mobilization and deployment of these critical federal resources.

A proactive response, or push system, is nothing new. In 1992, the nation's management of catastrophic disasters was intensely criticized after Hurricane Andrew leveled much of South Florida and Hurricane Iniki destroyed much of the Hawaiian island of Kauai. In particular, a 1993 GAO report points to the slow delivery of services vital to disaster victims as a major flaw in the response to Hurricane Andrew in South Florida. The report then contrasts this with the more effective response to Hurricane Iniki in Hawaii, where FEMA implemented a push system and sent supplies to the island of Kauai before local officials requested them. This occurred despite being implemented in an ad hoc manner—rather than as part of an orderly, planned response to catastrophic disasters. Furthermore, the long-standing authority for a proactive federal response resides in the Stafford Act. The current plan for how to utilize that authority is the NRP-CIA.

The pre-positioning of assets and commodities is a distinct action from the push or pull of those assets.   The federal government will often pre-position life-saving and life-sustaining disaster equipment and supplies prior to landfall of a hurricane as close to a potential disaster site as possible. This pre-positioning of supplies can substantially shorten response time and delivery of initial critical disaster supplies to the field.

Although part of a proactive response, this pre-positioning of disaster supplies and assets is not in and of itself a push of commodities. Once assets are pre-positioned to go into the field, they still need to be mobilized and deployed into the field either proactively by pushing the commodities to the state or reactively by waiting for a request from the state.

Operational procedures for a push are not well exercised, practiced, or utilized.   The majority of declared disasters are not catastrophic. Because of this, the pull system is most commonly used during disasters and training exercises and, therefore, is more familiar to disaster response personnel. In fact, the NRP-CIA has never been appropriately exercised. As a result, federal personnel have little experience or comfort with instituting a proactive response.

Additionally, if the Homeland Security Secretary does not invoke the NRP-CIA, federal personnel have no clear instruction to switch from a reactive approach to a proactive approach. Without this clear direction, federal personnel can be uncomfortable pushing resources into the state because of the inherent risks, such as complicating the disaster response by diverting needed resources from other areas or wasting millions of dollars in a duplication of effort.

Finding: The Secretary should have invoked the Catastrophic Incident Annex (NRP-CIA) to direct the federal response posture to fully switch from a reactive to proactive mode of operations

Perhaps the single most important question the Select Committee has struggled to answer is why the federal response did not adequately anticipate the consequences of Katrina striking New Orleans and, prior to landfall, begin to develop plans and move boats and buses into the area to rescue and evacuate tens of thousand of victims from a flooded city. At least part of the answer lies in the Secretary's failure to invoke the NRP-CIA, to clearly and forcefully instruct everyone involved with the federal response to be proactive, anticipate future requirements, develop plans to fulfill them, and execute those plans without waiting for formal requests from overwhelmed state and local response officials.

The NRP-CIA was specifically written for a disaster such as Katrina. According to the NRP:

- A catastrophic incident results in large numbers of casualties and displaced persons.
- The incident may cause significant disruption to the area's critical infrastructure.
- A credible operating picture may not be achievable for 24 to 48 hours or longer. As a result, response activities must begin without the benefit of a complete needs assessment.
- Federal support must be provided in a timely manner to save lives, prevent human suffering, and mitigate severe damage. This may require mobilizing and deploying assets before they are requested via normal NRP protocols.
- Large-scale evacuations, organized or self-directed, may occur.
- Large numbers of people may be left homeless and may require prolonged temporary housing.

It is clear the consequences of Hurricane Katrina exceeded all of these criteria and required a proactive response. According to the NRP, "Upon recognition that a catastrophic incident condition (e.g. involving mass casualties and/or mass evacuation) exists, the Secretary of DHS immediately designates the event an INS and begins, potentially in advance of a formal Presidential disaster declaration, implementation of the NRP-CIA." On Monday evening, when DHS received reports the levees had breached in multiple locations, it should have been clear to the department the nation's worst case hurricane scenario had occurred and a proactive federal response was required. Chertoff never invoked the NRP-CIA.

Smith, LOHSEP Deputy Director for Emergency Preparedness, believed, "the biggest single failure of the federal response was the Department of Homeland Security's failure to recognize that Katrina was a catastrophic event and implement the catastrophic incident annex to the National Response Plan. . . . Had DHS recognized Katrina for the event that it was, a truly catastrophic event, had DHS implemented the catastrophic incident annex to the NRP, Louisiana should have had a significant number of federal troops and federal assets, days prior to their actual arrival . . . . Instead federal troops did not arrive in number until Saturday, after the evacuations of the Superdome, Convention Center and cloverleaf were complete."

Finding: Absent the Secretary's invocation of the NRP-CIA, the federal response evolved into a push system over several days

Even though Chertoff never invoked the catastrophic annex, federal officials in the field began, in an ad hoc fashion, to switch from a pull response to a push system because of the operational demands of the situation. The switch was uncoordinated but widespread by the end of the first week. This has occurred in previous disasters. As previously mentioned, the response to Hurricane Iniki in Hawaii implemented an ad hoc push system as FEMA sent supplies to the island of Kauai before local officials requested them. Similarly, the response to Katrina evolved into an ad hoc push system, even though the NRP-CIA was not invoked.

* * * [The efforts behind] the switch to a push response [illustrate] important principles of effective emergency management. First, they demonstrate the importance of having qualified and experienced professionals in charge of operations. Second, these officials need to have the authority to commit resources as they see fit without waiting to seek approval from above. And, third, federal officials need to have good working relationships with their state counterparts. * * *

In Louisiana, FEMA response personnel tried on a number of occasions to push commodities and assets into the field. In cases where it was clear there was a need for life-saving and life-sustaining commodities but no clear state distribution system set up, FEMA acted proactively to provide assistance. For example, Louisiana FCO Bill Lokey noted there were situations where stranded individuals were not in immediate danger, but needed food and water. When FEMA gained access to several helicopters, FEMA began ferrying food and water to people stranded on high ground even though there was no formal request by the state to perform this function. In addition, FEMA contracted with over 100 ambulances to transport hospital evacuees. This mission was not requested by the state, but FEMA responded proactively because the situation demanded immediate action. * * *

[S]tate or local officials expressed frustration that requests for assistance were not processed because they did not follow the formal request process. For example, according to Louisiana and FEMA officials, state and local officials verbally requested specific assets or commodities during conference calls that were never fulfilled. In these cases no immediate action was taken because FEMA officials assumed the state would follow up the verbal requests with official written requests. If the catastrophic annex had been invoked, then perhaps FEMA would have expected requests outside the normal process and acted on them.

NOTES AND QUESTIONS

1. The Katrina experience arguably suggests that there should be not one but two federal emergency response systems: a "pull" system that awaits state requests for federal assistance with ordinary events, plus a "push" system under which the federal government proactively anticipates local conditions and delivers assistance without waiting for a request.

   a. The NRP, by all accounts, had already established separate pull and push systems. The NRP's default position is that of a "pull" system, as is the federal/state relationship established by the Stafford Act. The NRP's Catastrophic Incident Annex, by contrast, identifies the conditions under which federal emergency response may proceed proactively and prescribes expedited and streamlined protocols for performing Emergency Support Functions. Given the availability of the NRP-CIA, why did Secretary Chertoff fail to invoke the "push" protocol that evidently had been designed for precisely an event such as Katrina?

   b. How can the government know, *ex ante*, which events should be handled with the default "pull" system and which events qualify for the NRP-CIA's "push" treatment? Compounding the difficulty is the way in which hurricanes, earthquakes, and other natural disasters follow a right-skewed distribution characteristic of complex systems rather than the usual Gaussian ("bell curve") distribution. *See generally* Daniel A. Farber, *Probabilities Behaving Badly: Complexity Theory and Environmental Uncertainty*, 37 U.C. DAVIS L. REV. 145 (2003).

2. Complexity theory informs the law of disasters in another way. A "push" approach to emergency response developed during the relief efforts for Hurricanes Iniki and Hurricane Katrina even in the absence of clear legal authority, let alone coordinated direction from a hierarchical command structure. This epitomizes "emergent" behavior, in which uncoordinated actors following small-scale rules generate systemic effects transcending any one actor's local conduct. *See* JOHN H. HOLLAND, EMERGENCE: FROM CHAOS TO ORDER (1998); STEVEN JOHNSON, EMERGENCE: THE CONNECTED LIVES OF ANTS, BRAINS, CITIES, AND SOFTWARE (2001). The ability of on-site officials to make quick judgments, informed by firsthand observations not available to faraway supervisors, might have greater potential to effect good outcomes in emergencies than the designation of a federal coordinating officer under the Stafford Act or the designation of a principal federal official under the NRP.

B. STATE AND REGIONAL EMERGENCY RESPONSE AUTHORITY

Notwithstanding the elaborate legal structures of the Homeland Security Act, HSPD-5, and the National Response Plan, emergency response remains in the first instance the responsibility of state and local governments. Although the federal response to Katrina has attracted intense scrutiny in the popular press and by the federal government itself, much of the success or failure of the response to Katrina hinged on the actions—and omissions—of state and local officials such as Louisiana Governor Kathleen Babineaux Blanco and New Orleans Mayor Ray Nagin. This chapter therefore turns to state and regional emergency response authority. After reviewing Louisiana's response to Katrina, we will examine one source of emergency response, the interstate Emergency Management Assistance Compact (EMAC), which won praise for its effectiveness in delivering relief during Katrina.

1. STATE EMERGENCY RESPONSE AUTHORITY

ERNEST B. ABBOTT, OTTO J. HETZEL & ALAN D. COHN
STATE, LOCAL, AND FIRST RESPONDER ISSUES

American Bar Association, Hurricane Katrina Task Force
Subcommittee Report 13, 14-18 (Feb. 2006)

The authority of state and local elected officials to act under a state's police powers is at its apex during a disaster. Governors are given broad discretion under state constitutions and statutes to take actions deemed necessary to reduce imminent threats to life, property, and public health and safety. They have extraordinary powers, upon declaration of a state of emergency, to commandeer resources, control property, order evacuations, suspend laws and administrative requirements, and take other measures necessary to respond to the emergency. State and local authorities are of course the "first responders" to every emergency, since in all instances the event occurs initially in one or more local jurisdictions.

States devolve authority to local units of government in various ways. Some cities possess "home rule" authority, either by reason of predating the establishment of the state, or by operation of a state's constitution or law. Local governments in general may also possess authority specifically delegated by the state through charter or operation of state law. Virtually all states have also codified their emergency response powers in some combination of statutes and executive orders, and have developed plans and procedures for responding to catastrophic incidents that derive from these expressions of state authority. Most local governments have taken similar steps.

The federal government has interjected itself into the state and local government emergency planning process by conditioning the receipt of federal preparedness grant funding on review of state and urban area preparedness plans. This represents a federal exercise of its Tax and Spend power in the Constitution in order to encourage state compliance with such federal requirements. * * *

[F]our questions should guide an examination of the adequacy and use of state and local government authority to respond to catastrophic incidents: how did the state *express or clarify* its authority through statutes or executive orders; how was that authority *implemented* through plans, procedures, and protocols; in what manner did the state *execute* that authority during incidents; and how did the state *delegate* its authority to local units of government? * * * [These questions place] certain heavily reported aspects of the Louisiana response to Hurricane Katrina * * * in context, and * * * suggest[] how to examine whether that State's, and any state's, authorities are sufficient to respond to a disaster of this magnitude.

One example is the question of evacuation. Could Louisiana Governor Blanco have ordered a mandatory evacuation of Orleans Parish prior to Mayor Ray Nagin's evacuation order on Sunday, August 28, 2005, and was the decision not to do so due to a lack of authority?

The Louisiana Homeland Security and Emergency Assistance and Disaster Act ("Louisiana Disaster Act") [LA. REV. STAT. §§ 29:721-:733] empowers the governor to address emergencies and disasters, including those caused by flood or other natural disasters such as hurricanes. On Friday, August 26, 2005—three days before landfall of Hurricane Katrina and while there was still considerable uncertainty as to where Katrina would hit—Governor Blanco declared a state of emergency.

The Louisiana Disaster Act specifically empowers the Governor, upon the declaration of an emergency or disaster, to "[d]irect and compel the evacuation of all or part of the population from any stricken or threatened area within the state if he [or she] deems this action necessary for the preservation of life or other disaster mitigation, response, or recovery." [LA. REV. STAT. § 29:724(D)(5).] Thus, the Louisiana Disaster Act clearly authorizes the Governor to order a mandatory evacuation of any parish.

However, the Southeast Louisiana Hurricane Evacuation and Sheltering Plan ("Evacuation Plan") states that each parish, and not the state, will determine whether to issue a voluntary or mandatory evacuation order with respect to that parish. The Evacuation Plan has three phases: Precautionary/Voluntary; Recommended; and Mandatory. During these phases, the "Risk Area Parish" declares a state of emergency, marshals transportation resources, implements public transportation plans, coordinates evacuation orders with the state and other Risk Area Parishes, and instructs people to evacuate. The state plays only a supporting and consulting role, aside from the implementation of the contra-flow plan.

The Louisiana State Police initiated contra-flow on interstate highways running up from coastal Louisiana beginning on Saturday, August 27, 2005. However, the Governor did not order a mandatory evacuation of Orleans Parish at that time. The Evacuation Plan contemplates that the state "prepare proclamations for the State to intervene in local situations if local government fails to act." There is no indication in the official timelines of the State of Louisiana, however, that the State sought to override any parish's judgment as to whether or when to order a mandatory evacuation.

It cannot be known whether the Governor's action to order the mandatory evacuation of a parish prior to the parish government ordering such an evacuation would have resulted in a more complete evacuation, given the structure of the Evacuation Plan and the questions that existed until the last minute concerning the ultimate path of the hurricane. It is clear, however, that the Governor possessed the authority to order such an evacuation, although the state apparently chose, in making that authority operational in the form of the Evacuation Plan, to delegate that authority to local units of government (in this case, the parishes) without specifying the degree to which the State retained that authority, and criteria under which the State would exercise that retained authority.

A related example relates to the use of buses for evacuation. Aerial footage of floodwaters covering dozens of inoperative yellow school buses was shown repeatedly on news channels. Could the State or parish governments have forcibly commandeered these and other buses (and drivers) prior to the hurricane's landfall to help in evacuating residents who lacked other means of transportation to use for evacuation, and was the decision not to do so due to a lack of authority?

The Louisiana Disaster Act gives the Governor authority, under a declaration of emergency or disaster, to "[u]tilize all available resources of the state government and of each political subdivision of the state as reasonably necessary to cope with the disaster or emergency"; to "[t]ransfer the direction, personnel, or functions of state departments and agencies or units thereof for the purpose of performing or facilitating emergency services"; and to "commandeer or utilize any private property if he [or she] finds this necessary to cope with the disaster or emergency." [LA. REV. STAT. § 29:724(D)(2)-(4).] The Act gives parish presidents the same authority with respect to instruments of parish government and private property. [*See id.* § 29:727(F)(2)-(4).] Thus, both the State and parish governments had expressed authority to commandeer buses and drivers.

The Evacuation Plan states, as one of its operative assumptions, that "[s]chool and municipal buses, government-owned vehicles and vehicles provided by volunteer agencies may be used to provide transportation for individuals who lack transportation and require assistance in evacuating." It also assumes that "[m]anpower and equipment of the political subdivisions will be exhausted and outside support will be needed."

During the Precautionary/Voluntary Evacuation phase, the Risk Area Parish is responsible for alerting all emergency workers in the jurisdiction, reviewing evacuation procedures, making contact with "special facilities," and advising them to be ready to evacuate, marshalling local transportation resources, and implementing public transportation plans. The state is responsible for placing its departments and agencies on alert, calling nursing homes to ensure they are prepared to evacuate their residents, alerting DHS/FEMA that the state may need assistance, and preparing any required proclamations to make state resources available to support parish activities.

During the Recommended Evacuation phase, the Risk Area Parish is responsible for mobilizing parish and local transportation and announcing the location of staging areas for persons who need transportation. The state is responsible for mobilizing state transportation resources to support parish activities and mobilizing state evacuation route traffic control personnel and equipment. Finally, during the Mandatory Evacuation phase, the Risk Area Parish is responsible for mobilizing transportation resources and requesting assistance from the state, as needed. The state is responsible for coordination with and support of the parish in these activities. Thus, * * * these plans contemplate commandeering buses and drivers, if necessary, in support of evacuation efforts.

The timelines provided by the State of Louisiana make no mention of state authority being exercised to commandeer either school district or private resources, or to reassign or direct state employees holding appropriate driving credentials in the hours and days prior to landfall. It was not until August 31, 2005, that the Governor issued an Executive Order requiring each school district in Louisiana to make its school buses available to the Louisiana Office of Homeland Security and Emergency Preparedness, and authorized that office to commandeer those buses. * * *

In the crucible of a catastrophic incident response, it is very difficult, and indeed often inadvisable, to reverse the ways in which authority was previously implemented and delegated in plans, procedures, and protocols, since such reversal in the midst of crisis response can result in operational chaos. Failure to exercise authority as set forth in plans, procedures, and protocols can result in confusion and paralysis of decision-making. Thus, the time to ensure the adequacy of implementation of authority and its delegation, and the comprehension of such authority and its implementation by state and local government decision-makers, is prior to the onset of such an event * * * .

NOTES AND QUESTIONS

1. How would the federal response to Katrina have fared under the four criteria by which these observers evaluated Louisiana's effort: (1) the *expression and clarity* of authority to act, (2) the *implementation* of that authority, (3) the actual *exercise* of the authority, and (4) the appropriateness of the *delegation* of that authority?

2. On Saturday, August 27, 2005, Mayor Ray Nagin issued the first mandatory evacuation in the history of New Orleans. Aided by "contraflow," the practice of converting all highway lanes outbound, more than a million people evacuated southeastern Louisiana within 24 hours. Nearly 100,000 New Orleanians, however, remained in the city. Though some residents sought refuge at "shelters of last resort"—the Louisiana Superdome, the Convention Center, and the "cloverleaf"—others rode out the storm at home. *See* UNITED STATES SENATE COMMITTEE ON HOMELAND SECURITY AND GOVERNMENTAL AFFAIRS, HURRICANE KATRINA: A NATION STILL UNPREPARED 1-4 to 1-5, 16-1 to 16-14 (2006).

Why did so many New Orleanians play "hurricane roulette"? Many did so out of necessity. Lacking cars to leave, let alone the estimated $1,000 needed to shelter a family of four, the poorest residents of the city had no choice. City, state, and federal officials failed to coordinate bus evacuations until after the storm had struck and the levees had been breached. Still others elected to stay home. Snarled traffic associated with previous evacuations evidently persuaded some residents to stay, as did the experience of surviving earlier storms (particularly Camille, a Category 5 hurricane that struck the Gulf Coast in 1969).

How effective can any evacuation order be, at any level of government, if it is not backed by (1) transportation for those who lack the means to evacuate themselves and (2) perhaps some measure of coercion for those who might otherwise play the hurricane lottery?

3. Many residents of New Orleans apparently refused to evacuate because doing so would have forced them to abandon their pets:

> In hurricane-ravaged New Orleans, the lack of planning added to the burden and stress of both rescuers and residents. In a city of 500,000 as many as 69 percent of the people are pet owners and, by some estimates, there are as many as 600,000 pets and animals affected by the devastation of hurricane Katrina. Private rescue organizations estimate they have saved about 5,000 animals so far and have reunited only 600 animals with their owners. Estimates indicate there are an equal percentage of pet owners nationwide.

Introduction of the Pets Evacuation and Transportation Standards (PETS) Act of 2005, 151 Cong. Rec. E1943, E1943 (Sept. 22, 2005) (statement of Rep. Tom Laitos, D-Cal.); *see also* Pets Evacuation and Transportation Standards Act of 2005, 152 Cong. Rec. H2985, H2986 (May 22, 2006) (statement of Rep. Christopher Shays, R-Conn.). According to an animal search and rescue expert, "there is a direct correlation between people risking their lives in a disaster and the presence of pets in the home." Jay Romano, *Protecting Pets in a Disaster*, N.Y. TIMES, Sept. 25, 2005, at 14 (quoting Joseph Buttito). In the immediate aftermath of the storm, Representatives Lantos and Shays introduced the Pets Evacuation and Transportation Standards (PETS) Act. H.R. 3858, 109th Cong. (Sept. 22, 2005) (proposed amendment to 42 U.S.C. § 5196(b)); *see also* S. 2548, 109th Cong. (April 5, 2006). Characterizing the bill as "public safety" legislation, Representative Shays has described how the PETS Act would operate:

> In order to qualify for Federal Emergency Management Agency (FEMA) funding, a jurisdiction is required to submit a document detailing their disaster preparedness plan. The PETS Act would simply require state and local emergency preparedness authori-

ties to plan for how they will accommodate households with pets or service animals when presenting these plans to FEMA.

Christopher Shays, *Animal Law: Its Place in Legislation*, 12 ANIMAL L. 1, 1-2 (2005).

4. Many of the issues that plague the coordination of federal relief efforts with state-level efforts reappear in the coordination of statewide relief with local governments. Others, such as the Posse Comitatus Act's attempt to resolve the inherent tension between military and civilian authority, are noticeably absent in the relationship between state governments and their subdivisions. Some of the common issues involve questions of governmental structure. Traditional distinctions in local government law—between "Dillon's Rule" that local governments have only those powers that are explicitly assigned to them, on one hand, and "home rule" approaches that empower local governments absent contrary directions from their states—correspond to competing visions of federalism. Structural issues aside, questions of finance and competence are even more salient at the state level than they are in the relationship between the federal government and the states. Aside from granting money to local governments and conducting extensive training for local officials, which most states would gladly do if only they had unlimited resources, what concrete measures can help states coordinate emergency response efforts with their constituent localities?

2. MULTIJURISDICTIONAL RESPONSE AUTHORITY

The default "pull" structure of federal emergency response suggests that relief efforts for most noncatastrophic events should rely initially on local and state-level resources. It follows that some emergencies, even those affecting more than one state, may not warrant full federal involvement. In the anti-terrorism context, the Justice Department has fostered multijurisdictional partnerships for meeting regional threats. *See generally* DEPARTMENT OF JUSTICE, BUREAU OF JUSTICE ASSISTANCE, MUTUAL AID: MULTIJURISDICTIONAL PARTNERSHIPS FOR MEETING REGIONAL THREATS (September 2005). Even in circumstances meriting aggressive federal intervention, interstate cooperation can supplement federal aid. The Emergency Management Assistance Compact, an interstate compact ratified by Congress in 1996, provides the framework for mutual cooperation:

EMERGENCY MANAGEMENT ASSISTANCE COMPACT

Pub. L. No. 104-321, 110 Stat. 3877 (1996)

Article I   Purpose and Authorities

This compact is made and entered into by and between the participating member states which enact this compact, hereinafter called party states. For the purposes of this compact, the term "states" is taken to mean the several states, the Commonwealth of Puerto Rico, the District of Columbia, and all U.S. territorial possessions.

The purpose of this compact is to provide for mutual assistance between the states entering into this compact in managing any emergency disaster that is duly declared by the Governor of the affected state, whether arising from natural disaster, technological hazard, man-made disaster, civil emergency aspects of resources shortages, community disorders, insurgency, or enemy attack.

This compact shall also provide for mutual cooperation in emergency-related exercises, testing, or other training activities using equipment and personnel simulating performance of any aspect of the giving and receiving of aid by party states or subdivisions of party states during emergencies, such actions occurring outside actual declared emergency periods. Mutual assistance in this compact may include the use of the states' National Guard forces, either in accordance with the National Guard Mutual Assistance Compact or by mutual agreement between states.

Article II   General Implementation

Each party state entering into this compact recognizes that many emergencies transcend political jurisdictional boundaries and that intergovernmental coordination is essential in managing these and other emergencies under this compact. Each state further recognizes that there will be emergencies which require immediate access and present procedures to apply outside resources to make a prompt and effective response to such an emergency. This is because few, if any, individual states have all the resources they may need in all types of emergencies or the capability of delivering resources to areas where emergencies exist.

The prompt, full, and effective utilization of resources of the participating states, including any resources on hand or available from the federal government or any other source, that are essential to the safety, care, and welfare of the people in the event of any emergency or disaster declared by a party state, shall be the underlying principle on which all articles of this compact shall be understood.

On behalf of the Governor of each state participating in the compact, the legally designated state official who is assigned responsibility for emergency management will be responsible for formulation of the appropriate interstate mutual aid plans and procedures necessary to implement this compact.

Article III   Party State Responsibilities

A. It shall be the responsibility of each party state to formulate procedural plans and programs for interstate cooperation in the performance of the responsibilities listed in this article. In formulating such plans, and in carrying them out, the party states, insofar as practical, shall:

1. Review individual state hazards analyses and, to the extent reasonably possible, determine all those potential emergencies the party states might jointly suffer, whether due to natural disaster, technological hazard, man-made disaster, emergency aspects of resources shortages, civil disorders, insurgency, or enemy attack;

2. Review party states' individual emergency plans and develop a plan which will determine the mechanism for the interstate management and provision of assistance concerning any potential emergency;

3. Develop interstate procedures to fill any identified gaps and to resolve any identified inconsistencies or overlaps in existing or developed plans;

4. Assist in warning communities adjacent to or crossing the state boundaries;

5. Protect and assure uninterrupted delivery of services, medicines, water, food, energy and fuel, search and rescue, and critical lifeline equipment, services, and resources, both human and material;

6. Inventory and set procedures for the interstate loan and delivery of human and material resources, together with procedures for reimbursement or forgiveness; and

7. Provide, to the extent authorized by law, for temporary suspension of any statutes or ordinances that restrict the implementation of the above responsibilities.

B. The authorized representative of a party state may request assistance to another party state by contacting the authorized representative of that state. The provisions of this compact shall only apply to requests for assistance made by and to authorized representatives. Requests may be verbal or in writing. If verbal, the request shall be confirmed in writing within thirty days of the verbal request. Requests shall provide the following information:

1. A description of the emergency service function for which assistance is needed, including, but not limited to, fire services, law enforcement, emergency medical, transportation, communications, public works and engineering, building, inspection, planning and information assistance, mass care, resource support, health and medical services, and search and rescue;

2. The amount and type of personnel, equipment, materials and supplies needed, and a reasonable estimate of the length of time they will be needed; and

3. The specific place and time for staging of the assisting party's response and a point of contact at that location.

C. There shall be frequent consultation between state officials who have assigned emergency management responsibilities and other appropriate representatives of the party states with affected jurisdictions and the United States Government, with free exchange of information, plans, and resource records relating to emergency capabilities.

Article IV Limitations

Any party state requested to render mutual aid or conduct exercises and training for mutual aid shall take such action as is necessary to provide and make available the resources covered by this compact in accordance with the terms hereof; provided that it is understood that the state rendering aid may withhold resources to the extent necessary to provide reasonable protection for such state.

Each party state shall afford to the emergency forces of any party state, while operating within its state limits under the terms and conditions of this compact, the same powers, except that of arrest unless specifically authorized by the receiving state, duties, rights, and privileges as are afforded forces of the state in which they are performing emergency services. Emergency forces will continue under the command and control of their regular leaders, but the organizational units will come under the operational control of the emergency services authorities of the state receiving assistance. These conditions may be activated, as needed, only subsequent to a declaration of a state emergency or disaster by the governor of the party state that is to receive assistance or upon commencement of exercises or training for mutual aid and shall continue so long as the exercises or training for mutual aid are in progress, the state of emergency or disaster remains in effect, or loaned resources remain in the receiving state, whichever is longer.

Article V Licenses and Permits

Whenever any person holds a license, certificate, or other permit issued by any state party to the compact evidencing the meeting of qualifications for professional, mechanical, or other skills, and when such assistance is requested by the receiving party state, such person shall be deemed licensed, certified, or permitted by the state requesting assistance to render aid involving such skill to meet a declared emergency or disaster, subject to such limitations and conditions as the Governor of the requesting state may prescribe by executive order or otherwise.

Article VI Liability

Officers or employees of a party state rendering aid in another state pursuant to this compact shall be considered agents of the requesting state for tort liability and immunity purposes. No party state or its officers or employees rendering aid in another state pursuant to this compact shall be liable on account of any act or omission in good faith on the part of such forces while so engaged or on account of the maintenance or use of any equipment or supplies in connection therewith. Good faith in this article shall not include willful misconduct, gross negligence, or recklessness.

Article VII   Supplementary Agreements

Inasmuch as it is probable that the pattern and detail of the machinery for mutual aid among two or more states may differ from that among the states that are party hereto, this compact contains elements of a broad base common to all states, and nothing herein shall preclude any state entering into supplementary agreements with another state or affect any other agreements already in force between states. Supplementary agreements may comprehend, but shall not be limited to, provisions for evacuation and reception of injured and other persons and the exchange of medical, fire, police, public utility, reconnaissance, welfare, transportation and communications personnel, and equipment and supplies.

Article VIII   Compensation

Each party state shall provide for the payment of compensation and death benefits to injured members of the emergency forces of that state and representatives of deceased members of such forces in case such members sustain injuries or are killed while rendering aid pursuant to this compact, in the same manner and on the same terms as if the injury or death were sustained within their own state.

Article IX   Reimbursement

Any party state rendering aid in another state pursuant to this compact shall be reimbursed by the party state receiving such aid for any loss or damage to or expense incurred in the operation of any equipment and the provision of any service in answering a request for aid and for the costs incurred in connection with such requests; provided, that any aiding party state may assume in whole or in part such loss, damage, expense, or other cost, or may loan such equipment or donate such services to the receiving party state without charge or cost; and provided further, that any two or more party states may enter into supplementary agreements establishing a different allocation of costs among those states. Article VIII expenses shall not be reimbursable under this article.

Article X   Evacuation

Plans for the orderly evacuation and interstate reception [*sic*] of portions of the civilian population as the result of any emergency or disaster of sufficient proportions to so warrant, shall be worked out and maintained between the party states and the emergency management/services directors of the various jurisdictions where any type of incident requiring evacuations might occur. Such plans shall be put into effect by request of the state from which evacuees come and shall include the manner of transporting such evacuees, the number of evacuees to be received in different areas, the manner in which food, clothing, housing, and medical care will be provided, the registration of the evacuees, the providing of facilities for the notification of relatives or friends, and the forwarding of such evacuees to other areas or the bringing in of additional materials, supplies, and all other relevant factors. Such plans shall provide that the party state receiving evacuees and the party state from which the evacuees come shall mutually agree as to reimbursement of out-of-pocket expenses incurred in receiving and caring for such evacuees, for expenditures for transportation, food, clothing, medicines, and medical care, and like items. Such expenditures shall be reimbursed as agreed by the party state from which the evacuees come. After the termination of the emergency or disaster, the party state from which the evacuees come shall assume the responsibility for the ultimate support of repatriation of such evacuees.

Article XI   Implementation

A. This compact shall become effective immediately upon its enactment into law by any two states. Thereafter, this compact shall become effective as to any other state upon enactment by such state.

B. Any party state may withdraw from this compact by enacting a statute repealing the same, but no such withdrawal shall take effect until thirty days after the Governor of the withdrawing state has given notice in writing of such withdrawal to the Governors of all other party states. Such action shall not relieve the withdrawing state from obligations assumed hereunder prior to the effective date of withdrawal.

C. Duly authenticated copies of this compact and of such supplementary agreements as may be entered into shall, at the time of their approval, be deposited with each of the party states and with the Federal Emergency Management Agency and other appropriate agencies of the United States Government.

Article XII   Validity

This compact shall be construed to effectuate the purposes stated in Article I. If any provision of this compact is declared unconstitutional, or the applicability thereof to any person or circumstances is held invalid, the constitutionality of the remainder of this compact and the applicability thereof to other persons and circumstances shall not be affected.

Article XIII   Additional Provisions

Nothing in this compact shall authorize or permit the use of military force by the National Guard of a state at any place outside that state in any emergency for which the President is authorized by law to call into federal service the militia, or for any purpose for which the use of the Army or the

Air Force would in the absence of express statutory authorization be prohibited under § 1385 of Title 18 of the United States Code.

NOTES AND QUESTIONS

1. Mutual aid as a tool for emergency management traces its origins to global instability in 1949, when the Soviet Union exploded its first nuclear device and North Korea invaded South Korea. President Truman established the Federal Civil Defense Administration. In 1950 Congress passed the Federal Civil Defense Act, the Defense Production Act, and the Disaster Relief Act. Alone among these statutes, the Disaster Relief Act addressed natural as well as military disasters. In connection with these statutes, Congress also ratified the Civil Defense Compact of 1950.

    Nearly half a century later, the Emergency Management Assistance Compact (EMAC) became the first interstate compact since the Civil Defense Compact to facilitate interstate cooperation as a way to supplement federal emergency response. After Hurricane Andrew struck Florida in 1992, the Southern Governors' Association formed the Southern Regional Emergency Management Assistance Compact (SREMAC) in 1993. In 1995 the SREMAC opened membership to any state or territory that wished to join; one year thereafter, Congress ratified the broadened agreement as the Emergency Management Assistance Compact.

2. EMAC has drafted Model Intrastate Mutual Aid Legislation based on the interstate compact. *See* http://www.emacweb.org/?150. Compare EMAC's model statute to Louisiana's Disaster Act, LA. REV. STAT. §§ 29:721-:733. To what extent can and should these models guide emergency response legislation in other states?

3. Whether implemented on a regional or an intrastate basis, EMAC actively pursues a decentralized approach to emergency response. Does decentralization of response authority to states or to counties and municipalities supply a viable alternative to prevailing systems such as the Stafford Act, the NRP, and the Louisiana Disaster Act?

U.S. HOUSE OF REPRESENTATIVES, A FAILURE OF INITIATIVE

Final Report of the Select Bipartisan Committee to Investigate the
Preparation for and Response to Hurricane Katrina 144-145 (2006)

**Finding: Once activated, the Emergency Management Assistance
Compact (EMAC) enabled an unprecedented level of mutual aid assistance to reach the disaster area in a timely and effective manner**

EMAC provided invaluable interstate mutual aid in support of Hurricane Katrina by deploying more than 67,891 personnel (19,481 civilians and 48,477 National Guard) to Louisiana and Mississippi. EMAC facilitated mutual assistance from 48 states, the District of Columbia, the Virgin Islands and Puerto Rico.

In support of Hurricane Katrina, more than 2,188 resource requests (missions) were filled. Record numbers of National Guard troops, local responders, and health/medical personnel were deployed through the compact. EMAC also works in cooperation with the federal government by co-locating personnel, when requested, in the NRCC or Regional Response Coordination Center (RRCC) in order to share information on EMAC activities in the affected states, monitor the availability of needed resources being offered by assisting states, and facilitate overall emergency response and recovery activities.

Through state statute, EMAC addresses the legal issues of liability, workers compensation, reimbursement, and professional licensure—prior to a disaster or emergency when resource needs and timing are critical. State and territory members must pre-designate personnel with the authority to request and commit resources. Standard operating procedures exist for compact members and training and exercise of state personnel is required. While formalized protocols are in place, EMAC is designed to be adaptable and scaleable to meet the changing needs of each event.

Following each large scale activation of the compact, a review and evaluation of the response is conducted and standard operating procedures revised and updated to reflect lessons learned and best practices. For example, lessons learned from the 2004 Florida hurricanes led to an overhaul of some operational procedures related to mobilization and deployment of resources, an enhanced automation system to provide more accurate data and electronic tracking of resources, and a new standardized EMAC training curriculum and updated operations manual. These enhancements were either in progress or completed prior to Hurricane Katrina.

In Mississippi, EMAC assistance was considered a success. The assistance in Mississippi included help from other states' security agencies (such as their state police) as well as various states' National Guards (troops and hard assets). * * * Louisiana state officials also viewed EMAC assistance as very successful. One state official said there were almost 900 EMAC agreements for assistance. Although the EMAC response from surrounding states varied, state officials applauded EMAC for successfully getting law enforcement manpower assistance. According to state police officers Ralph Mitchell and Joseph Booth, Arkansas, Tennessee, New Jersey, and California all sent law enforcement officers through EMAC.

FEMA officials also noted the general success of EMAC. Because of the magnitude of the disaster, however, Louisiana was unable to handle all of the EMAC requests, requiring FEMA to become more involved in the process than normal. In particular, FCO Scott Wells noted some state offers of assistance through FEMA were rejected by Louisiana. He said these offers were rejected by SCO Smith because of concerns about the costs to the state.

NOTES AND QUESTIONS

1. Why did EMAC succeed where so many other response systems failed either partially or catastrophically? What distinguished EMAC, an inter-

state compact, from counterparts that covered either a smaller geographic footprint (local and state plans) or the entire United States (HSPD-5 and its components, especially the NIMS and the NRP)?

2. By the same token, EMAC did not perform flawlessly. Louisiana affirmatively rejected some offers of assistance from other states, evidently concerned that Louisiana would bear the eventual costs. Articles VIII and IX of EMAC respectively address "compensation" and "reimbursement." What is the distinction between these categories? Did EMAC offer Louisiana some alternative to refusing aid on grounds of cost? Article IX stipulates "that any aiding party state may assume in whole or in part such loss, damage, expense, or other cost, or may loan such equipment or donate such services to the receiving party state without charge or cost." It also provides "that any two or more party states may enter into supplementary agreements establishing a different allocation of costs among those states." "Compensation" under article VIII, however, may not be "reimbursable" under article IX.

3. Multijurisdictional emergency response systems, whether implemented through federal law (such as HSPD-5) or through an interstate compact (such as EMAC) may be viewed as a form of insurance among participating governments. Increasing the geographic footprint of an emergency response system has the effect of deepening an insurance pool: it allows participants to spread risks across a deeper and therefore more stable source of financial resources. The simultaneous presence of HSPD-5 and EMAC can be analogized to the presence of multiple layers of insurance against risk that defies any single state's ability to manage.

4. Of course, the insurance analogy suggests a fundamental weakness of these arrangements within a country with persistent differences along two dimensions. First, states have predictably different risk profiles. For instance, states with seashores are more vulnerable to hurricanes and typhoons, while states near geologically active faults, such as the San Andreas and New Madrid faults, are more prone to earthquakes. Second, states also have different levels of income and wealth. Environmental and economic differences impair the management of HSPD-5, EMAC, and other multijurisdictional emergency response systems. These schemes strongly resemble a health insurance system in which some beneficiaries are predictably poorer and sicker than others.

5. Reconsider article VII of EMAC:

> Inasmuch as it is probable that the pattern and detail of the machinery for mutual aid among two or more states may differ from that among the states that are party hereto, this compact contains elements of a broad base common to all states, and nothing herein shall preclude any state entering into supplementary agreements with another state or affect any other agreements already in force between states.

Is this provision an adequate tool for overcoming persistent differences in the economic and risk profiles among states?

C. REFORMING THE LAW OF EMERGENCY RESPONSE

The response to Katrina was so roundly denounced that proposals for reform arose almost immediately. The perceived failure of the law of emergency response prompted a long season of political introspection. This chapter concludes by examining two reform proposals. First, insofar as complex divisions of authority between federal, state, and local officials confounded efforts to coordinate a single, effective response to Katrina, an earlier calamity offers some lessons. In response to the Mississippi River flood of 1927, the federal government concentrated authority in a single "recovery czar," Secretary of Commerce Herbert Hoover. A second reading presents a comprehensive proposal to reinvent the federal emergency response system root and branch. After reviewing the failures of the existing system, a Senate committee has recommended the abolition of FEMA and the creation of a new National Preparedness and Response Authority.

> KEVIN R. KOSAR, DISASTER RESPONSE AND
> APPOINTMENT OF A RECOVERY CZAR: THE EXECUTIVE
> BRANCH'S RESPONSE TO THE FLOOD OF 1927
>
> ---
>
> (Oct. 25, 2005) (CRS Order Code RL33126)

In the wake of the destruction caused by Hurricanes Katrina and Rita, the press and policymakers have looked to the past for examples of federal responses to natural disasters that might serve as models for emulation today. A number of newspaper articles have referred to the executive branch's response to the 1927 Mississippi River flood. Some Members of Congress have expressed an interest in creating a cabinet-level "czar" to administer Hurricane Katrina and Hurricane Rita relief programs. Since the federal response to the flood of 1927 featured Secretary of Commerce Herbert Hoover as the director of the flood response and wielding immense executive powers, this episode * * * may be of particular interest * * * *

[The federal response to the 1927 flood] was primarily an executive branch response. President Calvin Coolidge created a quasi-governmental commission that included members of his Cabinet and the American National Red Cross. This commission encouraged the public to donate funds to the relief effort and utilized federal resources, American National Red Cross volunteers, and the private sector to carry out the relief and recovery program. The commission also gave Secretary of Commerce Herbert Hoover near-absolute authority.

The concentration of power and the blending of the governmental and private sectors in Hoover's hands enabled the relief effort to be carried out expeditiously and creatively. President Coolidge's empowerment of Hoover alone as director of the flood response clarified to federal, state, and local officials and the public who was in charge. As will be seen, historical accounts and assessments of the federal flood response failed to locate any instances of jurisdictional confusion or power struggles between agencies.

However, this administrative structure was not without costs. There was little direct federal oversight of actual relief provision. * * * Furthermore, the concentration of power in a single set of hands enabled Secretary Hoover to undertake inadvisable actions with nearly no constraints.

The Mississippi River Flood of 1927

* * * From late August 1926 through the spring of 1927, unusually heavy precipitation fell upon the Mississippi River Valley. "From January 1 to April 30, 1927, enough rain fell in various sections of [the Mississippi River basin] to cover the entire territory to a depth of 10.79 inches." * * *

In April 1927, the Mississippi River began bursting levees. The first was at Dorena, MO, where on April 16, 1,200 feet of levee crumbled. Five days later, massive crevasses opened in levees in Mounds Landing, MS, and then Pendleton, AR; hundreds of millions of gallons of water violently washed over the land. The flood had begun and its end was not declared until late July. People were drowned in the fields and in their homes. The rush of the water was so immense and violent that it permanently altered the topography in areas. Near the levee break at Mounds Landing, for example, the flood left a 65 acre lake that remains to this day.

In all, levees in Arkansas, Louisiana, Mississippi, and Missouri broke in 145 places. Over 26,000 square miles of land in seven states inhabited by some 930,000 persons were flooded. The damage was immense—41,487 buildings were destroyed, 162,017 homes flooded, and over $100 million [about $1.12 billion in 2005 dollars] in crops and farm animals destroyed. It is unclear how many persons were killed—accounts vary widely—but, it seems clear that at least 246 died. * * *

Federal Disaster Response, Relief, and Reconstruction

The federal government's response to the disaster was a mixture of pre-New Deal minimalist federal governance and, to use recent parlance, "governing by network." The federal government would make no immediate appropriations to the affected area. Instead, it would utilize federal resources and coordinate networks of federal, state, private, and not-for-profit organizations to deliver relief services. The President's Cabinet would direct the relief effort in close consultation with the American National Red Cross. Thus, flood response policy was centralized, but, its execution was decentralized.

In 1927, there was no federal disaster-response agency. Instead, the federal government had a partnership with the Red Cross, a congressionally chartered quasi-governmental entity, established for a number of purposes, including the carrying out of "a system of national and international relief in time of peace, and to apply the same in mitigating the suffering caused by pestilence, famine, fire, floods, and other great national calamities, and to devise and carry out measures for preventing the same." Under the charter, the President of the United States was to appoint six members, one of whom was to serve as chairman, of the eighteen-person central committee. The other five members were to be "named by him from the Departments of State, War, Navy, Treasury, and Justice." While the law did not provide a position for the President himself, Coolidge had been asked and agreed to serve as President of the Red Cross.

On April 22, 1927, President Calvin Coolidge issued a proclamation to the nation. He declared, "The Government is giving such aid as lies within its powers . . . . But the burden of caring for the homeless rests upon the agency designated by Government charter to provide relief in disaster—the American National Red Cross." He made no mention of emergency appropriations. Rather, Coolidge, as President of the United States and the Red Cross, asked for the public to donate $5 million [$55.9 million in 2005 dollars] to the Red Cross. Additionally, the President created a quasi-governmental commission to assist the Red Cross in the relief effort. Coolidge appointed Herbert Hoover, Secretary of Commerce, as chairman.

Hoover was an apt choice—he had been elected to the Central Committee of the Red Cross by the incorporators and he had experience managing post–World War I relief and reconstruction efforts in Europe. Hoover was directly assisted by James L. Fieser, acting chairman of the Red Cross. The remainder of the commission, whose roles, according to President Coolidge, were to lend expert advice and expedite resource provision, included the secretaries of the Departments of the Treasury, War, and Navy, and the members of the Red Cross Central Committee.

That same day—April 22—[the "Hoover Flood Commission"] met for the first time and made three major decisions. First, it effectively turned over direction of the Red Cross's relief effort to Secretary Hoover. Second, it appointed Henry M. Baker, disaster relief director for the Red Cross, as the actual administrator of the response effort. As "dictator," Baker would do the work to execute Hoover's directions. Third, the Flood Commission agreed that each of the affected states should appoint a "dictator"; this individual would serve as the point-person for the state, and who would see to it that state resources were provided to the centrally directed response. These decisions made Hoover, to use recent nomenclature, the "czar" for federal disaster response, likely the first.

This concentration of a wide array of governmental powers in a single set of hands enabled the federal government to respond rapidly without bureaucratic impediments. If Hoover asked for a federal resource, the Hoover Flood Commission would see that it was provided. The Memphis flood response headquarters served as an "administrative pump." A hodgepodge of resources from the many partners in the relief effort flowed in, as did advice from the Hoover Flood Commission and local relief workers. The headquarters, which was divided into operational units, including purchase and supply, river transportation and rescue work, rail transportation, and so forth, served as a processor. * * * Out of the pump flowed streams of coordinated responses. A single, official channel of communication—"Field Operations Letters"—was established; through it, the headquarters delivered relief plan directions to local personnel and groups by telephone calls and radio communications directed to regional Red Cross offices.

Furthermore, coordinating the federal response with the Red Cross gave the relief effort the power to draw upon thousands of already-trained Red Cross volunteers in affected areas. These volunteers on the scene provided information to the [Hoover Commission's] headquarters for use in planning and coordinating the response, and utilized relationships they had with affected residents and governments to help execute the response. Federal, state, and quasi-governmental entities and private citizens and businesses were linked to form an "administrative machine."

The President, for his part, let the Hoover Flood Commission run relief administration. He issued a further plea for another $5 million in donations to the Red Cross on May 2. Hoover, though, directed the expenditure of the funds, often shipping allotments to local Red Cross chapters to expend according to their directions.

The scale of the relief effort was massive. Approximately 640,000 displaced persons were aided by the Red Cross; 307,208 stayed in over 150 Red Cross camps, many for up to four months; the remainder of evacuees stayed elsewhere, but, received food from the Red Cross. The Red Cross provided those in the camps with food, tobacco, medical care, clothing, and some entertainment. Evacuees, typically, lived in tents donated by the Department of War, and had access to simple bathing and toilet facilities. They received rudimentary medical care; some entertainment and courses in home economics were provided.

While the relief operations were of considerable breadth, federal recovery and reconstruction efforts were quite modest. The Army Corp of Engineers, after some delay, repaired the levees. Hoover encouraged affected states to incorporate state reconstruction corporations. He also strongly encouraged banks in affected areas and the captains of industries of the day to provide working capital for the banks by buying stock in them. His plan was for state reconstruction corporations to lend money to farmers, sell these loans to the Federal Intermediate Credit Corporation, and use the proceeds to make more loans. The Red Cross, meanwhile, helped citizens rebuild some of their homes, and provided them with seeds, farm implements, basic household furnishings, and other items to help them regain the ability to sustain themselves. * * *

An Assessment of the Executive Branch's Response

The public donated and the Red Cross delivered over $21 million [$234.9 million] in aid. The federal government provided, perhaps, $10 million [$111.8 million] in resources and manpower—nearly $32 million [$346.7 million] in all.

On the whole, the response and relief provided by the federal government and Red Cross appear to have been well executed. The concentration of great power in the person of Secretary Hoover enabled quick and creative responses. By April 23, 1927, U.S. Coast Guard boats were rescuing citizens trapped in trees and on rooftops, bridges, and high grounds, the U.S. Army had shipped thousands of tents, cots, and blankets to areas where Red Cross camps were being set up, and the Navy had received Hoover's request to dispatch boats and rescue crews. * * *

The blending of governmental and private resources enabled creative responses. For example, the Red Cross Rescue Fleet was cobbled together from privately owned yachts, commercial barges, boats belonging to federal agencies such as the U.S. Army, Navy, Coast Guard, and river steamships. Railroads were employed to move * * * materials, manpower, and evacuees. Hoover also brought into the mix the Rockefeller Foundation, which provided public health assistance to affected counties.

Additionally, President Coolidge's employment of a Cabinet-based commission helped clarify to the public and local, state, and federal officials who was in charge of the flood response. Secretary Hoover was widely known throughout the nation, and the President made sure that everyone got the message that Hoover was in charge by utilizing the bully pulpit—he issued a presidential proclamation to the press. That same day—April 23—Hoover and Fieser made contact with governors to let them know that the federal government and Red Cross would jointly direct all activities. The scholarly and press accounts on the flood response cited above reveal no jurisdictional disputes between federal agencies or between federal and state agencies. Again, Hoover created an "administrative machine."

That said, the federal response has been faulted on at least four points. First, while the employment of governmental and private sector resources allowed for creative responses, it also opened the door to potential abuses. For example, Hoover, reportedly, empowered Baker to order the seizure of privately owned boats by relief workers. Thus, with no executive order or statute, private individuals were authorized to take the property of others. To whom individuals affected and aggrieved by civilian exercise of federal powers would protest or appeal is simply unclear.

Second, decentralized execution meant that the federal government had little oversight of the actual operations of the relief camps. Two significant incidents illustrate the limitations of this method of administration. First, critics accused the Red Cross of being slow to respond to the spread of venereal diseases among camp residents. Second, in some Red Cross camps, local officials brutalized Black evacuees and disallowed them to leave the camps.[2] * * * [T]he federal government had no one at these sites to provide accurate reports on the conditions or put a halt to these actions.[3]

---

2. Under the sharecropper relationship, a farmer would work land owned by another person and turn over to the landowner the products thereof. The landowner would sell the agricultural products and give the farmer a "share" of the proceeds. Under such an arrangement, many Blacks in the South had fallen into near or outright peonage. Farmers fell into debt when landowners would charge them for various items and services—such as loans for seed—and provided small returns. Bound by debt, farmers could not leave the land. After the flood of 1927, landowners had a strong interest in seeing that their sharecroppers returned to their fields.

Third, directions from headquarters and Hoover to field operations were very explicit as to the goals desired. In one instance, Hoover [ordered] a regional representative * * * to erect a camp to hold 10,000 persons and gave instructions on the proper construction and installation of the facilities, including tent platforms, latrines, pipelines, wells, and power lines. However, these same directions provided little direction as to the appropriate means. Locals were to figure it out themselves. Free to use whatever means they felt necessary to achieve these ends, local relief workers, in many instances, forced Black males, sometimes at gun point, to participate in flood response work. In short, workers carrying out ostensibly federal work were not federal workers, and did not have to follow federal administrative laws.

Finally, there is the matter of power concentration in the hands of a Cabinet-level czar. As head of the Hoover Flood Commission, head of the Red Cross flood relief effort, and the public face of flood relief—thanks to his tireless public relations efforts—Secretary Hoover held an immense amount of administrative and political power. * * * While this empowered him to do much good work, Hoover also made glaring mistakes, and made matters worse by refusing to admit his errors and make amends. Critically, nobody, the President excepted, could force Hoover to change course. For example,

> There is evidence that Hoover was aware of the mistreatment of Blacks in the camps and the shortcomings of his credit provision plan. Yet, he did little to fix these problems.
>
> In late May of 1927, the Secretary decided that the farmers of the area should plant soybeans, instead of cotton. He directed the Red Cross, which received public donations for the flood response, to buy enough soybean seed for 400,000 acres. When informed by agricultural scientists that soybeans were not an advisable crop choice for the affected areas, Hoover disregarded this counsel and contacted banks to urge them to loan monies to farmers for soybean crops.
>
> A destitute victim departing a relief camp might receive no more than "tickets that entitled him to railway fare * * * , and to a tent if his house was gone, tickets that gave him lumber, seeds, implements [for gardening], and a mule or cow." Many newspapers * * * argued that the federal government, which was running a massive surplus, should provide direct aid to flood victims in order to help them regain self-sustenance. Hoover disagreed—he thought flood victims had received enough to get back on their feet. Unfortunately, even these modest resources did not reach those in need. Red Cross officials distributed some evacuees' allotments to the planters for whom they worked. Some planters charged evacuees for the goods.

Therefore, they often employed threats of violence and called upon state and local governments to help them force farmers to return to work.

3. * * * President Coolidge empowered Hoover to issue reports on the progress of flood recovery. With an eye on a run for the presidency in 1928, this gave Hoover a strong incentive to be less than objective about inadequate results. Thus, he would often claim that six or fewer persons died once he was put in control of flood response. This figure is not deemed credible.

In summation, President Coolidge's version of a disaster response and recovery czar enabled quick and apparently efficient utilization of governmental and private sector resources and personnel. It also, though, gave a single administrator a large quantity of power with only presidential oversight, and, in some instances, that power appears to have been used inadvisably.

NOTES AND QUESTIONS

1. The definitive book on the 1927 flood is JOHN M. BARRY, RISING TIDE: THE GREAT MISSISSIPPI FLOOD OF 1927 AND HOW IT CHANGED AMERICA (1998). Kevin Kosar's CRS report draws heavily from Barry's book.
2. John Barry notes that the displacement of African Americans from flooded homes and their mistreatment in Hoover's camps pushed thousands of blacks out of the Mississippi Delta. *See* BARRY, *supra*, at 417. Coupled with the invention of the mechanical cotton picker and the boll weevil infestation, *see* NICHOLAS LEMANN, THE PROMISED LAND: THE GREAT BLACK MIGRATION AND HOW IT CHANGED AMERICA 5-6 (1991); Jim Chen, *Of Agriculture's First Disobedience and Its Fruit*, 48 VAND. L. REV. 1261, 1302-1312 (1995), the flood of 1927 sparked the eventual movement of more than 6 million Americans of African descent from the rural south to the urban north between the Great War and the Great Society.
3. How would the federal government appoint a "disaster czar"? He or she would surely "exercis[e] significant authority pursuant to the laws of the United States," Buckley v. Valeo, 424 U.S. 1, 126 (1976), and be subject to the appointments clause, U.S. CONST. art II, § 2, cl. 2. Unless the czar's mission can be characterized as limited in time and scope, *cf.* Morrison v. Olson, 487 U.S. 659, 671-673 (1988) (describing the traits of an "inferior" officer), or unless the czar is already a principal officer of the United States, the Senate must confirm his or her appointment.
4. The federal government relied almost exclusively on private-sector resources and personnel in responding to the flood of 1927. Hoover served as disaster czar, but the federal government supplied little else by way of muscle or materiel. Nongovernmental actors remain crucial today, especially in restoring critical infrastructure and services after a disaster. *See* Lee M. Zeichner, *Private Sector Integration*, in AMERICAN BAR ASSOCIATION, HURRICANE KATRINA TASK FORCE SUBCOMMITTEE REPORT 33, 34-38 (Feb. 2006). Almost all communications and energy facilities in the United States are privately controlled. *See* Jim Chen, *The Nature of the Public Utility: Infrastructure, the Market, and the Law*, 98 NW. U. L. REV. 1617, 1633-1640 (2004). Ensuring the continued supply of fuel and health care likewise demands more comprehensive interaction with the private sector. *Cf.* HOMELAND SECURITY COUNCIL, NATIONAL STRATEGY FOR PANDEMIC INFLUENZA (2005); U.S. DEPARTMENT OF HEALTH & HUMAN SERVICES, HHS PANDEMIC INFLUENZA PLAN (2005).

5. Though the United States is dependent on privately owned infrastructure, neither the Stafford Act nor the NRP explicitly authorizes private-sector involvement in emergency response. Legal confusion evidently impaired efforts by private entities to restore communications and other critical services in areas crippled by Katrina:

> Many companies turned to the Federal Government for support because the civil unrest, coupled with the unprecedented level of damage from the storm and subsequent flooding, hindered their access to the disaster site and to necessary resources, thus impairing their ability to repair the damaged critical infrastructure on their own. When requesting support from the Federal Government, many companies were unable to receive assistance because Federal agencies indicated that they did not have the authority to provide them support under the Stafford Act, and the NRP did not guide an interpretation that would enable that support. * * *
>
> Congress stated that its intent in creating the [Stafford] Act was "to provide an orderly and continuing means of assistance by the Federal Government to State and local Governments in carrying out their responsibilities to alleviate the suffering and damage which result from such disasters by," among other things, "achieving greater coordination and responsiveness of disaster preparedness and relief programs." [42 U.S.C. § 5121.] The Act acknowledges the need for robust coordination; however, it does not clearly address coordination with the private sector. The Stafford Act provides assistance to "State or local Governments for the repair, restoration, reconstruction, or replacement of a public facility damaged or destroyed by a major disaster and for associated expenses incurred by the Government." [*Id.* § 5172(a)(1)(A).]
>
> Although the language of the statute does not specifically preclude the private sector from receiving resources under the Act, it does not clearly grant the Federal Government authority to provide assistance to private entities, apart from nonprofit organizations. It states that the President can provide resources to "a person that owns or operates a private non-profit facility damaged or destroyed by a major disaster for the repair, restoration, reconstruction, or replacement of the facility and for associated expenses incurred by the person." [*Id.* § 5172(a)(1)(B).] In addition, the law states that the President can "coordinate all disaster relief assistance (including voluntary assistance) provided by Federal agencies, private organizations, and State and local Governments." [*Id.* § 5170(a)(2).] Section 5170(b)(3) of the Act also allows Federal departments and agencies to "provide assistance essential to meeting immediate threats to life and property resulting from a major disaster."
>
> This permission to "render assistance" to prevent loss of life or other serious harm stems from a long-standing tradition em-

bodied in policy, regulation, statute, and international obligation. Indeed, the focus of this discussion is properly on the existence of present authority to assure participation by necessary private sector infrastructure stewards in actions directed at such life saving activity, rather than eligibility of private sector entities for reimbursement. * * *

Absent from the Stafford Act is any direct reference to Federal assistance to "for-profit" entities, and it does not recognize that [telecommunications infrastructure providers], which own about 80 percent of the Nation's critical infrastructure, play a critical recovery role in disasters to address the threats to public health and safety, life, and property.

The President's National Security Telecommunications Advisory Committee, Legislative and Regulatory Task Force, *Federal Support to Telecommunications Infrastructure Providers in National Emergencies: Designation as "Emergency Responders (Private Sector)"* 7-9 (Jan. 31, 2006). Should the Stafford Act and the NRP be amended to authorize emergency response actions by private-sector, for-profit entities? If so, what measures can best facilitate voluntary relief efforts by the private parties entrusted during ordinary times to supply vital infrastructure and services? This advisory committee report advocates the creation of a new legal category, "emergency responders (private sector)," that would enable private owners of infrastructure to secure governmental protection and other "nonmonetary" assistance as their employees work to restore service.

6. The Department of Homeland Security's blueprint for protecting "critical infrastructure and key resources (CI/KR)," DEPARTMENT OF HOMELAND SECURITY, INTERIM NATIONAL INFRASTRUCTURE PROTECTION PLAN 1 (2005), acknowledges the importance of the private entities that "own[] and operate[] the vast majority of the Nation's CI/KR," *id.* at 4. DHS contemplates "CI/KR Sector Coordinating Councils" that would engage private owners and operators of infrastructure with their public-sector counterparts in emergency planning and response. *See id.* at 5, 33-34.

7. Perhaps the most important nongovernmental organization involved in emergency response and disaster relief is the American Red Cross:

The American Red Cross * * * is the only nongovernmental organization with lead agency responsibilities under the NRP. The Red Cross is an independent, non-governmental organization * * * that operates as a nonprofit, tax-exempt, charitable institution pursuant to a charter granted by the United States Congress. [*See* 36 U.S.C. § 300101.] It has the legal status of a "federal instrumentality" due to its charter requirements to carry out responsibilities delegated by the federal government.

[The Red Cross has the responsibility] to perform all duties incumbent upon a national society in accordance with the spirit and conditions of the Geneva Conventions to which the United

States is a signatory, to provide family communications and other forms of assistance to members of the U.S. military, and to maintain a system of domestic and international disaster relief, including mandated responsibilities under the Federal Response Plan coordinated by the Federal Emergency Management Agency.

The Red Cross is not a federal agency, nor does it receive federal funding on a regular basis to carry out its services and programs. It receives financial support from voluntary public contributions and from cost recovery charges for some services. Its stated mission is to "provide relief to victims of disasters and help people prevent, prepare for, and respond to emergencies."

To meet its mandated responsibilities under the NRP, the Red Cross functions as an ESF primary organization in coordinating the use of mass care resources in a presidentially declared disaster or emergency. As the lead agency for ESF #6, dealing with Mass Care, Housing and Human Services, the Red Cross assumes the role of providing food, shelter, emergency first aid, disaster welfare information and bulk distribution of emergency relief items.

U.S. HOUSE OF REPRESENTATIVES, A FAILURE OF INITIATIVE: FINAL REPORT OF THE SELECT BIPARTISAN COMMITTEE TO INVESTIGATE THE PREPARATION FOR AND RESPONSE TO HURRICANE KATRINA 42 (2006).

8. Originally chartered in 1900, the American Red Cross underwent a significant transformation in 1905, when Congress rechartered the Red Cross as a charitable organization to provide relief support during crises. The rechartering of the Red Cross proved crucial a year later, when an earthquake struck San Francisco and an ensuing fire engulfed the city. President Theodore Roosevelt announced that all federal aid would be channeled through the Red Cross. *See* NATIONAL ACADEMY OF PUBLIC ADMINISTRATION, COPING WITH CATASTROPHE: BUILDING AN EMERGENCY MANAGEMENT SYSTEM TO MEET PEOPLE'S NEEDS IN NATURAL AND MANMADE DISASTERS 10 (1993). As described in Chapter 2, the commander of the Pacific Division sent troops to San Francisco to relieve and reinforce civilian law enforcement officers. *See* Jim Winthrop, *The Oklahoma City Bombing: Immediate Response Authority and Other Military Assistance to Civil Authority (MAC)*, ARMY LAW., July 1997, at 3.

9. Throughout the twentieth century, especially after the Mississippi River flood of 1927, the federal government became progressively more involved in emergencies. The "role of the Federal government in disaster response has evolved significantly throughout the past 200 years":

In 1803, in what is widely seen as the first instance of Federal intervention in a disaster scenario, Congress approved the use of Federal resources to assist the recovery of Portsmouth, New Hampshire, following a devastating urban fire. Between 1803 and 1950, the Federal government intervened in over 100 incidents (earthquakes, fires, floods, and tornados), making Federal resources available to affected jurisdictions. These interventions were limited and were delivered in an ad hoc manner without an established Federal role or coordinated response plan. The Federal government also quickly recognized the role that private non-profit organizations can play. In 1905, Congress chartered the American Red Cross as a charitable organization to provide disaster relief support during crises. * * *

During the Great Depression, the approach of the Federal government became more proactive. For example, Congress endowed the Bureau of Public Roads with the authority to provide continuous grants to States for the repair of disaster-damaged infrastructure and charged the Army Corps of Engineers with the task of mitigating flood-related threats. This piecemeal legislative approach was eventually replaced by the Civil Defense Act of 1950[,] the first comprehensive legislation pertaining to Federal disaster relief.

In 1952, President Truman issued Executive Order 10427, which emphasized that Federal disaster assistance was intended to supplement, not supplant, the resources of State, local, and private sector organizations. This theme was echoed two decades later [by] President Nixon * * * . "Federal disaster assistance is intended to supplement individual, local and state resources." * * *

Th[e] piecemeal approach to disaster assistance was problematic and it prompted legislation that required greater cooperation between Federal agencies and authorized the President to coordinate these activities.

The 1960s and early 1970s brought massive disasters requiring major Federal response and recovery operations by the Federal Disaster Assistance Administration, established within the Department of Housing and Urban Development (HUD). Hurricane Carla struck in 1962, Hurricane Betsy in 1965, Hurricane Camille in 1969 and Hurricane Agnes in 1972. The Alaskan Earthquake hit in 1964 and the San Fernando Earthquake rocked Southern California in 1971. These events served to focus attention on the issue of natural disasters and brought about increased legislation. In 1968, the National Flood Insurance Act offered new flood protection to homeowners, and in 1974 the Disaster Relief Act firmly established the process of Presidential disaster declarations.

However, emergency and disaster activities were still fragmented. When hazards associated with nuclear power plants and the transportation of hazardous substances were added to natural disasters, more than 100 Federal agencies were involved in some aspect of disasters, hazards and emergencies. Many parallel programs and policies existed at the State and local level, compounding the complexity of Federal disaster relief efforts. The National

Governor's Association * * * asked President Jimmy Carter to centralize Federal emergency functions.

President Carter's 1979 executive order merged many of the separate disaster-related responsibilities into a new Federal Emergency Management Agency (FEMA). Among other agencies, FEMA absorbed: the Federal Insurance Administration, the National Fire Prevention and Control Administration, the National Weather Service Community Preparedness Program, the Federal Preparedness Agency of the General Services Administration and the Federal Disaster Assistance Administration activities from HUD. Civil defense responsibilities were also transferred to the new agency from the Defense Department's Defense Civil Preparedness Agency.

THE WHITE HOUSE, THE FEDERAL RESPONSE TO HURRICANE KATRINA: LESSONS LEARNED 11-12, 158-159 n.11 (2006). FEMA itself was absorbed in 2002 into a new bureaucracy that united emergency response and defense against terrorism within the Department of Homeland Security.

10. Given the scale and scope of federal involvement in emergencies, especially its escalation since 1927, a straightforward restoration of the Mississippi River flood's "disaster czar" approach seems fanciful. The experience of 1927 nevertheless retains enough allure to prompt a congressional inquiry after Katrina. Insofar as today's federal emergency response system aspires to "unified command" across jurisdictions and to a more rational coordination of 15 emergency support functions, in what respects does Herbert Hoover's 1927 experience remain pertinent?

UNITED STATES SENATE COMMITTEE ON HOMELAND SECURITY AND GOVERNMENTAL AFFAIRS

Hurricane Katrina: A Nation Still Unprepared 17-21 (2006)

Recommendations: A New National Emergency Management System for the 21st Century

The Committee's Report sets out seven foundational recommendations together with a series of supporting "building blocks," or tactical recommendations, all designed to make the nation's emergency preparedness and response system strong, agile, effective, and robust.

Hurricane Katrina exposed flaws in the structure of FEMA and DHS that are too substantial to mend. Our first foundational recommendation is to abolish FEMA and replace it with a stronger, more capable structure, to be known as the National Preparedness and Response Authority (NPRA). To take full advantage of the substantial range of resources DHS has at its disposal, NPRA will remain within DHS. Its Director would be assured of having sufficient access and clout by having the rank of Deputy Secretary, and having a direct line of communication to the President during catastrophes. The Director would also serve as the Advisor to the President for national emergency management, in a manner akin to the Chairman of the Joint Chiefs of Staff. To ensure capable and qualified leadership, senior NPRA officials would be selected from the ranks of professionals with experience in crisis management, in addition to substantial management and leadership experience, whether in the public, private, or nonprofit sector.

Our second foundational recommendation is to endow the new organization with the full range of responsibilities that are core to preparing for and responding to disasters. These include the four central functions of comprehensive emergency management—mitigation, preparedness, response and recovery—which need to be integrated. In addition, NPRA would adopt an "all-hazards plus" strategy for preparedness. In preparing our nation to respond to terrorist attacks and natural disasters, NPRA must focus on building those common capabilities—for example survivable, interoperable communications and evacuation plans—that are necessary regardless of the incident. At the same time, it must not neglect to build those unique capabilities—like mass decontamination in the case of a radiological attack or water search and rescue in the case of flooding—that will be needed for particular types of incidents. NPRA's mandate should also include overseeing protection of critical infrastructure, such as energy facilities and telecommunications systems, both to protect such infrastructure from harm and to ensure that such infrastructure is restored as quickly as possible after a natural disaster or terrorist attack.

Our third foundational recommendation is to enhance regional operations to provide better coordination between federal agencies and the states and establish regional strike teams. Regional offices should be adequately staffed, with representation from federal agencies outside DHS that are likely to be called on to respond to a significant disaster in the region. They should provide coordination and assist in planning, training, and exercising of emergency preparedness and response activities; work with states to ensure that grant funds are spent most effectively; coordinate and develop inter-state agreements; enhance coordination with NGOs and the private sector; and provide personnel and assets, in the form of Strike Teams, to be the federal government's first line of response to a disaster.

The Strike Teams would consist of, at a minimum, a designated Federal Coordinating Officer (FCO); personnel trained in incident management, public affairs, relief and recovery, and communications support; a Defense Coordinating Officer (DCO); and liaisons to other federal agencies. These regional Strike Teams should coordinate their training and exercises with the state and local officials and the private sector entities they will support when disasters occur.

Our fourth foundational recommendation is to build a true, government-wide operations center to provide enhanced situational awareness and manage interagency coordination in a disaster. Currently, there is a multiplicity of interagency coordinating structures, with overlapping missions, that attempt to facilitate an integrated federal response. Three of these structures —the Homeland Security Operations Center (HSOC), the National Response

Coordination Center (NRCC), and the Interagency Incident Management Group (IIMG)—should be consolidated into a single, integrated entity—a new National Operations Center (NOC). The NOC would include representatives of all relevant federal agencies, and should provide for one clearly defined emergency management line of communication from the states to the federal government and from the federal government to the states. It would also include a strong analytic team capable of sorting through and assessing information and determining which pieces would become part of the common operating picture.

To improve its performance in future disasters, the NOC should establish clear protocols and procedures to ensure that reports are received and reviewed, at appropriate levels, in a timely manner. When there is notice of a potential major disaster, the NOC should implement plans, including one for securing information from DOD, for obtaining postdisaster situational awareness, including identifying sources of information and data particular to the region in which the disaster may occur and, where appropriate, bringing in individuals with particular knowledge or expertise about that region.

Our fifth foundational recommendation is to renew and sustain commitments at all levels of government to the nation's emergency management system. FEMA emergency response teams have been reduced substantially in size, are inadequately equipped, and training for these teams has been all but eliminated. If the federal government is to improve its performance and be prepared to respond effectively to the next disaster, we must give NPRA— and the other federal agencies with central responsibilities under the NRP— the necessary resources to accomplish this. We must fund NPRA commensurate with the significance of its mission and ensure that those funds are well-spent. To be full partners in the national preparedness effort, states and localities will need additional resources as well.

The Administration and DHS must also ensure that federal leaders of all agencies with an emergency support role understand their key responsibilities under the NRP and the resources they need to effectively carry out the comprehensive planning required, while also training and exercising on NIMS, NRP and other operational plans. To fully integrate state and local officials into the system, there should be established an advisory council to NPRA made up of state and local officials and first responders. The advisory council should play an integral role in ensuring that the full range of activities of the new organization—including developing response plans, conducting training and exercises, formulating preparedness goals, effectively managing grants and other resources—are done in full consultation and coordination with, and take into account the needs and priorities of, states and localities.

DHS and the NPRA should more fully integrate the private and nonprofit sectors into their planning and preparedness initiatives. Among other things, they should designate specific individuals at the national and regional levels to work directly with private sector organizations. Where appropriate, private sector representatives should also be included in planning, training and exercises.

Our sixth foundational recommendation is to strengthen the underpinning of the nation's response to disasters and catastrophes. Despite their shortcomings and imperfections, the NRP and National Incident Management System (NIMS), including the Emergency Support Function (ESF) structure currently represent the best approach available to respond to multiagency, multi-jurisdictional emergencies. Federal, state, and local officials and other responders must commit to supporting the NRP and NIMS and working together to improve the performance of the national emergency management system. We must undertake further refinements of the NRP and NIMS, develop operational plans, and engage in training and exercises to ensure that everyone involved in disaster response understands them and is prepared to carry them out. In particular, the NRP should be strengthened to make the unity of effort concept very clear, so that everyone understands the concept and their roles in establishing unity, and there should be clarification of the importance of integrating agencies with ESF responsibilities into the ICS, rather than their operating in "stovepipes."

The roles and responsibilities of the PFO and FCO are overlapping and were a source of confusion during Hurricane Katrina. The Stafford Act should be amended to clarify the roles and responsibilities of the FCO, and the NRP should be revised to eliminate the PFO position for Stafford Act-declared emergencies and disasters. It should also be amended to ensure that the Act addresses response to all disasters and catastrophes, whether natural or man-made.

Our seventh foundational recommendation is to improve the nation's capacity to respond to catastrophic events. DHS should ensure that the Catastrophic Incident Annex (CIA) is fully understood by the federal departments and agencies with responsibilities associated with it. The Catastrophic Incident Supplement should be completed and published, and the supporting operational plans for departments and agencies with responsibilities under the CIA should be completed. These plans should be reviewed and coordinated with the states, and on a regional basis, to ensure they are understood, trained and exercised prior to an emergency.

DHS must also develop the national capabilities—especially surge capacity—it needs to respond to catastrophic disasters, ensuring it has sufficient full time staff, response teams, contracting personnel, and adequately trained and sufficiently staffed reserve corps to ramp up capabilities, as needed. These capabilities must be scalable so that NPRA can draw on the appropriate resources from supporting ESF agencies to respond to a disaster irrespective of cause, size, or complexity.

NOTE

The Senate report reviews many of the proposals discussed in this chapter. From the abolition of FEMA to better use of the Catastrophic Incident Index, the report embraces many recommendations by critics of the post–September 11 emergency response system. Most significantly, the report proposes a new National Preparedness and Response Authority, charged with integrating all "four central functions of comprehensive emergency management—mitigation, preparedness, response and recovery." The report also proposes "an 'all-hazards plus' strategy" that responds "to terrorist attacks and natural disasters" alike and stresses "common capabilities—for example survivable, interoperable communications and evacuation plans—that are necessary regardless of the incident." Yet the new NPRA would remain a branch of the Department of Homeland Security. How would the NPRA fulfill its "all hazards plus" mandate within a department dedicated primarily to preventing terrorism? Alternatively, would the Homeland Security aegis better enable the NPRA to exploit economies of scale and scope and learning-curve advantages accumulated within the entire department?

SOCIAL VULNERABILITY

"The moral test of government," said Hubert H. Humphrey, "is how it treats those who are in the dawn of life, the children; those who are in the twilight of life, the aged; and those who are in the shadows of life, the sick, the needy and the handicapped." Arnold v. Arizona Dept. of Health Servs., 160 Ariz. 593, 775 P.2d 521, 537 (1989) (quoting Humphrey). Natural disaster puts government to an extreme version of this test. This chapter addresses the relationship between social vulnerability and natural disasters. It begins with a global overview. Disasters are never strictly "natural"; they invariably stem from social as well as environmental factors. Because Hurricane Katrina unfolded as a tragedy of race and class, of official incompetence and social injustice, this chapter examines the racial and class-based dimensions of social vulnerability during and after the hurricane. This chapter then addresses other vectors of discrimination laid bare by the storm: sex, age, and immigrant status. A brief discussion of price-gouging laws rounds out this chapter's exploration of economic exploitation in its most general sense during disaster. This chapter's concluding section comes full circle by inquiring whether international human rights law might inform domestic efforts to minimize social vulnerability during natural disasters.

A. DISASTERS AS A FUNCTION OF INJUSTICE

Natural disaster supposedly does not discriminate; it putatively strikes everyone in its path, without regard to race, class, sex, age, or disability. In other words, "poverty is hierarchic, smog is democratic." ULRICH BECK, RISK

SOCIETY: TOWARD A NEW MODERNITY 36 (1986); *accord* Scott Frickel, *Our Toxic Gumbo: Recipe for a Politics of Environmental Knowledge*, http:// understandingkatrina.ssrc.org/frickel (Oct. 6, 2005). Closer examination of the natural and social factors in any disaster, however, belies this assumption. Disaster does not so much erase as expose social vulnerability. Though "'[n]atural disasters' such as hurricanes, earthquakes, and floods are sometimes viewed as 'great social equalizers'" that "strike unpredictably and at random, affecting black and white, rich and poor, sick and well alike," Katrina bluntly demonstrated that "the harms are not visited randomly or equally in our society." CENTER FOR PROGRESSIVE REFORM, AN UNNATURAL DISASTER: THE AFTERMATH OF HURRICANE KATRINA 34 (2005). Around the world, social injustice contributes so heavily to the incidence and intensity of natural disasters that the quest for equality may be regarded as a valuable tool for improving disaster preparedness, response, mitigation, compensation, and rebuilding.

This section begins with a global view of the relationship between natural disasters and social injustice. Katrina represented only a single episode in a grim season spanning from December 2004 through October 2005. Losses from events such as Katrina will not be stemmed until the law honestly confronts the contribution of "civilized" society to "natural" disasters:

THERESA BRAINE, WAS 2005 THE YEAR OF NATURAL DISASTERS?

84:1 Bull. World Health Org. 4 (Jan. 2006)

The year 2005 saw the aftermath of the 26 December 2004 earthquake and tsunami waves in Asia, hurricanes in central and north America, notably Katrina, * * * and the 8 October earthquake in Pakistan and India. The year also saw famine after crops were destroyed by locusts in Niger. Virtually unnoticed by the outside world was tiny El Salvador where the country's highest volcano, Ilamatepec, erupted on 1 October, displacing more than 7,500 people and killing two. A few days later Hurricane Stan swept through and killed about 70 people with floods and mudslides.

From January to October 2005, an estimated 97,490 people were killed in disasters globally and 88,117 of them in natural disasters * * * . [T]he number of natural disasters—floods, windstorms, droughts and geological disasters—recorded since 1900 have increased and the number of people affected by such disasters has also increased since 1975.

Is this as bad as it gets, or could it get worse? Why do natural disasters appear to be increasingly frequent and increasingly deadly?

Today's disasters stem from a complex mix of factors, including routine climate change, global warming influenced by human behaviour, socioeconomic factors causing poorer people to live in risky areas, and inadequate disaster preparedness and education on the part of governments as well as the general population.

Some disasters experts reject the term "natural disasters," arguing that there is almost always a man-made element. * * * Dr Ciro Ugarte [of the Pan

American Health Organization (PAHO)], explain[ed] that natural disasters would not have such a devastating effect on people's lives if they were not exposed to such risks in the first place.

Natural phenomena do not always generate human disasters. Ugarte noted that in 2005, several earthquakes that struck in South America were of a higher magnitude than the one that devastated northern Pakistan and parts of India in October, but these hit sparsely populated areas and therefore caused less damage. The same goes for several tsunamis in 2005 which were not deemed "disasters" because they didn't endanger anyone, Ugarte said.

Natural phenomena are likely to affect more people because Earth's population has increased. According to the United Nations Population Fund, this stands at about 6.5 billion people and is projected to reach 9.1 billion people in 2050.

Marko Kokic, spokesperson for WHO's Health Action in Crisis department, said that some communities are more vulnerable to the effects of natural disasters than 100 years ago because of ecological degradation. He said that, for example, when tropical storms hit the Caribbean in September 2004, there was nothing to stop storm waters gathering and wreaking devastation in Haiti because of deforestation. "We need to tackle the underlying issues, such as poverty and inequity," Kokic said, adding: "In many countries, people cut down trees because wood is the cheapest fuel."

Disasters are also a consequence of development and industrialization. In Europe, experts believe that countries such as France and Germany are more adversely affected by floods today because major rivers, such as the Rhine, have been straightened to ease commercial traffic.

Global warming as well as routine, cyclical climate changes are causing a higher number of strong hurricanes in the Caribbean, meteorologists say. Add to that the increasing number of people living in areas such as coastlines, in substandard housing and the destruction in a crisis of essential infrastructure, such as hospitals, and you have the potential for more devastating disasters than a few decades ago.

There have always been disasters. The bubonic plague wiped out more than 25 million people, or 37% of Europe's population, in the 1300s. More recently, the 1918-19 flu pandemic killed between 20 and 40 million people worldwide. One of the earliest recorded disasters, the eruption of Vesuvius in 79 AD, buried the ancient Roman city of Pompeii killing about 10,000 people. Today, two million people live within its possible range, illustrating one major difference between then and now.

About 75 disasters were reported globally in 1975 * * *. In 2000 the figure peaked at 525 and dropped to just under 400 in 2004. By far the highest number of fatalities—about 450,000—occurred in 1984. In 2004 nearly 300,000 died in disasters, but the number of people affected has soared since 1975 with about 600 million people affected by disasters of all kinds in 2002.

So complex and intertwined are the factors behind these disasters that some experts believe the most practical approach to preparedness may be to focus on reducing the risks rather than factors behind the risks.

Dave Paul Zervaas, regional coordinator for Latin America and the Caribbean at the United Nations' International Strategy for Disaster Reduction, argued that preparation should focus on making people less vulnerable to disasters. "We think it's much more important now to look at vulnerabilities, because you have factors you can control," Zervaas said. "You can work to lower vulnerability [to disasters]."

Hurricane Katrina in the United States is a good example, Zervaas said. A number of factors contributed to the damage and loss of life. The storm was huge. It struck a city whose levees had not been maintained or strengthened for years, and government agencies' response to the emergency was at first inadequate.

In Central America storms such as hurricanes Mitch and Stan have wrought damage with rain and landslides rather than wind. "The poverty issue and the social inequity situation have not become much better in most places," said Zervaas, adding that migration to cities conspires with a lack of urban planning to put people in danger.

Clearly, climate change—whether helped by human behaviour or not—is playing a role. Hurricane experts say the world is in the midst of a routine, cyclical climate change that causes the Caribbean to heat up, increasing the frequency of powerful storms. The effect of this is greater than that of global warming * * * *

Experts agree that the poor are disproportionately hit. "In several of these countries, the poor people are looking for spaces to build their houses or their communities [and] they find spaces that are not already used," Ugarte said. "And those spaces that are not already used are usually the spaces at higher risk for natural phenomena. There's a huge relationship between this kind of damage and poverty."

For this reason financial services play a role in both prevention, and damage limitation and recovery. * * * [T]he risks generated by climate change [include] * * * "blows to the world economy sufficiently severe to cripple the resilience that enables affluent countries to respond to catastrophes." * * * * While it is important to encourage people, governments and companies to buy insurance, not everyone can afford it or see the need.

Microfinancing is another avenue, giving poor people the means to improve their economic situation so that a disaster does not hit them as hard as it would otherwise, and also by lending them money to use in recovering from it. * * *

PAHO has expanded its programmes to focus not only on preparedness but also on mitigation. This involves reducing secondary deaths and destruction that can occur in the aftermath of a disaster, and implementing building codes that require hospitals, schools, military bases, and other vital structures to be built to withstand such disasters.

Many countries say they can't afford more preparation, but some measures are simple and can be inexpensive, such as a tsunami warning system, Ugarte said. "But from there to Banda Aceh, that is another step," Ugarte said, referring to the capital of the Indonesian province that was worst hit by the earthquake and tsunami of December 2004. "And from Banda Aceh to all the little communities on the coast, that's another issue. That last link of the chain is not in place. And that is the system that we need to build."

Disaster experts say early warning systems and education are essential to prevent and mitigate against the effects of natural disasters. * * * [A] simple phone call saved thousands of lives when the giant tsunami waves hit India in 2004. A fisherman's son named Vijayakumar Gunasekaran, who lives in Singapore, heard about the tsunami early on the radio and phoned relatives living on the east coast of India. Following his warning, all 3,630 residents evacuated their village there before the waves arrived.

NOTES AND QUESTIONS

1. The increase in the frequency and intensity of natural disasters depends on a complex web of interrelated factors. Climate change, environmental degradation, population growth, social and economic inequality, and governmental policy all contribute. These factors span a spectrum that can be calibrated according to the degree of putative control that governments can exert. Although Chapter 8 will explore many of these issues, it may be useful to identify the crucial factors in connection with this chapter's discussion of social vulnerability[JC4].

   a. *Climate change*. Though "environmental geographers [say] there is no such thing as a natural disaster," Neil Smith, *There's No Such Thing as a Natural Disaster*, http://understandingkatrina.ssrc.org/Smith (Sept. 26, 2005), the factors that contribute to disasters do vary in the degree of effective control that humans can exert. Perhaps the most complex and therefore most unmanageable natural phenomenon, climate change is affected by a staggering range of factors. Since the Industrial Revolution, however, the earth's climate has begun to exhibit two disturbing trends. First, overall temperature has risen. Second, departures from "normal" conditions are becoming more frequent and more intense. Storms and temperature extremes—in both directions—are rapidly becoming the norm rather than the exception. *See generally, e.g.*, INTERGOVERNMENTAL PANEL ON CLIMATE CHANGE, CLIMATE CHANGE 2001: WORKING GROUP II, IMPACTS, ADAPTATION AND VULNERABILITY (2001); SPENCER WEART, THE DISCOVERY OF GLOBAL WARMING (2003).

   Assume, at least for argument's sake, that the principal drivers of climate change are anthropocentric. Greenhouse gas emissions represent the very sort of "diffuse, cross-jurisdictional" crises that defy "haphazard local encouragement" and require cooperative solutions. Stephen M. Nickelsburg, Note, *Mere Volunteers? The Promise and Limits of Community-Based Environmental Protection*, 84 VA. L. REV. 1371, 1409 (1998); *see also* Daniel A. Farber, *Stretching the Margins: The Geographic Nexus in Environmental Law*, 48 STAN. L. REV. 1247, 1271 (1996). Because in dividual contributions to climate change are hard to quantify and even harder to control, whether through incentives or coercive regulation, governments will have great difficulty fashioning satisfactory *ex post* remedies, let alone effective *ex ante* prevention.

b. *Localized environmental degradation*. Environmental conditions on a smaller footprint also affect the probability and impact of natural disasters. Wealth and poverty are each capable of degrading the environment and thereby contributing to disaster. Whereas poverty and desperation have driven deforestation in Haiti, the urge to move more barge traffic in western Europe has driven the straightening of the Rhine. For strikingly different reasons, both regions find themselves more vulnerable to storms, flooding, and other putatively natural phenomena.

c. *Population growth and distribution*. The mere existence of more humans increases the number of potential casualties. *See generally* JOEL COHEN, HOW MANY PEOPLE CAN THE EARTH SUPPORT? (1995); PAUL EHRLICH & ANNE EHRLICH, THE POPULATION EXPLOSION (1990). These population increases are not distributed evenly. The rich and the poor alike are crowding seashores and other environmentally vulnerable areas. Poverty arguably poses a greater challenge for disaster management, since the poor often have no choice but to live in risky areas. The inability of the poor to heed evacuation orders, examined in Chapter 3, finds a distressing corollary in the continued presence of the poor in areas prone to storms, flooding, earthquakes, and other disasters.

d. *Governmental policies*. Katrina represented merely one prominent instance of legal failure. The federal government and the most directly affected states shared responsibility for failure on at least three distinct levels. First, these governments fell short of optimal *preparedness*, in the sense of educating themselves and the public on ways to minimize risk and on the division of authority in the event of disaster. Early warning systems and evacuation protocols had to be improvised, even though the probability of a strong hurricane hitting New Orleans was substantial and anticipated, and even though officials at all levels of government knew that such a strike would inflict grave casualties. Second, once Katrina struck, officials did not carry out the best available plans for *response and mitigation*. For instance, Secretary of Homeland Security Michael Chertoff failed to invoke the National Response Plan's Catastrophic Incident Annex. Finally, the Gulf Coast sustained intense *secondary damage* to hospitals and other elements of public infrastructure that contribute most to mitigation and recovery. Governments should strive to minimize secondary casualties attributable more directly to these losses than to the disaster itself.

To be sure, failed policies are more readily remedied than broader social and environmental problems, such as economic inequality or global climate change. The structure of this chapter and of this book as a whole reflects this instinct. We have focused so far on the initial allocation of governmental authority and the actual implementation of emergency response measures, leaving to later chapters more diffuse issues of compensation, risk spreading, prevention, mitigation, and long-term environmental protection. The immediate subject of social vulnerability and its contribution to a natural disaster illustrates the interplay of governmental, economic, social, and environmental forces. Precisely because there is no such thing as a strictly natural disaster, government should focus in the first instance on matters more within its control, hopeful that success in overcoming economic and social injustice will lessen the suffering from disasters.

2. Consider this summary of human factors that contribute to the "mortality, displacement, economic destruction" wrought by disasters:

> The first of these is pre-disaster preparedness and mitigation. From constructing housing (or levees) to withstand natural [shocks] to pre-positioning adequate relief supplies and preparing realistic evacuation plans, the ability of communities and societies to plan ahead to resist disaster is critical.
>
> Second, the in-disaster coping capacities of affected populations: are there resources on which they are able to fall back? In some hunger-prone regions of the world, for example, 'famine foods'—not eaten in good times but growing wild and freely available—can provide some meager support in periods of scarcity. In developed ones, have communities been able to build up and ensure access to stockpiles of canned goods, drinking water and first aid supplies? Or has their ability to build up a margin of safety been whittled away by poverty and marginalisation?
>
> Third, the immediacy, quantity, efficiency and coverage of the disaster response: each element is critical. Response may be timely but insufficient, ignoring key communities; or, as is all too frequent in the case of major "CNN catastrophes" which creep onto the world's television screens, the response may eventually be large but months too late. * * *
>
> Finally, the longer term commitment of governments and other actors to post-disaster recovery: long after the flood waters and the TV cameras both recede, reconstruction and rehabilitation are critical in rebuilding shattered lives and livelihoods. But continued commitment (and investment) at this point can capitalise on a unique opportunity to build towards the reduction of future disasters.

Stephen Jackson, *Un/natural Disasters, Here and There*, http://understandingkatrina.ssrc.org/jackson (Sept. 12, 2005).

3. Katrina capped a global year of misery that began with a natural disaster of even greater geographic and social scale. Roughly a quarter of a million people died in the Indian Ocean tsunami of December 26, 2004. Another million people were displaced. Though spread across three continents, the populations most directly affected by the tsunami were united in poverty and their vulnerability to one of the most destructive disasters in history:

HUMAN RIGHTS CENTER, UNIVERSITY OF CALIFORNIA, BERKELEY

After the Tsunami: Human Rights of Vulnerable Populations 1 (October 2005)

The tsunami of December 26, 2004, devastated thousands of communities along the coastline of the Indian Ocean. More than 240,000 people were killed. Tens of thousands went missing and are presumed dead, and more than a million people were displaced. Those most affected by the tsunami were the poor, including fisher folk, coastal workers with small retail or tourist businesses, workers in the tourism industry, migrants, and those who farmed close to coastal areas. The majority of those who died were women and children.

Immediately following the tsunami, international aid agencies feared that human traffickers might seize the opportunity to compel those most vulnerable (women, children, and migrant workers) into situations of forced labor. * * * [O]ther human rights problems, including arbitrary arrests, recruitment of children into fighting forces, discrimination in aid distribution, enforced relocation, sexual and gender-based violence, loss of documentation, as well as issues of restitution, and land and property tenure soon emerged in certain tsunami-affected areas.

As we have seen in the aftermath of hurricane Katrina, which devastated coastal areas in the southern United States, natural disasters often catch national and local governments and relief agencies unprepared to deal with the massive exigencies of emergency relief and management, and can expose victims of these catastrophes to violations of human rights.

Victims of natural disasters are protected by a host of human rights treaties and agreements. Both the UN Guiding Principles on Internal Displacement and the Sphere Project's Humanitarian Charter and Minimum Standards in Disaster Response protect victims of natural disaster and guide relief efforts to ensure that those displaced receive access to adequate and essential relief—including food, shelter, and medical care. These guiding principles maintain that internally displaced persons (IDP) have the right to request and to receive protection and assistance from national authorities who, in turn, have the primary duty and responsibility to protect and assist populations within their jurisdiction.

Natural disasters can exacerbate pre-existing vulnerabilities of populations already at risk. Poverty-stricken groups living in substandard housing, on unstable ground, or in flood plains are usually the principal victims of these disasters. Often these groups have experienced ongoing discrimination because of their ethnicity, religion, class, or gender, which has left them living in fragile physical environments. Moreover, pre-existing civil war or a history of ongoing human rights abuses can complicate or interfere with aid relief and reconstruction.

In countries where corruption and bureaucratic incompetence are rife, certain individuals and groups may manipulate their political connections to receive or distribute aid at the expense of others. Still other groups may receive little or no aid because of their ethnicity, religion, gender, age, or social standing. These abuses can leave individuals and families at risk and prolong the time they have to stay in poorly built and even dangerous camps and shelters for internally displaced people.

Isolated in camps, the internally displaced often are sidelined as government officials in distant towns and cities formulate and implement resettlement and rebuilding programs, sometimes in favor of special interests. Uncoordinated relief efforts run the risk of exacerbating these problems, especially where there is weak government oversight of the activities of international agencies and aid organizations. A tension can develop between government appropriating all decision-making to itself or allowing nongovernmental organizations to carry out their missions as they see fit. Lack of a middle ground leaves survivors with no one to turn to for assistance.

NOTES AND QUESTIONS

1. Compare Hurricane Katrina with the Indian Ocean tsunami. What might American policy makers learn from an even greater tragedy that spanned the entire Indian Ocean rim? Conversely, can global efforts against staggering losses to natural disaster learn from domestic failures in one of the world's wealthiest nations? The parallels between Katrina and the tsunami are fairly obvious: catastrophic loss of life and property, disparate impact based on social and economic status, and a distressing degree of official incompetence. Some salient differences, however, do distinguish the two disasters:

     a. *Preexisting human rights violations*. Whatever else might be said of inequality, civil rights, and human dignity in the United States, none of Katrina's victims were exposed to conscription into civil wars or opportunistic human trafficking. North America, to put it mildly, knows nothing of the misery that afflicts less developed parts of the world.

     b. *Corruption and lack of transparency and accountability in government*. Again, official fecklessness in America falls short of the sheer ineptitude of governments in many of the world's poorest countries. Katrina's impact on New Orleans and the Gulf Coast was the subject of extensive public discussion. The House of Representatives, the Senate, and the White House all delivered scathing reports on the failures of the response effort, complete with concrete platforms for reform. Some officials perceived as having performed poorly during Katrina, such as former FEMA chairman Michael Brown, lost power.

     c. *Wealth, poverty, and inequality*. According to the World Bank's gauges of absolute poverty, the world's poorest subsist on $1 per day in purchasing power parity (relative to the value of U.S. dollars in 1985). Such extreme levels of poverty are unknown—and politically unthinkable—in the United States. By the same token, *relative* poverty exists everywhere, and by this standard the United States fares poorly, at least as compared with other industrialized countries. According to the United Nations, *see* UNITED NATIONS, HUMAN DEVELOPMENT INDICATORS 270

(2005), the United States reported a Gini coefficient of 40.8, which corresponds to a higher level of economic inequality than either India (32.5) or Bangladesh (31.8), two significantly poorer countries that suffered mightily during the 2004 tsunami, *see id.* at 272.[1]

   d. *War.* Nearly a century and a half after Appomattox Court House, every American combat veteran is eligible for membership in the Veterans of *Foreign* Wars. Many other countries, sadly, continue to experience war as a thoroughly domestic phenomenon. Most Americans have no personal experience with the conscription of children or the exploitation of civilians as human shields against organized violence.

2. In the end, Katrina and the Indian Ocean tsunami should not be compared as part of an exercise to determine which victims suffered more, but rather as part of a learning experience by which policymakers might minimize future suffering. Taking account of geographic, social, economic, and political differences represents an important step in that learning process. "If the Indian Ocean Tsunami and Hurricane Katrina can be said to have any 'lessons' for us, it is to suggest that western developed countries may have as much to learn about disaster preparedness, management and recovery from non-western developing countries in terms of community-based assistance and the integrated flexible use of technology as the latter do from the former in terms of technocratic know-how and scientific expertise." Greg Bankoff, *The Tale of the Three Pigs: Taking Another Look at Vulnerability in the Light of the Indian Ocean Tsunami and Hurricane Katrina*, http://understandingkatrina.ssrc.org/bankoff (Dec. 12, 2005).

3. The Berkeley tsunami report identifies two sources of international norms that might govern disaster relief efforts. One of these is the United Nations' Guiding Principles on Internal Displacement, which will receive more consideration in this chapter. The other is the handbook of the Sphere Project, a collaborative effort of the Red Cross, Red Crescent, and other humanitarian organizations. A substantial portion of the Sphere Project's handbook outlines the "Humanitarian Charter" to which participating organizations aspire. The handbook's "Minimum Standards," by contrast, "are based on agencies' experience of providing humanitarian assistance":

> Though the achievement of the standards depends on a range of factors, many of which may be beyond our control, we commit ourselves to attempt consistently to achieve them and we expect to be held to account accordingly. We invite other humanitarian actors, including states themselves, to adopt these standards as accepted norms. * * *

---

1. The Gini coefficient is a measure of economic inequality; a higher score on this gauge indicates greater disparities in income within a country. See Philip M. Dixon, Jacob Weiner, Thomas Mitchell-Olds & Robert Woodley, *Bootstrapping the Gini Coefficient of Inequality*, 68 ECOLOGY 1548 (1988).

[W]e commit ourselves to make every effort to ensure that people affected by disasters have access to at least the minimum requirements (water, sanitation, food, nutrition, shelter and health care) to satisfy their basic right to life with dignity. To this end we will continue to advocate that governments and other parties meet their obligations under international human rights law, international humanitarian law and refugee law.

THE SPHERE PROJECT HANDBOOK: HUMANITARIAN CHARTER AND MINIMUM STANDARDS IN DISASTER RESPONSE 19 (2004).

4. One theme running through this chapter is the notion that social vulnerability in times of disaster raises questions of human rights. How can international human rights law balance the proposition that environmental quality is "essential to . . . the enjoyment of human rights," Stockholm Declaration, Report of the United Nations Conference on the Human Environment, U.N. Doc. A/Conf.48/14, 11 I.L.M. 1416, 1416 (1972) (preamble), with the equally solemn pronouncement that economic development is also a "universal and inalienable right and an integral part of fundamental human rights," Vienna Declaration and Programme of Action, U.N. Doc. A/CONF.157/24, *adopted at* Vienna, June 14-25, 1993, *reprinted in* 32 I.L.M. 1661 (1993)? Environmental sustainability may hinge on a global transition from poverty to affluence and from authoritarianism to democracy rather than the suppression of economic development. *See* JACK M. HOLLANDER, THE REAL ENVIRONMENTAL CRISIS: WHY POVERTY, NOT AFFLUENCE, IS THE ENVIRONMENT'S NUMBER ONE ENEMY (2003). Of the world's myriad environmental problems, "persistent poverty may turn out to be the most aggravating and destructive." Patrick Low, *Trade and the Environment: What Worries the Developing Countries?*, 23 ENVTL. L. 705, 706 (1993).

5. Katrina and the tsunami exposed serious flaws in several nations' capacity for preparedness, response, mitigation, and recovery in the event of natural disaster. Many of those flaws are attributable to—or at least exacerbated by—social, economic, and political inequalities expressed by the catchall phrase, "social vulnerability." To what extent is the global community willing to engage problems of social vulnerability once a single, catastrophic event has subsided? Or is the world doomed to remain inherently unequal and unjust—and correspondingly unprepared for the next tragedy that blends natural calamity with human injustice?

B. THE SCARS OF RACE, CLASS, AND INJUSTICE

Among Hurricane Katrina's first casualties was any expectation that the storm and the governmental response to it would deal equally with all victims, without regard to race or class. In a survey of Katrina evacuees living in

Houston, "68 percent of respondents thought the federal government would have responded more quickly if people trapped in the floodwaters were 'wealthier and white rather than poorer and black.'" U.S. HOUSE OF REPRESENTATIVES, A FAILURE OF INITIATIVE: FINAL REPORT OF THE SELECT BIPARTISAN COMMITTEE TO INVESTIGATE THE PREPARATION FOR AND RESPONSE TO HURRICANE KATRINA 19 (2006). At its worst, the storm exposed longstanding racial, social, and economic inequities. To be effective and legitimate, the legal response to disasters must address these injustices.

SUSAN L. CUTTER, THE GEOGRAPHY OF SOCIAL VULNERABILITY: RACE, CLASS, AND CATASTROPHE

http://understandingkatrina.ssrc.org/Cutter (Sept. 23, 2005)

The revelations of inadequate response to the hurricane's aftermath are not just about failures in emergency response at the local, state, and federal levels or failures in the overall emergency management system. They are also about failures of the social support systems for America's impoverished—the largely invisible inner city poor. The former can be rectified quickly (months to years) through organizational restructuring or training; the latter requires much more time, resources, and the political will to redress social inequities and inequalities that have been sustained for more than a half century and show little signs of dissipating.

How did we arrive at such a confluence of natural and social vulnerabilities manifested as the Hurricane Katrina disaster? This complex emergency began with geography—the spatial interaction of humans and their environment over time. Officially founded in 1718 by Jean-Baptiste Le Moyne de Bienville, New Orleans was strategically located at the crossroads of three navigable water bodies, Lake Pontchartrain, the Gulf of Mexico, and the Mississippi River. Important primarily as a trading depot for French fur trappers, the city evolved into one of the most important ports in America providing a gateway to the nation's agricultural riches.

The original settlement was on the highest ground in the bayou, Vieux Carré (the French Quarter), which later became the heart and soul of the modern city. How prescient for the early settlers to build on the highest ground available. As the settlement grew in the ensuing decades, New Orleans became a major American port city and a sprawling metropolis sandwiched between and surrounded by water. * * *

To reduce the natural risks of flooding, the physical environment surrounding New Orleans was re-engineered, spawning an era of structural river control. Levees were built to control the flow of the mighty Mississippi, but they were also built to contain flooding from Lake Pontchartrain, especially useful during hurricane season. * * * Instead of seeing the deposition of alluvium that one expects in a deltaic coastline, the levees channeled the river and its sediment, destroying protective wetlands south and east of the city. With many areas of the city below sea level, even heavy rainfall became a problem filling the city with water just like a giant punchbowl. An elaborate pumping system was required to keep the city dry during heavy rains, let alone tropical storms. What would happen during a hurricane, a levee failure, or an intentional levee breach used to divert floodwaters away from the city as was done in 1927?

Concurrent with the physical transformation of the city, a new social geography was being created as well. The South's segregated past was best seen in the spatial and social evolution of southern cities, including New Orleans. Migration from the rural impoverished areas to the city was followed by white flight from urban areas to more suburban communities. Public housing was constructed to cope with Black population influxes during the 1950s and 1960s and in a pattern repeated throughout America, the housing was invariably located in the most undesirable areas—along major transportation corridors, on reclaimed land, or next to industrial facilities. Employment opportunities were limited for inner city residents as jobs moved outward from the central city to suburban locations, or overseas as the process of globalization reduced even further the number of low skilled jobs. The most impoverished lived in squalor-like conditions concentrated in certain neighborhoods within cities, with little or no employment, poor education, and little hope for the future for their children or grandchildren. It is against this backdrop of the social geography of cities and the differential access to resources that we can best understand the Hurricane Katrina disaster.

Socially created vulnerabilities are largely ignored in the hazards and disaster literature because they are so hard to measure and quantify. Social vulnerability is partially a product of social inequalities—those social factors and forces that create the susceptibility of various groups to harm, and in turn affect their ability to respond, and bounce back (resilience) after the disaster. But it is much more than that. Social vulnerability involves the basic provision of health care, the livability of places, overall indicators of quality of life, and accessibility to lifelines (goods, services, emergency response personnel), capital, and political representation.

Race and class are certainly factors that help explain the social vulnerability in the South, while ethnicity plays an additional role in many cities. When the middle classes (both White and Black) abandon a city, the disparities between the very rich and the very poor expand. Add to this an increasing elderly population, the homeless, transients (including tourists), and other special needs populations, and the prospects for evacuating a city during times of emergencies becomes a daunting challenge for most American cities. What is a major challenge for other cities became a virtual impossibility for New Orleans. Those that could muster the personal resources evacuated the city. With no welfare check (the hurricane struck near the end of the month), little food, and no help from the city, state, or federal officials, the poor were forced to ride out the storm in their homes or move to the shelters of last resort. This is the enduring face of Hurricane Katrina—poor, black, single mothers, young, and old—struggling just to survive; options limited by the ineffectiveness of preparedness and the inadequacy of response. * * *

As a nation, we have very little experience with evacuating cities from natural hazards * * *. Crisis relocation planning was the norm during the height of the Reagan administration, but many social scientists scoffed at the implausibility of the effort as a precautionary measure against a nuclear attack. Our collective experience with evacuations is based on chemical spills or toxic releases, planning for nuclear power plant accidents, and hurricanes. In most cases, but certainly not all, the evacuations have been in rural or suburban places, not a major U.S. city. * * * The potential differences in response are critical and highlight the difficulties in emergency preparedness for major cities. The number of large urban hospitals, the dependence on public transportation, and the need for mass sheltering all complicate preparedness efforts in these dense multi-ethnic and multi-racial cities. In addition to the sheer number of people at risk, emergency managers have the additional task of identifying those residents who may be the most vulnerable—the poor, the infirm, the elderly, the homeless, women, and children. The nescient result is an ever-widening disparity in society's ability to cope with more persistent social and economic problems in urban areas, let alone a potential mass impact event of unknown origin. This is the story of Hurricane Katrina and its aftermath. * * *

Just as there is variation in the physical landscape, the landscape of social inequity has increased the division between rich and poor in this country and has led to the increasing social vulnerability of our residents, especially to coastal hazards. Strained race relations and the seeming differential response to the disaster suggest[] that in planning for future catastrophes, we need to not only look at the natural environment in the development of mitigation programs, but the social environment as well. It is the interaction between nature and society that produces the vulnerability of places. While physical vulnerability is reduced through the construction of disaster-resistant buildings, changes in land use, and restoration of wetlands and floodways, a marked reduction in social vulnerability will require an improvement in the overall quality of life for the inner city poor. We should not have the equivalent of developing world conditions in a nation as wealthy as the United States. This is the tragedy of Hurricane Katrina. * * *

Disasters will happen. To lessen their impacts in the future, we need to reduce our social vulnerability and increase disaster resilience with improvements in the social conditions and living standards in our cities. We need to build (and rebuild) damaged housing and infrastructure in harmony with nature and design cities to be resilient to environmental threats even if it means smaller, more livable places, and fewer profits for land and urban developers and a smaller tax base for the city. Disasters are income neutral and color-blind. Their impacts, however, are not.

NOTES AND QUESTIONS

1. Reconsider this statement by Susan Cutter: "Social vulnerability is partially a product of social inequalities—those social [JC5]factors and forces that create the susceptibility of various groups to harm, and in turn affect their ability to respond, and bounce back (resilience) after the disaster."

This pivotal passage suggests that social vulnerability consists of two distinct components: the *susceptibility* of certain groups to harm and the *resilience* of these groups. *See generally* Susan L. Cutter, Bryan. J. Boruff & W. Lynn Shirley, *Social Vulnerability to Environmental Hazards*, 84 SOC. SCI. Q. 242 (2003).

a. *Susceptibility* is an *ex ante* quality; it is already in place when disaster strikes. Inequality in New Orleans and other parts of the South has taken hundreds of years to build. Differences in living conditions, wealth, and power rendered the poorest, often black victims of Katrina susceptible to disproportionate loss.

b. *Resilience*, by contrast, assumes importance after the fact. Rebuilding destroyed communities demands extraordinary human and material resources. Capital available—and often taken for granted—for recovery in more affluent communities may simply not exist in poorer communities. Crucial physical and social infrastructure, often strained or undermined by disaster and its aftermath, is not as readily reestablished.

2. Consider also this definition of vulnerability:

> By vulnerability we mean the characteristics of a person or group in terms of their capacity to anticipate, cope with, resist, and recover from the impact of a natural hazard. It involves a combination of factors that determine the degree to which someone's life and livelihood is put at risk by a discrete and identifiable event in nature or in society.

PIERS BLAIKIE, TERRY CANNON, IAN DAVIS & BEN WISNER, AT RISK: NATURAL HAZARDS, PEOPLE'S VULNERABILITY AND DISASTERS 9 (1994).

3. Could the victims of Hurricane Katrina seek legal relief from the officials who supervised an emergency preparedness and response effort that appears not only to have been wholly inadequate, but also arguably to have exposed blacks to greater harm than similarly situated whites? Aside from the question of whether government had a duty to act, *cf.* DeShaney v. Winnebago County Dept. of Soc. Servs., 489 U.S. 189 (1989), formidable barriers block the path to relief. A direct claim that violated the hurricane victims' civil rights seems remote at best.

a. Constitutional law does not recognize an equal protection claim based solely on the claim that otherwise neutral conduct has a racially disparate impact. *See* Washington v. Davis, 426 U.S. 229, 242 (1976). An equal protection violation typically hinges on "[p]roof of racially discriminatory intent or purpose." Village of Arlington Heights v. Metropolitan Housing Dev. Corp., 429 U.S. 252, 265 (1977); *accord, e.g.*, City of Cuyahoga Falls v. Buckeye Community Hope Found., 538 U.S. 188, 194 (2003). The government must have chosen a particular course "because of" and not merely "in spite of" the decision's adverse impact on "an identifiable group." Personnel Adm'r v. Feeney, 442 U.S. 256, 279 (1979); *accord* McCleskey v. Kemp, 481 U.S. 279, 298 (1987).

b. On the other hand, when even neutral legislation or governmental conduct produces a clear pattern that cannot be explained except on racial grounds, a constitutional violation may lie. *See* Gomillion v. Lightfoot, 364 U.S. 339 (1960); Yick Wo v. Hopkins, 118 U.S. 356 (1886); *cf.* Lane v. Wilson, 307 U.S. 268 (1939); Guinn v. United States, 238 U.S. 347 (1915). The appearance of "a clear pattern, unexplainable on grounds other than race," makes the "evidentiary inquiry . . . relatively easy." *Arlington Heights*, 429 U.S. at 266. Because cases presenting "a pattern [this] stark" are "rare," however, "impact alone is [seldom] determinative, and [a reviewing] Court must look to other evidence." *Id.*

c. In most cases, evidence of "invidious discriminatory purpose" demands a deeper inquiry into the "historical background" underlying official conduct. *Arlington Heights*, 429 U.S. at 267. "The specific sequence of events leading up the challenged decision also may shed some light on the decisionmaker's purposes." *Id.* Departures from "the normal procedural sequence" or from substantive decisionmaking criteria "also might afford evidence that improper purposes are playing a role." *Id.* Finally, "[t]he legislative or administrative history may be highly relevant, especially where there are contemporary statements by members of the decisionmaking body, minutes of its meetings, or reports." *Id.* at 268. What evidence can be found in the record of official conduct during the preparation for a hypothetical hurricane hitting New Orleans, during Katrina itself, and throughout recovery after the storm?

d. The use of legislative or administrative history gives rise to another basis for relief, albeit one rarely encountered. The Supreme Court has invalidated an otherwise facially neutral law that disenfranchised all persons convicted of crimes of moral turpitude, citing statements showing that the law's proponents intended to prevent blacks from voting. *See* Hunter v. Underwood, 421 U.S. 222 (1985). *But cf.* Palmer v. Thompson, 403 U.S. 217, 224 (1971) ("[N]o case in this Court has held that a legislative act may violate equal protection solely because of the motivations of the men who voted for it.").

e. "In many instances, to recognize the limited probative value of disproportionate impact is merely to acknowledge the 'heterogeneity' of the Nation's population." *Arlington Heights*, 429 U.S. at 266 n.15 (quoting Jefferson v. Hackney, 406 U.S. 535, 548 (1972)).

f. Notwithstanding *Washington v. Davis* and *Arlington Heights*, the Supreme Court is more willing in certain contexts to infer discriminatory purpose from disparate impact. *See, e.g.*, Shaw v. Reno, 509 U.S. 630 (1993) (gerrymandering); Batson v. Kentucky, 476 U.S. 79 (1986) (peremptory jury challenges); Rogers v. Lodge, 458 U.S. 613 (1982) (vote dilution); Swann v. Charlotte-Mecklenburg Bd. of Educ., 402 U.S. 1 (1971) (school desegregation). Does anything about natural disasters, the nature of social vulnerability during disaster, or the role of government warrant a comparable judicial willingness to infer purpose from effect? Or, as in the context of selective prosecution, must a claim alleging a racially uneven response to a disaster "draw on 'ordinary equal protection standards'"? United States v. Armstrong, 517 U.S. 456, 465 (1996).

4. The Eighth Amendment supplies another constitutional analogy by which policy *vis-à-vis* vulnerable populations during a disaster may be judged. A prison official's "deliberate indifference" to a substantial risk of serious harm to an inmate violates the prohibition on "cruel and unusual punishments." *See, e.g.*, Helling v. McKinney, 509 U.S. 25 (1993); Wilson v. Seiter, 501 U.S. 294 (1991); Estelle v. Gamble, 429 U.S. 97 (1976).

   a. "Deliberate indifference" demands that an official have a state of mind more blameworthy than negligence. In considering a claim that inadequate medical care violated the Eighth Amendment, the Supreme Court has distinguished "deliberate indifference to serious medical needs of prisoners," *Estelle*, 429 U.S. at 104, from mere "negligen[ce] in diagnosing or treating a medical condition," *id.* at 106. Transcending the "ordinary lack of due care for the prisoner's interests or safety," Whitley v. Albers, 475 U.S. 312, 319 (1986), deliberate indifference ultimately requires subjective intent:

   > [A] prison official cannot be found liable under the Eighth Amendment for denying an inmate humane conditions of confinement unless the official knows of and disregards an excessive risk to inmate health or safety; the official must both be aware of facts from which the inference could be drawn that a substantial risk of serious harm exists, and he must also draw the inference.

   Farmer v. Brennan, 511 U.S. 825, 837 (1994).

   b. Perhaps the officials in charge of preparing for and responding to Katrina can be accused of *passive* rather than deliberate indifference:

   > [R]acial exclusion * * * today happens not so much through active bigotry as it does through the tacit exclusions created by these sorts of unstated, unconsidered social habits. * * * [I]f your social network is, for purely historical reasons, defined by color lines that were drawn long ago in a different and undeniably widely bigoted age, then you don't have to be a bigot yourself to be perpetuating the institutional structures of racial exclusion * * * * This was exactly Illinois Senator Barack Obama's point when he declared on the Senate floor that the poor response to Katrina was not "evidence of active malice," but merely the result of "a continuation of passive indifference." These structural exclusions matter very much for one's total life opportunities, including crucially one's economic opportunities—and thus greatly affect one's opportunities to, say, escape from deadly hurricanes.

   Nils Gilman, *What Katrina Teaches about the Meaning of Racism*, http://understandingkatrina.ssrc.org/Gilman (Sept. 14, 2005). Is "passive indifference" less blameworthy than its deliberate counterpart?

5. For yet another legal perspective on vulnerability, consider U.S. SENTENCING GUIDELINES § 3A1.1, which instructs judges to enhance the sentence of a federal criminal defendant who "intentionally selected

any victim or any property as the object of the offense of conviction because of the actual or perceived race, color, religion, national origin, ethnicity, gender, disability, or sexual orientation of any person" or who "knew or should have known that a victim of the offense was a vulnerable victim."

a. The Guidelines are structured so that the presence of "race, color, religion, national origin, ethnicity, gender, disability, or sexual orientation" automatically qualifies a defendant for an enhanced sentence, independent of any inquiry into the victim's vulnerability.

b. With respect to the sentencing enhancement for a "vulnerable victim," the following three-prong test applies:

> The enhancement may be applied where: (1) the victim was particularly susceptible or vulnerable to the criminal conduct; (2) the defendant knew or should have known of this susceptibility or vulnerability; and (3) this vulnerability or susceptibility facilitated the defendant's crime in some manner; that is, there was "a nexus between the victim's vulnerability and the crime's ultimate success."

United States v. Iannone, 184 F.3d 214, 220 (3d Cir. 1999); *accord, e.g.,* United States v. Zats, 298 F.3d 182, 186 (3d Cir. 2002). At least the first two prongs of this test can be applied by analogy to officials accused of failing to address social vulnerabilities during a natural disaster. Certain victims are "particularly susceptible or vulnerable" in times of disaster, and public officials "kn[o]w or should have known of this susceptibility or vulnerability." Because the Sentencing Guidelines are an artifact of criminal law, the analogy degrades somewhat with respect to the third prong, but some connection remains. The presence of a "nexus between the victim's vulnerability" and the social harm attributable to a natural disaster arguably should bear on the degree of official responsibility for shortcomings in remedying social vulnerabilities through preparation, response, mitigation, or recovery.

6. In assessing the moral (if not legal) culpability that should be assigned for the socially lopsided effects of Katrina, consider the following account:

> It is society's most vulnerable who were "left behind" by government efforts to assess, to plan for, and to respond to a storm of Katrina's magnitude. And this was predictably so. A host of government decisions were made—each of which had the potential to mitigate or exacerbate the effects of a hurricane for the people of New Orleans—against a social, economic, and political backdrop that made the disproportionate impacts of certain government choices virtually inevitable. Where the choice was to forego the basic services and protections typically provided by a government, it should have been clear to decision makers precisely who would be left to fend for themselves.

Twenty-eight percent of people in New Orleans live in poverty. Of these, 84 percent are African-American. Twenty-three percent of people five years and older living in New Orleans are disabled. An estimated 15,000 to 17,000 men, women, and children in the New Orleans area are homeless. The lowest lying areas of New Orleans tend to be populated by those without economic or political resources. The city's Lower Ninth Ward, for example, which was especially hard hit and completely inundated by water, is among its poorest and lowest lying areas. Ninety-eight percent of its residents are African-American. * * * "[I]n New Orleans, water flows away from money. Those with resources who control where the drainage goes have always chosen to live on the high ground. So the people in the low areas were the hardest hit."

Of the households living in poverty, many have no access to a car: 21,787 of these households without a car are black; 2,606 are white. This lack of access became crucial, given an evacuation plan premised on the ability of people to get in their cars and drive out of New Orleans.

CENTER FOR PROGRESSIVE REFORM, AN UNNATURAL DISASTER: THE AFTERMATH OF HURRICANE KATRINA 34-35 (2005).

7. The Congressional Research Service has quantified the unequal social impact of Hurricane Katrina:

Hurricane Katrina disproportionately impacted communities where the poor and minorities, mostly African-Americans, resided. The three states where communities were damaged or flooded by the hurricane rank among the poorest in the nation. According to the 2000 Census, Mississippi ranked second only to the District of Columbia in its poverty rate; Louisiana was right behind it ranking third, and Alabama ranked sixth. CRS estimates that about one-fifth of the population most directly impacted by the storm was poor. That poverty rate (21%) was well above the national poverty rate of 12.4% recorded in the 2000 Census. * * * In addition, over 30% of the most impacted population had incomes below one-and-one-half times the poverty line and over 40% had income below twice the poverty line * * * .

The hurricane's impact on New Orleans also took a disproportionate toll on African Americans. An estimated 310,000 black people were directly impacted by the storm, largely due to flooding in Orleans Parish. Blacks are estimated to have accounted for 44% of storm victims. In Orleans Parish, an estimated 272,000 black people were displaced by flooding or damage, accounting for 73% of the population affected by the storm in the parish. In contrast, an estimated 101,000 non-black people in Orleans Parish were displaced by flooding or damage, accounting for about 63% of the non-black population living in the parish; still a high proportion affected, but somewhat less than that experienced by blacks.

Among blacks living in Orleans Parish who were most likely displaced by the storm, over one-third (89,000 people, or 34.0% of displaced blacks) were estimated to have been poor, based on 2000 Census data. Among non-black (predominantly white) persons living in the parish who were likely displaced by the storm, an estimated 14.6% (14,000) were poor.

Thomas Gabe, Gene Falk & Maggie McCarty, *Hurricane Katrina: Social-Demographic Characteristics of Impacted Areas* 14, 16-17 (Nov. 4, 2005) (CRS Order Code RL33141).

8. Katrina's disparate impact on poor and nonwhite individuals has been characterized as part of a larger pattern of "environmental injustice":

Katrina * * * was an exceptionally large echo of a socioeconomic political condition known popularly as environmental injustice, the longstanding pattern whereby people of color and the poor are exposed to greater environmental risk while receiving fewer environmental amenities. Between the two, race has a statistically stronger link than class, and recent reports reveal that the association between race and environmental hazards is increasing. If we examine the background policies and decisions that ultimately led to the devastation in the wake of Katrina, we begin to see the event as part of this larger pattern.

For example, planners anticipated that approximately 100,000 transit-dependent residents of New Orleans, mostly poor and black, would have no private transportation out of the city in an emergency. The federal, state and local governments made no provision for them. Instead, evacuation plans relied on private automobiles. Environmental justice activists, citing Hurricane Hugo in 1989 and the 2005 release of chlorine gas from a train crash in South Carolina, note that this is not the first time people of color have been overlooked by emergency planners and then received slower assistance afterwards.

Eileen Gauna, *Katrina and Environmental Injustice*, http://jurist.law .pitt.edu/forumy/2005/10/katrina-and-environmental-injustice.php (Oct. 10, 2005). Other critics have argued that Katrina's indignities are "part of a pattern of environmental disasters in which low-income communities and communities of color are overlooked in the preparations before such disasters occur and receive less rapid assistance afterwards." CENTER FOR PROGRESSIVE REFORM, AN UNNATURAL DISASTER: THE AFTERMATH OF HURRICANE KATRINA 35-36 (2005). *See generally* ROBERT D. BULLARD, DUMPING IN DIXIE: RACE, CLASS AND ENVIRONMENTAL QUALITY (3d ed. 2000); LUKE W. COLE & SHEILA FOSTER, ENVIRONMENTAL RACISM AND THE RISE OF THE ENVIRONMENTAL JUSTICE MOVEMENT (2000).

9. In addition to environmental injustice, racial bias manifested itself in the New Orleans housing market before and after Katrina:

> [M]any residents lacked the insurance and assets needed to recover from the storm. New Orleans had a relatively low home-ownership rate—just 47 percent compared to 67 percent nationally. * * * And much of the housing stock was old (though not necessarily in bad condition), with 45 percent of the units constructed before 1950, more than twice the national figure (21 percent). Without mortgages, many low-income longtime home-owners opted out of costly homeowners insurance or flood insurance. Moreover, FEMA had designated many of these areas to be at "low" flood risk, so lenders did not require flood insurance.
>
> Like most cities across the country, New Orleans already had an affordable housing crisis before Katrina. According to the 2000 Census, two-thirds (67 percent) of extremely low income households in New Orleans bore excessive housing cost burdens (by federal standards, housing costs that exceed 30 percent of income), a figure slightly higher than average for Louisiana and slightly lower than that for the nation as a whole. More than half (56 percent) of very low income households in New Orleans were paying more than half their income for housing, also comparable to national figures. Both owners and renters were equally disadvantaged, with majorities of both groups facing excessive housing cost burdens.
>
> Only a small proportion of needy households received federal housing assistance—a public housing apartment, other federally subsidized housing, or Housing Choice Voucher (Section 8). Those that did receive assistance had lower housing costs, but many had to cope with living in some of the nation's worst public housing. * * *
>
> Historically, the city's public housing projects were sited in low-income neighborhoods, isolating low-income residents from the rest of the city and exacerbating both racial segregation and the concentration of black poverty. Decades of neglect and mismanagement had left these developments in severe distress. Residents of projects like Desire, Florida, and Iberville endured intolerable physical conditions, high levels of violent crime, rampant drug trafficking, and myriad other social ills. These distressed public housing communities blighted the surrounding neighborhoods and exacerbated the overall racial and economic segregation in the city.

Susan J. Popkin, Margery A. Turner & Martha Burt, *Rebuilding Affordable Housing in New Orleans: The Challenge of Creating Inclusive Communities* 2-3 (Jan. 2006) (available at http://www.urban.org/UploadedPDF/900914_affordable_housing.pdf).

10. Of the more than $20 billion in direct property damage caused by Katrina, nearly four-fifths ($16 billion) involved residential property. *See* 1 ARMY CORPS OF ENGINEERS, FINAL REPORT OF THE INTERAGENCY PERFORMANCE EVALUATION TASKFORCE (IPET) 8 (June 1, 2006). In Katrina's immediate aftermath, FEMA placed an estimated 125,000 evacuees in hotels; "an untold number" of additional evacuees "stay[ed] with friends and family or liv[ed] in cars, tents, or damaged homes." National Fair Housing Alliance, *No Home for the Holidays: Report on Housing Discrimination Against Hurricane Katrina Survivors* 4-5 (Dec. 20, 2005) (available at http://newreconstruction.civilrights.org/ NFHAKatrinaDiscriminationReport.pdf).

11. "The longer-term challenge" is to rebuild New Orleans "without recreating intense concentrations of minority poverty and distress":

> Instead of isolating needy families in pockets of extreme poverty, affordable housing should be provided throughout the metropolitan area so low-income households choosing to return to New Orleans have safe and secure places to live, along with access to the good jobs and schools needed to get ahead. And for those who do not return, affordable housing policies should help ensure that people left homeless by Katrina enjoy the same opportunities in their new communities, do not wind up concentrated in the poorest neighborhoods, and receive the supports they need so they do not end up even worse off than they were in New Orleans.
>
> To expand the stock of moderately priced rental and for-sale housing, while allowing returning residents flexibility and choice about where to live, we recommend a strategy that addresses both the supply side and the demand side of the housing market. More specifically, regulatory incentives and capital subsidies should be used to encourage and support the construction of affordable housing units throughout the metropolitan region (by both for-profit and nonprofit developers). At the same time, low-income households returning to the area should receive vouchers to supplement what they can afford to pay to rent or buy modest housing in neighborhoods of their choice. * * *
>
> Whatever decisions are ultimately made about how to move forward, reconstruction should be based on what is known about how to incorporate high-quality, affordable housing into healthy mixed-income communities that offer real opportunities for low-income families. * * * [T]he city may not be able to recover economically unless its low-wage workforce returns—both the reconstruction effort itself and the city's tourism industry depend on them. And much of what creates the unique and vibrant New Orleans culture grows directly out of its lower-income and minority communities with their many deeply rooted families.

Popkin et al., *supra*, at 8-9. *See generally* Myron Orfield, *Land Use and Housing Policies to Reduce Concentrated Poverty and Racial Segregation*, 33 FORDHAM URB. L.J. (forthcoming 2006).

12. One proactive way to assimilate lessons from Katrina and other disasters is to think of ways that the government and other parties involved in preparing for, responding to, and recovering from disasters can develop greater cultural competence in order to minimize the effects of social vulnerability. The "cultural competence continuum" developed in TERRY L. CROSS ET AL., TOWARDS A CULTURALLY COMPETENT SYSTEM OF CARE, VOLUME I: A MONOGRAPH OF EFFECTIVE SERVICES FOR MINORITY CHILDREN WHO ARE SEVERELY EMOTIONALLY DISTURBED (1989) describes a spectrum ranging from least to greatest cultural competence: (1) destructiveness, (2) incapacity, (3) blindness, (4) precompetence, (5) competence, and finally (7) proficiency.

The following excerpt, though aimed at the narrower question of mental health services, illustrates how greater cultural competence can improve disaster assistance of all kinds:

U.S. DEPARTMENT OF HEALTH AND HUMAN SERVICES, DEVELOPING CULTURAL COMPETENCE IN DISASTER MENTAL HEALTH PROGRAMS: GUIDING PRINCIPLES AND RECOMMENDATIONS 14-17 (2003)

(DHHS Pub. No. SMA 3828)

Culture as a source of knowledge, information, and support provides continuity and a process for healing during times of tragedy. Survivors react to and recover from disaster within the context of their individual racial and ethnic backgrounds, cultural viewpoints, life experiences, and values. Culture offers a protective system that is comfortable and reassuring. It defines appropriate behavior and furnishes social support, identity, and a shared vision for recovery. For example, stories, rituals, and legends that are part of a culture's fabric help people adjust to catastrophic losses by highlighting the mastery of communal trauma and explaining the relationship of individuals to the spiritual. Despite the strengths that culture can provide, responses to disaster also fall on a continuum. Persons from disadvantaged racial and ethnic communities may be more vulnerable to problems associated with preparing for and recovering from disaster than persons of higher socioeconomic status.

Because of the strong role that culture plays in disaster response, disaster mental health services are most effective when survivors receive assistance that is in accord with their cultural beliefs and consistent with their needs. As disaster mental health service providers seek to become more culturally competent, they must recognize three important social and historical influences that can affect the success of their efforts.

These three influences are the importance of community, racism and discrimination, and social and economic inequality.

The Importance of Community

Disasters affect both individuals and communities. Following a disaster, there may be individual trauma, characterized as "a blow to the psyche that breaks through one's defenses so suddenly and with such brutal force that one cannot react to it effectively." There also may be collective trauma—"a blow to the basic tissues of social life that damages the bonds attaching people together and impairs the prevailing sense of community." Cultural and socioeconomic factors contribute to both individual and community responses to the trauma caused by disaster.

The culture of the community provides the lens through which its members view and interpret the disaster * * * * [A] disrupted and fragmented [community] will be able to provide less support than a cohesive community.

A classic example is * * * the devastating 1972 flood in Buffalo Creek, West Virginia. The flood led to relocation of the entire community [and] a "loss of community," in which people lost not only their sense of connection with the locale but also the support of people and institutions. Results of this community's fragmentation included fear, anger, anxiety, and depression.

Other studies have emphasized positive effects that can result from disaster experiences in communities that perform a protective role and cushion the stress of the disaster. Compared with nondisaster-related suffering, which is isolating and private, the suffering of disaster survivors can be collective and public. However, devastating disasters can have positive outcomes. They can bring a community closer or reorient its members to new priorities or values. Individuals may exhibit courage, selflessness, gratitude, and hope that they may not have shown or felt before the disaster.

Community often is extremely important for racial and ethnic minority groups, and it may dramatically affect their ability to recover from disaster. For example, a racial or ethnic minority community may provide especially strong social support functions for its members, particularly when it is surrounded by a hostile society. However, its smaller size may render it more fragile and more subject to dispersion and destruction after a disaster. Members of some racial and ethnic minority groups, such as refugees, previously have experienced destruction of their social support systems, and the destruction of a second support system may be particularly difficult.

Racism and Discrimination

Many racial and ethnic minority groups, including African Americans, American Indians, and Chinese and Japanese Americans, have experienced racism, discrimination, or persecution for many years. * * * [R]acial discrimination persists in housing rentals and sales, hiring practices, and medical care. Racism also takes the form of demeaning comments, hate crimes, and other violence by institutions or individuals, either intentionally or unintentionally.

As a result of past or present experiences with racism and discrimination, racial and ethnic minority groups may distrust offers of outside assistance at any time, even following a disaster. They may not be accustomed to receiving support and assistance from persons outside of their own group in non-disaster circumstances. Therefore, they may be unfamiliar with the social and cultural mechanisms of receiving assistance and remain outside the network of aid. * * * For example, following the 1994 California earthquake, * * * many immigrants' distrust of government posed a barrier to their use of disaster services. Likewise, some of the survivors of a hurricane in Alabama were immigrants from Asian Communist countries who did not trust any government and were not accustomed to receiving Government assistance.

Social and Economic Inequality

Poverty disproportionately affects racial and ethnic minority groups. For example, in 1999, 8 percent of whites, 11 percent of Asian Americans and Pacific Islanders, 23 percent of Hispanic Americans, 24 percent of African Americans, and 26 percent of American Indians and Alaska Natives lived in poverty. Significant socioeconomic differences also exist within racial and ethnic minority groups. For example, although some subgroups of Asian Americans have prospered, others remain at low socioeconomic levels.

Social and economic inequality also leads to reduced access to resources, including employment; financial credit; legal rights; and education, health, and mental health services. Poor neighborhoods also have high rates of homelessness, substance abuse, and crime.

Poverty makes people more susceptible than others to harm from disaster and less able to access help. Low-income individuals and families typically lose a much larger part of their material assets and suffer more lasting negative effects from disaster than do those with higher incomes. Often, disadvantaged persons live in the least desirable and most hazardous areas of a community, and their homes may be older and not as sound as those in higher income areas. * * *

[S]ome groups cannot readily access [disaster relief] services. Negative perceptions derived from pre-disaster experiences may serve as a barrier to seeking care. Lack of familiarity with sources of community support or lack of transportation are common barriers for many immigrants and unwillingness to disclose their immigration status is a major barrier.

Middle-class disaster survivors are more likely than lower-income people * * * to know how to complete forms, communicate adequately, talk to the "right" people, or otherwise maneuver within the system. Thus, they may be more likely to receive aid than survivors with fewer means or those from different cultures. On the other hand, affluent groups * * * may fear a loss of control and find it humiliating to accept emergency assistance such as clothing, food, loans, and emotional support from disaster workers.

In some instances, people of lower socioeconomic status exhibit strong coping skills in disaster situations because they have seen difficult times before and have survived. In other instances, the loss of what little one had may leave an individual feeling completely hopeless.

NOTES

1. Mental health experts have identified certain characteristics of disasters that bear heavily on the emotional distress felt by survivors and on health professionals' efforts to assist in their recovery:

    a. *Intensity of the impact.* Disasters that effect intense destruction within a brief period are likelier to cause emotional distress than slower, less destructive disasters.

    b. *Impact ratio.* When a significant proportion of a community sustains losses, there are fewer survivors available to lend material and emotional support to others.

    c. *Potential for recurrence.* The threat of recurrence, real or perceived, of the disaster or of associated hazards can increase stress in survivors.

    d. *Cultural and symbolic aspects.* Survivors may be deeply disturbed by disaster-related changes in their lives, even in their routines. Natural and human-caused disasters can have great symbolic effects.

    e. *Extent and type of loss.* Deaths of loved ones, personal injury, property damage or loss, and job loss can affect emotional recovery.
See Robert Bolin & Lois Stanford, *The Northridge Earthquake: Community-Based Approaches to Unmet Recovery Needs*, 22 DISASTERS 21 (1998); Department of Health & Human Services, *Assuring Cultural Competence in Health Care: Recommendations for National Standards and an Out-comes-Focused Research Agenda* 6 (2000).

2. How did Katrina measure on these gauges? Consider the Corps of Engineers' assessment of the storm's physical and social consequences:

> The most serious direct impact of Katrina was the high number of deaths. While large numbers of people were able to evacuate, the groups least likely to be able to do so on their own, the poor, elderly, and disabled, were hardest hit. * * * [F]looding was highly correlated to land elevation, and the areas with the lowest elevations were largely residential. This places the residential population who cannot readily evacuate at the greatest risk.

> Katrina caused direct property losses (excluding Plaquemines Parish) of over $20 billion, approximately 78 percent ($16 billion) of which was attributed to residential losses. The next largest component was the 11.5 percent ($2.4 billion) attributed to commercial losses. There was an additional $6.0 to $6.7 billion in losses attributed to public infrastructure, including the hurricane protection system itself. The most significant infrastructure im-

pact was incurred by the hurricane protection system (1.8 to 2.08 billion) followed by roadway networks and assets of the regional electrical distribution/transmission grid. Together, the damages to these categories of infrastructure totaled approximately $2.0 billion. This estimate is followed by damages to public transit assets of approximately $690 to $730 million followed by damages to rail lines, airport facilities, gas and water distribution, telecommunications assets, and assets for waterborne transportation totaling an additional $1.7 to $1.9 billion. Approximately half of the direct economic losses, excluding public and utilities infrastructure, can be associated with breaching of levees and floodwalls. The remaining losses alone, attributable to rainfall and overtopping, constitute the largest losses experienced in any disaster in the New Orleans vicinity.

Combined with the significant and far-reaching impact of Hurricane Katrina regarding initial displacement of population, workforce, and businesses, the impacts to infrastructure and affiliated public welfare and services will contribute to slowed phasing of recovery with regard to return of populace and business activities. Orleans Parish alone is estimated to have lost over 60 percent of its population and St. Bernard Parish nearly 80 percent. On the other hand, St. Charles and Tammany Parishes have increased in population since before the storm. * * *

[T]he social organization of the community and region has been compromised by the mass exodus of the population, the structural damage, and the demands to respond and rebuild. The flooding caused a breakdown in New Orleans' social structure, a loss of cultural heritage, and dramatically altered the physical, economic, political, social, and psychological character of the area. * * *

The immediate physical damage made large portions of the city uninhabitable, with thousands of residential, commercial, and public structures destroyed. Basic infrastructure facilities, such as power, water, sewer, and natural gas lines, were made inoperable and continued to be out of service for months after the event. Many victims not only lost their homes, but also their schools, health care, places of worship, places of trade, and jobs. The forced relocations disrupted family and friend networks. As a result, the event not only had an immediate impact on the well being of the population of those living and working in the metropolitan area, but also resulted in basic changes in the social organization of all aspects of that population.

1 ARMY CORPS OF ENGINEERS, FINAL REPORT OF THE INTERAGENCY PERFORMANCE EVALUATION TASKFORCE (IPET) 8-9 (June 1, 2006). "These impacts are unprecedented in their social consequence and unparalleled in the modern era of the United States." *Id.* at 9.

C. SEX, AGE, AND IMMIGRANT STATUS

Bias has many manifestations. Women, children, the elderly, and immigrants (documented and otherwise) all suffered from Hurricane Katrina in ways that other victims did not. Justice John Paul Stevens's frequent admonition, that there indeed "is only one . . . Equal Protection Clause,"[2] serves as a reminder that the aspiration to equality persists no matter what the source of injustice. This chapter therefore examines social vulnerability by sex, age, and immigration status.

1. SEX: WOMEN AND WOMEN'S CONTRIBUTIONS TO POST-DISASTER RECOVERY

Although Katrina is most often framed as a tragedy of race and class, at least one commentator argues that it should also be regarded as a tragedy of sex:

ELAINE ENARSON, WOMEN AND GIRLS LAST? AVERTING THE SECOND POST-KATRINA DISASTER

http://understandingkatrina.ssrc.org/Enarson (Nov. 15, 2005)

The fault lines of American society, as much as the failings of its infrastructure, are shamefully on display in the aftermath of Hurricane Katrina. Race, class, age and (dis)ability are now at the heart of the public debate about vulnerability, preparedness and emergency response, but this is also a story, as yet untold, about women and men.

It was low-income African American women, many single mothers among them, whose pleas for food and water were broadcast around the world from the Superdome, women more than men who were evacuated from nursing homes, and women more than men whose escape of sorts was made with infants, children and elders in tow. Now we see on nightly TV the faces of exhausted women standing in seemingly endless lines seeking help of any kind. In the long run, as we have learned from studies of past disasters, women will be at the heart of this great city's rebirth, and the emotional center of gravity for their families on the long road to the "new normal." They will stitch the commemorative quilts, organize community festivals and hurricane anniversary events, support their schools and faith-based organizations and relief agencies, and compose and sing many of the Katrina songs to come. Though not this simple, it is often said that men rebuild buildings while women reweave the social fabric of community life.

---

2. Adarand Constructors, Inc. v. Pena, 515 U.S. 200, 246 (1995) (Stevens, J., dissenting); *see also* City of Richmond v. J.A. Croson Co., 488 U.S. 469, 514 n.5 (1989) (Stevens, J., concurring in part and concurring in the judgment); Karcher v. Daggett, 462 U.S. 725, 749 (1983) (Stevens, J., concurring); Craig v. Boren, 429 U.S. 190, 211 (1976) (Stevens, J., concurring).

We are transfixed now by images of needy women and strong men (a few with female partners) wearing badges, carrying weapons and riding in armored vehicles, and will soon be treated to endless photos of hardworking men hauling garbage, replacing roofs, making speeches and decisions. Behind the scenes (taking nothing away from others), women labor, too. In the dreary months ahead, after the nation's attention wanes, the burdens on women will be exceptional and exceptionally invisible. Imagine cleaning just one flooded room, helping just one toddler or teen to sleep well again, restoring the sense of security to a widowed mother's life. The basic domestic chores of "homemaking" gain new significance and are vastly more difficult in a FEMA trailer, a friend's apartment or the basement of a church—and parents will call upon daughters more than sons for help. Nothing will change in a hurry as women pack and unpack, moving from place to place across the nation with distracted partners, bewildered children, pets and whatever possessions remain or are gathered piecemeal. The demands on the women who take them in and make them at home are incalculable, and displaced families will stay longer than anyone now imagines. Women across the nation are also the lifeblood of voluntary organizations of all descriptions, now being pulled inexorably into relief work. They will continue to do this work when the funds dry up and women (and to a lesser extent men) marginalized by race and class fall between the (gaping) cracks of the relief system. Long after we think Katrina over and done with, women whose jobs and professions in teaching, health care, mental health, crisis work, and community advocacy bring them into direct contact with affected families will feel the stress of "first responders" whose work never ends.

NOTES AND QUESTIONS

1. Disaster affects women and men differently. *Compare, e.g.*, Jane C. Ollenburger & Graham A. Tobin, *Women and Postdisaster Stress*, *in* THE GENDERED TERRAIN OF DISASTER: THROUGH WOMEN'S EYES 95 (Elaine Enarson & Betty Hearn Morrow eds., 1998) *and* Jane C. Ollenburger & Graham A. Tobin, *Women, Aging, and Post-Disaster Stress: Risk Factors*, 17 INTL. J. MASS EMERGENCIES & DISASTERS 65 (1999) *with, e.g.*, Lawrence A. Palinkas et al., *Social, Cultural, and Psychological Impacts of the Exxon Valdez Oil Spill*, 52 HUMAN ORG. 1 (1993). Nor have observers failed to account for differences in women's *vis-à-vis* men's contributions to disaster relief and recovery. *See, e.g.*, AYSE YONDER, SENGUL AKCAR & PREMA GOPALAN, WOMEN'S PARTICIPATION IN DISASTER RELIEF AND RECOVERY (2005). Enarson transcends these first-order differences. Unless women recover on terms equivalent to men after a disaster, the area's social fabric will suffer long-term secondary damage.
2. Recall how *susceptibility* and *resilience* represent distinct components of vulnerability. The disproportionate number of women trapped inside New Orleans suggests that women were more *susceptible* during the hurricane. Enarson argues that New Orleans will not be as *resilient* unless

women contribute significantly to the recovery. Women play a pivotal role in combating poverty and other social ills. "Teach a man to fish, and he eats. Teach a woman to fish, and everyone eats." Elizabeth Palmberg, *"Teach a Woman to Fish . . . and Everyone Eats." Why Women Are Key to Fighting Global Poverty*, SOJOURNERS MAG., June 2005 (quoting Ritu Sharma of the Women's Edge Coalition). *See generally* ELIZABETH M. KING & ANDREW D. MASON, ENGENDERING DEVELOPMENT—THROUGH GENDER EQUALITY IN RIGHTS, RESOURCES, AND VOICE (2001).

3. Are there other groups or individuals whose post-disaster welfare heavily affects a community's resilience? How might the law recognize "keystone" actors who are likeliest to make the greatest contribution to recovery?

2. AGE: CHILDREN AND THE ELDERLY

THOMAS GABE, GENE FALK & MAGGIE MCCARTY, HURRICANE KATRINA: SOCIAL-DEMOGRAPHIC CHARACTERISTICS OF IMPACTED AREAS 17-19 (NOV. 4, 2005)

(CRS Order Code RL33141)

The Aged. The aged may have been especially affected by Katrina. Many had close ties to their communities, having resided there for years, and for some, their entire lifetimes. Some may have found it more difficult than others to evacuate. The elderly are more likely to live alone, and less likely to own a car, or be able to drive. Some may have been more isolated, living alone, or homebound due to frailty or disability.

Home Ownership Status and Community Ties. Among households headed by persons age 65 or older who were likely displaced by the storm, 70% are estimated to have owned their own home—an ownership rate higher than any other age group. Among aged homeowners likely displaced by the storm, over 70% had lived in their homes for over 20 years, and 47% over 30 years, in the year 2000. Among likely displaced aged renters, an estimated 55% had lived in their rental units for over 20 years, and 36% over 30 years, based on 2000 Census data.

Living arrangements. An estimated 88,000 persons age 65 and older were likely displaced by Hurricane Katrina, or 12.4% of the population affected by flooding and/or storm damage. Among the aged population affected, an estimated 27,000 lived alone, in one-person households, which accounted for 41% of households with an aged member.

The hurricane likely displaced an estimated 45,000 persons age 75 and older, a population prone to frailty. Among this group, nearly 15,000 are estimated to have lived alone, in one-person households, which accounted for 45% of the households with a member age 75 or older.

Disability status. Nearly half (48%) of all persons age 65 or older living in flooded or damage-affected areas reported having a disability, and over one-quarter (26%) reported two or more types of disability. Reported disabilities included sensory disabilities (blindness, deafness, or severe hearing impairment), and other disabilities reflecting conditions lasting more than six months that limit various activities. These activity-limiting disabilities include mental disabilities (difficulty learning, remembering, or concentrating); self-care disabilities (difficulty dressing, bathing, or getting around inside the home); and, going outside disabilities (difficulty going outside the home alone to shop or visit a doctor's office). An estimated 13% of persons age 65 and older in the flood or damage-affected areas reported a self-care disability, and 19% of those age 75 and older; one-quarter of those age 65 and older reported a disability that made it difficult to go outside, unassisted, and of those age 75 and older, one-third reported such a disability.

Poverty status. Among aged persons likely displaced by the storm, an estimated 12,600, based on 2000 Census data, were poor, or about 14.7% of the aged displaced population, and nearly 23,600 (27.6%) had incomes below 150% of the poverty line.

Vehicle Availability. Among all households living in the flood or damage-affected areas, an estimated 19% had no vehicle available to the household. Among households with heads age 65 or older, over one-quarter (26%) were without a vehicle, and among those age 75 or older, one-third (33%). In order to evacuate from the storm, these households would have been dependent on other nonresident family members, friends, neighbors, or public or specially arranged transportation.

Children. About one-fourth of the people who lived in areas damaged or flooded by Hurricane Katrina were children (under age 18). Hurricane Katrina struck at the beginning of the school year, potentially displacing an estimated 183,000 children, * * * including an estimated 136,000 children who were of school age. An estimated 47,000 children under the age of 5 lived in neighborhoods that experienced flooding or damage from the hurricane.

Child Poverty Rates in Areas Acutely Affected by Hurricane Katrina. The characteristics of the children in the damaged and flooded areas reflect greater disadvantage compared with the characteristics of children in the nation as a whole. Many of the children in affected areas were poor. [Among 180,102 children in areas flooded or damaged by Hurricane Katrina, 54,646, or 30.3 percent, were poor. Among children aged 0-4, 32.8 percent, or 15,079 out of 46,025, were poor.] * * * The poverty rate of 30% for children in hurricane-flooded or damaged areas is almost twice the 2000 Census child poverty rate for the nation as a whole of 16.6%. * * *

[A]bout 15,000 children of preschool age (age 0-4), or about one-third of all children in that age group, were poor. Another 40,000 school age children who lived in flooded or hurricane-damaged areas were poor. Over half (55%) of the children most likely to have been displaced by the hurricane were African-American * * * . Approximately 45% of the displaced black children were estimated to have been poor (about 45,000 children), accounting for 25% of all children displaced by the storm, and 82% of all poor displaced children.

Living Arrangements of Children in Hurricane-Affected Areas. Children in the areas damaged and flooded by Hurricane Katrina were more likely than children nationwide to live in female-headed families. * * * Overall, 38% of children under the age of 18 in the hurricane-affected areas lived with a female head; nationally, this percentage is 20%. Children in female-headed families are more likely to be poor than children living in married couple or other families. * * * [N]ationwide, 41% of children in female-headed families were in poverty versus an overall poverty rate of 16%. Further, a single mother often needs child care to enter the workforce or remain working. In the Hurricane Katrina-damaged and flooded areas, there were 12,000 preschool children living in families headed by a single mother. The high rate of children living with single mothers also is consistent with the hurricane having disproportionately affected African-Americans, as African-American children are more likely than children of other racial and ethnic groups to be raised by a single mother.

NOTES AND QUESTIONS

1. Age classifications warrant no special scrutiny as a matter of equal protection jurisprudence. *See* Massachusetts Bd. of Retirement v. Murgia, 427 U.S. 307 (1976). Limits on constitutional relief do not necessarily govern other sources of law. Should problems of age—whether applied to the elderly or to children—warrant special attention during disasters? In what ways are the aged and the young especially *susceptible*? To what extent are these groups less *resilient* than others during recovery? You may find it helpful to distinguish between the general difficulties posed by poverty (which disproportionately affect children and the elderly) and unique problems associated with youth or old age.

2. In political, social, and physical terms, children face drastically different challenges in times of disaster than do the elderly. Even if the very young and the very old posed challenges of precisely the same difficulty, however, the law could be more responsive to one class at the apparent expense of the other. Because children cannot vote, whereas the elderly represent a politically potent constituency, children rarely secure as much legal protection as do their elders. How seriously does American society take its nominal commitment to "the upbringing and education of children"? Pierce v. Society of Sisters, 268 U.S. 510, 534-535 (1925).

3. Certain types of bias, though expressed along some vector besides age, reap their heaviest toll from the very young and the very old. Discrimination in health care is one example. Another is housing. What both types of bias have in common is their disparate impact on the physically vulnerable, a condition that corresponds (roughly) with youth and senescence. Laws against health care and housing discrimination target the use of race as an illicit factor in allocating these scarce, potentially life-saving resources. The primary beneficiaries, however, tend to be the youngest and oldest members of the protected groups.

3. ALIENAGE AND IMMIGRATION

Immediately after Hurricane Katrina, the Department of Homeland Security announced that it would "refrain from initiating employer sanction enforcement actions for the next 45 days for civil violations, under Section 274A of the Immigration and Nationality Act [8 U.S.C. § 1324a], with regard to individuals who are currently unable to provide identity and eligibility documents as a result of the hurricane." Department of Homeland Security, *Notice Regarding I-9 Documentation Requirements for Hiring Hurricane Victims* (Sept. 6, 2005). The decision to suspend enforcement of the immigration laws triggered an uptick in Latino immigration:

> In the weeks following the storm, the construction industry quickly became a magnet for Latino immigrants who were lured by the promise of paychecks and an emergency federal decree temporarily suspending immigration-enforcement sanctions. * * *
> The media picked up on the trend in early October 2005 and described how employers were seeking Latino immigrants to help rebuild the affected areas. Together with a cartoon in the *Los Angeles Times* that depicts an African American walking out of New Orleans holding two suitcases and a Mexican laborer walking in holding tools to repair a broken levee, articles with titles such as "Illegal Workers Eying the Gulf Coast," "Big Easy Uneasy about Migrant Wave," "La Nueva Orleans" and "A New Spice in the Gumbo" all signal the role that immigrants, many of them Latino laborers, will play in the efforts to rebuild.
> Yet Latinos responding to labor-market demand have not been all that welcome. New Orleans Mayor Ray Nagin famously asked at a forum with business leaders, "How do I make sure New Orleans is not overrun with Mexican workers?" Although he quickly distanced himself from the remark—which provoked a joint statement about unity by civil rights and Latino organizations—many in the region believe contractors favor cheap, foreign labor over local, native workers.

Katharine Donato & Shirin Hakimzadeh, *The Changing Face of the Gulf Coast: Immigration to Louisiana, Mississippi, and Alabama,* http://www.migrationinformation.org/Feature/display.cfm?id=368 (Jan. 1, 2006).

Conflict with Latino newcomers illustrates merely one of the many legal issues surrounding immigrants, immigration, and Hurricane Katrina:

Ruth Ellen Wasem, Katrina-Related Immigration Issues and Legislation

(Sept. 19, 2005) (CRS Order Code RL33091)

Caught in the web of [Katrina's] tragedy and its sweeping dilemmas are a unique subset of immigration-related issues. The loss of livelihood, habitat, and life itself has very specific implications for foreign nationals who lived in the Gulf Coast region. * * *

This report focuses on four immigration policy implications of Hurricane Katrina. It opens with a discussion of employment verification and other documentary problems arising for those who have lost their personal identification documents. It follows with an overview of the rules for noncitizen eligibility for federal benefits. Issues pertaining to how the loss of life or livelihood affects eligibility for immigration visa benefits are discussed next. The report closes with * * * background on relief from removal options for Katrina-affected aliens. * * *

Personal Identification and Employment Eligibility.   Many of the victims of Hurricane Katrina lack personal identification documents as a result of being evacuated from their homes, loss or damage to personal items and records, and ongoing displacement in shelters and temporary housing. As a result of the widespread damage and destruction to government facilities in the area affected by the hurricane, moreover, many victims will be unable to have personal documents re-issued in the near future. Lack of adequate personal identification documentation * * * has specific consequences under immigration law, especially when it comes to employment.

The Immigration and Nationality Act (INA) requires employers to verify employment eligibility and establish identity through specified documents presented by the employee—citizens and foreign nationals alike. Specifically, § 274(a)(1)(B) of the INA makes it illegal for an employer to hire any person —citizen or alien—without first verifying the person's authorization to work in the United States. * * *

Noncitizen Eligibility for Federal Assistance.   Lack of sufficient documentation to confirm eligibility for federal programs and assistance is a core issue for all victims, not merely those who are noncitizens. The eligibility of noncitizens for public assistance programs, moreover, is based on a complex set of rules that are determined largely by the type of noncitizen in question and the nature of services being offered. The Personal Responsibility and Work Opportunity Reconciliation Act of 1996 [Pub. L. No. 104-193] is the key statute that spells out the eligibility rules for noncitizens seeking federal assistance. * * *

Legal Permanent Residents.   Under current law, noncitizens' eligibility for the major federal means-tested benefit programs largely depends on their immigration status and whether they arrived in the United States (or were on a program's rolls) before August 22, 1996, the enactment date of the Personal Responsibility and Work Opportunity Reconciliation Act of 1996. * * * Several bills that would waive the categorical [eligibility] requirements for various federal programs in the case of Hurricane Katrina victims have been introduced, but most are silent on the issue of noncitizens. On September 13, however, legislation to provide the Secretary of Agriculture with additional authority and funding to provide emergency relief to victims of Hurricane Katrina (S. 1695) was introduced, and, among other provisions, this bill would treat legal immigrants in the United States who are victims of Hurricane Katrina as refugees for the purposes of food stamps.

Unauthorized Aliens. The PRWOR of 1996 * * * also denies most federal benefits, regardless of whether they are means tested, to unauthorized aliens * * * . The class of benefits denied is broad and covers: (1) grants, contracts, loans, and licenses; and (2) retirement, welfare, health, disability, housing, food, unemployment, postsecondary education, and similar benefits. So defined, this bar covers many programs whose enabling statutes do not individually make citizenship or immigration status a criterion for participation. Thus, programs that previously were not individually restricted—the earned income tax credit, social services block grants, and migrant health centers, for example—became unavailable to unauthorized aliens, unless they fall within the act's limited exceptions. These programmatic exceptions include: treatment under Medicaid for emergency medical conditions (other than those related to an organ transplant); short-term, in-kind emergency disaster relief; immunizations against immunizable diseases and testing for and treatment of symptoms of communicable diseases; [certain] services or assistance (such as soup kitchens, crisis counseling and intervention, and short-term shelters) * * * *

P.L. 104-193 also permits unauthorized aliens to receive Old Age, Survivors, and Disability Insurance benefits under Title II of the Social Security Act (SSA), if the benefits are protected by that title or by treaty or are paid under applications made before August 22, 1996. Separately, the P.L. 104-193 states that individuals who are eligible for free public education benefits under state and local law shall remain eligible to receive school lunch and school breakfast benefits. (The act itself does not address a state's obligation to grant all aliens equal access to education under the Supreme Court's decision in Plyler v. Doe, 457 U.S. 202 (1982).) P.L. 104-193 expressly bars unauthorized aliens from most state and locally funded benefits. The restrictions on these benefits parallel the restrictions on federal benefits.

Disaster Assistance. * * * [N]oncitizens—regardless of their immigration status—are not barred from short-term, in-kind emergency disaster relief and services or assistance that deliver in-kind services at the community level, provide assistance without individual determinations of each recipient's needs, and are necessary for the protection of life and safety. Moreover, the [Stafford Act] * * * requires nondiscrimination and equitable treatment in disaster assistance:

> The President shall issue, and may alter and amend, such regulations as may be necessary for the guidance of personnel carrying out Federal assistance functions at the site of a major disaster or emergency. Such regulations shall include provisions for insuring that the distribution of supplies, the processing of applications, and other relief and assistance activities shall be accomplished in an equitable and impartial manner, without discrimination on the grounds of race, color, religion, nationality, sex, age, or economic status.

FEMA assistance provided under the Stafford Act includes (but is not limited to) grants for immediate temporary shelter, cash grants for uninsured emergency personal needs, temporary housing assistance, home repair grants, unemployment assistance due to the disaster, emergency food supplies, legal aid for low-income individuals, and crisis counseling. * * *

Relief from Removal. At various times in the past, the Attorney General has provided, under certain conditions, discretionary relief from deportation so that aliens who have not been legally admitted to the United States or whose temporary visa has expired nonetheless may remain in this country temporarily. * * * The Attorney General has provided blanket relief by means of the suspension of enforcement of the immigration laws against a particular group of individuals. In addition to Temporary Protected Status (TPS) which may be provided by the Secretary of DHS, the two most common discretionary procedures to provide relief from deportation have been deferred departure or deferred enforced departure (DED) and extended voluntary departure (EVD). Unlike TPS, aliens who benefit from EVD or DED do not necessarily register for the status with [U.S. Citizenship and Immigration Services], but they trigger the protection when they are identified for deportation. * * *

NOTE

Migrants rarely come from the poorest sectors of society. The truly abject have too few resources to move. Migrants typically have at least modest resources and social networks at their disposal. *See* Elizabeth Fussell, *Leaving New Orleans: Social Stratification, Networks, and Hurricane Evacuation*, http://understandingkatrina.ssrc.org/ Fussell (Sept. 26, 2005); Douglas S. Massey & Kristin Espinosa, *What's Driving Mexico-US Migration?: A Theoretical, Empirical and Policy Analysis*, 102 AM. J. SOCIOLOGY 939 (1997); J. Edward Taylor, *Differential Migration, Networks, Information and Risk*, in MIGRATION THEORY, HUMAN CAPITAL AND DEVELOPMENT 147 (Oded Stark, ed., 1986).

D.   PRICE GOUGING AFTER NATURAL DISASTERS

Natural disasters routinely create shortages. High prices are the predictable response of markets to shortages. Although price gouging affects all survivors of a disaster, policymakers often worry that it falls most heavily upon the most vulnerable survivors. In the immediate aftermath of a disaster, legislatures often restrict the ability of vendors to charge what the market will bear for food, water, medicine, and other essential supplies. This section reviews those laws, their constitutionality, and their efficacy.

ANGIE A. WELBORN & AARON M. FLYNN, PRICE INCREASES IN THE AFTERMATH OF HURRICANE KATRINA: AUTHORITY TO LIMIT PRICE GOUGING 1-4 (SEPT. 2, 2005)

(CRS Order Code RS22236)

There are no federal laws that specifically address price gouging. Price gouging laws exist at the state level and are generally applicable in situations arising from a declared emergency. An increase in prices alone does not necessarily constitute price gouging, and technically, price gouging only occurs when the trigger event has been met in a particular state. If there exists evidence of collusive activity among retailers, suppliers, or manufacturers, federal antitrust laws could be applicable. The Federal Trade Commission monitors gas prices and investigates possible antitrust violations in the petroleum industry. * * *

While there is no federal price gouging law, many states have enacted some type of prohibition or limitation on price increases during declared emergencies. All of the affected states—Louisiana, Mississippi, Alabama, and Florida—have price gouging laws that are triggered by the declaration of an emergency in the state. Generally, the laws prohibit the sale of goods and services in the designated emergency area at prices that exceed the prices ordinarily charged for comparable goods or services in the same market area at or immediately before the declaration of an emergency. However, there exists a general exemption for increased prices that are the result of additional costs incurred for procuring the goods or services in question, or "national or international market trends."

The Florida statute [FLA. STAT. § 501.160] is the most detailed of the four. It establishes a prima facie case of unconscionable pricing, if:

> 1) The amount charged represents a gross disparity between the price of the commodity or rental or lease of any dwelling unit or self-storage facility that is the subject of the offer or transaction and the average price at which that commodity or dwelling unit or self-storage facility was rented, leased, sold, or offered for rent or sale in the usual course of business during the 30 days immediately prior to a declaration of a state of emergency, and the increase in the amount charged is not attributable to additional costs incurred in connection with the rental or sale of the commodity or rental or lease of any dwelling unit or self-storage facility, or national or international market trends; or

> 2) The amount charged grossly exceeds the average price at which the same or similar commodity was readily obtainable in the trade area during the 30 days immediately prior to a declaration of a state of emergency, and

the increase in the amount charged is not attributable to additional costs incurred in connection with the rental or sale of the commodity or rental or lease of any dwelling unit or self-storage facility, or national or international market trends.

Commodity is broadly defined to include "any goods, services, materials, merchandise, supplies, equipment, resources, or other article of commerce," and specifically includes, "without limitation, food, water, ice, chemicals, petroleum products, and lumber necessary for consumption or use as a direct result of the emergency." * * *

Typically, state price gouging laws are triggered only when there has been a declaration of emergency in the state. The laws, therefore, are only applicable in areas affected by the declared emergency. Thus, in other parts of the country, not directly affected by Hurricane Katrina, state price gouging laws, where they exist, are not likely to be generally applicable to any price increases occurring subsequent to the hurricane. While price increases may not fall within the definition of price gouging, if the raising of prices by retailers, suppliers, or manufacturers is the result of collusive activity, the federal antitrust laws could be applicable.

Under special circumstances and depending on the scope of the statute in question, state price gouging laws could be triggered by the declaration of an emergency not specifically related to a natural disaster occurring in the state. For example, Georgia's price gouging statute can be triggered by the declaration of an "energy emergency," which is defined as "a condition of danger to the health, safety, welfare, or economic well-being of the citizens of this state arising out of a present or threatened shortage of usable energy resources." [GA. CODE ANN. §§ 10-1-393, 38-3-3.] The Governor of Georgia declared such an emergency on August 31, 2005, triggering the state's price gouging statute.

NOTES AND QUESTIONS

1. At least 15 states and Guam have statutes that specifically address price gouging during emergencies. *See* ALA. CODE § 8-31-3; ARK. CODE ANN. § 4-88-301 to -305; CAL. PENAL CODE § 396; CONN. GEN. STAT. § 42-232; FLA. STAT. ANN. §§ 501.160, .201-.213; GA. CODE ANN. § 10-1-393; GUAM CODE ANN. § 32201; IND. CODE §§ 4-6-9.1-1 to -7; LA. REV. STAT. ANN. § 29:732; MISS. CODE ANN. § 75-24-25; N.Y. GEN. BUS. LAW § 396-r; N.C. GEN. STAT. ANN. § 75-37; S.C. CODE 1976 § 39-5-145; TEX. BUS. & COM. CODE ANN. § 1746(25); VA. CODE ANN. § 59.1-525 to -529; W. VA. CODE § 46A-6J-1 to -6. Ordinary trade regulation laws may also address price increases during disasters and other emergencies. For an evaluation of Florida's price-gouging statute, see Gary E. Lehman, *Price Gouging: Application of Florida's Unfair Trade Practices Act in the Aftermath of Hurricane Andrew*, 17 NOVA L. REV. 1029 (1993).
2. Tennessee and Virginia regulate price gouging in vaccines during medical emergencies. *See* TENN. CODE ANN. § 47-18-2801 to -2805; VA. CODE ANN.

§ 59.1-533 to -37. California penalizes an engineer who offers to practice engineering without legal authority, impersonates or uses the seal of another practitioner, or uses an expired or revoked certificate in connection with repairing structures damaged by natural disasters. *See* CAL. BUS. & PROF. CODE § 6788.

3. On June 28, 2005, two months before Hurricane Katrina, Louisiana very presciently amended its price-gouging statute. 2005 La. Sess. Law Serv. Act No. 149 (S.B. No. 162) reenacted LA. REV. STAT. ANN. § 29:732 and added the following italicized language:

> During a state of emergency as declared by the governor or as declared by the parish president, *or during a named tropical storm or hurricane in or threatening the Gulf of Mexico,* the value received for goods and services sold within the designated emergency area may not exceed the prices ordinarily charged for comparable goods and services in the same market area at, or immediately before, the time of the state of emergency. However, the value received may include reasonable expenses and a charge for any attendant business risk, in addition to the cost of the goods and services which necessarily are incurred in procuring the goods and services during the state of emergency.

4. Retail gasoline prices, already a subject of political concern, rose after Katrina. The federal government has occasionally imposed price controls on petroleum products. *See generally* Welborn & Flynn, *supra*, at 4-6. The Economic Stabilization Act of 1970, Pub. L. No. 91-379, 84 Stat. 796, authorized the President to control commodity prices, including crude oil and refined petroleum. President Nixon exercised this authority in 1971 before it expired in 1974. The Emergency Petroleum Allocation Act of 1973 (EPAA), Pub. L. No. 93-159, 87 Stat. 627 (codified at 15 U.S.C. §§ 751-760), directed the President to adopt temporary measures "to deal with shortages of crude oil, residual fuel oil, and refined petroleum products or dislocations in their national distribution system" and to "minimiz[e] the adverse impacts of such shortages or dislocations on the American people and the domestic economy." Until it expired in 1981, the EPAA authorized the President to allocate oil and to set its price. Finally, the federal government can influence oil supplies and prices by manipulating the Strategic Petroleum Reserve (SPR). *See* Energy Policy and Conservation Act of 1975, Pub. L. No. 94-163, 89 Stat. 871 (codified as amended at 42 U.S.C. §§ 6231-6247).

5. Scholars have speculated that price-gouging laws emerge in response to recent, salient experiences with calamity. *See* Christine Jolls, Cass R. Sunstein & Richard Thaler, *A Behavioral Approach to Law and Economics*, 50 STAN. L. REV. 1471, 1513 (1998). Of the 16 jurisdictions with all-purpose price-gouging statutes, 9 are prone to hurricanes: Alabama, Florida, Georgia, Louisiana, Mississippi, North Carolina, South Carolina, Texas, and Virginia. Guam is prone to typhoons. So is California, although earthquakes probably figure more prominently in that state's con-

sciousness. Of the remaining 5 states, Connecticut and New York are marginally susceptible to hurricanes. The presence of landlocked Arkansas, Indiana, and West Virginia counsels "[m]ore in-depth empirical research . . . to determine" whether behavioral considerations provide the most convincing explanation, or "whether conventional interest-group theories provide an alternative account." *Id.*

6. Price-gouging laws are rationalized as a tool for correcting a temporary market failure. The market's ordinary ability to allocate goods and services to buyers who value them most is thought to be impaired by a temporary spike in prices. Price-gouging statutes and their functional equivalents (such as state trade regulation laws and federal antitrust laws) are thought to strip sellers of a windfall attributable solely to high prices that cannot spur further output within an emergency's time frame. *See, e.g.*, United States v. Eli Lilly & Co., 1959 Trade Cas. (CCH) ¶69,536 (D.N.J. 1959); Almarin Phillips & George R. Hall, *The Salk Vaccine Case: Parallelism, Conspiracy and Other Hypotheses*, 46 VA. L. REV. 717 (1960). Conventional economic wisdom, however, disfavors price-gouging statutes. During shortages, high prices are the most efficient market-clearing mechanism. Suppressing prices serves solely to discourage vendors of essentials from entering the market. *See, e.g.*, RICHARD G. LIPSEY & PETER O. STEINER, ECONOMICS 83-88 (5th ed. 1978); P.D. Byrnes, W.J. Lowry & E.J. Bondurant II, *Product Shortages, Allocation and the Antitrust Laws*, 20 ANTITRUST BULL. 713 (1975); James I. Serota, *Monopoly Pricing in a Time of Shortage*, 33 LOY. U. CHI. L.J. 791 (2002).

7. To what extent does the Constitution constrain the regulation of price - gouging? The Supreme Court has addressed this question in the context of laws designed to curb windfall profits during wartime:

UNITED STATES V. COMMODITIES TRADING CORP.
SUPREME COURT OF THE UNITED STATES

339 U.S. 121, 70 S. Ct. 547, 94 L. Ed. 707 (1950)

MR. JUSTICE BLACK delivered the opinion of the Court.

Commodities Trading Corporation brought this suit in the Court of Claims to recover "just compensation" for about 760,000 pounds of whole black pepper requisitioned by the War Department in 1944 * * * * The United States contended that the [Office of Price Administration] ceiling price of 6.63 cents per pound was just compensation. Commodities denied this, claiming 22 cents per pound. It argued that Congress did not and could not constitutionally fix the ceiling price as a measure for determining what is just compensation under the Constitution. * * *

[This case is] controlled by the clause of the Fifth Amendment providing that private property shall not be "taken for public use, without just compensation." This Court has never attempted to prescribe a rigid rule for determining what is "just compensation" under all circumstances and in all cases.

Fair market value has normally been accepted as a just standard. But when market value has been too difficult to find, or when its application would result in manifest injustice to owner or public, courts have fashioned and applied other standards. Since the market value standard was developed in the context of a market largely free from government controls, prices rigidly fixed by law raise questions concerning whether a "market value" so fixed can be a measure of "just compensation." * * *

The word "just" in the Fifth Amendment evokes ideas of "fairness" and "equity," and these were the primary standards prescribed for ceiling prices under the Emergency Price Control Act. As assurance that prices fixed under its authority by the administrative agency would be "generally fair and equitable," Congress provided that price regulations could be subjected to judicial review. All legitimate purchases and sales had to be made at or below ceiling prices. And most businessmen were compelled to sell because, for example, their goods were perishable or their businesses depended on continuous sales. Thus ceiling prices of commodities held for sale represented not only market value but in fact the only value that could be realized by most owners. Under these circumstances they cannot properly be ignored in deciding what is just compensation.

The extent to which ceiling prices should govern courts in such a decision is another matter. Congress did not expressly provide that prices fixed under the Price Control Act should constitute the measure of just compensation for property taken under the Fifth Amendment. And § 4(d) provides that the Act shall not be construed as requiring any person to sell. But § 1(a) declared the Act's purposes "to assure that defense appropriations are not dissipated by excessive prices" and to "prevent hardships . . . to the Federal, State, and local governments, which would result from abnormal increases in prices . . . ." Congress thus plainly contemplated that these governments should be able to buy goods fulfilling their wartime needs at the prices fixed for other purchasers. The crucial importance of this in the congressional plan for a stabilized war economy to limit inflation and prevent profiteering is shown by the fact that during the war approximately one-half of the nation's output of goods and services went to federal, state and local governments. And should judicial awards of just compensation be uniformly greater in amount than ceiling prices, expectations of pecuniary gains from condemnations might prompt many owners to withhold essential materials until the Government requisitioned them. We think the congressional purpose and the necessities of a wartime economy require that ceiling prices be accepted as the measure of just compensation, so far as that can be done consistently with the objectives of the Fifth Amendment.

[Dissenting opinions by Justices Frankfurter and Jackson are omitted.]

NOTE

Commodities Trading appears to foreclose takings clause objections to price-fixing statutes adopted in response to war, disaster, or other emergency. Suppose that the government, as an alternative to regulating prices, purchased supplies for distribution on some basis other than willingness and ability to pay. If the government is the primary or exclusive purchaser of a commodity, vendors may respond by raising prices. This issue arose in United States v. Cors, 337 U.S. 325 (1949), a case involving the pricing of tugboats purchased by the federal government during wartime:

> The special value to the condemner as distinguished from others who may or may not possess the power to condemn has long been excluded as an element from market value. In time of war or other national emergency the demand of the government for an article or commodity often causes the market to be an unfair indication of value. The special needs of the government create a demand that outruns the supply. The market, sensitive to the bullish pressure, responds with a spiraling of prices.
>
> The normal market price for the commodity becomes inflated. And so the market value of the commodity is enhanced by the special need which the government has for it. * * * [A]t the time of the requisition there was "a rising market and a strong demand for tugs of all types" in and around the Port of New York, due in part at least to the shortage of tugs resulting from the government's requisitioning program.
>
> It is not fair that the government be required to pay the enhanced price which its demand alone has created. That enhancement reflects elements of the value that was created by the urgency of its need for the article. It does not reflect what "a willing buyer would pay in cash to a willing seller" in a fair market. It represents what can be exacted from the government whose demands in the emergency have created a sellers' market. In this situation, as in the case of land included in a proposed project of the government, the enhanced value reflects speculation as to what the government can be compelled to pay. That is a hold-up value, not a fair market value. That is a value which the government itself created and hence in fairness should not be required to pay.

Id. at 333-334. For an analysis of *Commodities Trading* and *Cors*, see Gregory R. Kirsch, Note, *Hurricanes and Windfalls: Takings and Price Controls in Emergencies*, 79 VA. L. REV. 1235 (1993).

E. INTERNATIONAL HUMAN RIGHTS LAW AS A MODEL FOR DOMESTIC REFORM

Soon after it began reporting on Katrina, the media started debating the appropriateness of using the term *refugees* to refer to persons evacuated from areas affected by the storm. The term *refugees* carries great significance in international law, as does the concept of an "internally displaced person."

How might international human rights law inform the treatment of persons displaced by natural disasters?

DONNA E. ARZT, SOUND AND FURY: KATRINA AND THE "REFUGEES" DEBATE

Jurist Legal News & Research, http://jurist.law.pitt.edu/forumy/ 2005/10/sound-and-fury-katrina-and-refugees.php (Oct. 3, 2005)

In the midst of the Katrina disaster [arose] * * * a debate over what to call the survivors. Shortly after news media began using the term "refugees," the Rev. Jesse Jackson, among others, protested that it was racist to call American citizens "refugees." Rep. Diane Watson (D-Ca.) even said the label was "almost a hate crime." The victims of Katrina, after all they had gone through, did not appreciate being compared to people fleeing from Third World countries * * * * For lack of a better term, the awkward "evacuees" became the word most often used to refer to anyone who had been displaced by Katrina and its aftermath.

By now, it is more than evident that "refugee" does not technically apply to persons who remain in their own country and that the legally correct term would be the inelegant phrase, "Internally Displaced Person" or "IDP." A refugee is someone who:

owing to well-founded fear of being persecuted for reasons of race, religion, nationality, membership of a particular social group or political opinion, is outside the country of his nationality and is unable, or owing to such fear, is unwilling to avail himself of the protection of that country; or who, not having a nationality and being outside the country of his former habitual residence as a result of such events, is unable or, owing to such fear, is unwilling to return to it. [Convention Relating to the Status of Refugees, art. 1(A)(2), 189 U.N.T.S. 150, *entered into force* April 22, 1954.]

Refugees are not necessarily stateless; "refugee" is not the opposite of "citizen." However, the term reflects a certain reality, evident in the clause * * * "unable, or owing to such fear, is unwilling to avail himself of the protection of that country." Katrina's victims who did not receive the expected aid were, indeed, unable to avail themselves of governmental protection. * * *

Internally displaced persons are

persons or groups of persons who have been forced or obliged to flee or to leave their homes or places of habitual residence, in particular as a result of or in order to avoid the effects of armed conflict, situations of generalized violence, violations of human rights or natural or human-made disasters, and who have not crossed an internationally recognized State border. [Guiding Principles on Internal Displacement, U.N. Doc. E/CN.4/1998/53/Add.2 (1998), ¶2, *noted in* Comm. Hum. Rts. res. 1998/50, para. 2.]

There [are] currently an estimated 25 million IDPs around the world— twice as many as international refugees. Because they are internally located, their government must consent to the assistance of an international agency * * * * That is more likely in the case of a natural disaster than when a military conflagration is occurring.

Hypothetically, let's assume that many of Katrina's evacuees had indeed crossed an international frontier—either that Texas is an independent country or that they had reached Mexico, which had taken them in. Then suppose they had sought asylum in a third country, such as Canada. Would they then be properly classified as "refugees"?

Probably not. Flight from a natural disaster is not normally considered "persecution" or "torture," which are intentional acts caused by a human persecutor. While it would be a stretch, they could argue that the persecution was not the hurricane and flood but the government's neglect of them after the natural disaster occurred, because of their predominantly African-American race. But the burden of proof, which is on the persons claiming refugee status, would be hard to meet, since non-black evacuees, though they may have had more resources to evacuate on their own, usually encountered the same governmental incompetence. Refugee law provides protection from intentional mistreatment, not disparate impact.

ROBERTA COHEN, TIME FOR THE UNITED STATES TO HONOR INTERNATIONAL STANDARDS IN EMERGENCIES

The Brookings-Bern Project on Internal Displacement, http://www.brookings.edu/views/op-ed/cohenr/20050909.htm (Sept. 9, 2005)

The Congressional Black Caucus is right. The more than one million Americans so painfully uprooted by Hurricane Katrina are not refugees * * * * Rather, they are internally displaced persons * * * * A refugee is someone who flees across borders because of persecution, and once over the border, benefits from a well-established international system of protection and assistance. For those displaced internally, their governments have the main responsibility to assure their well-being and security.

The Guiding Principles on Internal Displacement, introduced into the United Nations in 1998, are international standards for persons forcibly uprooted from their homes by conflict and natural disaster who remain within their own countries. Given the disastrously inadequate initial performance in dealing with this catastrophe, our government would do well to become familiar with these guidelines both for the current rescue effort and for future emergencies.

The guidelines * * * are "the basic international norm for protection" of internally displaced persons. Although not a binding treaty, UN resolutions regularly call them a "standard." The US Agency for International Development calls them "a useful tool and framework" in its 2004 policy on assistance to internally displaced persons in foreign countries.

It is now time for the U.S. government to apply these standards to displaced Americans here at home. * * * [G]overnments have a responsibility to prevent or mitigate the conditions that lead to displacement. In natural disasters, this means heeding early warnings, developing adequately funded and effective disaster preparedness plans at the local, state and national levels, ensuring that there are means to carry out the response, and evacuating people who cannot leave on their own and are in harm's way. Such steps should be seen as the fundamental right of populations living in high-risk areas. When public officials fail to take reasonable measures to protect them, claims for compensation need to be considered.

In distributing aid, fairness is essential. Discrimination on the basis of race, color, national, ethnic or social origin, social status, political opinion, disability or similar criteria must be prohibited. This means that the poor, who in the Gulf Coast are mainly black and Hispanic, should also have received help in being evacuated, while the most vulnerable—children, expectant mothers, the disabled, sick, and elderly—should have been attended to with the least possible delay. A review process should be set up to hear charges of discriminatory treatment and ensure remedial action.

The guidelines also address protecting and assisting the victims of disasters. Those uprooted have the right to expect to receive humanitarian aid in the form of essential food, potable water, clothing, medical services, sanitation, and basic shelter and housing as well as assistance later in rebuilding their lives. They are to be protected from acts of violence, rape, and lawlessness. When governments are not able to fulfill these responsibilities, they must promptly call upon the international community for assistance. In extreme situations, if governments refuse outside help yet fail to fulfill their commitments, the international community has the responsibility to intercede.

Consultation with the displaced is of cardinal importance. It may not be practical in the immediate aftermath of the Hurricane Katrina disaster, but in the recovery and reconstruction phases, when people begin to decide whether to return to ravaged Gulf Coast areas or resettle, and homes, businesses and local economies begin to be rebuilt, consultative mechanisms are essential. Exclusion from the decisions that affect their lives will not only heighten helplessness but undermine the effectiveness of the aid provided. The government must also help the displaced to recover, where possible, their property and possessions or provide or assist the persons in obtaining compensation or some form of reparation.

The UN guidelines are a valuable tool for federal, state, and local government officials. They are being adopted in one form or another by a growing number of countries. Were the United States to follow the guidelines, it would find itself on firmer ground for reacting to the current emergency and planning for future ones.

NOTES AND QUESTIONS

1. It is now clear that the legally significant term for Hurricane Katrina's evacuees was not *refugees*, but rather *internally displaced persons*. The evacuees were neither stateless persons "outside the country of [their]

former habitual residence" nor U,S. citizens "unable" or, "owing to well-founded fear of being persecuted for reasons of race, religion, nationality, membership of a particular social group or political opinion, . . . unwilling to avail" themselves of their country's protection. Moreover, as Donna E. Arzt observes, Katrina's evacuees would face a steep climb in arguing that officials singled them out for abuse on grounds of race or class. By all accounts, federal, state, and local authorities responding to Katrina were uniformly inept in handling all evacuees. The Convention Relating to the Status of Refugees appears inapplicable.

2. The immigration laws of the United States reinforce this restrained interpretation of the Convention. In interpreting domestic immigration laws that permit the grant of asylum based on persecution or a well-founded fear of persecution on account of race, religion, nationality, membership in a particular social group, or political opinion, *see* 8 U.S.C. §§ 1101(a)(42), 1158(a), the Supreme Court has held that fear of conscription in a guerrilla group's military operations does *not* qualify an alien for asylum. *See* INS v. Elias-Zacarias, 502 U.S. 478 (1992); *cf.* INS v. Cardoza-Fonseca, 480 U.S. 421 (1987).

3. By contrast, the Guiding Principles on Internal Displacement do apply to "persons or groups of persons who have been forced or obliged to flee or to leave their homes of habitual residence . . . in order to avoid the effects of . . . natural or human-made disasters, and who have not crossed an internationally recognized State border." How might emergency response proceed if American governments were to consult the Guiding Principles? To what extent does existing law comply with the Principles? What might need to be revised or replaced? If the Principles had guided Katrina's response, might it have been more effective?

GUIDING PRINCIPLES ON INTERNAL DISPLACEMENT

U.N. Doc. E/CN.4/1998/53/Add.2 (1998)

Introduction: Scope and Purpose

1. These Guiding Principles address the specific needs of internally displaced persons worldwide. They identify rights and guarantees relevant to the protection of persons from forced displacement and to their protection and assistance during displacement as well as during return or resettlement and reintegration.

2. For the purposes of these Principles, internally displaced persons are persons or groups of persons who have been forced or obliged to flee or to leave their homes or places of habitual residence, in particular as a result of or in order to avoid the effects of armed conflict, situations of generalized violence, violations of human rights or natural or human-made disasters, and who have not crossed an internationally recognized State border. * * *

SECTION I—GENERAL PRINCIPLES

Principle 1

1. Internally displaced persons shall enjoy, in full equality, the same rights and freedoms under international and domestic law as do other persons in their country. They shall not be discriminated against in the enjoyment of any rights and freedoms on the ground that they are internally displaced. * * *

Principle 2

1. These Principles shall be observed by all authorities, groups and persons irrespective of their legal status and applied without any adverse distinction. * * *

Principle 3

1. National authorities have the primary duty and responsibility to provide protection and humanitarian assistance to internally displaced persons within their jurisdiction.

2. Internally displaced persons have the right to request and to receive protection and humanitarian assistance from these authorities. They shall not be persecuted or punished for making such a request.

Principle 4

1. These Principles shall be applied without discrimination of any kind, such as race, colour, sex, language, religion or belief, political or other opinion, national, ethnic or social origin, legal or social status, age, disability, property, birth, or on any other similar criteria.

2. Certain internally displaced persons, such as children, especially unaccompanied minors, expectant mothers, mothers with young children, female heads of household, persons with disabilities and elderly persons, shall be entitled to protection and assistance required by their condition and to treatment which takes into account their special needs.

SECTION II—PRINCIPLES RELATING TO PROTECTION FROM DISPLACEMENT

Principle 5

All authorities and international actors shall respect and ensure respect for their obligations under international law, including human rights and humanitarian law, in all circumstances, so as to prevent and avoid conditions that might lead to displacement of persons.

Principle 6

1. Every human being shall have the right to be protected against being arbitrarily displaced from his or her home or place of habitual residence.
2. The prohibition of arbitrary displacement includes displacement: * * *
(d) In cases of disasters, unless the safety and health of those affected requires their evacuation; * * * .
3. Displacement shall last no longer than required by the circumstances.

Principle 7

1. Prior to any decision requiring the displacement of persons, the authorities concerned shall ensure that all feasible alternatives are explored in order to avoid displacement altogether. Where no alternatives exist, all measures shall be taken to minimize displacement and its adverse effects.
2. The authorities undertaking such displacement shall ensure, to the greatest practicable extent, that proper accommodation is provided to the displaced persons, that such displacements are effected in satisfactory conditions of safety, nutrition, health and hygiene, and that members of the same family are not separated. * * *

Principle 8

Displacement shall not be carried out in a manner that violates the rights to life, dignity, liberty and security of those affected.

Principle 9

States are under a particular obligation to protect against the displacement of indigenous peoples, minorities, peasants, pastoralists and other groups with a special dependency on and attachment to their lands.

SECTION III—PRINCIPLES RELATING TO PROTECTION DURING DISPLACEMENT

Principle 10

1. Every human being has the inherent right to life which shall be protected by law. No one shall be arbitrarily deprived of his or her life. * * *

Principle 11

1. Every human being has the right to dignity and physical, mental and moral integrity. * * *

Principle 12

1. Every human being has the right to liberty and security of person. No one shall be subjected to arbitrary arrest or detention.

2. To give effect to this right for internally displaced persons, they shall not be interned in or confined to a camp. If in exceptional circumstances such internment or confinement is absolutely necessary, it shall not last longer than required by the circumstances.

3. Internally displaced persons shall be protected from discriminatory arrest and detention as a result of their displacement. * * *

Principle 14

1. Every internally displaced person has the right to liberty of movement and freedom to choose his or her residence.

2. In particular, internally displaced persons have the right to move freely in and out of camps or other settlements.

Principle 15

Internally displaced persons have:

(a) The right to seek safety in another part of the country;

(b) The right to leave their country;

(c) The right to seek asylum in another country; and

(d) The right to be protected against forcible return to or resettlement in any place where their life, safety, liberty and/or health would be at risk.

Principle 16

1. All internally displaced persons have the right to know the fate and whereabouts of missing relatives.

2. The authorities concerned shall endeavour to establish the fate and whereabouts of internally displaced persons reported missing * * *. They shall inform the next of kin on the progress of the investigation and notify them of any result.

3. The authorities concerned shall endeavour to collect and identify the mortal remains of those deceased, prevent their despoliation or mutilation, and facilitate the return of those remains to the next of kin or dispose of them respectfully. * * *

Principle 17

1. Every human being has the right to respect of his or her family life.

2. To give effect to this right for internally displaced persons, family members who wish to remain together shall be allowed to do so.

3. Families which are separated by displacement should be reunited as quickly as possible. All appropriate steps shall be taken to expedite the reunion of such families, particularly when children are involved. The responsible authorities shall facilitate inquiries made by family members and encourage and cooperate with the work of humanitarian organizations engaged in the task of family reunification.

4. Members of internally displaced families whose personal liberty has been restricted by internment or confinement in camps shall have the right to remain together.

Principle 18

1. All internally displaced persons have the right to an adequate standard of living.

2. At the minimum, regardless of the circumstances, and without discrimination, competent authorities shall provide internally displaced persons with and ensure safe access to:
   (a) Essential food and potable water;
   (b) Basic shelter and housing;
   (c) Appropriate clothing; and
   (d) Essential medical services and sanitation. * * *

Principle 19

1. All wounded and sick internally displaced persons as well as those with disabilities shall receive to the fullest extent practicable and with the least possible delay, the medical care and attention they require, without distinction on any grounds other than medical ones. * * *

3. Special attention should * * * be given to the prevention of contagious and infectious diseases, including AIDS, among internally displaced persons.

Principle 20

1. Every human being has the right to recognition everywhere as a person before the law.

2. To give effect to this right for internally displaced persons, the authorities concerned shall issue to them all documents necessary for the enjoyment and exercise of their legal rights, such as passports, personal identification documents, birth certificates and marriage certificates. In particular, the authorities shall facilitate the issuance of new documents or the replacement of documents lost in the course of displacement, without imposing unreason-

able conditions, such as requiring the return to one's area of habitual residence * * * *

Principle 21

1. No one shall be arbitrarily deprived of property and possessions.
2. The property and possessions of internally displaced persons shall in all circumstances be protected, in particular, against the following acts:
   (a) Pillage; [and]
   (b) Direct or indiscriminate attacks or other acts of violence; * * * .
3. Property and possessions left behind by internally displaced persons should be protected against destruction and arbitrary and illegal appropriation, occupation or use. * * *

Principle 23

1. Every human being has the right to education.
2. To give effect to this right for internally displaced persons, the authorities concerned shall ensure that such persons, in particular displaced children, receive education which shall be free and compulsory at the primary level. * * *

SECTION IV—PRINCIPLES RELATING TO HUMANITARIAN ASSISTANCE

Principle 24

1. All humanitarian assistance shall be carried out in accordance with the principles of humanity and impartiality and without discrimination. * * *

Principle 25

1. The primary duty and responsibility for providing humanitarian assistance to internally displaced persons lies with national authorities.
2. International humanitarian organizations and other appropriate actors have the right to offer their services in support of the internally displaced. Such an offer shall not be regarded as an unfriendly act or an interference in a State's internal affairs and shall be considered in good faith. * * *
3. All authorities concerned shall grant and facilitate the free passage of humanitarian assistance and grant persons engaged in the provision of such assistance rapid and unimpeded access to the internally displaced.

Principle 26

Persons engaged in humanitarian assistance, their transport and supplies shall be respected and protected. They shall not be the object of attack or other acts of violence. * * *

SECTION V—PRINCIPLES RELATING TO RETURN, RESETTLEMENT AND REINTEGRATION

Principle 28

1. Competent authorities have the primary duty and responsibility to establish conditions, as well as provide the means, which allow internally displaced persons to return voluntarily, in safety and with dignity, to their homes or places of habitual residence, or to resettle voluntarily in another part of the country. Such authorities shall endeavour to facilitate the reintegration of returned or resettled internally displaced persons.

2. Special efforts should be made to ensure the full participation of internally displaced persons in the planning and management of their return or resettlement and reintegration.

Principle 29

1. Internally displaced persons who have returned to their homes or places of habitual residence or who have resettled in another part of the country shall not be discriminated against as a result of their having been displaced. They shall have the right to participate fully and equally in public affairs at all levels and have equal access to public services.

2. Competent authorities have the duty and responsibility to assist returned and/or resettled internally displaced persons to recover, to the extent possible, their property and possessions which they left behind or were dispossessed of upon their displacement. When recovery of such property and possessions is not possible, competent authorities shall provide or assist these persons in obtaining appropriate compensation or another form of just reparation. * * *

5

COMPENSATION AND RISK SPREADING

There are limits to how successfully we can prevent harm from disasters. When harm actually occurs, the next question is compensation. Should we use private insurance, government programs, or the tort system to provide a safety net for victims? This subject intersects with the previous one: The prospect of compensation may undermine the motivation of potential victims to invest in increased safety. This chapter considers methods of victim compensation and their pitfalls.

As we have seen, FEMA provides grants and loans to disaster victims to help with recovery. Moreover, many victims have insurance of one kind or another. But the insurance is often limited to wind damage as opposed to flood damage. After Katrina, there are bound to be thousands, if not hundreds of thousands, of disputes on the wind versus flood issue, as well as other insurance issues such as coverage and valuation. And after floods, FEMA typically requires localities to upgrade their building codes for rebuilding—but the added expenses are not covered by the typical insurance policy, even if the policy covers "replacement cost." An additional problem is that insurance companies tend to withdraw from the market after catastrophes— so people may be very vulnerable if another big hurricane hits in the next few years. For all of these reasons, designing a system for compensating catastrophe victims involves significant complications.

The issues discussed in this chapter connect with some of the questions of race and class discussed earlier. Consider the following observations:

- Home ownership is still the cornerstone of the American dream. It is the largest investment most families will make in their lifetimes. Home ownership is a cushion against inflation, the cornerstone of wealth creation, and a long-term asset that can secure advantages and transfer across generations. Home ownership is a critical pathway for "transformative" assets—inherited wealth that lifts a family beyond their own achievements.

- Ownership of property, land, and business is still a central part of the American dream of success—a dream that has eluded millions of Americans. The growing economic disparity between racial/ethnic groups has a direct correlation to institutional barriers in housing, lending, employment, education, health, and transportation. Housing discrimination denies a substantial segment of people of color communities a basic form of wealth accumulation and investment through home ownership. The average Black family holds only ten cents of wealth for every dollar that Whites possess.

- About 60 percent of America's middle-class families' wealth is derived from their homes. Much of the increase in Black wealth is due to rising home ownership, which increased from 42 percent in 1990 to 48 percent in 2003—still far behind the nationwide home-ownership rate of 68 percent. Addressing "wealth disparity" is one of the biggest issues facing urban, suburban, and rural areas for the next 50 years.[1]

Of course, the problem of compensation for catastrophic loss cuts across all groups and income levels. But for those groups whose hold on assets may have been the most tenuous in the first place, the problem of compensation may loom even larger.

A. METHODS OF COMPENSATING VICTIMS

ROBERT L. RABIN AND SUZANNE A. BRATIS
FINANCIAL COMPENSATIN FOR CATASTROPHIC
LOSS IN THE UNITED STATES

Financial Compensation For Victims After Catastrophe, M. Faure,
T. Honlief, eds., Springer Verlag, 2005

We have selected for closer examination three distinct illustrations of approaches taken by the U.S. legal system to compensation for financial loss in particularly notable instances: 1) the personal injury and death toll stemming from the terrorist attacks on September 11, 2001; 2) the property damage suffered in the single most costly hurricane in recent U.S. history, Hurricane Andrew; and 3) the profile of recovery in the prototypical mass tort disaster, a commercial airline crash.

---

1. Robert D. Bullard & Beverly Wright, The *Real* Looting: Katrina Exposes a Legacy of Discrimination and Opens the Door for 'Disaster Capitalism,' http://www.seeingblack.com/2005/x101105/411_oct05.shtml (last visited Apr. 4, 2006).

A. The September 11 Victim Compensation Fund

In the immediate aftermath of September 11, a no-fault compensation plan was enacted that closely reflected the anxieties and emotions stirred up by the horrendous toll of deaths and injuries occurring on that fateful day. The September 11 Victim Compensation Fund (the Fund), signed into law just eleven days after the terrorist attacks, addressed only personal injury and fatality claims. Losses related to property damage, as well as business losses or interruptions, remained compensable only in tort, if at all. Moreover the Fund was part of a broader legislative scheme, the Air Transportation Safety and System Stabilization Act, offering a package of loans and subsidies to the airlines to avoid a potential collapse of the U.S. commercial air transport system.

Within limits, the Fund was meant to create baseline assurance that victims of physical injury and their survivors would receive benefits.[2] More precisely, the Fund established eligibility for individuals "present at [any of the three crash sites] at the time, or in the immediate aftermath, of the terrorist-related aircraft crashes,"[3] and who "suffered physical harm or death" as a result of the crashes. For this circumscribed class, the Fund provided benefits for both economic and noneconomic losses on a no-fault basis.

In spelling out those benefits, however, the Fund appeared to be far more generous than earlier-enacted no-fault systems in the United States, virtually all of which follow the traditional model established in the early twentieth century for addressing the toll of industrial injuries: workers' compensation schemes. Under workers' compensation, eligible claimants recover medical expenses and a percentage of lost income (generally based on a schedule of awards in cases of permanent disabling conditions and in death benefit cases), subject to a statutory ceiling.

By contrast, under the Fund economic loss was defined to include not just medical expenses and loss of present earnings, but "loss of business or employment opportunities to the extent recovery for such loss is allowed under applicable state law"—presumably, a reference to individual, case-by-case tort principles. And noneconomic loss was broadly defined to include "losses for physical and emotional pain, suffering, inconvenience, physical impairment, mental anguish, disfigurement, loss of enjoyment of life, loss of society and companionship, loss of consortium (other than loss of domestic service), hedonic damages, injury to reputation, and all other non-pecuniary losses of any kind or nature." Interestingly, no parallel to the economic loss definition that referenced "[as] allowed under applicable state law" was included in this latter definition of noneconomic loss. Nonetheless, the pervasive influence of the tort perspective of doing individualized justice—disparaged by critics of

---

2. The description of the Fund and regulations that follows draws in part on an earlier treatment, *see* Robert L. Rabin, *The Quest for Fairness in Compensating Victims of September 11*, 49 CLEV. ST. L. REV. 573 (2001).

3. Air Transportation Safety and System Stabilization Act, Pub. L. No. 107-42, 405(b)(2), 115 Stat. 230, 238 (2001) (codified as amended at 49 U.S.C. § 40101 (2004)).

the tort system, trumpeted by its advocates—was apparent on the face of both provisions.

But there was one substantial qualification to this apparent generosity of spirit. Under traditional tort principles, there is recovery in tort of out-of-pocket expenses even if they have been reimbursed by "collateral" sources such as health and disability insurance. Under the Fund, there is no recovery for these items. Indeed, the restriction on "double recovery," as tort critics would put it, was written in exceedingly broad terms to cover "all collateral sources, including life insurance, pension funds, death benefit programs, and payments by Federal, State, or local governments related to the terrorist-related aircraft crashes. . . ."

Thus, the Fund steered a somewhat uncertain course between collective principles that would emphasize timely compensation and filling the gaps of unmet need, on the one hand, and individualized recovery that would pull in the direction of the tort model, on the other. Before examining this tension in somewhat more detail, however, consider the escape hatch provided in the Act: the prospect of lodging a tort claim instead of proceeding under the Fund.

One can only speculate about why a statutory tort cause of action for claimants was established in the Fund legislation; perhaps in recognition of the fact that some victims with substantial collateral source recoveries—most notably, victims with major life insurance holdings, accrued pension benefits, or accidental death coverage—might well have anticipated no recoverable benefits under the Fund. Or realistically, Congress may have simply recognized that substantial categories of September 11 victims—most clearly, those suffering property damage and psychological harm without accompanying physical injury—were simply not covered by the Fund. Of course, tort, as the default system, would have been available for addressing these claims—how successfully is another matter—without the need for establishing a federal cause of action under the Act. But this would arguably have created the appearance of treating Fund beneficiaries as second-class citizens if they were offered no tort option.

Whatever the case, Congress's ambivalent embrace of tort is highlighted by the title of section 408, which created the federal cause of action: "*Limitation* on Air Carrier Liability." If Congress was determined to leave tort as an option, it was equally determined to constrain tort along lines familiar to observers of late twentieth-century U.S. tort reform. The Act established a ceiling on tort liability of the air carriers, providing that liability "shall not be in an amount greater than the limits of the liability coverage maintained by the air carrier."[4] In subsequent legislation, this protective cap on liability, linking it to the limits of insurance coverage, was carried over to aircraft manufacturers, property owners in the World Trade Center, airport owners, and governmental entities.

---

4. *Id.* § 408(a). The amount of insurance coverage was reported to be $1.5 billion per plane. *See* Jim VandeHei and Milo Geyelin, *Economic Impact: Bush Seeks to Limit Liability of Companies Sued as Result of Attacks*, WALL ST. J., Oct. 25, 2001, at A6.

Ceilings aside, exclusive jurisdiction to hear "all actions brought for any claim (including any claim for loss of property, personal injury, or death) resulting from or relating to the terrorist-related aircraft crashes" was located in the federal district court for the Southern District of New York. But no federal common law was created; rather, the court was to apply the substantive law of the state in which the crash occurred. Finally, just to leave no doubt about it, section 408(b)(1) declared that the federal cause of action was to be "the exclusive remedy for damages arising out of the hijacking and subsequent crashes of such flights."

Thus, claimants eligible under the Fund were put to a choice—they had either to elect a claim for benefits under the Fund or to waive their rights and pursue a tort claim. At the same time, for those falling outside the eligibility limits of the Fund—such as those claiming solely economic loss—tort, as circumscribed in the Act, remained available. Interestingly, the tort option provided in the Fund legislation is not found in the traditional workers' compensation model, which precludes recourse to tort altogether (other later-enacted, no-fault schemes vary in this regard). Nonetheless, in its benefit provisions, as indicated, the Fund was far more generous than any other existing no-fault scheme in the United States.

These singular aspects of the Fund were not lost on the Special Master, appointed under the Act, who faced the immediate task of developing a concrete program for determining benefit awards for victims of September 11. His efforts offer an alternative vision of how one might design a no-fault model for future victims of terrorism, or catastrophic loss more broadly conceived.

When the Special Master, Kenneth Feinberg, was appointed on November 26, 2001, his initial task was to promulgate regulations resolving the principal tensions in the Act and filling in some important blanks. He issued a set of draft regulations ("Interim Final Rule") for commentary on December 21, 2001, and subsequently, on March 8, 2002, he issued final regulations ("Final Rule"), spelling out his interpretations of Fund provisions.

Feinberg's reading of the main provisions of the Fund reveals an interesting effort to strike a balance between understanding the Act in traditional no-fault terms that would have emphasized meeting scheduled basic loss of victims, and interpreting the Act in an open-ended fashion that essentially would have offered tort-type, individualized compensation in a no-fault setting. His manner of resolving this tension is evident in the approach taken to the three key substantive benefit provisions already discussed: collateral source offset, economic loss, and noneconomic loss.

As mentioned earlier, the Act explicitly called for the offset of life insurance and pension benefits. These provisions raised a firestorm of criticism from victims' families (in particular, the well endowed), concerned that they were likely to receive nothing in Fund benefits because of the foresight of the deceased, who it was argued, had earned or set aside funds for just such a contingency as occurred. These protests were sharpened to a fine point by prospective claimants observing that unconstrained tort—the absence of a Fund—would be a superior option, since life insurance and pension benefits traditionally are not offset under the tort system.

The Special Master responded to these criticisms in the Final Rule, by interpreting the Act to allow reduction of the offset to the extent of victims' self-contributions. More generally, Feinberg announced that it would be "very rare" for *any* eligible claimant to receive less than $250,000. It should be noted that neither of these interpretive moves is grounded in the language of the act.

Rather, the Special Master's actions reflected a fundamental philosophical difference buried in the esoteric legal language of collateral offset. On the one hand, a need-based approach to compensation would point to full offset of all collateral sources, as the Act appeared to require, since these outside benefits do contribute to meeting basic needs. On the other hand, under an individual claimant-focused, tort-type inquiry as to the "deserving" status of the victim, offsets arguably would be ignored entirely. In the end, the Special Master arrived at something of a compromise, liberalizing the statute from the victims' perspective by reducing the offset through recognition of victims' contributions and ignoring entirely outside private charity received by Fund-eligible claimants, as well as establishing a quite substantial presumptive minimum recovery.

As indicated, in addressing economic loss the Act appears to be at cross-purposes with the literal terms of the collateral source offset provision, in referring to recovery of "loss of business or employment opportunities" as defined in state tort law. On its face, this would seem to suggest an individualized inquiry in every case into the lifetime earnings prospects of each deceased victim, entirely at odds with the traditional no-fault approach of scheduled benefits.

In the Final Rule, the Special Master again crafted a compromise. Although there is no mention of scheduling in the statute, Feinberg established a grid applicable to the range of potential claimants—a "presumed economic loss" schedule—based on age, size of family, and recent past earnings, along with a presumptive cap applicable to the upper 2 percent of income earners. In devising this strategy, he provided for awards that recognized very considerable future earnings disparities, an announced range of $250,000 to between $3 and $4 million. But at the same time, he rejected an approach that would have recognized entirely open-ended, case-by-case speculation about future earnings prospects.

Although there are exceptions, no-fault schemes typically do not provide for pain and suffering loss, apart from optional or supplemental recourse to tort. In fact, tort law itself, as encapsulated in wrongful death statutes, did not traditionally provide any pain and suffering loss for survivors—that is, loss of companionship. Indeed, many states still do not recognize nonpecuniary loss as compensable to survivors in tort, limiting recovery to economic loss. And some other states, such as California, refuse to recognize pain and suffering of the deceased *victim* prior to death as recoverable in tort.

Nonetheless, the Special Master provided for *scheduled* noneconomic benefit awards under the Fund, for each victim and every surviving eligible family member. In the Interim Final Rule, $250,000 was to be awarded for each victim; a figure that remained unchanged in the Final Rule. With respect to survivors, the Interim Final Rule provided $50,000 for the spouse and each dependent, a figure that was increased to $100,000 each in the Final Rule. Thus, a surviving spouse with two children would receive benefits of $550,000 for noneconomic loss in a claim under the Fund.

* * *

B. Compensating Hurricane Damage: Hurricane Andrew

On August 24, 1992, Hurricane Andrew made landfall in the United States. This Category 4 hurricane struck just east of Homestead Air Force Base in Florida, passed through the southern Florida peninsula and moved onto south-central Louisiana. When it hit Florida, the storm had sustained wind speeds of approximately 145 mph, with gusts of at least 175 mph, and storm surges up to 16.9 feet.

Natural events only become "disasters" because of the impact that they have on human settlements. And disaster events are typically ranked relative to one another based on the costs associated with the damage that they cause. When it struck, Hurricane Andrew became the costliest natural disaster in U.S. history, both in terms of the FEMA relief required and total estimates of property damaged. Total property damage was estimated to be more than 25 billion dollars. Florida witnessed 28,066 of its homes destroyed and another 107,380 damaged. 180,000 people were left homeless, 82,000 businesses were destroyed or damaged, 1.4 million residents were left without power and 32,000 acres of farmland were damaged. In addition, twenty-six deaths were found directly attributable to the hurricane's impact and another 39 lives were lost as an indirect result of the storm.

Hurricane Andrew caused $17 billion in insured damage. Homeowner policy holders in Florida submitted 280,000 claims and recovered over $11 billion or 65% of total insured losses resulting from Andrew. The other types of insurance coverage triggered by the event included commercial multiperil ($3.767 billion), commercial fire ($1.062 billion) automobile/physical damage ($365 million) mobile-home owners ($204 million), and farm owners ($16 million).

The size of the disaster caught many insurance companies unprepared, which affected the efficiency of claims processing. First, insurers were, themselves, victims of the disaster. Many of the insurers' employees who lived in the south Florida area suffered property damage, making it difficult for them to attend to their business duties and their own home crises. Additionally, the storm damaged office buildings, communications services, and data storage facilities of the insurance companies. This damage created hurdles for efficient operation of business.

There was also simply a dearth of claims adjusters in relation to the magnitude of claims filed. Florida's Department of Insurance streamlined its process of licensing claims adjusters in the days following the storm, enabling insurers to use emergency adjusters to deal with the volume of claims. Some insurers did not take advantage of this emergency provision, and the shortage of adjusters introduced delays in the system. With so many policyholders left homeless or severely in need in the first few days after the storm, these delays resulted in many people having to wait for the temporary living expense funds they needed to pay for basic necessities like food, shelter, and clothing.

In 1992, property insurers in Florida collected $1.5 billion in premiums. They paid out about 10 times that amount to victims of Hurricane Andrew. The costs of the hurricane were greater than any company expected and forced members of the Florida insurance industry to recalculate their risks. In the aftermath of Hurricane Andrew, the landscape of Florida's insurance industry changed dramatically. Before Andrew struck, nearly 300 insurers provided a variety of coverage options to Florida's citizenry. As a result of the losses caused by Andrew, seven small insurers became insolvent, 34 insurers informed Florida's Department of Insurance of their intent to withdraw from the market entirely, and 29 reduced their coverage options in the state. Reinsurers also contributed to the situation. Primary insurers are restricted in the coverage that they can offer by the reinsurance available to them and many reinsurers became reluctant to provide coverage after the events of Hurricane Andrew.

The Florida Legislature responded to the state's insurance crisis by creating the Residential Property and Casualty Joint Underwriting Association and the Florida Hurricane Catastrophe Fund, which are currently of major importance.

* * *

The risk of hurricane events occurring in Florida is continuous. If anything, climate change studies indicate that the frequency and severity of such storms will increase in the future. And the potential damage that a storm of Andrew's caliber could inflict today far exceeds the destruction that occurred in 1992. One study estimated that if Hurricane Andrew hit with the same force in the same location today, it would cause close to $70 billion in damage, nearly twice the 1992 figure. As coastal area populations continue to increase and infrastructure continues to grow denser, the potential impact of future hurricanes becomes more devastating.

The catastrophe-response infrastructure of both Florida and FEMA were heavily analyzed in the aftermath of the storm. Since 1992, FEMA has updated the Federal Response Plan twice, attempting to strengthen federal coordination, management, and leadership. Likewise, Florida's insurance industry underwent a major overhaul, along the lines discussed above.

The 2004 summer hurricane season put both the national and the state relief reforms to an unprecedented test. Beginning with Hurricane Charley, the southeast coastal states suffered through four significant hurricanes between August and October. As of late October, 2004, combined state and federal disaster aid for Florida alone reached more than $2 billion.

This cluster of hurricanes will provide a test for Florida's insurance industry, as well as FEMA. Florida's government will be challenged both in its role as a primary catastrophe insurer, through the state's newly formed Citizens Property Insurance Corporation, and as a reinsurer, through the Florida Hurricane Catastrophe Fund. These programs were created by the state in direct response to the lessons learned from Hurricane Andrew. As the state cleans up from Hurricane Charley and its three successors, and Florida's residents begin rebuilding their homes and their lives, onlookers will have the opportunity to assess whether Andrew's lessons were well-heeded.

C. Catastrophic Loss in Tort: The Case of Commercial Airline Crashes

Whatever the doctrinal limitations, tort is frequently criticized from the broader perspectives of economic efficiency, distribution of risk, and fairness. Certainly from a compensation vantage point, the latter two concerns loom large. Tort only provides compensation: 1) when the *wrongdoing* of a defendant can be established, and 2) when the defendant is *solvent* (again, recall the discussion in the introductory section of this report). These limitations, along with the no-duty rules just discussed, mean that it is often the case that victims suffering similar injuries are not treated in a like fashion—and indeed that the disparities are sometimes glaring (ranging from no recovery to millions of dollars for similar accidental injuries or deaths). Thus, both in terms of risk distribution and fairness, it can be argued that tort leaves much to be desired.

Moreover, these limitations spill over into a critique from an economic, deterrence-oriented perspective, as well: No-duty rules, as well as insolvency, that insulate risk generators from bearing the cost of accidents for which they are responsible, translate into inadequate incentives on risk generators to provide safety precautions. In addition, the high administrative cost of shifting losses in tort is frequently invoked as an independent shortcoming of the system—undermining both its deterrence function and its efficacy from a risk-distribution and fairness perspective.[5]

As indicated in the section on insurance, the limitations of tort do not mean that those suffering personal injury loss as a consequence of catastrophic harm go entirely uncompensated.[6] About 85% of the U.S. population is covered to some extent by private health insurance, and Medicare offers public health insurance coverage to those over 65 years of age. The resulting gap in medical coverage—while still fairly substantial—is not as wide as the shortfall in coverage for wage loss. Private disability insurance coverage in the U.S. is quite uncommon, and while state disability and unemployment insurance benefits provide short-term partial relief, they do not fill the gap in cases of longer-term or very serious injuries. On this latter score, the federal SSDI insurance program, as indicated earlier, does offer scheduled benefits—

---

5. It is generally thought that injury victims in tort receive roughly 50% of total expenditures by tort defendants. *See* J. KAKALIK & N. PACE, RAND INST. CIV. JUST., COSTS AND COMPENSATION PAID IN TORT LITIGATION (1985).

6. Indeed, a 1991 study conducted by RAND Institute for Civil Justice found that overall areas of personal injury, payments in tort comprised 11% of total benefits received by accident victims—although the percentage would almost certainly be higher for victims in catastrophic loss cases. D. HENSLER, ET AL., RAND INST. CIV. JUST. COMPENSATION FOR ACCIDENTAL INJURIES IN THE UNITED STATES (1991).

although considerably short of full economic restoration—to those experiencing permanent total disability. In sum, the public welfare schemes in the U.S. leave quite large gaps in coverage for the economic consequences of personal injury, and private insurance sources fill only part of the gap, primarily for those carrying generous health insurance.

With regard to residential and commercial property and casualty loss, private insurance is the avenue of recourse. In the case of residential property, it is likely to be held by homeowners; much less likely to be held by renters. There are no general exclusions in the standard policies that would apply to catastrophic loss—just as there is none for third-party liability in the personal injury setting.

NOTES

1. The 9/11 compensation fund has not been seen as a model for compensating Katrina victims. Most of the attention has been on compensation for property loss. Should we consider a fund to compensate the families of those who were killed, or was 9/11 a unique event because of its national security dimension? Of course 9/11 was different in other ways: the harm was caused by an identifiable enemy, possible liability by the airlines could have had devastating economic effects, and the families of the victims were often affluent and legally sophisticated.

2. Could the federal government be held liable for defectively designing or constructing the New Orleans flood control system? Could state or local governments be held liable for similar problems with nonfederal levees or for failing to inspect and maintain federal levees? Consider your answers in light of the next two cases.

PATERNO v. STATE OF CALIFORNIA

113 Cal. App. 4th 998; 6 Cal. Rptr. 3d 854; 2003 (2003)

Morrison, J. The environmental aftermath of the Gold Rush continues to plague California. Hydraulic mining debris caused flooding which led to the building of levees at the confluence of the Yuba and Feather Rivers. Almost a century ago the Linda levee was built with uncompacted mining debris, and the use of that debris caused the levee to collapse on February 20, 1986.

About 3,000 plaintiffs sued the State of California (State), Reclamation District 784 (District) and others not now parties, seeking damages. In Paterno v. State of California (1999), 74 Cal. App. 4th 68 [87 Cal. Rptr. 2d 754] (*Paterno I*), we affirmed a defense jury verdict finding no dangerous condition of public property and reversed an inverse condemnation liability finding against defendants, and remanded for another trial on inverse liability. A new coordination judge (Hon. John J. Golden), conducted a lengthy court trial and issued a defense judgment against sample plaintiffs (collectively, Paterno) who filed this appeal.

Paterno embraces Judge Golden's factual findings, which in his view, create inverse liability on the part of the State as a matter of law. We agree. When a public entity operates a flood control system built by someone else, it accepts liability as if it had planned and built the system itself. A public entity cannot be held liable for failing to upgrade a flood control system to provide additional protection. But the trial court found the levee was built with porous, uncompacted mining debris, in a location which encouraged seepage, leading directly to the failure of the levee, and that long before the failure, feasible cures could have fixed the problems. Use of such technology would not have been an upgrade, but would have ensured the planned flood control capacity was achieved.

(2) Inverse liability stems from the California Constitution and is not dependent on tort or private property principles of fault. California Supreme Court precedent dictates that a landowner should not bear a disproportionate share of the harm directly caused by failure of a flood control project due to an unreasonable plan. Whether the plan is unreasonable is not measured by negligence principles, as in a tort case alleging a dangerous condition of public property, but by balancing a number of specific factors referred to as the *Locklin* factors. (Locklin v. City of Lafayette (1994) 7 Cal. 4th 327 [27 Cal. Rptr. 2d 613, 867 P.2d 724] (*Locklin*).) Based on the facts found by the trial court and application of the *Locklin* factors, we conclude Paterno's damages were directly caused by an unreasonable State plan which resulted in the failure of the Linda levee and the State is liable to pay for Paterno's damages. In large part our conclusion is based on the fact that the levee system benefited all of California and saved billions of dollars, and to require Paterno to bear the cost of the partial failure of that system—a failure caused by construction and operation of an unstable levee—would violate *Locklin*. A basic part of the State's flood plan was to accept existing levees as much as possible, to reduce the cost of an extensive, coordinated, flood control system. The People benefited from that cost-saving feature. However, the record shows the State never tested the Linda levee, or reviewed the records of its construction, to see if it was as strong as the global plans assumed it was, and the State even ignored specific warnings about the levee's weaknesses. In such circumstance, the costs of the levee failure must be deemed part of the deferred costs of the project. We do not separately address an alternate theory that the State is liable because of an inadequate levee inspection plan, although we discuss the lack of any plan to examine the heart of the levee.

Although in some ways the District is a coparticipant with the State in operating the levee, we conclude it is entitled to judgment. The District was responsible for and only for ordinary maintenance and could not alter the structure of the levee, even if it had the financial means to do so.

We will affirm the judgment in favor of the District, reverse the judgment in favor of the State with directions to enter judgment in favor of Paterno, and remand for further proceedings. In making this order, we realize this case is as hoary as Jarndyce v. Jarndyce. We expedited this appeal, and counsel assisted this court by providing much of the record and the briefs in computerized format. We will direct that this case be given priority in the trial court and that all available means to expedite the remaining triable issues be implemented.

* * *

In 1904 Yuba County adopted a resolution authorizing construction of a levee known as the Morrison Grade, which became the Linda levee. It was built by men and horses using scrapers to borrow nearby material, mostly mining debris. The trial court found: "In the process, little or no compaction of the material was attempted or achieved. As built, Morrison Grade was highly susceptible to seepage failure because of its siting on top of fifteen feet of porous hydraulic mining debris, the porosity of the material of which it was constructed, and the absence of any compaction of that material during construction." The Linda levee was part of the District, formed in 1908, and incorporated into the SRFCP.

Pursuant to the Grant Report the Corps improved the levee in 1934 and 1940 but the trial court found "the existing levee was incorporated into the finished work" without change. The floods of 1955 sorely tested the SRFCP and exposed many deficiencies, but no problems were revealed in the Linda levee, in particular the south levee on the Yuba between the Southern Pacific Railroad and the E Street Bridge (before the Feather confluence). Although the flood stage *exceeded* design capacity and water came within a foot of the top, it held. In the 1964 flood year the Linda levee was also subjected to higher waters than in 1986, yet held.

In February 1986, a tropical weather system brought much warm rain, which in turn caused snow melt triggering massive flooding in California For three days the Linda levee held water reaching to 76 feet (U.S. Engineering Datum), but it failed when the water had receded to about 74.3 feet; it is designed to hold up to 80 feet. The State concedes the levee failed at about *half* its designed capacity. The trial court found "the resulting 150 foot gap in the embankment allowed roughly 20,000 acre-feet of water . . . to inundate some 7,000 acres of land situated in the communities of Linda and Olivehurst, lying across the river south of Marysville in a territory which had been protected by the [levee] from flooding for many years. The flooding resulted in damage . . . estimated to be in the range of one hundred million dollars." "By 1986, the value of property protected by the levee . . . was about $ 409,400,000. There was evident no general perception that the area was not a safe place for urban development."

* * *

On appeal the State (but not the District) asserts the levee broke due to unforeseeable causes (e.g., "hydro-consolidation") and therefore the State cannot be liable to Paterno. We tend to agree with Paterno that the State has waived this argument. At trial the State objected to the trial court's proposal that it consider the Albers factors, which included foreseeability. Elsewhere at trial the State asserted it "has never contended that foreseeability was an issue in this case, ever." The State appears to be improperly changing its theory on appeal by claiming lack of foreseeability as a defense. But the point is important and raises no new factual issues, so we will address it.

The State misapprehends the role of foreseeability. As Paterno points out, foreseeability plays no role in the causation analysis and is not determinative in the balancing step, only informative. This is not a case involving a dangerous condition of public property, and we are not applying tort or water law standards of liability. We are implementing the constitutional command that the State must compensate landowners when it damages their property. As Paterno points out, "Even if the State failed to appreciate the risk of failure, this is not a defense to proximate cause. In other words, the levee's planned design and construction throughout its life 'endangered the levee in a way not adequately valued by the planners.'" We agree with Paterno's interpretation and the point has been made elsewhere.

The "reasonableness" balanced here is not a negligence standard of care, which might turn on foreseeability, but is "determined by balancing the public benefit and private damage in each case." The causation element is restated with greater precision in terms of 'substantial causation.'"

Thus, while foreseeability may weigh in favor of the landowner, lack of foreseeability does not defeat the claim.

In this case the evidence overwhelmingly shows the failure of the levee was foreseeable. The State says "There were no events that reasonably put the State on notice before Linda levee failed that its capability to safely carry flood flows was or was becoming compromised." Paterno does not argue the State actually foresaw the levee failure. But the State must be charged with knowledge of how the levee was built. It operated the levee for decades and had ample opportunity to examine it. If it chose not to do so for fiscal reasons, that would indicate the loss should be absorbed by the State.

NOTES

1. Could victims of Katrina recover against state or local authorities for negligence in designing or maintaining levees? Consider Bernard v. Thigpen Constr. Co., 702 So. 2d 1387 (La. 1997), and Bernard v. Thigpen Constr. Co., 695 So. 2d 518 (La. Ct. App. 1997), vacated by 702 So. 2d 1387 (La. 1997). The appellate court had approved certification of the class injured in the 1995 flood, but then the Louisiana Supreme Court set aside the certification after ruling in another decision that "the existence of individual causation and liability issues as to each potential class member may so predominate over common issues that class certification is inappropriate." Bernard v. Thigpen Construction Co., 702 So.2d 1387, 1388 (La. 1997). The appellate opinion is more interesting in imagining how plaintiffs could come together as a class following a natural disaster.

2. What about tort actions by FEMA against state and local governments to recover for its expenditures? In United States v. Parish of St. Bernard, 756 F.2d 1116 (5th Cir. 1985), the Fifth Circuit affirmed the district

court's grant of summary judgment to various local governments and public entities. FEMA had sued to recover over $100 million from the defendants for noncompliance with the National Flood Insurance Program. The court held that Congress had not expressly authorized a contract theory for a right of action under the NFIP, but the federal government could pursue common law claims to recover the defendants' NFIP-insured property. The NFIP will be discussed in more detail in the next section and again in Chapter 6.

Would it be helpful for the federal government to have a cause of action against local governments for negligently maintaining levees or failing to implement measures required by federal law? Would this provide an incentive for improved performance at the local level? Or would it just saddle already battered municipalities with a heavy litigation burden?

3.   The next case considers the potential liability of the federal government itself for flood damages. Note that while the California constitution requires compensation whenever the government "damages" property, the federal Constitution does not impose such a requirement. Instead, it merely provides liability when property is deliberately "taken" by the government. Thus, any recovery for the failure of flood control must be based on tort rather than on inverse combination.

UNITED STATES V. JAMES

478 U.S. 597, 106 S. Ct. 3116, 92 L. Ed. 2d 48 (1986)

JUSTICE POWELL delivered the opinion of the Court.

[This litigation arose from serious accidents that occurred in the reservoirs of federal flood control projects in Arkansas and Louisiana. In both accidents, recreational users (water-skiers in Arkansas and a fisherman in Louisiana) of the reservoirs were injured or drowned when they were swept through retaining structures after those structures were opened by the United States Corps of Engineers to control flooding. Separate actions were brought against the United States under the Federal Tort Claims Act. In the Arkansas case, the court held that although Government agents had willfully and maliciously failed to warn of a known danger, the Government was immune from damages under 33 U.S.C. § 702c, which provides in part that "[no] liability of any kind shall attach to or rest upon the United States for any damage from or by floods or flood waters at any place." In the Louisiana case, the court similarly granted summary judgment for the United States despite the Government's concession that it negligently failed to warn of the danger from the current caused by open gates. In a consolidated appeal, the Court of Appeals reversed the judgments. The Court of Appeals held that Congress had not intended to shield the negligent or wrongful acts of Government employees either in the construction or continued operation of flood control projects, including the failure to warn the public of hazards to their use of reservoirs.]

The starting point in statutory interpretation is "the language [of the statute] itself." "[We] assume that the legislative purpose is expressed by the ordinary meaning of the words used." The immunity provision in § 702c, enacted as part of the Flood Control Act of 1928, outlines immunity in sweeping terms: "No liability of *any* kind shall attach to or rest upon the United States for *any* damage from or by floods or flood waters at *any* place." It is difficult to imagine broader language.

On its face, this language covers the accidents here. Respondents' injuries occurred as a result of the release of waters from reservoirs that had reached flood stage. Given the nature of the accidents at issue, and given the plain terms of the statute, "it requires some ingenuity to create ambiguity."

Although the Court of Appeals found, for example, that the word "damage" was ambiguous because it might refer only to damage to property and exclude damage to persons, the ordinary meaning of the word carries no such limitation. Damages "have historically been awarded both for injury to property and injury to the person—a fact too well-known to have been overlooked by the Congress . . . Moreover, Congress' choice of the language "*any* damage" and "liability of *any* kind" further undercuts a narrow construction. (Emphasis added.)

Nor do the terms "flood" and "flood waters" create any uncertainty in the context of accidents such as the ones at issue in these cases. The Act concerns flood control projects designed to carry floodwaters. It is thus clear from § 702c's plain language that the terms "flood" and "flood waters" apply to all waters contained in or carried through a federal flood control project for purposes of or related to flood control, as well as to waters that such projects cannot control. As both District Courts found, the waters here clearly fall within the ambit of the statute.

We have repeatedly recognized that "[when] . . . the terms of a statute [are] unambiguous, judicial inquiry is complete, except 'in "rare and exceptional circumstances."'" In the absence of a "clearly expressed legislative intention to the contrary," the language of the statute itself "must ordinarily be regarded as conclusive." Despite respondents' contentions and the reasoning of the Court of Appeals, we do not find that the legislative history of the statute justifies departure from the plain words of the statute. Indeed, on balance we think the legislative history of the Flood Control Act of 1928 *reinforces* the plain language of the immunity provision in § 702c.

The Flood Control Act enacted "a comprehensive ten-year program for the entire [Mississippi River] valley, embodying a general bank protection scheme, channel stabilization and river regulation, all involving vast expenditures of public funds. "The Act was the Nation's response to the disastrous flood in the Mississippi River Valley in 1927. That flood resulted in the loss of nearly 200 lives and more than $200 million in property damage; almost 700,000 people were left homeless. The flood control system in the Mississippi River Valley in response to this catastrophe was the largest public works project undertaken up to that time in the United States.

It is not surprising, in the light of the devastation wrought by the 1927 flood and the magnitude of Congress' undertaking, that the legislative history of § 702c shows a consistent concern for limiting the Federal Government's financial liability to expenditures directly necessary for the construction and operation of the various projects. Numerous statements concerning the immunity provision confirm that it was intended to reaffirm sovereign immunity in such a dangerous and extensive project. The Chairman of the House Rules Committee, in opening the discussion on the rule governing debate on the 1928 Act, stated:

> I want this bill so drafted that it will contain all the safeguards necessary for the Federal Government. If we go down there and furnish protection to these people—and I assume it is a national responsibility—I do not want to have anything left out of the bill that would protect us now and for all time to come. I for one do not want to open up a situation that will cause thousands of lawsuits for damages against the Federal Government in the next 10, 20, or 50 years.

A number of other Congressmen unequivocally stated that the United States should not be liable for any expense other than the direct cost of constructing the project.

These statements show that the sweeping language of § 702c was no drafting inadvertence. Congress clearly sought to ensure beyond doubt that sovereign immunity would protect the Government from "any" liability associated with flood control. As the Court of Appeals for the Eighth Circuit explained three decades ago in *National Mfg.*, § 702c's language "safeguarded the United States against liability of any kind for damage from or by floods or flood waters in the broadest and most emphatic language." The equally broad and emphatic language found in the legislative history shows that Congress understood what it was saying. We therefore conclude that the legislative history fully supports attributing to the unambiguous words of the statute their ordinary meaning.

JUSTICE STEVENS, with whom JUSTICE MARSHALL and JUSTICE O'CONNOR join, dissenting.

As a part of the major undertaking authorized by the Mississippi Flood Control Act of 1928, Congress directed the Secretary of War and the Chief of Engineers to take special steps to acquire lands that were subject to "overflow and damage" along the banks of the Mississippi River where it was impracticable to construct levees. In the section of the Act containing that specific direction concerning the acquisition of "lands so subjected to overflow and damage," there is a sentence stating that "[no] liability of any kind shall attach to or rest upon the United States for any damage from or by floods or flood waters at any place."

According to the Court, Congress intended by this sentence to immunize the Federal Government from liability for *any* claim for personal injury, even though Congress provided expressly for compensation for property damage in excess of that required by the Constitution. n2 In my view, neither the plain language of the statute nor the legislative history behind it supports imputing such a perverse design to the Legislature. In my opinion, this provision applies only to property damage, and the judgment below should be affirmed.

* * *

It would be regrettable but obligatory for this Court to construe the immunity provision to bar personal injury claims if such was the intent of Congress. But when a critical term in the statute suggests a more limited construction, and when the congressional debates are not only consistent with this construction, but nowhere reveal a recognition, let alone an intention, that the immunity provision would deprive those injured by governmental negligence of any remedy, a narrower interpretation is more faithful to the objective of Congress. It defies belief—and ascribes to the Members of Congress a perverse, even barbaric, intent—to think that they spent days debating the measure of extraconstitutional compensation they would provide riparian landowners but intended—without a single word of dissent—to condemn the widows, orphans, and injured victims of negligent operation of flood control projects to an irrational exclusion from the protection of the subsequently enacted Tort Claims Act.

NOTES

1. The Flood Control Act was passed in a different era, when the federal government was generally immune from liability for negligence. It was also an era when a federal involvement in flood control was considered quite extraordinary. Should Congress revisit § 702 in light of these changed circumstances? Should the Court have considered these changes in interpreting the existing statute?

2. In Mocklin v. Orleans Levee District, 877 F.2d 427, (5th Cir. 1989), the plaintiffs brought suit against several defendants, including the Army Corps of Engineers, for the wrongful death of their son and sought damages under the Federal Torts Claim Act. The child had drowned when he slipped from a sand bar caused by the dredging into one of the flotation channels used to prevent further flood damage; the Corps had dredged the lake (Lake Pontchartrain) to make flotation channels during the construction phase of levees. The government's defense relied on § 702c. The Court concluded that the child died "from or by" flood water within the meaning of the FCA, because the flotation channel where the plaintiffs' son died contained water related to flood control; the flood channels were "inescapably" part of the flood control project.

3. For other examples of the difficulty of suing the federal government for disaster related activities, see Ames Farms v. United States, 1995 U.S. Dist. LEXIS 9827, 94-1448-Civ-Moreno (S.D. Fla. 1995) (dismissing suit for damages to property as a result of debris placement and removal after Hurricane Andrew); B & D Farms Inc. v. United States, 94-1449-Civ-Marcus (S.D. Fla. Dec. 21, 1994) (dismissing suit for damages to property as a result of debris removal after Hurricane Andrew); Dureiko v. Phillips & Jordan, Inc., 1996 U.S. Dist. LEXIS 22365 (S.D. Fla. 1996) (dismissing

suit for damages following a claim against government for negligent supervision of contractor which performed clean-up after Hurricane Andrew); Kirchmann v. United States, 8 F.3d 1273 (8th Cir. 1993), (affirming trial court's ruling that federal government was not liable for negligent supervision of a contractor which failed to safely dispose of hazardous waste in farmland).

B. FLOOD INSURANCE

FEMA has succinctly summarized the basics of flood insurance:

> In 1968, Congress created the National Flood Insurance Program (NFIP) in response to the rising cost of taxpayer funded disaster relief for flood victims and the increasing amount of damage caused by floods. The Mitigation Division, a component of the Federal Emergency Management Agency (FEMA), manages the NFIP, and oversees the floodplain management and mapping components of the Program. Nearly 20,000 communities across the United States and its territories participate in the NFIP by adopting and enforcing floodplain management ordinances to reduce future flood damage. In exchange, the NFIP makes federally backed flood insurance available to homeowners, renters, and business owners in these communities.
>
> Flood damage is reduced by nearly $1 billion a year through partnerships with communities, the insurance industry, and the lending industry. Further, buildings constructed in compliance with NFIP building standards suffer approximately 80 percent less damage annually than those not built in compliance. The NFIP is self-supporting for the average historical loss year, which means that operating expenses and flood insurance claims are not paid for by the taxpayer, but through premiums collected for flood insurance policies. The Program has borrowing authority from the U.S. Treasury for times when losses are heavy, however, these loans are paid back with interest. To get secured financing to buy, build, or improve structures in Special Flood Hazard Areas (SFHA's) you will be required to purchase flood insurance. Lending institutions that are federally regulated or federally insured must determine if the structure is located in a SFHA and must provide written notice requiring flood insurance.
>
> Flood insurance is available to any property owner located in a community participating in the NFIP. All areas are susceptible to flooding, although to varying degrees, in fact, 25% of all flood claims occur in the low-to-moderate risk areas. Flooding can be caused by heavy rains, melting snow, by inadequate drainage systems, failed protective devices such as levees and dams, as well as by tropical storms and hurricanes.[7]

This all seems simple enough, but there are actually some tricky policy issues involved, and the NFIP has been subject to serious criticisms.

---

7. FEMA, About Flood Insurance, http://www.fema.gov/hazard/flood/index.shtm.

WILLIAM O. JENKINS, JR., FEDERAL EMERGENCY MANAGEMENT AGENCY: OVERSIGHT AND MANAGEMENT OF THE NATIONAL FLOOD INSURANCE PROGRAM

Testimony Before the Subcommittee on Housing and Community Opportunity, Committee on Financial Services, U.S. House of Representatives) (Oct. 20, 2005).

As GAO has reported, the NFIP, by design, is not actuarially sound. The program does not collect sufficient premium income to build reserves to meet long-term future expected flood losses, in part because Congress authorized subsidized insurance rates to be made available for some properties. FEMA has generally been successful in keeping the NFIP on a sound financial footing, but the catastrophic flooding events of 2004 (involving four separate hurricanes) required FEMA, as of August 2005, to borrow $300 million from the U.S. Treasury to help pay an estimated $1.8 billion on flood insurance claims. Following Hurricane Katrina in August 2005, legislation was enacted to increase FEMA's borrowing authority from $1.5 billion to $3.5 billion through fiscal year 2008.

Properties that suffer repeated flooding but generally pay subsidized flood insurance rates—so-called repetitive-loss properties—constitute a significant drain on NFIP resources. These properties account for roughly 1 percent of properties insured under the NFIP, but account for 25 percent to 30 percent of all claim losses. The Flood Insurance Reform Act of 2004 established a pilot program requiring owners of repetitive-loss properties to elevate, relocate, or demolish houses, with NFIP bearing some of those costs. Future studies of the NFIP should analyze the progress made to reduce the inventory of subsidized repetitive-loss properties, and determine whether additional regulatory or congressional action is needed.

In 1973 and again in 1994, legislation was enacted requiring the mandatory purchase of NFIP policies by some property owners in high-risk areas. In June 2002, GAO reported that the extent to which lenders were required to enforce mandatory purchase requirements was unknown. While FEMA officials believed that many lenders often were noncompliant, neither side could substantiate its claims regarding compliance.

FEMA did not use a statistically valid method for sampling files to be reviewed in its monitoring and oversight activities. As a result, FEMA cannot project the results of these reviews to determine the overall accuracy of claims settled for specific flood events or assess the overall performance of insurance companies and their adjusters in fulfilling responsibilities for the NFIP—actions necessary for FEMA to have reasonable assurance that program objectives are being achieved.

FEMA has not yet fully implemented provisions of the Flood Insurance Reform Act of 2004 requiring the agency to develop new materials to explain coverage and the claims process to policyholders when they purchase and renew policies, establish an appeals process for claimants, and provide insurance agent education and training requirements. The statutory deadline for implementing these changes was December 30, 2004, and as of September

2005 FEMA had not developed documented plans with milestones for meeting the provisions of the act.

* * *

A key characteristic of the NFIP is the extent to which FEMA must rely on others to achieve the program's goals. FEMA's role is principally one of establishing policies and standards that others generally implement on a day-to-day basis and providing financial and management oversight of those who carry out those day-to-day responsibilities. These responsibilities include ensuring that property owners who are required to purchase flood insurance do so, enforcing flood plain management and building regulations, selling and servicing flood insurance policies, and updating and maintaining the nation's flood maps. In our prior work, we have identified several major challenges facing the NFIP:

- **Reducing losses to the program resulting from policy subsidies and repetitive loss properties**. The program is not actuarially sound because of the number of policies in force that are subsidized—about 29 percent at the time of our 2003 report. As a result of these subsidies, some policyholders pay premiums that represent about 35-40 percent of the true risk premium. Moreover, at the time of our 2004 report, there were about 49,000 repetitive-loss properties—those with two or more losses of $1,000 or more in a 10-year period—representing about 1 percent of the 4.4 million buildings insured under the program. From 1978 until March 2004, these repetitive-loss properties represented about $4.6 billion in claims payments.
- **Increasing property owner participation in the program**. As little as half of eligible properties may participate in the flood insurance program. Moreover, the extent of noncompliance with the mandatory purchase requirement by affected property owners is unknown.
- **Developing accurate, digital flood maps**. In our report on the NFIP's flood map modernization program, we discussed the multiple uses and benefits of accurate, digitized flood plain maps. However, the NFIP faces a major challenge in working with its contractor and state and local partners of varying technical capabilities and resources to produce accurate, digital flood maps. In developing those maps, we recommended that FEMA develop and implement data standards that will enable FEMA, its contractor, and its state and local partners to identify and use consistent data collection and analysis methods for developing maps for communities with similar flood risk.
- **Providing effective oversight of flood insurance operations**. In the report we are releasing today, we note that FEMA faces a challenge in providing effective oversight of the 95 insurance companies and thousands of insurance agents and claims adjusters who are primarily responsible for the day-to-day process of selling and servicing flood insurance policies.

* * *

The most immediate challenge for the NFIP is processing the flood insurance claims resulting from Hurricanes Katrina and Rita. Already, according to FEMA, the NFIP has received about twice as many claims in 2005 as it did in all of 2004, which was itself a record year. The need for effective communication and consistent and appropriate application of policy provisions will be particularly important in working with anxious policyholders, many of whom have been displaced from their homes. In the longer term, Congress and the NFIP face a complex challenge in assessing potential changes to the program that would improve its financial stability, increase participation in the program by property owners in areas at risk of flooding, reduce the number of repetitive-loss properties in the program, and maintain current and accurate flood plain maps. These issues are complex, interrelated, and are likely to involve trade-offs. For example, increasing premiums to better reflect risk may reduce voluntary participation in the program or encourage those who are required to purchase flood insurance to limit their coverage to the minimum required amount (i.e., the amount of their outstanding mortgage balance). This in turn can increase taxpayer exposure for disaster assistance resulting from flooding. There is no "silver bullet" for improving the current structure and operations of the NFIP. It will require sound data and analysis and the cooperation and participation of many stakeholders.

NOTES

1. Flood insurance presents a tricky set of problems. If it is priced too high, people simply may fail to insure. If it is priced too low, society is in effect subsidizing individuals to build in high-risk areas. Obviously, the solution is to price it "just right"—but finding the right level may not be easy, especially because there is no private market to use as a benchmark.

2. There has been serious criticism of how private insurance companies, which act as agents for the program, conduct business. In Howell v. State Farm Insurance Companies, Civil Action No. 1:04-CV-01494-BEL, several policyholders filed a class-action suit against eight insurers (including State Farm, Omaha Property and Casualty, and Allstate Insurance). The 2004 lawsuit alleged that the eight insurers used inaccurate and unrealistic pricing data to calculate repair and replacement costs on covered flood losses and that this method of calculating claimants' losses generated artificially low damage estimates and settlement offers. Plaintiffs also allege that insurers pressured them into signing proof-of-loss statements within 60 days after flooding, even though plaintiffs suspected that adjusters had underestimated scope of damage; plaintiffs felt that they had no choice but to sign the proof-of-loss statements because they feared that they would lose their chance to claim insurance. Moreover, plaintiffs alleged that

compensation of claims adjusters created a conflict of interest between policyholders and adjusters, which denied policyholders contractual benefits.

3. Despite all these failings, the flood control program has had some successes, as the following excerpt discusses.

OLIVER A. HOUCK, RISING WATER: THE NATIONAL FLOOD INSURANCE PROGRAM AND LOUISIANA

60 Tulane Law Review 61–164 (1985)

One of the surprises of this research, notwithstanding its negative findings, has been the extent to which the NFIP, in fact, works. It would be hard to find a program which cuts against more fundamental grains: freedom to choose where to live and build, freedom from government restriction (the federal government, at that), and freedom to maximize a profit from the land, buyer beware. Yet, without a strong economic constituency, this program has managed to survive in Congress and to have evolved at least to the flood-map and local-ordinance phase in thousands of communities. The NFIP is a remarkable phenomenon in American politics—an unpopular, grudgingly accepted program making its modest way. The conclusions and criticisms which follow should be taken in that light. This program undertakes a terribly difficult job. One has to remember that doughnut when looking at the hole.

The first impression one carries away from this research is that Congress, for all of its support for the NFIP, has yet to commit fully to making the NFIP's approach to the flood control problem work. The nation can approach flooding in only a few ways: (1) ignore it, (2) keep the water away from the people, (3) pay the people who get wet, or (4) keep the people away from the water. For one hundred years we tried option (1). As a matter of politics and humanity, (1) is no longer an option; given enough disasters—and flood disasters continue on a rising curve—the nation will respond. Options (2) and (3) represent the historic responses, and they are both attractive. Their difficulty is that they are both expensive, and their spectacularly unsuccessful history proves that they can never solve the problem. One is left with option (4). So is Congress, but with a more than wistful eye on the never-ending dams and levees and politically attractive disaster relief grants of (2) and (3).
* * *

Congress appears to have made the reasonable choice of the means available under option (4) to guide development away from floodplains. The NFIP is, to the maximum extent imaginable, a local program. One could scarcely think of a lesser federal presence short of, perhaps, simply mailing the insurance checks. Unfortunately, insurance checks will not avert future losses. Indeed, as predicted early on in the testimony which gave birth to the NFIP, insurance payments can encourage future losses. It is up to FEMA, with congressional support, to make the guided development part work. Congress can do more to provide that support, and FEMA can do considerably more to implement it.

Recommendations for action at the congressional level, while unconstrained by existing legislation, are limited by the art of the possible. Congress is not about to forgo new water project construction, or to withhold future disaster relief, nor should it. It should, however, structure these two programs so that they aid rather than frustrate the NFIP. With regard to water projects, it should require, as a condition for authorization of flood control dams, levees, and other structures, evidence that they be: (1) limited to that protection which could not be afforded by full NFIP compliance, (2) authorized only upon a demonstration that no other means of protection are feasible or prudent, and (3) conditioned, even then, upon binding agreements to discourage new development in surrounding flood-hazard areas. No flood-protection rationale for a structural project should be eligible for inclusion in any cost/benefit ratio absent these showings.

Congress should also examine other federal assistance and disaster relief benefits to flood-prone areas. The 1977 amendments to the NFIP, which permitted federally insured financing of development in nonparticipating communities, should be re-examined and repealed. No compelling argument—other than the profits to be made by individual developers—supports federal facilitation of new floodplain development that will lead to inevitable flood losses. Similarly, the more recent amendments proposed to limit disaster relief to participating communities should be adopted. The motives here are neither punitive nor even fiscal. Federal funds simply should be distributed in a way which maximizes local prevention of local flood losses, and the NFIP presents the means to that end.

Lastly, Congress should mandate a study of the degree to which upstream levees and channelization affect water stages downstream. Information on increased stages is available only from small, isolated watersheds. The analysis which accompanies an individual project goes no further. The cumulative effects of thousands of these projects, in virtually every watershed from Ohio to Montana, are largely unrecognized. Decisionmakers at all levels should be aware of the true costs of local, structural strategies to communities downstream, including, of course, the ultimate downstream community, Louisiana.

Turning to improvements available to FEMA and to local authorities within the existing NFIP, there is no part of the program which could not be better performed. In its most jaundiced light, the Emergency Program lags, the mapping is dubious, and the requirements of even the Regular Program are misunderstood, misapplied, and ignored. The deficiencies noted in this report are not new to FEMA: they confirm findings by the Comptroller General on at least two occasions, as well as an independent survey of the National Science Foundation. What may be new to FEMA is the scale of these deficiencies and, as illustrated in United States v. Parish of St. Bernard—and Hurricane Juan—their potential consequences. Rather than repeating these findings in full, two bear mention because of their particular significance to Louisiana: the treatment of coastal high-hazard areas and the adequacy of enforcement.

The effect of the NFIP on coastal development remains, to this observer, quite uncertain. In Louisiana, the program has only recently begun to be applied to coastal areas in a way that reflects actual storm damages. The accuracy of mapping remains contested, and there is virtually no experience by which to measure the success of local ordinances. From a purely analytical perspective, no good reason appears for providing federal assistance of any kind to high-hazard coastal development. There is every chance that, over a life of the structure, it will meet hurricane forces and will come off second best. Coastal high-hazard areas are as dynamic and storm-threatened as the barrier islands, and the same logic which led to legislation barring federal assistance to barrier island development should bar federal assistance in these areas as well

From Louisiana's perspective, coastal prospects look particularly bleak given the phenomenal rate of coastal subsidence, the addition of sea-level rise, and FEMA's reluctance to take either into account. At the least, the structural elevation and storm-proofing requirements for insurance eligibility should reflect the anticipated conditions over the life of the structure. Maps updated at a later time provide no remedy; construction will at that point already be grandfathered into the program. The cure starts only when future conditions are looked squarely in the eye. For much of coastal Louisiana they are a grim sight. However, they are no grimmer than the sight of evacuees.

The last word is reserved for enforcement. It is difficult to speak harshly of the efforts of an agency with so much to oversee and so little means. FEMA's regional staff has been decimated in recent years. Here more than anywhere, the unavoidable question is whether Congress and the administration really want the program to work. If they do, they will need to provide resources for the program on the theory that, over time, the enforcement of realistic ordinances will ultimately save the government money.

The most dramatic recent development in the NFIP has not been storm surge mapping or adjusted actuarial rates but, rather, litigation. Whatever the ultimate disposition of United States v. Parish of St. Bernard, its theory, and to an equal extent that of Gabler v. Regent Development Corp.,[9] brings a sort of free market to bear on the flood insurance program: if one does not perform to standard, one may be sued. This awareness is not all bad. In the context of the NFIP, it could do more to stimulate adherence to the content of local ordinances than all of the reports and inspectors imaginable, at considerably less expense.

The final act of United States v. Parish of St. Bernard has, of course, yet to be played. The Supreme Court may or may not hear the matter. It may or may not reverse. The Congress may then act to change the result again. Whatever scenario unfolds, it should end with the authorization of litigation as an enforcement tool. Compliance with the NFIP's ordinances is at the very heart of the program and is crucial to its financial success and its efficacy in reducing human suffering. Even with an army of inspectors to review what each of the thousands of NFIP communities is doing, a sanction which merely removes a noncomplying community from the program until it cleans house

---

9. Gabler v. Regent Dev. Corp., No. 216-002, slip op. at 2 (24th Judicial Dist. Ct., Parish of Jefferson, Division F, Oct. 4, 1983), *rev'd*, 470 So. 2d 149 (La. Ct. App. 5th Cir. 1985).

would, in effect, be license to get away with the maximum infractions before the inspectors arrived. The least obtrusive federal presence is, by chance, also the one likely to be most effective in stimulating compliance: the appearance at the courthouse to recover damages for practices which, however styled, amount to a wrong against the federal government, local residents, insurance ratepayers, and disaster relief taxpayers nationwide.

The NFIP is not a glamorous program. It is also not an easy program to understand. One tends to approach it, as this researcher did several years ago, with high skepticism. One tends to emerge, or at least this researcher did, with the conviction that, perversely, its implementation is successful in almost inverse proportion to the risk of flooding in a given area. Where the risk is low, compliance is generally good; no one's shoe is pinched. Where the risk is high, however, as in much of South Louisiana, tomorrow's development still overrides next year's inevitable losses. We know this much from the positive side: the program can work. What is still unknown is whether Congress will support the program sufficiently to allow it to work in those very places where making it work is the most difficult, and the most necessary.

NOTES

1. Flood insurance covers property loss, but not loss of life. Should the federal government try to fill that gap?
2. Should the government protect people from the consequences of their own choices? When individuals knowingly build in flood-prone areas, should they be held responsible for the risks they are taking?
3. Should the flood insurance program be abandoned, in favor of reliance on private insurance? You may want to consider that question in light of the next section.

C. PRIVATE INSURANCE

We begin with an excerpt that discusses the impact of Hurricane Katrina on the insurance industry, and some possible legislative solutions. We will then look more carefully at some insurance issues raised by Katrina, before turning in the next section to the question of legislation.

HURRICANE KATRINA: INSURANCE LOSSES AND
NATIONAL CAPACITIES FOR FINANCING DISASTER
RISK (SEPT. 15, 2005)

Congressional Research Service

[Private] insurer losses from Hurricane Katrina are estimated to be $40-$60 billion. This would make the tropical storm the costliest natural disaster in

U.S. history, exceeding Hurricane Andrew in 1992 and the September 2001 terrorist attacks. These insured loss figures include damages caused by storm's landfall in Florida on August 25, 2005, that led to an estimated $600 million to $2 billion in insured losses, as well as dozens of offshore oil and gas platforms reported either lost, damaged, or missing and believed sunk. Total damages are expected to exceed $200 billion, with the federal government expected to spend over $100 billion for response and recovery efforts associated with Hurricane Katrina in Alabama, Florida, Louisiana, Mississippi, and other affected areas. These amounts will exceed the initial cost for recovery from the September 11 terror attacks.

* * *

Insured loss estimates are likely to change as the extent of losses becomes better known. Disaster experts and modeling firms expect the numbers to change as more is known about the levels of water contamination and economic losses from business interruption and displacement of residents in New Orleans, Biloxi, Pascagoula, and Gulfport. These figures will also change when more accurate information about the economic costs of interruption of oil supply and exports of commodities such as grain becomes available. Most of the U.S. energy operations are in the Gulf Coast region.

Most insurance market analysts would agree that insurers will be able to pay all Katrina-related claims without triggering insurer insolvencies or market disruption. Despite the severity of damages, insurers are well-equipped to manage the financial impact of a catastrophe of this scale. The U.S. personal lines insurers have benefited from recent favorable market conditions and have built up policyholder surplus for an unexpected event like Katrina. [T]he industry as a whole earned $38.7 billion in net after-tax income in 2004, and policyholder surplus increased by 13.4%, or $46.5 billion, to a record $393.5 billion for the same year. A. M. Best, an insurance rating and information agency, reports that almost all rated companies will be able to meet their commitments. A few individual companies' ratings may, however, be lowered.

Although the insurance industry will emerge largely intact from Hurricane Katrina and is better capitalized now than ever, the industry simply does not have sufficient capital to fund a mega-catastrophe. This fact is not new. Insurers and financial market experts knew after Hurricane Andrew in 1992 that outside capital was needed to supplement industry capacity. Since then, new capital entered the catastrophe insurance market.

Insurers learned important lessons from Hurricane Andrew that prompted them to make changes to both protect the industry's balance sheets and stabilize the property insurance markets in the aftermath of a small-to-moderate hurricane. For example, after Hurricane Andrew, the Florida state legislature worked with insurers and regulators to create a hurricane catastrophe system designed to mitigate losses to the insurance industry and prevent insurers from withdrawing from the Florida insurance market. The Florida Hurricane Catastrophe Fund was created as a reinsurance-like entity funded by a portion of insurance premiums and managed by the Florida State Board of Administration. Florida also began using percentage deductibles tied to the value of homes instead of a dollar amount such as $500 per claim. Florida created a state-regulated insurer of last resort to provide insurance when no company is willing to underwrite disaster risks. These measures saved the property insurance industry from financial disaster after the four major hurricanes in 2004. Neither Louisiana, Mississippi, nor Alabama, however, have a similar catastrophe fund to compensate hurricane victims at a level comparable to what is available in Florida.

Most insurance analysts predict that Hurricane Katrina will likely result in higher pricing and restricted coverage in the hardest-hit areas. Insurers who specialize in coverage for offshore oil rigs and platforms, for example, have already announced 50% increases in premium prices. In addition, insurance rating agencies are now comparing their insurers' modeled catastrophe exposures to the potential market share exposure to determine the need for rating action. Insurance market analysts note that insurers with accurate loss exposure projections will be able to manage their losses within their capital base. Those that are shown to not have accurate loss exposure projections could suffer a rating downgrade.

When claims adjusters are finally able to assess the hundreds of thousands of damaged structures, they will likely face major challenges in distinguishing the portion of damage attributable to wind or flood. What was the wind damage before the levees broke and flooding began? This is important because wind damages are covered under standard commercial and residential property insurance policies, but floods are not. The central question of when the wind-driven rain or rising floodwater came in and when the wind came in will determine how flood claims are apportioned among the National Flood Insurance Program (NFIP), private insurers, and individuals.

It is quite likely that policyholders who lack federal flood insurance coverage might take advantage of vague policy language in their homeowners insurance policies to argue that the ultimate cause of damage was not flooding, but breaches of the New Orleans levees. Insurers are likely, however, to argue that they did not price the flood risk in the homeowners policy, and hence did not set aside reserves to pay such claims.

Although the purchase of federal flood insurance is mandatory for certain property owners as a condition of eligibility for loans from federally regulated lending institutions, many residents in flood-prone areas impacted by Katrina did not have flood insurance. According to the Insurance Information Institute, only about 30% of homes in Louisiana are protected by flood coverage, and even fewer homeowners in Mississippi and Alabama purchased the coverage. A problem is that, although mortgage lenders required homeowners in flood zones to buy flood coverage, these institutions reportedly have no system in place to ensure that homeowners keep the coverage in force. In addition, banks that provide mortgage loans on property found to be uninsured for flood damage might incur losses should homeowners who cannot afford reconstruction abandon both the property and the mortgage commitment.

* * *

The increasing magnitude of both insured and uninsured losses from natural disasters represents an ongoing challenge for both governments and the private sector. Natural disasters typically result in large government out-lays for disaster relief assistance, and they place a financial strain on private disaster insurance markets. The federal government alone, facing fiscal con-straints to cover the losses to the private sector, will find it costly and chal-lenging to meet long-term disaster related spending. In addition, insurers have been and will continue to be reluctant to cover properties in high-risk areas because of high long-run costs (which translates into high prices for disaster insurance) and low demand for disaster insurance.

Most insurance market analysts note that there is no state in the Union that is not subject to catastrophe exposure, and the current situation sug-gests that the projected exposures are far greater than the insurance indus-try is currently prepared to handle. The insurance industry's financial capacity and surplus to underwrite a $100 billion-plus mega-catastrophic event remains in doubt.

* * *

Opponents of federal disaster insurance say such measures conflict with long established sociological, economic, and actuarial principles that focus on the "true" cost of government programs (the opportunity cost of the funds), the foregone benefits of a competitive insurance marketplace (e.g., cost effi-ciency and rate competition), and the absence of consumer choice (the ability to decide whether to purchase coverage). Citing the development of new fi-nancial instruments to fund catastrophe coverage and expanded reinsurance capacity, critics of public insurance systems say there is no need for a federal insurance program at this time. They insist that such programs would shield the private sector from loss while creating sizable taxpayer-financed subsi-dies that undermine private-sector incentives for efficient risk management. Moreover, it has been argued that these programs would encourage popula-tion growth and development in high-risk, hurricane-prone areas that should not be developed, and would allow insurers to "cherry pick" the best risks and send the federal government the poor risks. Rather than providing insurance protection for natural hazard losses, J. Robert Hunter, Director of Insurance for Consumer Federation of America, for example, argues that the federal government should take actions to expand private-sector capacity for insur-ing disaster losses. Proponents of federal disaster insurance have argued that such a scheme would reduce dependence on "free" disaster assistance and support efficient risk management by households and businesses.

* * *

Historically, Congress has been reluctant to enact federal disaster insur-ance legislation because of (1) a lack of consensus on what will work and (2) concerns about adequate provisions for mitigation and avoidance of unneces-sary government intrusion into markets being adequately served by private sector financial entities. Congressional reluctance to establish a federal dis-aster insurance program has been based on the recognition that such a pro-gram would conflict with sociological, economic, and actuarial principles that emphasize the "true" cost of government programs (the opportunity cost of the funds), the foregone benefits of a competitive insurance marketplace (e.g., cost efficiency and rate competition), and the absence of consumer choice (the ability to decide whether to purchase coverage).

The federal government has played an important role in the U.S. economic system by assuming risks that the private sector either will not undertake at any price, or will accept but at a price so high that most potential beneficiaries will not purchase the coverage. For example, government risk-bearing now occurs in environmental disasters, nuclear-plant accidents, toxic waste dumps, and flooding. Establishing an explicit federal disaster insurance system to ameliorate the potential damages to homes and commercial buildings stemming from natural disasters would represent another government risk-bearing program—one that could expose taxpayers to funding demands if program revenues fail to cover costs, or if returns are lower than expected. Nevertheless, supporters of a federal disaster insurance program argue that it would be justified by the national scope of the Hurricane Katrina disaster, and by the inability of the private insurance industry to handle future high payouts from a mega-catastrophic event without federal government involvement.

As Members of Congress explore long-term ways to respond to Hurricane Katrina, consideration might be given to whether there is a need to improve the nation's ability to finance catastrophic risk and, if so, how. Previous Congresses responded to similar concerns by considering legislation to create a federal catastrophe reinsurance program for residential property. Despite broad support for several bills over the past few Congresses, the full Congress did not authorize a federal reinsurance program until the enactment of the Terrorism Risk Insurance Act of 2002. Finally, most observers would agree that for the very highest layers of catastrophe risk, the government (and consequently the taxpayer) is now, by default, the insurer of last resort. In the 109th Congress, any one of a number of policy options could be pursued, and will likely be influenced by whether it can be shown that potential losses from Hurricane Katrina are beyond the capacity of private markets to diversify natural hazard risks. Members will likely be grappling with several policy questions. For example, will reinsurance and securitization be enough to maintain insurance solvency after a mega-catastrophic hurricane or earthquake? How can the various funding sources available for catastrophe insurance be expanded and refined to cope with a catastrophic hurricane? Finally, what role, if any, should the federal government play in catastrophe insurance?

NOTES

1. From the point of view of the property owner, whether property is destroyed by wind or water is largely irrelevant. But insurers have not wanted to participate in the market for flood insurance, and exclusions for damages caused by water are their effort to avoid coverage for flood risks. Thus, there is a mismatch between the insured's expectation that

insurance will cover major risks and the insurer's desire to manage risk exposure.

2. The issue of "wind versus water" can arise in many different settings. Consider the following factual scenarios:

- The roof is blown off the house by wind. Some water also entered the house from flooding. It is unclear how much of the flooding was due to wind and how much to rain. Who has the burden of proof, the insured or the insurer?

- A house is flooded first, but then the roof blows off, so the house would have suffered the same water damage even without the flood. Should the fact that the flooding occurred first relieve the insurer from liability, considering that the same damage would have resulted from wind anyway?

- Rain first floods a lake, but then wind drives the flood waters against levees, bursting the levees and resulting in water damage to a house. Is the proximate cause wind or water?

3. In theory, individuals should know that their insurance does not cover flooding, but consumer knowledge on this point may be somewhat spotty. Should this affect the insurance company's liability? Consider the following excerpt.

PRESS RELEASE: ATTORNEY GENERAL JIM HOOD FILES COMPLAINT AND MOTION FOR TEMPORARY RESTRAINING ORDER AGAINST INSURANCE INDUSTRY TO PROTECT MISSISSIPPI'S VICTIMS OF HURRICANE KATRINA (SEPT. 15, 2005)

Mississippi Attorney General's Office

Biloxi, Miss.—Attorney General Jim Hood today announced that his office has filed a civil action in the Chancery Court of Hinds County, Mississippi, First Judicial District against the insurance industry seeking to declare void and unenforceable certain provisions contained in property casualty insurance policies issued to Mississippi Gulf Coast residents excluding coverage from damage caused by Hurricane Katrina.

Attorney General Jim Hood stated, "All that the people have left is hope and I'm not going to allow an insurance company to wrongfully take that hope away. Although some insurance companies are trying to do the right thing, I won't allow the others to take advantage of people hurt by Hurricane Katrina."

The complaint asks the Court to declare that certain insurance contract provisions are void and unenforceable as the same are contrary to public policy, are unconscionable, and are ambiguous. The provisions at issue attempt to exclude from coverage loss or damage caused directly or indirectly by water, whether or not driven by wind. The Complaint states that these provisions should be strictly construed against the insurance companies who drafted the insurance policies and their exclusions. The Complaint also states that the issuance of such insurance policies violates the Mississippi Consumer Protection Act. The Complaint also asks the Court, among other things, to enter a Temporary Restraining Order to immediately stop insurance companies from asking property owners to sign documents stating that their loss was caused by flood or water as opposed to wind, and to stop using water exclusions to deny or reduce coverage for hurricane damage or loss. The Court is also being asked to enter a preliminary and permanent injunction with regard to these same matters.

"I'm hopeful that next week we will be able to stop unscrupulous insurance adjusters from requiring people to sign away their rights to 'flood damage' claims in exchange for a significantly smaller amount which will be used for immediate living expenses. I want to encourage the people to continue to fight and I'll do everything I can to make sure that insurance companies pay what they owe." Hood said.

NOTES

1. In addition to the "wind versus water" issues, another frequent insurance issue involves the "ordinance or law" exclusion:

    > A typical Ordinance or Law exclusion clause reads: "We do not cover loss . . . resulting in any manner from . . . Enforcement of any ordinance or law regulating the construction, reconstruction, maintenance, repair or demolition of buildings or other structures." The insurance industry has articulated several reasons for the exclusion. However, as discussed below, the reasons fail to explain the distinction between costs of complying with the building codes and costs associated with coverage under "Replacement Cost" policies, which are fairly standard in today's market.
    >
    > Insurance companies most frequently state that the purpose of the exclusion is to prevent an insured from obtaining a "windfall" through the enforcement of a local or state ordinance or law. For example, in Bradford v. Home Insurance Co.,[10] the insured sustained damage to his leaching field. The cost of replacing the field with material similar to the original would have been $1,000. However, a local ordinance required that the insured also install a septic tank at a cost of $2,300. The insurer denied coverage for the cost of the tank based on an Ordinance or Law exclusion in the insured's policy and the court upheld the insurer's decision. Another court articulated the purpose of the exclusion as follows:

---

10. 384 A.2d 52 (Me. 1978).

> [T]he insurer is required . . . to indemnify the insured for the cost of repairing or replacing a building which was lost or destroyed by fire with materials of like kind and quality, but it is not required to assume repair or replacement costs which would provide the insured with a more structurally valuable building than the one that was damaged or destroyed. . . . The owners of new buildings which conform with state or local building laws are merely reimbursed for costs which they actually incurred. On the other hand, the owner of buildings which do not conform with such laws are not permitted to recover costs which they never assumed in the first place.[11]

Such windfalls, however, are inherent in "replacement cost" policies, which obligate insurers to reimburse the insured for the actual cost of repairs and construction without deducting any amount for depreciation. For example, if an insured needed to replace a damaged roof, the insurer would be liable for the cost of the entire new roof, even if the damaged roof had been ten years old. This begs the question: Why is paying to replace a ten-year-old roof with a new roof less objectionable than paying to replace a home built under an old building code with a home that complies with a current building code?

Insurers also justify the exclusion by stating that they must limit their exposure to the risk of having to pay for costs that are uncertain. Moreover, insurers claim that it is expensive to keep track of, and properly estimate, the impact of building codes. Ironically, uncertainty created the need for insurance in the first place and inspires many homeowners to purchase insurance. The basic purpose of insurance is to pool and distribute the risk of uncertain losses over a large number of people so that an individual will not bear the entire impact of a loss. Who better to evaluate and spread risk than insurance companies?

Because insurance companies have the knowledge and ability to pool and spread risk, and because ordinances and laws—e.g., building codes—are enacted for the health, safety, and welfare of the public, the following questions must be asked: Why is coverage of building code upgrades not automatically included in insurance policies? Why have insurance companies fought so ardently to support the exclusions despite the fact that courts have been ambivalent toward the exclusions? The fact that some individuals may benefit from an increase in the value of their property because of an upgrade required by an ordinance or law is unimportant when weighed against the potentially devastating effect the exclusions can have when they are enforced.[12]

---

11. Breshears v. Indiana Lumbermens Mut. Ins. Co., 63 Cal. Rptr. 879, 883 (Cal. Ct. App. 1967).

12. Hugh L. Wood, Jr., *The Insurance Fallout Following Hurricane Andrew: Whether Insurance Companies Are Legally Obligated to Pay for Building Code Upgrades Despite the "Ordinance Or Law" Exclusion Contained in Most Homeowners Policies*, 48 U. MIAMI L. REV. 949 (1994)(student comment).

2. Apart from the substance of insurance claims, their sheer number may overwhelm the litigation system. Consider the following alternative:

> In response to Hurricanes Katrina and Rita and the devastation left in their wake, the AAA has developed AAA Disaster Recovery Claims Resolution Services, a permanent program to address insurance claim disputes quickly and fairly. At present, more than 400 neutrals have agreed to serve at reduced rates on the panel for this special dispute management program. The insurance providers have agreed to pay the AAA's case administration fees and the neutral's compensation and expenses. Information about this program can be found at www.adr.org/sp.asp?id=26808/; www.adr.org/si.asp?id=2025; and adr.org/si.asp?id=2024/ (Guide to AAA Disaster Recovery Claims).
>
> The AAA previously helped victims of Hurricanes Andrew and Iniki, the Northridge earthquake, and the Grand Forks flood resolve insurance disputes. However, unlike those temporary programs, the new program is permanent. It will have its own formal set of procedures, available at www.adr.org/sp.asp?id=26802/. Under these procedures, the AAA will assist individuals with their property claims regardless of the amount involved. It will also assist businesses with claims under $75,000. This program will use telephone and in-person mediations to resolve disputes.[13]

D. DESIGNING INSURANCE FOR CATASTROPHIC RISKS

DAVID L. BRUMBAUGH, & RAWLE O. KING,
CONGRESSIONAL RESEARCH SERVICE

TAX DEDUCTIONS FOR CATASTROPHIC RISK
INSURANCE RESERVES: EXPLANATION AND
ECONOMIC ANALYSIS, SEPTEMBER 2, 2005

The devastation caused by Hurricane Katrina which struck along the Gulf of Mexico and Atlantic coast on August 29, 2005, highlights the fact that the United States continues to be subject to natural hazard risks, primarily weather-related risks such as hurricanes and windstorms, but also seismic risk (earthquakes, tsunami, volcanic eruptions) and flood hazard risks. Such natural disaster risks result in deaths, property damage, and economic dislocation. Federal outlays for disaster victims have been increasing, and the fre-

---

13. *AAA OFFERS New Disaster Recovery Services*, 60-JAN Dispute Res. J. 4 (2005).

quency of weather-related natural disasters generally perceived to be rising. The combination of economic dislocation from natural disasters and high federal and private costs has generated interest in Congress and elsewhere in proposals designed to change the way individuals and communities evaluate and protect themselves against the risk of natural disasters (i.e., financing risk with insurance). Given the increasing concentration of insured property values and sophisticated computer models that suggest an increased frequency of hurricanes and high probable maximum losses (PML) from catastrophic earthquakes, respectively, there has been some sense of urgency in Congress, state legislatures and the private sector to address the nation's financial exposure to catastrophic risks.

* * *

In broad terms, catastrophic risk is distinct from other risks simply because of its large size—catastrophes affect a large number of persons and firms simultaneously, imposing huge losses. Traditional examples include natural disasters such as Hurricanes Andrew (1992) and Katrina (2005), the Northridge earthquake (1994), and the Midwest floods (1993). Another example is the risk of loss from the World Trade Center terrorist attacks on September 11, 2001, although this particular type of risk has certain unique characteristics that place it beyond the scope of the analysis here.

In terms of economic analysis, the large size of catastrophes produces a particular result for insurance: it makes the elimination of uncertainty by an individual insurance firm difficult. The market for insurance is based on insurance firms being able to pool risks faced by a large number of policyholders whose risks are not related to each other. When a large number of uncorrelated risks are pooled, insurance firms can predict with relative certainty the average occurrence of a particular insured event (say, an accident) occurring among insured persons, and can provide insurance based on the reduction of that uncertainty. But the ability of pooled risks to reduce uncertainty diminishes when the risks of policyholders are correlated, and in the case of catastrophes, the risk of large numbers of insurance buyers is, indeed, related. (For example, large groups of homeowners may simultaneously incur damage from a hurricane or earthquake.) Thus, to sell catastrophe insurance, insurance firms must pool an exceedingly large group of risks in order to avoid correlated risks and develop marketable insurance. In keeping with this feature of catastrophe insurance, an important characteristic of the market is its reliance on what is known as "reinsurance" in insurance parlance. That is, a particular insurance firm, in writing policies for catastrophic risk, may not be able to find a sufficiently large pool of uncorrelated risks in its own marketing area. For example, a company whose market is limited to a particular coastal area may have difficulty developing a pool of customers whose risk of facing hurricane damage is unrelated. The company may accordingly sell hurricane insurance policies, but may itself purchase insurance ("reinsurance") against the catastrophe, in effect expanding the pool to unrelated risks beyond its own market.

Another technique insurance firms have used in recent years to provide catastrophe insurance is "securitization." Here, insurance firms turn to general capital markets to diversify their risks by marketing securities (for example, "catastrophe bonds," whose interest rate is contingent on the likelihood of a catastrophe's occurrence) that are attractive to investors because market risk is not related to catastrophe risk, and the catastrophe securities may thus provide a means of portfolio diversification for investors.

Notwithstanding these methods of financing catastrophe insurance, concern has been expressed by some analysts and policymakers about the ability of the industry to satisfactorily meet the challenges of a major catastrophe. Concern has focused on two factors that are sometimes termed the industry's "capacity" to face catastrophic risk: whether the insurance industry provides a sufficient level of catastrophe coverage; and whether a catastrophe would result in a large number of insolvencies among insurance firms. Proposals for tax-deductible reserve accounts have been advanced as a means of increasing the industry's capacity.

ROBERT L. RABIN AND SUZANNE A. BRATIS
FINANCIAL COMPENSATION FOR CATASTROPHIC
LOSS IN THE UNITED STATES

Financial Compensation for Victims After Catastrophe, M. Faure,
T. Honlief, eds., Springer Verlag, 2005

The Terrorism Risk Insurance Act of 2002 (TRIA) exemplifies the federal government assuming the role of excess liability insurer, in effect providing a cap on the losses for which the private insurance industry will be responsible in the event of a major act of terrorism.

In terms of insurance losses, the terrorist attacks on the World Trade Center and Pentagon on September 11, 2001, rank as the most costly catastrophe in U.S. history. This is without reference to the personal injury claims compensated under the Victim Compensation Fund, totaling nearly $7 billion, discussed in a separate section of this report. By the middle of October 2003, private insurance companies had received 35,094 claims related to the September 11 attacks on the World Trade Center alone, representing a total of $19.07 billion, including massive numbers of personal property and business interruption claims (the latter including claims for lost income and expenses related to restarting or reinvigorating affected businesses). Workers compensation claims paid by the industry came to 5,660. These aggregate costs far exceeded past terrorism-related damage claims in the U.S.

In the aftermath of the attacks, even before massive numbers of claims began to be filed, the U.S. Congress was faced with widespread concern about the solvency of the American insurance industry. On November 26, 2002, President George W. Bush signed into law the Terrorism Risk Insurance Act of 2002. TRIA was created to ensure the continuing availability of insurance for terrorism risk. Its goals encompassed both protecting the American public, by ensuring continued insurance coverage, and protecting the insurance industry as it rebuilt after the losses caused by September 11. The Act created a mechanism by which the federal government and private insurance providers would share the burden of property and casualty losses resulting from any future terrorist attacks.

Essentially, all commercial insurers doing business within the U.S are required to participate in the program. Under the Act's provisions, insurers are required to make available coverage for insured losses resulting from acts of terrorism in all of their commercial property and casualty insurance policies. The coverage cannot differ materially from the terms, amounts, and other limitations of policies written to cover losses arising from nonterrorist causes. In addition to the continued availability of coverage, insurers must inform policyholders of the premium charged for coverage and the federal share of compensation provided for under the Act.

In return for such actions on the part of insurers, the federal government assumes a percentage of an insurer's losses from compensating claims arising from terrorist acts. Each insurer is responsible for a deductible amount. But once that threshold is reached, federal funds are used to reimburse the insurer 90% of the insured losses in excess of the deductible. Importantly, the Act imposes a $100-billion annual industry-aggregate limit on federal reimbursements.

The program's reimbursement provision is triggered only by the occurrence of an "act of terrorism." To qualify, an event must meet a three-part definition, in addition to a threshold dollar amount of $5 million. The act must: (1) be "a violent act or an act that is dangerous to human life, property or infrastructure"; (2) result in damage within the US. (or outside of the United States in the case of air carriers, vessels, and U.S. missions), committed by one or more individuals, on behalf of foreign interests, in an "effort to coerce the civilian population of the United States or to influence the policy or affect the conduct of the United States Government by coercion"; and (3) be certified as an "act of terrorism" by the secretary of the treasury in concurrence with the secretary of state and the attorney general. Reimbursement of the insured (including the federal contribution), and risk management administration, remains in the hands of the private insurer.

In addition to providing for reimbursement, the act also contains provisions for managing litigation arising out of certified acts of terrorism. Once an act of terrorism is certified, the Act creates an exclusive federal cause of action and remedy for property damage, personal injury, or death arising out of or relating to the terrorist act. The federal cause of action preempts certain state law claims and provides for the consolidation of all civil claims. Additionally, the Act provides that punitive damages awarded in actions for property damage, personal injury, or death are not to be counted as "insured losses" and are not paid under the Program. Finally, the United States is provided the right of subrogation with respect to any payment made by the United States under the Program.

The provisions of the Act make it clear that Congress did not intend the program to be a primary source of compensation. Compensation provided for by other federal programs cannot be duplicated by funds from the Program. For example, disaster relief provided under FEMA or benefit awards under the September 11th Victim Compensation Fund must be deducted from the total amount otherwise payable under TRIA. Moreover, the TRIA program is a stopgap measure. The Act expires in 2005 and the deductible amount attributed to the insurers increases annually until that point to reduce the total amount of losses subject to federal reimbursement.

* * *

The 1994 Northridge Earthquake in California caused more than $15 billion in insured losses. After that event, many private insurers in the state attempted to terminate their earthquake coverage offerings. The state was challenged to find a solution that would keep its citizenry protected from future earthquake-related losses while also protecting the state's insurance industry. In 1996, California revamped its insurance laws related to earthquake coverage and created the California Earthquake Authority (CEA).

Insurance providers that sell "residential property insurance" in the state of California are permitted to exclude earthquake-related losses from their standard policy coverage, but are required by law to offer their customers earthquake insurance in some form. An insurer must notify its customer that the primary residential property insurance policy issued by the insurer does not contain a provision for earthquake damage and must make an offer of an independent policy (or an addition to the primary policy) for such coverage. The insurer can meet its obligations in several ways. It can offer to underwrite the earthquake coverage itself or it can arrange for coverage by another affiliated (or unaffiliated) insurance provider. Most residential property insurers—those comprising about 80% of the market, including the largest homeowners' insurers in the state—have chosen to opt out of providing coverage themselves, and instead simply administer policy coverage for the CEA, which assumes primary risk-bearing responsibility.

Homeowners and renters are not required by law to carry earthquake insurance. Thus, once the requisite offer of coverage is made by the insurance provider, the insured is free to accept or reject the offer. If the insured does decide to purchase earthquake insurance, the insurance provider must provide coverage that complies with the applicable CEA regulations. In its administrative capacity (for the CEA), an insurance provider is not required to abandon its usual underwriting standards in issuing earthquake insurance. Rather, it can use these standards to determine whether or not it is willing to provide an earthquake policy for each particular customer. However, if the insurer determines that a home does not meet its underwriting standards and decides not to issue earthquake insurance, the provider also becomes foreclosed from providing a primary residential property insurance policy for the home. Nor can an insurance provider cancel a residential property insurance policy on the grounds that the customer accepted the offer for earthquake insurance. But the critical point is that the CEA assumes the risk within the stated policy limits if an earthquake should occur—as mentioned, the private insurer plays an exclusively administrative role.

The Authority is a privately financed entity that provides earthquake insurance to California residents. It is composed of insurance companies licensed to do business in California and is governed by a three-member board of state officials including the Governor, the State Treasurer and the State Insurance Commissioner. The Board has the authority to conduct certain oversight and financial duties, but the issuance and management of earthquake policies is done by the private member companies. The Authority is charged with setting a rate for earthquake insurance and writing a residential earthquake insurance policy that is in compliance with the insurance laws discussed above and approved by the Board. Insurance policies are available for homeowners, renters, mobile home owners, and condominium owners. Coverage generally extends to costs of repair or replacement of property damaged by earthquake activity.

The authority is funded by participating insurers, along with bond sales, reinsurance, and the premiums charged for policies sold. Initial operating capital was provided through mandatory contributions by the participating insurers. If the Board determines, at any time, that claims will exceed the working capital of the Authority and that no additional sources of funding (e.g. assessments, reinsurance, private capital market monies) will be available to the Authority to pay claims, the Board can present a plan for pro-rata or installment payments of claims for approval by the Insurance Commissioner. The Board is obligated to ensure the authority has sufficient capital to maintain operation. The State itself has no liability to pay claims in excess of the Authority's capability.

Thus, by establishing a ceiling on the mandated contributions from private insurers, and pooling these risks, the CEA represents a model under which the state has relieved the private insurers of the uncertainty and potentially catastrophic losses associated with a major earthquake. Similar options are available for insurers of commercial property. In practice, however, major commercial insurance brokers have created pools of private insurers to offer coverage on large commercial properties.

NOTES

1. There have been some important changes in catastrophic risk insurance since Hurricane Andrew:

   • *Hurricane Insurance Deductibles.* Seventeen states and the District of Columbia (Alabama, Connecticut, Florida, Georgia, Hawaii, Louisiana, Maine, Maryland, Massachusetts, Mississippi, New Jersey, New York, North Carolina, Rhode Island, South Carolina, Texas, and Virginia) now require property owners to pay hurricane or windstorm deductibles from 1 percent to 15 percent of the insured value of the property, depending on the type of home (e.g., mobile homes carry a higher percentage deductible) and where the property is located, rather than traditional dollar deductibles used for other types of claims, such as fire damage and theft. Higher deductibles have also been imposed for wind damage. These deductibles allow private insurers to shift the risk onto homeowners.

- *Capital Market for Catastrophe Securities.* Starting in the late 1980s, insurers, reinsurers, and investment banks began offering catastrophe securities (sometimes known as insurance-linked securities, ILS) that transfer risk of natural calamities to the capital market. These securities sell because they offer unusually high returns and because the rates of return are not correlated with returns in the stock and bond markets.
- *Building Codes and Construction Standards.* In hurricane-prone areas, home insurance rates are now linked to new building codes and structural standards based on a building's ability to withstand wind damage. Following Hurricane Andrew, the Insurance Institute for Property Loss Reduction (IIPLR) launched a study to develop better wind and seismic building codes so structures could better withstand the force of storms and earthquakes. This led to the Building Code Effectiveness Grading Schedule (BCEGS), which takes into account many factors such as the skill of building inspectors, budgets of communities, etc. The Florida legislature requires insurers to take into account the BCEGS system when pricing rates.
- *Catastrophe Simulation Modeling Flourished after Hurricane Andrew.* These models allow insurers to better predict future windstorm losses based on current demographics and construction methods rather than rely on historical data. However, the damages forecasted by these models are often wrong by many orders of magnitude.

2. Congress has been considering legislative responses to the issue of catastrophic risk insurance:

- H.R. 21 in the 106th Congress and H.R. 1552 in the 108th Congress: encompass an "all-hazard" approach to covering most natural hazards, including hurricanes, earthquakes, and volcanoes. Both H.R. 21 and H.R. 1552 would have established a federal program to provide reinsurance to improve the availability of homeowners' insurance.
- H.R. 21 Approach: would have established a new federal disaster reinsurance fund to provide up to $25 billion in annual coverage to state insurance pools.
- H.R. 1552 Approach: would have authorized the secretary of the treasury to establish a program to make reinsurance coverage available through the auctioning of contracts.
- Homeowners' Insurance Availability Act of 2005 (H.R. 846), 109th Congress: identical to H.R. 21 to establish a federal program that provides catastrophe reinsurance to state insurance programs and private insurers.
- Tax Deductibility of Disaster Reserves: The 108th Congress has also considered changing federal tax policy to authorize tax-deferred treatment of private insurers' catastrophe reserves. Al-

lowing private insurers to build up catastrophe reserves to pay natural disaster-related claims that have a low probability of occurrence, it is argued, would lower insurers' costs of holding capital and, in turn, lower the premiums they must charge for a given level of disaster coverage.

3. For more in-depth coverage of these issues, see HOWARD KUNREUTHER AND RICHARD J. ROTH, SR., PAYING THE PRICE: THE STATUS AND ROLE OF INSURANCE AGAINST NATURAL DISASTERS IN THE UNITED STATES (1998).

6

PREVENTION AND MITIGATION

We cannot prevent earthquakes or hurricanes. What we can do is design communities so as to limit the damage that they cause. For some disasters, such as flooding, we may be able to eliminate the damage by insulating human communities from natural events. Indeed, some "natural" disasters can be considered as human in origin as natural, because prudent measures were not made to mitigate the risks. For example, the Army Corps of Engineers has now virtually conceded that it failed to design and construct an adequate control system for New Orleans.

Mitigation is a crucial part of managing the risk of disaster. But it involves making economic sacrifices today for benefits at some unknown time in the future, a trade-off that does not seem to come naturally to humans. This chapter discusses some of the forms that mitigation can take and some efforts to create incentives to mitigate.

One of the key connections between this chapter and the last one is the problem of "moral hazard." The more effectively we compensate people for the damage created by disasters, the less their incentive to take preventive action such as building elsewhere. Thus, in order to prevent this form of moral hazard, counter-incentives or regulatory mandates may be needed to encourage measures that would prevent or limit damage.

A. FORMS OF MITIGATION

If we think about the dangers of flooding in a city like New Orleans, we can imagine concentric rings of protection. In the outer ring are coastal structures and wetlands that might dampen storm surges. In the next ring are levees and floodgates to hold back the waters. But even well-designed structures cannot always prevent flooding – someday, the "design storm" (be 100-year storm or a 500-year storm) will come. So the next ring inside consists of land use restrictions and secondary buffer areas within the city itself, so that fewer communities are at severe risk of flooding. Finally, in the inner circle, houses can be designed to be more flood resistant (for example, by raising them above ground level). These forms of mitigation are discussed in more detail in the following excerpt.

HURRICANES KATRINA & RITA: USING MITIGATION TO REBUILD A SAFER GULF COAST (SEPT. 9, 2005)[1]

Association of State Flood Plain Managers, White Paper

Huge amounts of funding will go into reconstruction of these devastated areas over the next weeks, months and years. We must ensure that reconstruction will be done to create safer, more disaster resistant homes, businesses and infrastructure. These actions are not only needed in the affected Gulf Coast area, but in all coastal areas of the nation, where the population at risk is increasing daily as people move to the coast. A number of steps in this process will be necessary:

1. **Assess the damage to each structure** to determine if it should be reconstructed. If reconstruction is appropriate, the rules and standards for safe construction must be adhered to.

2. **Evaluate the current maps and construction standards for needed adjustments to protect lives and property.** FEMA should perform an analysis of the flood maps and damages in the Gulf Coast to determine if the current standards for mapping and managing those areas are adequate. Did the maps correctly reflect the expected storm surge and flood hazard? Did the existing flood maps show properties not at risk that were destroyed or badly damaged? Did those maps accurately reflect the 1% chance (100-year) flood? Will the new mapping process address any such problems? Did those structures on the coast built to existing standards survive? If not, do the standards need to be strengthened? Did the development along the coast expose supporting infrastructure to costly damages? This analysis can provide information for stronger reconstruction, and possible adjustments. Is the 1% chance flood an adequate standard? (See the Forum report on the 1% adequacy).

3. **Mitigate wherever possible.**   Reconstruction in coastal areas must incorporate the tenets of natural hazards mitigation. All options for mitiga-

---

1. ASFPM, WHITE PAPER, HURRICANES KATRINA & RITA: USING MITIGATION TO REBUILD A SAFER GULF COAST, Sept. 9, 2005, *available at* http://www.floods.org.

tion must be considered, including elevating or floodproofing the structure, or acquiring and relocating those in areas too hazardous for habitation. In some cases it may be more economical to demolish a damaged building and replace it with another one built to disaster resistant standards. Those that can be repaired must be carefully cleaned and dried to eliminate moisture and mold. While mitigating the structures against flooding, also modify them to protect against wind and storm surge.

* * *

5. **Communities and states should adopt higher standards for reconstruction to reflect their hazards.** The standards of the National Flood Insurance Program are minimum nation-wide standards. Each community and state should review its hazards in light of recent events and determine if higher standards are necessary to protect its citizens, properties and infrastructure. Many states and communities throughout the nation have adopted better protection standards, such as prohibiting construction in the high hazard areas, requiring "freeboard" above the 100-year flood level for structures, and ensuring that land use development is compatible with expected hazards. It has been stated that New Orleans was already considering higher construction and building codes. This is the time to make those adjustments. FEMA's Community Rating System rewards higher standards with lower flood insurance costs in those communities.

Provide funding for federal mitigation cost sharing programs

Post-disaster mitigation funding must be restored. The Hazard Mitigation Grant Program (HMGP) provides mitigation funds after a disaster as part of the Disaster Relief Act. Funding for that program was started in 1988, but was inadequate to be effective until the Midwest floods of 1993, when Congress increased funding to 15% of the disaster costs. In FY 2003, the funding level was reduced to 7.5%, and has again proved inadequate. Property owners are most receptive to mitigating their property at a time when they have to rebuild anyway. Communities are more responsive to assisting in cost sharing mitigation in the wake of disasters. Mitigation cost sharing with federal funds under this program is only done after a rigorous test to ensure that benefits over the life of a project exceed the cost of the mitigation. This opportunity for mitigation should not be missed. Rebuilding after Hurricanes Dennis and Katrina will be expensive enough once, lets [sic] not set ourselves up to do it again when the next major hurricane takes aim at the Gulf Coast.

Repetitive loss structures—programs must be funded so they can be mitigated. Many of the nation's repetitive loss structures (those with repeated flood insurance claims) are in the areas hit by Hurricanes Dennis and Katrina. Now is the time to mitigate the damages to those structures. Many property owners will have problems finding the resources to simply rebuild, let alone mitigate their structures. The 2004 NFIP Reform Act provides authority for added funding to help property owners mitigate repetitive loss structures, through a variety of generally non-structural means, including voluntary buyouts and relocations, elevation of buildings and floodproofing. That funding needs to be provided in the FY 06 budget so the NFIP can help reduce this drain. This matter should be of concern to everyone in a flood zone. Repetitive claims and large numbers of claims will drive up the cost of flood insurance for everyone.

Protecting and restoring natural systems and water resource projects policy.

Natural systems such as wetlands, marshes and barrier beaches provide a level of protection against coastal storm events. The Gulf Coast is rapidly losing barrier islands and the coastal wetlands that buffer the impact of hurricanes and flooding of the gulf [sic] coast and Southeast Louisiana. The State of Louisiana and Federal agencies in conjunction with parishes and public developed the Louisiana Coastal Area Ecosystem Restoration Plan to address these losses. In order to have a sustainable working Gulf Coast and New Orleans area, we must invest now in sound redevelopment and restoration practices. Future public financial investment in redevelopment along the Gulf Coast and New Orleans area must be completed in a manner that respects the natural processes occurring along the Gulf Coast. Reconstruction must balance the critical nature of coastal wetlands and other shoreline processes with the economic uses unique to coastal Louisiana and the Gulf. If we do not account for the delicate nature of this balance, we will simply be reconstructing a coast that will be even more vulnerable to the destruction caused by natural disasters.

Modernize the national Guidance for Floodplains and Reducing Flood Damages. Procedures for planning and implementing water resources developments, including flood damage reduction projects, should be modernized with much greater attention to setting priorities for investments. The current rules for planning and evaluating federal water resource projects have not been updated for 22 years, since 1983. In addition, the current Executive Order on Floodplain Management outlining federal polices and goals for managing the nation's floodplains has not been updated for 28 years, since 1977. Despite a flood of high-level reports from agencies, the National Academy of Sciences and professional organizations calling for an updating effort, neither Congress nor the Executive Branch [has] taken critical actions to ensure that these guiding documents incorporate key lessons that have been learned since the rules were established.

Levees and Structural protection works.

The Association of State Floodplain Managers (ASFPM) does not advocate new levees to protect undeveloped areas, and finds that using levees to protect existing development often results in creating situations where the expense of ongoing operation and maintenance costs may, over time, exceed the costs of other mitigation alternatives such as acquisition and relocation or elevation. Combinations of setback levees with some floodplain clearance can avoid pinching rivers in and creating added problems elsewhere. Even the

Corps of Engineers staff has been known to say "there are only two kinds of levees, those that have failed and those that will fail." Levees are only built to a certain level of protection, which will be exceeded at some point in the future. Reliance on levees should be an option of last resort.

Current levee design and construction standards are inadequate. Levees that protect critical facilities, such as hospitals, emergency operations centers, police, emergency medical services and fire stations, major infrastructure and large and vulnerable urban centers such as New Orleans must be constructed to a higher level of protection than those protecting rural or sparsely populated areas. A comprehensive and adequate levee policy would recognize the need for these differences. Levees in rural areas can utilize the 100-year flood (1% chance flood) level of protection, but only if local land use requirements prevent the area from becoming a highly urbanized area. Existing urban areas and critical facilities need protection to at least the 500-year (0.2% chance flood, and in coastal areas a category 5 hurricane) standard to avoid the catastrophic consequences, such as those experienced in the New Orleans area. It is important to recognize that levee failures in the New Orleans area [are] simply the tip of the iceberg—-we have thousands of miles of levees "protecting" large and critical urban communities in this nation. We must prevent this sort of damage and suffering.

Residual risk insurance and minimum construction standards should be required for structures behind levees.   Under current standards, structures behind a levee providing 100-year "protection" are not required to purchase flood insurance and are not required to be elevated. When the bigger flood occurs (and it will), and the levee is overtopped or fails, that development may be flooded not just with a foot or so of water, but to the rooftops, such as we've seen in New Orleans. This all or nothing approach in current national policy encourages communities to seek federal funding for just the 100-year levee, leaving not only the property owners and community, but federal taxpayers exposed to the catastrophic event. At a minimum, those structures protected by levees must pay a small amount (**residual risk insurance**) into a fund for when that catastrophic event occurs that exceeds the levee capacity. Structures behind levees should also be required to be elevated a minimum of two feet above natural ground to protect against low level incidents and internal drainage.

A National Levee Safety Program is needed.   We have no national inventory of levees, nor do we know the condition (the adequacy or safety) of many of these levees. Property owners behind levees assume they are protected, and are surprised and angry when levees fail. The state of California has been told by its courts that the state is responsible for damages caused due to failure of levees for which they are the sponsors. That exposes the state to perhaps billions of dollars in liability. Communities with levees throughout the nation face these issues. Congress should hold hearing[s] on this issue with the intent to identify actions that will be initiated to address documented deficiencies.

The Corps of Engineers should be charged and funded to undertake a National Levee Safety Inspection Program similar to the national Dam Safety Program. No federal funding should be provided for levees unless standards for the construction, operation and maintenance of the levee are in place and maintained, and unless states and communities accept their share of the costs and responsibilities. Emergency action plans in the event of failure or overtopping of those levees must be in place and exercised yearly. These standards can differentiate between rural and urban levees, but must require that communities have land use standards in place which would prevent a rural levee at lower standards from becoming an urban levee, where large urban areas and critical facilities would not then be adequately protected.

NOTES

1. A constant theme in this book has been federalism. How much of the responsibility for monitoring flood safety should be placed on the federal government and how much at the state level? What about funding for levee repairs? At least in the case of interstate waterways, one argument for federal intervention may be that levees in one place can increase the risk of flooding elsewhere, requiring some form of central planning.
2. Property owners are unlikely to be enthusiastic about investing large sums in upgrading their property's flood protection. Indeed, even designating property as being within a floodplain may diminish its market value. How can the government create incentives to engage in this behavior, or at least ease the pain?
3. Our primary focus has been on floods, but similar problems in the arid western United States exist for fire hazards—and indeed, the two can be related, as the next excerpt explains.

JACK AINSWORTH & TROY ALAN DOSS,
CALIFORNIA COASTAL COMMISSION
CALIFORNIA COASTAL COMMISSION, NATURAL HISTORY
OF FIRE & FLOOD CYCLES POST FIRE MITIGATION EFFORTS

Presentation to The Post-Fire Hazard Assessment
Planning and Mitigation Workshop, University
of California, Santa Barbara (August 18, 1995).

Development in the Urban/Wildland Interface

Over 1,000 homes were destroyed by fire in six Southern California counties between October 25 and November 10, 1993. During the Old Topanga Firestorm alone at least 3,500 homes were directly threaten[ed] with destruction. The Oakland/Berkeley Hills Fire of 1991 destroyed 2,449 single family residences. 437 apartment dwellings and condominium units, burned over 1,600 acres, killing 25 people, and injured another 150 people (NFPA 1992).

In the summer of 1994, over 50,000 acres and 37 homes were destroyed by fire (Planning 1995). With such staggering statistics it is a wonder to many why one would choose to live in the urban/wildland interface, but many do. Over six million Californian [sic] residents live in wildland areas, with another four million along the wildland urban/interface.

The urban/wildland interface is a wonderful place to live from an aesthetic point of view, and these areas provide a rural environment to many who have given up on the lifestyle of the urban flat lands of areas like the Los Angeles basin. Yet, natural processes are seldom understood or taken into consideration by those who develop or live in the urban/wildland interface. Millions of dollars are spent every year in fire suppression, flood control, and by tax subsidized insurance programs paid for off the backs of the majority of "flatlanders" who don't live with such risks, and by those who cannot afford to live in such locations. In a recent letter to the City of Malibu, the National Foundation for Environmental Safety, Inc., stated:

> Man-made calamities should not be continuously confused with "Acts of God." The life style of people living in slide, flood, and fire prone communities where periodic and largely foreseeable "man-made" disasters occur on a seemingly regular basis (such as in many areas of the Santa Monica Mountains and much of Malibu) is supported by the general public in the form of FEMA (Federal) and OES (State) disaster aid and State-mandated subsidies.

These areas are a dangerous place to put a home, and require that many pay with tax dollars and sometimes their lives for a privilege experienced by only a few. Furthermore, it is difficult and costly for government to prevent the spread of development into these areas as any conflict between government and the property owner over the development in such areas may result in a "takings" case, resulting in the further spending of tax dollars. Additionally, past development in the interface has occurred, far too often, with little planning for the inherent risk associated with living in these areas. Small wildland fires may quickly be extinguished, but this only results in the further build up of dead woody materials unless the fuel is removed by hand, or allowed to burn during a seasonal summer fire or as the result of a controlled burn. When large conflagrations occur it may be impossible for fire fighters to much more than observe a blaze, as they are charged with protecting life before property, and this includes their own lives.

Fire Suppression. As development has extended, or exploded as it has in some areas, into the chaparral environment, residents and government agencies have had to respond to the hazards associated with living in the urban/wildland interface. The majority of urban settlers who moved into these wildland areas are ignorant of the environment they are moving into and ill equipped to live in this wildland environment. Too often home buyers fail to realize that fire protection agencies may not be able to save their home from fire, and that agencies charged with building and safety and flood control may be powerless to save them from floods, mudflows, and landslides.

The primary response from government has been to [initiate] aggressive fire suppression and management in an attempt to eliminate fire from native lands. In spite of these aggressive fire suppression efforts large wildfires continue to consume vast acreages of chaparral in Southern California. After nearly a century of suppression, there has been increasing debate that fire control efforts have altered chaparral fire regimes in ways that magnify the threat of burning, erosion, sedimentation, and flooding at the urban/wildland interface. Fire suppression in Southern California appears to be producing older growth stands of chaparral which result in larger more intense fires. Younger chaparral stands (less than 20 years) are less likely to burn due to lower ratios of dead fuel to live fuels and reduced horizontal and vertical continuity of fuels. In northern Baja California where fire suppression has not been practiced to the extent it has in Southern California a mosaic pattern of differing age stands of chaparral appears to have developed resulting in smaller fire events of less intensity. Minnich . . . comparing the chaparral fire regimes in southern California and Baja California found that in Baja California numerous small fire events fragment stands into a fine mixture of age classes, a process which appears to help preclude large fires. While the pattern of large fires in Southern California appears to be an artifact of suppression.

Fire suppression is extremely effective at the ignition stages of a fire and where climatic conditions are favorable. Therefore, fires occurring in Southern California in the summer during periods of higher humidity, lower wind speeds and temperatures are much more easily controlled. Most of Southern California's major fires occur in the very late summer and fall periods during off-shore wind conditions (Santa Ana Winds) which are characterized by high temperatures, low humidity and very high wind speeds. Fires in [these types] of severe weather conditions are extremely difficult and in many cases impossible to control. This type of weather scenario, in conjunction with extensive areas of older chaparral stands, result[s] in fire magnitudes so great that entire watersheds are completely denuded of vegetation. This intense type of fire can even consume young moist stands of chaparral.

The extent of burned watershed can magnify flash-flood runoff behavior and high sediment yield in an exponential fashion. Higher regional fire intensities may also result in more extensive hydrophobic soil impermeability and high runoff (Minnich, 1989). These adverse watershed impacts can be moderated by implementing a sustained-yield program of small to medium size planned burns to produce the stand mosaic similar to the Baja California chaparral model.

Prescribed burns adjacent to the urban wildland interface can present some challenging problems. The common complaints voiced by residents of these areas are the annoyance and potential health effects of the smoke, reduced visibility and potential danger of the controlled fire escaping and endangering their residences. Furthermore, air quality regulations, particularly in Southern California, severely limit the time of year these burns may occur. Given these constraints the prescribed burning near the urban wildland interface can be carried out only on a very limited basis. However, even on a limited basis prescribed burning in the urban wildland interface can be a valuable cost effective fire management tool for protection agencies.

The proximity of the Malibu/Santa Monica Mountains to the Los Angeles metropolitan region coupled with its coastal location, breathtaking views, access to undisturbed natural areas, and sense of rural living make this a very desirable area. With proper land use planning, site planning, building codes and vegetation clearance it is possible to significantly reduce the threat of fire in the Chaparral community. However, the problem in the Santa Monica Mountains is [that] there are literally thousands of existing legal undeveloped parcels comprising hundreds of acres of land area that are located in very remote, topographically constrained, and environmentally sensitive areas. These factors make it quite difficult to mitigate the threat of fire and adverse environmental impacts.

There are also a number of very poorly planned subdivisions which were divided in the late 1920s and 30s with lot sizes of less than an acre and many more typically 5,000 to 10,000 sq. ft. in size. These subdivisions were primarily designed for weekend cabin type[s] of use. However, today the expensive homes built on these parcels are occupied on a year-round basis. There are approximately 6,000 of these ill-conceived small parcels in the Santa Monica Mountains. These subdivisions have very narrow winding roads which cannot accommodate fire equipment and are for the most part very heavily wooded with both natural and exotic plant species. These types of subdivisions are disasters just waiting to happen.

Proper site design on a large parcel can reduce fire danger to some extent. [H]owever, in these small lot subdivisions it is impossible in many cases to significantly reduce the fire hazards given the very steep site topography, lack of adequate water supply, proximity to other structures and limited access for fire equipment.

Given that the threat of fire alone has not provide[d] an adequate basis to prohibit development on these parcels and given the more rigorous requirements placed on regulatory agencies by recent court decisions regarding constitutional takings of private property, these parcels are and will continue building out. Furthermore, as most of us know today regulatory agencies are facing even more severe limitations and restrictive requirements regarding regulation of private property. Therefore, the oversimplified argument, which is voiced quite often—"just deny all development of homes on these parcels" —is just not realistic or legally justifiable.

In order to reduce the buildout of these subdivisions and remote environmentally sensitive parcels the California Coastal Commission developed the Transfer of Development program in the Malibu/Santa Monica Mountains Area of the Coastal Zone. Simply, the Transfer of Development program requires that any time a new parcel is created through the subdivision process, the equivalent development rights on designated small lot subdivision lots or remote environmentally sensitive parcels have to be retired. In theory, the newly created subdivisions are located in areas more suitable for this type of development. To date 924 substandard lots have been retired in small lot subdivisions and some 800 acres of remote environmentally sensitive parcels have been retired, [m]aking the Malibu/Santa Monica Mountains Transfer of Development program one of the most successful in the United States.

NOTES

1. Controlling development would be much easier in a legal system that did not recognize property rights. We will return later to the question of whether development restrictions unconstitutionally invade the property rights of landowners.
2. Inadequate fire protection creates an "externality" by increasing the risk to neighbors. This seems to call for a collective response. Is this equally true of other risks, such as earthquakes and flooding? If not, should we rely on the private market to a greater extent to encourage mitigation for those risks?

B. PRESERVING BUFFER ZONES

When we think about flood prevention, we naturally think of levees, sea-walls, and dikes. But nature also provides other forms of protection against flooding. Since Hurricane Katrina, the possible role of wetlands in controlling storm surges has received particular attention. Unfortunately, in just the areas where such wetlands might be the most useful, they seem to be the most imperiled.

**THE CENTER FOR PROGRESSIVE REGULATION, AN UNNATURAL
DISASTER: THE AFTERMATH OF HURRICANE KATRINA**

http://www.progressiveregulation.org/articles/ Unnatural_Disaster_512.pdf (Sept.
2005) 10–11

Louisiana's coastal plain contains one of the largest expanses of coastal wetlands in the contiguous United States. Sadly, 90 percent of the nation's coastal wetlands *loss* occurs here too. Built by the deltaic processes of the Mississippi River, Louisiana's coastal plain hosts an extraordinary diversity of coastal habitats, ranging from natural levees and beach ridges to large swaths of forested swamps, to freshwater, intermediate, brackish, and saline marshes. These features—which nourish wildlife, filter water, and dampen storm surges—help make the coastal plain, to use the Corps' words, one of "the most productive and important natural assets" in the country.

While most people do not realize it, one of the most important services provided by coastal marshes involves storm protection. Imagine blasting water through a garden hose at full force onto a cement driveway. The water splashes and surges, fanning out in many directions. Now imagine spraying water from the same hose onto a thick, dense lawn. The difference between the cement and the lawn is the difference between a storm path composed of open water and denuded coast and one composed of lush forests and marsh.

Louisiana's coastal wetlands act as vast sponges, absorbing billions of gallons of rainfall and shielding people and property from storms. The effect is impressive, even for city dwellers who have never seen a marsh: every two miles of wetlands south of New Orleans reduces tropical storm surges there by half a foot. Louisiana's coastal wetlands and barrier islands also help shield an internationally significant commercial-industrial complex from the destructive forces of storm-driven waves and tides.

In addition to storm protection services, the Louisiana coastal plain also provides numerous other benefits. It offers habitat for countless species, including commercially significant sea life and waterfowl. With more than five million birds wintering in Louisiana, the Louisiana coastal plain provides crucial rest stops to migrating birds. Finally, Louisiana's coastal marshes provide services vital to water quality. The marshes function as giant "water treatment plants," filtering out vast quantities of nitrogen, phosphorous, and other pollutants from incoming water bodies. Taken together, the many services of Louisiana's coastal wetlands make them a treasure every bit as unique and breathtaking as the city of New Orleans itself. The coast's storm protection, habitat, and water treatment services, while impossible to precisely quantify, surely amount to billions of dollars of commercial benefit per year.

The Failures of Wetlands Law and Policy: Bayou Farewell

Unbelievably, this giant of all coastal wetlands, this biotic and commercial treasure, is disappearing before our very eyes. Since the 1930s Louisiana has lost more than 1.2 million acres of coastal wetlands. Today, the Corps believes Louisiana is losing about 6,600 acres per year, a rate that if unchecked will result in a net loss of 328,000 acres – or an area roughly the size of Rhode Island – by 2050.

Why is this happening? The effect is partly due to natural subsidence: the soft soils of the coastal plain naturally shift and sink over time. But this phenomenon, at best, explains only a small fraction of the loss. The real culprits are human-made: Louisiana's vast network of levees, navigational channels, and oil-and-gas infrastructure. While all of these things are important to safety and commerce, their significant effects on Louisiana's wetlands required intense study, mitigation, and remediation.

The levee system accelerates coastal land loss by reducing the natural flow of a river's freshwater and sediment to wetland areas where lost land would then naturally be replenished. Instead, that valuable water and sediment is funneled down the Mississippi and shot into the Gulf, toward the outer continental shelf, where the formation of barrier islands is impossible.

Louisiana's coastal plain is crisscrossed with a vast matrix of navigational canals, including ten major navigational channels and literally thousands of smaller access canals serving navigation, allowing oil rig access, and cradling oil and gas pipelines. This network severely disrupts the natural flow of water and nutrients in wetland areas, isolating and starving them. The major navigational channels pose their own special threat to flood control by sometimes acting as "hurricane highways," allowing storms to sweep inland, past marshland, like liquid bulldozers.

In the 1980s, prompted by scientific studies documenting Louisiana's land loss, local groups made up of environmentalists, shrimpers, scientists, and business people began pushing for plans to save what would later be called "America's Wetland." One result of such efforts was the federal Coastal Wetlands Planning, Protection and Restoration Act of 1990 (the "Breaux Act"), which created a federal and state task force to implement wetlands restoration projects with annual funds of around $40 million. Although the projects saved hundreds of acres of wetlands, advocates soon realized that a $40 million program was insufficient. A much more ambitious plan was needed if the coast would ever be saved.

In 1998, state and federal agencies, with the participation of a diverse group of local churches, scientists, environmentalists, and fishermen, developed a book-length plan called "Coast 2050: Toward a Sustainable Coastal Louisiana," which offered a host of ecosystem restoration strategies. The underlying principles of the Coast 2050 Plan were to restore or mimic the natural processes that built and maintained coastal Louisiana. The complete plan, to be implemented over the next 50 years carried a price tag of $14 billion, more than twice as much as the Everglades restoration project (nearly $8 billion) and about the same as Boston's new underground highway, "The Big Dig." Though expensive, Coast 2050 actually seemed a bargain, considering the costs of doing nothing threatened to exceed $100 billion in lost jobs, lost infrastructure, lost fishing, and increased hurricane damage.

But Coast 2050 was never funded. In 2004, hamstrung by climbing deficits, the White House demanded, under pressure from the Office of Management and Budget and the Council for Environmental Quality, that the Corps lower its sights and propose a scaled-down 10 year plan that focused only on a few projects that would cost between $1 to 2 billion.

Still, state officials had hopes of securing more funds to restore the wetlands' storm-shielding capabilities. Louisiana Governor Kathleen Blanco pleaded with the federal government to grant her state "just a fraction" of the $5 billion it annually received from oil and gases leases on the outer continental shelf off of Louisiana's coast. Louisiana, of course, never received a greater share of oil and gas royalties for wetlands protection. In the end, it did not even receive the anticipated $1 to 2 billion. The President's 2005 Energy Bill provided only $540 million for Louisiana's coastal restoration over four years. In the wake of the current disaster, it is time to renew the promise of Coast 2050, completely funding it.

NOTES

1. There is only a limited empirical basis for determining the protective effect of coastal wetlands in storms. There is also some evidence from Hur-

ricane Katrina that levees protected by wetlands were better able to survive wave action. Thus, besides coastal wetlands, more urban ones may also be significant.

Some supportive evidence about wetlands comes from the 2004 tsunami:

> The scale of the 26 December 2004 Indian Ocean tsunami was almost unprecedented. In areas with the maximum tsunami intensity, little could have prevented catastrophic coastal destruction. Further away, however, areas with coastal tree vegetation were markedly less damaged than areas without. Mangrove forests are the most important coastal tree vegetation in the area and are one of the world's most threatened tropical ecosystems.
>
> Measurement of wave forces and modeling of fluid dynamics suggest that tree vegetation may shield coastlines from tsunami damage by reducing wave amplitude and energy. * * *
>
> Our results suggest that mangroves and *Casuarina* plantations attenuated tsunami-induced waves and protected shorelines against damage. * * * Conserving or replanting coastal mangroves and greenbelts should buffer communities from future tsunami events.

Finn Danielsen et al., *The Asian Tsunami: A Protective Role for Coastal Vegetation,* 310 SCIENCE 643 (2005).

2. The federal government can control development of wetlands under section 404 of the Clean Water Act. There has been considerable controversy over the scope of this jurisdiction. In United States v. Riverside Bayview Homes, Inc., 474 U.S. 121 (1985), the Court held that federal jurisdiction extended to wetlands that are adjacent to navigable waters or their tributaries. In Solid Waste Agency v. U.S. Army Corps of Engineers, 531 U.S. 159 (2001), the Court held that the statute did not apply to "isolated" wetlands that are not linked to navigable waters; the Court intimated that it might exceed Congress's power under the Constitution to regulate those wetlands.

3. In Chapter 7, we will consider plans to restore the Louisiana wetlands in more detail as part of our discussion of rebuilding.

C. LAND USE CONTROLS

Perhaps the most effective way of preventing disaster is to stay out of the danger zone. Land use controls can prevent development in disaster-prone areas such as flood plains or along major tectonic faults. However, this is easier said than done, given the realities of a market economy. For this reason, it is helpful to begin by looking at how a nonmarket economy has approached the task.

MARTHA THOMPSON & IZASKUN GAVIRIA, OXFAMAMERICA, WEATHERING THE STORM: LESSONS IN RISK REDUCTION FROM CUBA

http://www.oxfamamerica.org/newsandpublications
/publications/research_reports/pdfs/cuba_hur_eng.pdf
(Apr. 2004), 6–26.

Cuba is a small and poor country whose geographical location gives it a high and recurrent risk of hurricanes. In the seven years between 1996 and 2002, six major hurricanes have hit Cuba, yet a total of only 16 people have died (see Table 1). By comparison, when Hurricane Isabel hit the mid-Atlantic United States in September 2003, it alone was directly responsible for 22 deaths and indirectly responsible for 6 deaths (AP 2003). The question fairly posed is: What is Cuba doing right in terms of disaster mitigation and preparedness?

There is no "secret" to Cuba's success. Instead, the nation's exceptional dedication of risk reduction incorporation into its structures and risk consciousness can and should be studied for lessons learned and for opportunities to replicate its life-saving strategies. Today, the number of people affected by disasters worldwide is increasing; many of those affected are people from the global south (IFRC 2002, 10). In that light, it is imperative to share strategies and successes in risk reduction among nations whose populations are most affected by these hazards. Cuba's experience is an extremely valuable case from which to extract lessons that can (and have already) reduced the loss of life, even in a world that faces increasingly frequent, violent, and often unpredictable natural disasters.

This report examines the Cuban experience from three angles:

- Analyzing the elements of Cuba's model of risk reduction.
- "Unpacking" the Cuban model to examine its components and their effectiveness.
- Investigating elements that can be cultivated from the Cuban experience and shared with other Southern countries trying to improve disaster preparedness. This report focuses on adapting elements of the Cuban model to Central America, but obviously it is equally possible to adapt elements of the model in many other regions or countries.

* * *

Hurricane season in the Caribbean officially begins every year on June 1st and ends on November 30th. Hurricanes are part of Cuba's geographic destiny; Cuba lies right across the mouth of the Gulf of Mexico, directly in the path of any hurricane aiming toward the Gulf. Hurricanes crossing Central America also often head toward Cuba. Hundreds of deaths have been attributed to hurricanes in Cuba over the years, as recorded in the Cuban national archives. According to the National Hurricane Center meteorological records show that hurricanes are occurring increasingly often and with increasing intensity in the Atlantic Basin where Cuba lies. Out of a total of 240 hurricanes from 1983 to 2003 in the basin, 111 occurred between 1984 and 1993 while 129 occurred between 1994 and 2003 (See Figure 1). However, through their development of risk reduction, the Cuban government and people have prevented the recurring hazard of hurricanes from continuing to bring the same disastrous consequences in terms of loss of human life.

Hurricanes affecting Cuba from 1996-2002

NOTE: *Hurricanes Lili and Isidore passed over the western provinces of Cuba within a period of 10 days. Hurricane damage assessment calculated the two disasters together.

HURRICANE	MONTH / YEAR	CATE-GORY	DEATHS	PEOPLE EVACU-ATED	HOMES DE-STROYED	HOMES DAMAGED
Lili	10/2002	2	1	165,830	5,640*	50,855*
Isidore	09/2002	2	0	280,000	5,640*	50,855*
Michelle	11/2001	4	5	712,000	8,700	90,000
Irene	10/1999	1	4	162,664	224	3,000
Georges	10/1998	3-4	6	818,000	2,100	40,000
Lili	09/1996	3	0	200,000	2,922	22,066

Only 16 people have been killed by the six hurricanes that hit Cuba from 1996-2002. These low death rates are especially remarkable when placed into the context of Cuba's economic crisis, constraints on transportation and other resources, and the almost annual occurrence of a hurricane over the past seven years.

These hurricane mortality rates become even more remarkable when compared with the totals of neighbors in Central America, the Caribbean, and even the United States. 1996 was a record year for hurricanes in the Atlantic Basin as 150 people died throughout the region (NHC 1996). In the same year, at the height of the economic crisis in Cuba, there were no hurricane deaths despite category 3 Hurricane Lili hitting the island in October. When Hurricane Georges hit Cuba in 1998, six people were killed; Georges killed 597 people in the rest of the Caribbean, mainly Haiti and the Dominican Republic (NHC 1998). Table 2 provides a comparison of death rates in Cuba and other countries by hurricane:

HURRI-CANE AND YEAR	CATEGORY WHEN IT HIT CUBA	FATALI-TIES IN CUBA	CATEGORY WHEN IT HIT ELSEWHERE	FATALITIES ELSEWHERE	TOTAL OF FATALI-TIES
Lili 2002	2	1	Tropical Storm	Jamaica 4, Haiti 4, St. Vincent 4	13
Isidore 2002	2	0		US 4, Mexico 2	6
Michelle 2000	4	5	Tropical Depression	Honduras 6, Nicaragua 4, Jamaica 2	17
Irene 1999	1	4	1	US 8	12
Georges 1998	3-4	6	3-4	Antigua 2, St. Kitts & Nevis 4, Dom. Rep. 380, Haiti 209, Bahamas 1, US 1	603
Lili 1996	3	0		Honduras 5, Costa Rica 3, Great Britain 6	14
Total of fatalities	15-16	16		649	665

Hurricane Michelle in 2001 is a good example of Cuba's disaster preparedness in action. Hurricane Michelle was one of only seven Category 4 hurricanes of the 240 that have hit the Atlantic basin between 1983 and 2003 (NHC 1983-2003). This was the worst hurricane to affect Cuba since 1944. Hurricane Michelle made landfall with winds of 216 km/hr at the Bay of Pigs on Cuba's southern coast. Traveling north across the island, the storm eventually caused heavy damage to homes (22,400 damaged; 2,800 destroyed), agriculture, industry, and infrastructure in five provinces, including the City of Havana. In all, only five deaths were reported. By contrast, a few days earlier, when Michelle had traveled through Central America as a tropical depression, 36 people were killed or reported missing.

The Cuban government has put a number of national institutions and mechanisms in place for disaster mitigation in the case of any emergency. These institutions and mechanisms are quite comprehensive and not limited to mitigating hurricanes. Several entities that contribute to disaster mitigation, such as the Institute for Physical Planning, are also part of the vision of sustainable development in the country. Their efforts correspond to several important aspects of good governance for risk reduction cited in the "golden dozen." The most fundamental of these is the political commitment on the part of the government to safeguard human lives, but other key aspects of good governance demonstrated in disaster mitigation in Cuba are:

- The laws, regulations and directives that specifically address disaster mitigation, preparedness and response.
- Investments in economic development that explicitly take potential consequences for risk reduction or increase into account. To be effective, the commitment to regulate and enforce planning for physical vulnerability has to extend to economic development.
- Investment in institutional capital (e.g. capable, accountable, and transparent government institutions for mitigating disasters). Land use regulations, building codes and hazard-proof infrastructure are key to disaster mitigation. Once they are on the books, they are only effective if there is government commitment to their enforcement.
- Investment in human development and institutional capacity for research on hazards and research reduction is critical.

a. Legal Framework

Cuba's legal framework is one of its key assets in risk reduction. The country's disaster mitigation, preparedness, response, and recovery measures and structures are enshrined in law, and those laws are enforced. The most important legislation approved the formation and organization of the Cuban National Civil Defense (DCN) in 1966. A 1976 mandate requires that all adult citizens receive civil defense training. More recently (in 1994), National Defense Law 75 was passed. In 1997, Legal Decree 170 was passed to complement the important 1976 law. Legal Decree 170 specifically describes the goal of protecting the population, the economy, and the environment from the destructive effects of natural disasters and other types of catastrophes through a combination of prevention, preparedness, response, and recuperation.

In sum, the legal framework sets up a blueprint for prevention, mitigation, preparation and action in times of emergency. The High Command of the Cuban National Civil Defense is charged by law with overseeing Cuba's compliance with measures of civil defense and all relationships with international aid and cooperation in times of disasters. The laws, particularly legal decree 170, detail the role of the ministries, social organizations, and all public entities in case of emergency, including the use of their resources. The law also defines the four phases of emergency mobilization: information, alert, alarm, and recovery.

Finally, the laws define a centralized decision-making structure during the emergency: the High Command of the National Civil Defense in consultation with the President of the Republic through the Minister of the Armed

Forces. These laws also lay out decision-making (the enactment of different phases and measures) by local authorities when circumstances so require.
* * *

b. Physical Planning and Land Use Regulations

Physical planning and land use regulations have been created in the Cuban legal system and are firmly embedded in governmental structures. The Institute of Physical Planning (IPF) and the National Housing Institute (INV) are two government institutes in the Ministry of Planning whose work addresses hazard resistant planning and reducing physical vulnerability in all construction and physical planning projects in the country.

The Institute of Physical Planning (IPF)   The IPF is in charge of formulating, implementing, and monitoring physical planning policies as well as creating the corresponding regulations and measures. The goal of IPF's physical planning policies and regulations is to reduce the technical vulnerability of physical structures. Any national or international individual or entity planning to build anything—be it a store or a dam—needs IPF approval before construction begins. The plans must fulfill the Institute's criteria for reduction of technical vulnerability. Once the IPF approves a project, it is also responsible for monitoring its development. In addition, the IPF designates the levels of risk for settlement of coastal areas, riversides, hillsides, etc., which determine whether or not populations may occupy them. A clear priority for human safety is placed over unbridled economic development.

A special physical planning commission within the IPF is designated to manage land use, natural resources, and economic and environmental transformations in areas of high vulnerability. The commission's work led to a 1995 agreement to decrease the vulnerability of high-risk areas in Havana by protecting aging structures and raising new construction above sea level.

National Institute of Housing   The INV Institute leads housing construction in the country. Once a disaster hits, the INV coordinates with the provincial and municipal authorities, the Civil Defense, and the Ministry of Economy and Planning to evaluate residential damages. The Institute decides which houses need to be rebuilt, which should be structurally strengthened, and which repaired. INV municipal and provincial employees design a working plan for every house affected, allocating the distribution of the scarce resources. Unfortunately, the scarcity of building materials severely limits initiatives by the Institute and other authorities to improve structures.

c. Measures to Prevent Overpopulation of High Risk Areas

The global south's rapid urbanization in the past few decades translates into large numbers of poor people living in high-risk areas. Cuba has historically addressed this issue by developing rural areas and making services accessible enough to slow the population from migrating and overwhelming the cities. Government commitment to rural development was a fundamental objective of revolutionary policy in 1959, and development in the countryside has dramatically improved over the past forty years. Government policy also seeks to create employment opportunities for professionals in the countryside so that sons and daughters of rural farmers who gain education and professional degrees have the possibility of obtaining professional employment in their home areas.

The government closely monitors high-risk areas in the country with existing population. Levels of risk in these areas are periodically measured and evaluated. According to the High Command of the National Defense, 2,137,000 of 11 million people in Cuba are classified as "vulnerable population living in high-risk areas," as shown below in Table 3.

TABLE 3   Vulnerable Population in Cuba.

NUMBER OF PEOPLE	HAZARD TO WHICH THEY ARE VULNERABLE
902,000	Dams or reservoirs breaking or overflowing
650,000	Partial or total collapse of residence/building
540,000	Flooding
45,000	Mudslides
Total: 2,137,000	

With the constant threat of hurricanes, the National Civil Defense pays particular attention to communities that are classified as vulnerable to coastal flooding. Special attention is given to those situated less than one meter above sea level or within 1,000 meters of the sea.

NOTES

1. The Cuban example suggests that rigorous control of land use can be a valuable mitigation technique. However, in a more open society, such land use control becomes more difficult. Local politicians may not be motivated to enact unpopular development restrictions. What kinds of incentives can the state and federal governments provide to encourage such restrictions?

2. Efforts at land use control have sometimes proved problematic. In 1993, a midwestern flood caused $16 billion in damage, leading to efforts to reduce infrastructure on floodplains. However, these efforts have not proved effective:

Since 1993, the amount of such infrastructure has increased dramatically: 28,000 new homes were built, population increased 23%, and 26.8 km^2 (6,630 acres) of commercial and industrial development were added on land that was inundated during the 1993 flood. In all, $2.2 billion in new development has occurred in the St. Louis area alone on land that was under water in 1993.

* * *

Thanks to Federal guidelines, buyouts, and enlightened management in many localities, successes in managing U.S. floodplains outnumber the failures. The problem is that when these measures succumb to local economic self-interest and development pressure, small local failures—like cracks in levees themselves—allow massive increases in floodplain infrastructure that can rob the nation of all the net improvements painstakingly won elsewhere. In spite of the lessons learned during the 1993 flood, the St. Louis region and selected other localities across the United States are seeing their floodplains disappear behind new and enlarged levees and under new urban and suburban development.

Nicholas Pinter, *One Step Forward, Two Steps Back on U.S. Floodplains*, 308 SCIENCE 207 (2005).

3. In the United States, property rights have a great deal of political weight. They also have some degree of constitutional protection. Blocking development can sometimes be an unconstitutional taking of property. Some background may be helpful in understanding the next three cases, which deal with that issue.

The Takings Clause of the Fifth Amendment provides that private property shall not "be taken for public use, without just compensation." The seminal decision was Pennsylvania Coal v. Mahon, 260 U.S. 393 (1922). This case involved a Pennsylvania statute making it unlawful for coal companies to cause the collapse or subsidence of any overlaying structure, such as a residence. In the case before the Court, the coal company contended that the effect would be to make mining completely infeasible, wiping out the value of the mining rights that they had purchased from the owner of the surface rights. In an opinion by Justice Holmes, the Court held that this was a taking of property because the statute had "very nearly the same effect for constitutional purposes as appropriating or destroying it." Since then, courts have struggled to determine when a regulation "goes too far" and becomes a taking. The most important modern case, Penn Central Transportation Co. v. New York, 438 U.S. 104 (1978), attempted to provide a synthesis of the law. According to *Penn Central*, except where a regulation physically invades property (as by providing public access), the test is whether the regulation unreasonably "interfered with distinct investment-backed expectations." In the following case, however, the Court attempted to provide more of a bright-line test.

LUCAS V. SOUTH CAROLINA COASTAL COUNCIL

Supreme Court of the United States, 1992.
505 U.S. 1003, 112 S. Ct. 2886, 120 L. Ed.2d 798.

JUSTICE SCALIA delivered the opinion of the Court.

In 1986, petitioner David H. Lucas paid $975,000 for two residential lots on the Isle of Palms in Charleston County, South Carolina, on which he intended to build single-family homes. In 1988, however, the South Carolina Legislature enacted the Beachfront Management Act, which had the direct effect of barring petitioner from erecting any permanent habitable structures on his two parcels. A state trial court found that this prohibition rendered Lucas's parcels "valueless." This case requires us to decide whether the Act's dramatic effect on the economic value of Lucas's lots accomplished a taking of private property under the Fifth and Fourteenth Amendments requiring the payment of "just compensation."

* * *

[O]ur decision in *Mahon* [an early takings decision by Justice Holmes] offered little insight into when, and under what circumstances, a given regulation would be seen as going "too far" for purposes of the Fifth Amendment. In 70–odd years of succeeding "regulatory takings" jurisprudence, we have generally eschewed any " 'set formula' " for determining how far is too far, preferring to "engag[e] in * * * essentially ad hoc, factual inquiries." We have, however, described at least two discrete categories of regulatory action as compensable without case-specific inquiry into the public interest advanced in support of the restraint. The first encompasses regulations that compel the property owner to suffer a physical "invasion" of his property. * * *

The second situation in which we have found categorical treatment appropriate is where regulation denies all economically beneficial or productive use of land. As we have said on numerous occasions, the Fifth Amendment is violated when land-use regulation "does not substantially advance legitimate state interests *or denies an owner economically viable use of his land.*"[4]

---

4. Regrettably, the rhetorical force of our "deprivation of all economically feasible use" rule is greater than its precision, since the rule does not make clear the "property interest" against which the loss of value is to be measured. When, for example, a regulation requires a developer to leave 90% of a rural tract in its natural state, it is unclear whether we would analyze the situation as one in which the owner has been deprived of all economically beneficial use of the burdened portion of the tract, or as one in which the owner has suffered a mere diminution in value of the tract as a whole. (For an extreme—and, we think, unsupportable—view of the relevant calculus, see Penn Central Transportation Co. v. New York City, 42 N.Y.S.2d 324, 333–334, 397 N.Y.S.2d 914, 920, 366 N.E.2d 1271, 1276–1277 (1977), aff'd, 438 U.S. 104, 98 S. Ct. 2646, 57 L.Ed.2d 631 (1978), where the state court examined the diminution in a particular parcel's value produced by a municipal ordinance in light of total value of the taking claimant's other holdings in the vicinity.) Unsurprisingly, this uncertainty regarding the composition of the denominator in our "deprivation" fraction has produced inconsistent pronouncements by the Court. The answer to this difficult question may lie in how the owner's reasonable expectations have been shaped by the State's law of property—i.e., whether and to what degree the State's law has accorded legal recognition and protection to the particular interest in land with respect to which the takings claimant alleges a diminution in (or elimination of) value. In any event, we avoid this difficulty in the present case, since the "interest in land" that Lucas has pleaded (a fee simple interest) is an estate with a rich tradition of protection at common law, and since the South

We have never set forth the justification for this rule. Perhaps it is simply, as Justice Brennan suggested, that total deprivation of beneficial use is, from the landowner's point of view, the equivalent of a physical appropriation. * * * Surely, at least, in the extraordinary circumstance when *no* productive or economically beneficial use of land is permitted, it is less realistic to indulge our usual assumption that the legislature is simply "adjusting the benefits and burdens of economic life," [*Penn Central*], in a manner that secures an "average reciprocity of advantage" to everyone concerned. And the *functional* basis for permitting the government, by regulation, to affect property values without compensation—that "Government hardly could go on if to some extent values incident to property could not be diminished without paying for every such change in the general law"—does not apply to the relatively rare situations where the government has deprived a landowner of all economically beneficial uses.

On the other side of the balance, affirmatively supporting a compensation requirement, is the fact that regulations that leave the owner of land without economically beneficial or productive options for its use—typically, as here, by requiring land to be left substantially in its natural state—carry with them a heightened risk that private property is being pressed into some form of public service under the guise of mitigating serious public harm. *See, e.g.,* Annicelli v. South Kingstown, 463 A.2d 133, 140–141 (R.I. 1983) (prohibition on construction adjacent to beach justified on twin grounds of safety and "conservation of open space"); Morris County Land Improvement Co. v. Parsippany–Troy Hills Township, 40 N.J. 539, 552–553, 193 A.2d 232, 240 (1963) (prohibition on filling marshlands imposed in order to preserve region as water detention basin and create wildlife refuge). As Justice Brennan explained: "From the government's point of view, the benefits flowing to the public from preservation of open space through regulation may be equally great as from creating a wildlife refuge through formal condemnation or increasing electricity production through a dam project that floods private property." The many statutes on the books, both state and federal, that provide for the use of eminent domain to impose servitudes on private scenic lands preventing developmental uses, or to acquire such lands altogether, suggest the practical equivalence in this setting of negative regulation and appropriation.

We think, in short, that there are good reasons for our frequently expressed belief that when the owner of real property has been called upon to sacrifice *all* economically beneficial uses in the name of the common good, that is, to leave his property economically idle, he has suffered a taking.
* * *

It is correct that many of our prior opinions have suggested that "harmful or noxious uses" of property may be proscribed by government regulation without the requirement of compensation. For a number of reasons, however, we think the South Carolina Supreme Court was too quick to conclude that that principle decides the present case. The "harmful or noxious uses" princi-

---

Carolina Court of Common Pleas found that the Beachfront Management Act left each of Lucas's beachfront lots without economic value.

ple was the Court's early attempt to describe in theoretical terms why government may, consistent with the Takings Clause, affect property values by regulation without incurring an obligation to compensate—a reality we nowadays acknowledge explicitly with respect to the full scope of the State's police power. * * *

The transition from our early focus on control of "noxious" uses to our contemporary understanding of the broad realm within which government may regulate without compensation was an easy one, since the distinction between "harm-preventing" and "benefit-conferring" regulation is often in the eye of the beholder. It is quite possible, for example, to describe in *either* fashion the ecological, economic, and aesthetic concerns that inspired the South Carolina legislature in the present case. One could say that imposing a servitude on Lucas's land is necessary in order to prevent his use of it from "harming" South Carolina's ecological resources; or, instead, in order to achieve the "benefits" of an ecological preserve. Whether one or the other of the competing characterizations will come to one's lips in a particular case depends primarily upon one's evaluation of the worth of competing uses of real estate. * * *

Where the State seeks to sustain regulation that deprives land of all economically beneficial use, we think it may resist compensation only if the logically antecedent inquiry into the nature of the owner's estate shows that the proscribed use interests were not part of his title to begin with.[5] This accords, we think, with our "takings" jurisprudence, which has traditionally been guided by the understandings of our citizens regarding the content of, and the State's power over, the "bundle of rights" that they acquire when they obtain title to property. It seems to us that the property owner necessarily expects the uses of his property to be restricted, from time to time, by various measures newly enacted by the State in legitimate exercise of its police powers; "[a]s long recognized, some values are enjoyed under an implied limitation and must yield to the police power." [*Mahon.*] And in the case of personal property, by reason of the State's traditionally high degree of control over commercial dealings, he ought to be aware of the possibility that new regulation might even render his property economically worthless (at least if the property's only economically productive use is sale or manufacture for sale). In the case of land, however, we think the notion pressed by the Council that title is somehow held subject to the "implied limitation" that the State may

---

5. Drawing on our First Amendment jurisprudence, Justice Stevens would "loo[k] to the *generality* of a regulation of property" to determine whether compensation is owing. The Beach-front Management Act is general, in his view, because it "regulates the use of the coastline of the entire state." There may be some validity to the principle Justice Stevens proposes, but it does not properly apply to the present case. The equivalent of a law of general application that inhibits the practice of religion without being aimed at religion, is a law that destroys the value of land without being aimed at land. Perhaps such a law—the generally applicable criminal prohibition on the manufacturing of alcoholic beverages challenged in *Mugler* [v. Kansas, 123 U.S. 623, 8 S. Ct. 273, 31 L. Ed. 205 (1887)] (1887), comes to mind—cannot constitute a compensable taking. But a regulation *specifically directed to land use* no more acquires immunity by plundering landowners generally than does a law specifically directed at religious practice acquire immunity by prohibiting all religions. Justice Stevens' approach renders the Takings Clause little more than a particularized restatement of the Equal Protection Clause.

subsequently eliminate all economically valuable use is inconsistent with the historical compact recorded in the Takings Clause that has become part of our constitutional culture.

* * *

It seems unlikely that common-law principles would have prevented the erection of any habitable or productive improvements on petitioner's land; they rarely support prohibition of the "essential use" of land. The question, however, is one of state law to be dealt with on remand. We emphasize that to win its case South Carolina must do more than proffer the legislature's declaration that the uses Lucas desires are inconsistent with the public interest, or the conclusory assertion that they violate a common-law maxim such as *sic utere tuo ut alienum non laedas.* As we have said, a "State, by *ipse dixit,* may not transform private property into public property without compensation * * *." Instead, as it would be required to do if it sought to restrain Lucas in a common-law action for public nuisance, South Carolina must identify background principles of nuisance and property law that prohibit the uses he now intends in the circumstances in which the property is presently found. Only on this showing can the State fairly claim that, in proscribing all such beneficial uses, the Beachfront Management Act is taking nothing.[6]

JUSTICE KENNEDY, concurring in the judgment.

In my view, reasonable expectations must be understood in light of the whole of our legal tradition. The common law of nuisance is too narrow a confine for the exercise of regulatory power in a complex and interdependent society. The State should not be prevented from enacting new regulatory initiatives in response to changing conditions, and courts must consider all reasonable expectations whatever their source. The Takings Clause does not require a static body of state property law; it protects private expectations to ensure private investment. I agree with the Court that nuisance prevention accords with the most common expectations of property owners who face regulation, but I do not believe this can be the sole source of state authority to impose severe restrictions. Coastal property may present such unique concerns for a fragile land system that the State can go further in regulating its development and use than the common law of nuisance might otherwise permit.

The Supreme Court of South Carolina erred, in my view, by reciting the general purposes for which the state regulations were enacted without a determination that they were in accord with the owner's reasonable expectations and therefore sufficient to support a severe restriction on specific parcels of property. The promotion of tourism, for instance, ought not to suffice to deprive specific property of all value without a corresponding duty to compensate. Furthermore, the means as well as the ends of regulation must accord with the owner's reasonable expectations. Here, the State did not act until after the property had been zoned for individual lot development and

---

6. * * * We stress that an affirmative decree eliminating all economically beneficial uses may be defended only if an *objectively reasonable application* of relevant precedents would exclude those beneficial uses in the circumstances in which the land is presently found.

most other parcels had been improved, throwing the whole burden of the regulation on the remaining lots. This too must be measured in the balance.

JUSTICE BLACKMUN, dissenting.

[T]he Court justifies its new rule that the legislature may not deprive a property owner of the only economically valuable use of his land, even if the legislature finds it to be a harmful use, because such action is not part of the "long recognized" "understandings of our citizens." These "understandings" permit such regulation only if the use is a nuisance under the common law. Any other course is "inconsistent with the historical compact recorded in the Takings Clause." It is not clear from the Court's opinion where our "historical compact" or "citizens' understanding" comes from, but it does not appear to be history.

The principle that the State should compensate individuals for property taken for public use was not widely established in America at the time of the Revolution. * * *

Even into the 19th century, state governments often felt free to take property for roads and other public projects without paying compensation to the owners. As one court declared in 1802, citizens "were bound to contribute as much of [land], as by the laws of the country, were deemed necessary for the public convenience." * * *

* * *

In short, I find no clear and accepted "historical compact" or "understanding of our citizens" justifying the Court's new taking doctrine. Instead, the Court seems to treat history as a grab-bag of principles, to be adopted where they support the Court's theory, and ignored where they do not. If the Court decided that the early common law provides the background principles for interpreting the Taking Clause, then regulation, as opposed to physical confiscation, would not be compensable. If the Court decided that the law of a later period provides the background principles, then regulation might be compensable, but the Court would have to confront the fact that legislatures regularly determined which uses were prohibited, independent of the common law, and independent of whether the uses were lawful when the owner purchased. What makes the Court's analysis unworkable is its attempt to package the law of two incompatible eras and peddle it as historical fact.

JUSTICE STEVENS, dissenting.

In considering Lucas' claim, the generality of the Beachfront Management Act is significant. The Act does not target particular landowners, but rather regulates the use of the coastline of the entire State. Indeed, South Carolina's Act is best understood as part of a national effort to protect the coastline, one initiated by the Federal Coastal Zone Management Act of 1972. * * * Moreover, the Act did not single out owners of undeveloped land. The Act also prohibited owners of developed land from rebuilding if their structures were destroyed, and what is equally significant, from repairing erosion control devices, such as seawalls. In addition, in some situations, owners of developed land were required to "renouris[h] the beach * * * on a yearly basis with an amount * * * of sand * * * not * * * less than one and one-half times the yearly volume of sand lost due to erosion." In short, the South Carolina

Act imposed substantial burdens on owners of developed and undeveloped land alike. This generality indicates that the Act is not an effort to expropriate owners of undeveloped land.

Admittedly, the economic impact of this regulation is dramatic and petitioner's investment-backed expectations are substantial. Yet, if anything, the costs to and expectations of the owners of developed land are even greater: I doubt, however, that the cost to owners of developed land of renourishing the beach and allowing their seawalls to deteriorate effects a taking. The costs imposed on the owners of undeveloped land, such as petitioner, differ from these costs only in degree, not in kind.

NOTES

1. After Hurricane Hugo, so many structures were damaged in the area that the state relented on its ban on rebuilding existing houses. After further negotiations, South Carolina eventually bought the lots for over $1.5 million. The area has been flooded many times since the Supreme Court's ruling, and the inhabitants have constructed walls of two-ton and three-ton sandbags. Carol M. Rose, *The Story of* Lucas: *Environmental Land Use Regulation Between Developers and the Deep Blue Sea*, in RICHARD J. LAZARUS & OLIVER A. HOUCK, ENVIRONMENTAL LAW STORIES 268-269 (2005).

2. One noteworthy aspect of *Lucas* is Justice Scalia's use of a narrowly construed "nuisance exception," at least in total takings cases. This is in sharp contrast to the call by Byrne and others for an expansive new land ethic focusing on ecological interdependency. Justice Scalia's use of nuisance law has attracted attention from commentators, who have suggested that nuisance law has been far more fluid and adaptable than Scalia suggests.

D. INCENTIVES

The question of incentives has been in the background of much of our discussion of mitigation. This section considers the effort to use flood insurance to provide incentives for municipalities to impose land use controls and for landowners to engage in mitigation.

GAO, OVERSIGHT AND MANAGEMENT OF THE NATIONAL
FLOOD INSURANCE PROGRAM

http://www.gao.gov/new.items/do6183t.pdf (Oct. 20, 2005)

In reauthorizing the NFIP in 2004, Congress noted that "repetitive-loss properties"—those that had resulted in two or more flood insurance claims payments of $1,000 or more over 10 years—constituted a significant drain on the resources of the NFIP. These repetitive loss properties are problematic not only because of their vulnerability to flooding but also because of the costs of repeatedly repairing flood damages. While these properties make up only about 1 percent of the properties insured under the NFIP, they account for 25 to 30 percent of all claims losses. At the time of our March 2004 report on repetitive-loss properties, nearly half of all nationwide repetitive loss property insurance payments had been made in Louisiana, Texas, and Florida. According to a recent Congressional Research Service report, as of December 31, 2004, FEMA had identified 11,706 "severe repetitive-loss" properties defined as those with four or more claims or two or three losses that exceeded the insured value of the property. Of these 11,706 properties almost half (49 percent) were in three states—3,208 (27 percent) in Louisiana, 1,573 (13 percent) in Texas, and 1,034 (9 percent) in New Jersey.

As the destruction caused by horrendous 2004 and 2005 hurricanes are a driving force for improving the NFIP today, devastating natural disasters in the 1960s were a primary reason for the national interest in creating a federal flood insurance program. In 1963 and 1964, Hurricane Betsy and other hurricanes caused extensive damage in the South, and, in 1965, heavy flooding occurred on the upper Mississippi River. In studying insurance alternatives to disaster assistance for people suffering property losses in floods, a flood insurance feasibility study found that premium rates in certain flood-prone areas could be extremely high. As a result, the National Flood Insurance Act of 1968, which created the NFIP, mandated that existing buildings in flood-risk areas would receive subsidies on premiums because these structures were built before the flood risk was known and identified on flood insurance rate maps. Owners of structures built in flood-prone areas on or after the effective date of the first flood insurance rate maps in their areas or after December 31, 1974, would have to pay full actuarial rates. Because many repetitive-loss properties were built before either December 31, 1974, or the effective date of the first flood insurance rate maps in their areas, they were eligible for subsidized premium rates under provisions of the National Flood Insurance Act of 1968.

The provision of subsidized premiums encouraged communities to participate in the NFIP by adopting and agreeing to enforce state and community floodplain management regulations to reduce future flood damage. In April 2005, FEMA estimated that floodplain management regulations enforced by communities participating in the NFIP have prevented over $1.1 billion annually in flood damage. However, some of the properties that had received the initial rate subsidy are still in existence and subject to repetitive flood losses, thus placing a financial strain on the NFIP.

For over a decade, FEMA has pursued a variety of strategies to reduce the number of repetitive-loss properties in the NFIP. In a 2004 testimony, we noted that congressional proposals have been made to phase out coverage or begin charging full and actuarially based rates for repetitive-loss property owners who refuse to accept FEMA's offer to purchase or mitigate the effect of floods on these buildings. The 2004 Flood Insurance Reform Act created a

5-year pilot program to deal with repetitive-loss properties in the NFIP. In particular, the act authorized FEMA to provide financial assistance to participating states and communities to carry out mitigation activities or to purchase "severe repetitive loss properties." During the pilot program, policyholders who refuse a mitigation or purchase offer that meets program requirements will be required to pay increased premium rates. In particular, the premium rates for these policyholders would increase by 150% following their refusal and another 150% following future claims of more than $1,500. However, the rates charged cannot exceed the applicable actuarial rate.

It will be important in future studies of the NFIP to continue to analyze data on progress being made to reduce the inventory of subsidized NFIP repetitive-loss properties, how the reduction of this inventory contributes to the financial stability of the program, and whether additional FEMA regulatory steps or congressional actions could contribute to the financial solvency of the NFIP, while meeting commitments made by the authorizing legislation.

In 1973 and 1974, Congress enacted requirements for mandatory purchase of NFIP policies by some property owners in high-risk areas. From 1968 until the adoption of the Flood Disaster Protection Act of 1973, the purchase of flood insurance was voluntary. However, because voluntary participation in the NFIP was low and many flood victims did not have insurance to repair damages from floods in the early 1970s, the 1973 act required the mandatory purchase of flood insurance to cover some structures in special flood hazard areas of communities participating in the program. Homeowners with mortgages from federally regulated lenders on property in communities identified to be in special flood hazard areas are required to purchase flood insurance on their dwellings for the amount of their outstanding mortgage balance, up to a maximum of $250,000 in coverage for single-family homes. The owners of properties with no mortgages or properties with mortgages held by lenders who are not federally regulated were not, and still are not, required to buy flood insurance, even if the properties are in special flood hazard areas—the areas NFIP flood maps identify as having the highest risk of flooding. FEMA determines flood risk and actuarial ratings on properties through flood insurance rate mapping and other considerations including the elevation of the lowest floor of the building, the type of building, the number of floors, and whether or not the building has a basement, among zones. For example, areas subject to damage by waves and storm surge are in zones with the highest expectation for flood loss.

Between 1973 and 1994, many policyholders continued to find it easy to drop policies, even if the policies were required by lenders. Federal agency lenders and regulators did not appear to strongly enforce the mandatory flood insurance purchase requirements. According to a recent Congressional Research Service study, the Midwest flood of 1993 highlighted this problem and reinforced the idea that reforms were needed to compel lender compliance with the requirements of the 1973 Act. In response, Congress passed the National Flood Insurance Reform Act of 1994. Under the 1994 law, if the property owner failed to get the required coverage, lenders were required to purchase flood insurance on their behalf and then bill the property owners. Lenders became subject to civil monetary penalties for not enforcing the mandatory purchase requirement.

In June 2002, we reported that the extent to which lenders were enforcing the mandatory purchase requirement was unknown. Officials involved with the flood insurance program developed contrasting viewpoints about whether lenders were complying with the flood insurance purchase requirements primarily because the officials used differing types of data to reach their conclusions. Federal bank regulators and lenders based their belief that lenders were generally complying with the NFIP's purchase requirements on regulators' examinations and reviews conducted to monitor and verify lender compliance. In contrast, FEMA officials believed that many lenders frequently were not complying with the requirements, which was an opinion based largely on noncompliance estimates computed from data on mortgages, flood zones, and insurance policies; limited studies on compliance; and anecdotal evidence indicating that insurance was not always in place where required. Neither side, however, was able to substantiate its differing claims with statistically sound data that provide a nationwide perspective on lender compliance.

NOTES

1. For further discussion of the problem of repeated claimants, see Congressional Research Service, Federal Flood Insurance: The Repetitive-Loss Problem (June 30, 2005).
2. The flood insurance program seems to have had only limited success in providing incentives to mitigate, and to some extent it may have encouraged landowners to remain in dangerous areas. Is the problem incurable or simply an aspect of moral hazard inherent in any compensation program?
3. What about stronger incentives for lenders? For example, the law might provide that a lender who failed to require flood insurance would lose the benefit of the mortgage to the extent of any flood damage. In effect, the lender would be forced to "insure" the property up to the value of its mortgage. Would this be effective or too draconian?
4. The mitigation system clearly seems to be broken. Consider the following recommendations for improvement:

> Mitigation practice could be strengthened through "accountable devolution" of responsibility and authority to states and localities. Under this approach, FEMA's role would be to create incentives and tools for effective performance, to assist state and local mitigation agencies in planning and carrying out mitigation strategies, and to evaluate the outcomes in light of national standards. . . . [FEMA] would focus on helping to reduce cumulative vulnerability to risk through implementation of comprehensive

federal, state, and local pre- and post-disaster mitigation plans and strategies. Its regional teams would play a vital role in building state and local mitigation commitment and capacity.

Three practice changes could make a lot of difference. Provision of hazard information for state and local mitigation planning would help to overcome this Achilles' heel of present practice. Requiring regional-scale mitigation plans would extend the vision of planners and decision makers beyond their jurisdiction to include the complete natural system that spawns the hazard risks. And issuing best practice manuals would help inspire and educate mitigation planners in large and small agencies across the country as well as save them time and money.

DAVID R. GODSCHALK ET AL., NATURAL HAZARD MITIGATION: RECASTING DISASTER POLICY AND PLANNING 545 (1999).

7

REBUILDING NEW ORLEANS

After the flood has happened, the task becomes rebuilding. We must then confront a host of questions: Should we rebuild New Orleans, and if so, how much of the old city should be restored? How should **land uses** be changed from residential to other uses? How can the city be protected from a repeat of Katrina? Who will live in the "new" New Orleans, and what will happen to the people who never return? This chapter confronts some of those issues.

A. WHY REBUILD? HOW MUCH?

The first question is obviously whether to rebuild at all. Would it be better to simply maintain the port facility, or the tourist destinations, or the above-sea level parts and abandon the rest of the city? What would abandoning the rest of New Orleans mean for former residents? Consider the contrasting views in the following excerpts.

ROBERT W. HAHN, THE ECONOMICS OF REBUILDING CITIES: REFLECTIONS AFTER KATRINA

The Economists' Voice Vol. 2 [2005], No. 4, Article 1 (at http://www.bepress.com/ev/vol2/iss4/art1)

No doubt, the United States has the capacity to respond quickly and decisively to catastrophe. Yet, in the horrible aftermath of Katrina—particularly given what may be in store in an era of terrorism and weapons of mass destruction—we ought to pause to ask a question before spending billions on repairs: Is it always worth rebuilding a city after nature (or an enemy) wreaks havoc? The answer, I would argue, is not as obvious as it might first seem.

Until recently, even asking this question appeared to be politically verboten. Then, House Speaker Dennis Hastert did the unthinkable. He created a ruckus by suggesting the issue of rebuilding New Orleans is "a question that certainly we should ask." While the Speaker received a stinging rebuke from former Louisiana Senator John Breaux, he was right to raise the issue.

The cost to rebuild the city could top 75 billion dollars. According to the *Wall Street Journal*, disaster relief and rebuilding costs for the entire region could be twice that amount. With that much money at stake, decision makers should ask whether the gargantuan project represents the best possible use of taxpayer dollars. To make that assessment, they need a framework for decision making and some data on costs and benefits.

The Basic Framework

The economists' framework provides a useful starting point: select policies that will maximize or increase net benefits—defined as economic benefits less costs. One way of increasing net benefits is to get people to take into account both the private and social cost of their decisions. This clearly has not been the case in places like New Orleans, where the federal government foots the bill for a major part of the flood protection system, subsidizes flood insurance, and hands out cash cards after the disaster. More generally, if insurance for disasters related to hurricanes, earthquakes, and even terrorist-prone regions is subsidized, we can expect inefficiencies following from too many people choosing to live in high-risk areas.

Of course, sometimes the government should intervene in markets. For example, providing some liability protection for firms manufacturing anti-terrorist devices after 9-11 may have been sensible. But the onus should generally be on those favoring intervention to show why the benefits are likely to justify the costs.

Toting up Benefits and Costs

The first priority is to weigh the desirability of varying degrees of government commitment to restoring New Orleans (and the other Gulf Coast cities) to pre-Katrina status. Ideally, though, that assessment should be just the beginning of a more fundamental analysis of the government's economic response to natural (and unnatural) disasters.

* * *

Let me suggest two ways for experts to help the public think through the dimensions of this issue before the next disaster. First, economists could use cost-benefit analysis to compare options for rebuilding, relocating, or abandoning cities when disasters like Katrina occur. Second, they could help formulate ways in which market tests could inform the comparisons.

For example, it would be possible to hold auctions for permits that allow developers to rebuild designated parts of the city. The government could use its power of eminent domain to auction off large blocks of land that were largely destroyed by the storm. The bids from these auctions could be used to estimate the overall economic benefits from rebuilding the city.

By the same token, auctions for infrastructure contracts would offer insights into what private contractors betting their own money think the new infrastructure would cost. The idea is not that far-fetched. Washington already has considerable experience in this area, auctioning rights to emit sulfur dioxide emissions and rights to use the electromagnetic spectrum for cell phones and the like. A parallel approach could be to use prediction markets modeled after markets that now allow individuals to bet on elections—to forecast the costs of rebuilding or the consequences in terms of increased economic output.

Combining market and non-market estimates for benefits and costs would provide valuable information for decision makers. If, in total, the bids for permits were too low to pay for rebuilding the public infrastructure and the levees, this may be a sign that it isn't worth doing.

Of course, such markets can hardly be expected to provide perfect measures of either societal benefits or costs. For one thing, expectations of future government subsidies would affect bids. The long-term economic solution to the subsidy problem is to design the subsidies so they have a minimal impact on relocation decisions and economic growth. Better yet, courageous politicians should remove them altogether.

In the meantime, economists could estimate the impact of current subsidies on market prices to obtain a better estimate of the net benefits of rebuilding a city. The general impact of subsidies would be to raise bids for property, because bidders will factor in the expected windfall from the subsidies.

A potential drawback of markets is that they may not adequately take into account the preferences of future generations. Rebuilding New Orleans may not be worth the cost to current residents. But who is to speak for future generations in deciding how much it would be worth to our grandchildren to have an intact French Quarter to enjoy?

While such considerations underscore the need to interpret results with care, they should not be show-stoppers. Economic analysis of rebuilding options could inform the policy process and make it more transparent.

In the end, value judgments will inevitably need to be made by our elected leaders. We should not, however, assume that these judgments cannot change. The Dutch, who live with a system of dikes, have recently changed their strategy to reduce the human costs associated with floods. Likewise, the U.S. government could change its strategy for rebuilding after disasters, as we learn more about what works.

Clearly, economics can't tell us all we need to know in deciding whether to spend billions of dollars in rebuilding a great city. Yet, the failure to frame the issues in terms of costs and benefits leaves us flying blind.

NOTES

1. Is cost-benefit analysis an appropriate way of determining whether to rebuild a city? Are there intangible benefits to the rebuilding of New Orleans that cannot be easily assigned monetary value?
2. Could the kinds of markets that Hahn discusses be used to decide which particular areas of the city should be rebuilt? Would there be equity problems to such an approach.
3, Compare the post-Katrina rebuilding discussions with the post-9/11 discussion regarding rebuilding Lower Manhattan. Why do you think rebuilding New Orleans has generated so much more controversy?

EDWARD L. GLAESER, SHOULD THE GOVERNMENT REBUILD NEW ORLEANS, OR JUST GIVE RESIDENTS CHECKS?

The Economists' Voice, Vol. 2 [2005], No. 4, Article 4 (at http://www.bepress.com/ev/vol2/ iss4/art4)

In the wake of Hurricane Katrina, President Bush declared that a "Great City Will Rise Again." He promised, "Throughout the area hit by the hurricane, we will do what it takes—we will stay as long as it takes—to help citizens rebuild their communities and their lives."

Lawmakers have stumbled over each other to suggest greater and greater public spending to rebuild New Orleans. While details remain to be settled, the current estimates are that federal spending will be close to $200 billion.

Senator Edward Kennedy has proposed a $150 billion agency specifically dedicated to Gulf area infrastructure. This spending is being justified as federal insurance against disaster.

* * *

The case for rebuilding New Orleans, then, depends on whether the residents of New Orleans will be made better off by this spending, than by being given checks or vouchers.

* * *

Vouchers or Checks Would Be Life-Changing For Poor New Orleans Residents

To put the numbers in context, imagine that we were to spend $100 billion dollars on infrastructure for the residents of the city. An alternative to this spending is to give each one of the city of New Orleans' residents a check for more than $200,000.

Annual per capita income in that city is less than $20,000, so this check would amount to ten years' income, on average—a hefty, and potentially life-changing sum. That is enough to send several children to college, to buy a modest home, and/or to relocate and start a dreamed-of business.

If this money were spread over the 1.33 million residents in the New Orleans metropolitan area, each resident would still receive $75,000, still enough to pay for a home in many areas of the country.

Can the benefits to the residents' of local infrastructure possibly equal the benefits for receiving three or ten years' income as a lump sum? One has to wonder.

Could Public Spending Possibly Benefit Residents More than Checks or Vouchers Could?

Indeed, there are many reasons to suspect that spending vast sums to rebuild the city may not make sense. New Orleans is like many great American cities that were built during previous eras and have become somewhat obsolete.

Before 1900, moving goods by water was much cheaper than moving goods by land. As a result, all of the great American cities were built on rivers, or where an important river meets the sea. From that perspective, the location of New Orleans was unbeatable: it is the port at the mouth of America's greatest river system.

New Orleans reached its peak of economic importance relative to the U.S. in 1840. But the Civil War and the relative decline of water-based transportation relative to rail caused the city to lose ground, relative to Northern cities, through much of the Nineteenth century.

In 1840, New Orleans was America's third-largest city (after New York and Baltimore); by 1920, it had dropped to being only its *seventeenth* largest city. Still, the city's edge as a port continued to ensure that its population increased until the 1950s.

New Orleans began to decline, in absolute terms, in 1960. The port remains important, but increasing mechanization and containerization, together meant that fewer and fewer people were needed to work in that port. Today, according to the 2003 County Business Patterns, less than one-twentieth of the employees in New Orleans are in transportation industries, and more than a quarter of these aren't even working in the port or pipelines.

Even the vaunted energy industry employs a remarkably small number of people. County Business Patterns reports that there are fewer than 2,000 people in New Orleans working in oil and gas extraction, and fewer than 100 people working on pipeline transportation.

While there are fewer than 7,500 people working in the port, there are 32,000 employees in health care and social assistance. New Orleans' biggest industry is tourism, and there are 37,000 employees working in food services and accommodation.

New Orleans remains an important port, but this port doesn't need a large city, and over time, the city has contracted. New Orleans' population has declined steadily—from 627,000 residents in 1960 to 485,000 residents in 2000.

If the American Community Survey is to be believed (this is based on a smallish sample), New Orleans has lost another 40,000 inhabitants between

2000 and 2004. The 4.1 percent growth of the New Orleans metropolitan area in the 1990s put it far below the average U.S. population growth. It is hard to find a sunbelt city that is doing as badly as New Orleans.

All of this information cuts strongly against any claim that the rebuilding of New Orleans would be more beneficial for its residents, than their receiving a large check or voucher that would enable them not only to rebuild, but to transform, their lives.

Could New Orleans, with Spending, Somehow Return to Its Long-Past Glory?

Granted, some previously great ports have managed to rebuild themselves around new industries. New York is now devoted to finance. San Francisco is the center for information technology.

But New Orleans was never able to reinvent itself, perhaps because it lacked the human capital that has been so heavily correlated with urban success over the past 50 years.

Moreover, New Orleans' port locale raises construction costs, relative to, say, the flat, featureless plains of Las Vegas. And New Orleans' climate is problematic relative to California. My own guess is that the city would have declined by more than it has, if it were not for the durability of its housing stock and other infrastructure. And now, thanks to Hurricane Katrina, that last asset has been decimated.

Nor was New Orleans' housing stock very valuable, in the market, to begin with. The decline in New Orleans' population has been accompanied by economic distress and by low housing prices.

The 2000 Census reported that more than 27 percent of New Orleans residents were in poverty (relative to 12 percent for the U.S. as a whole). Median family income was only 64 percent of the median family income in the U.S.

In 2004, according to the American Community Survey, the unemployment rate for the city was over 11 percent. And New Orleans' housing prices, pre-hurricane, remained far below those of the nation as a whole, providing further evidence of weak pre-existing demand for living in the city.

By most objective measures, the city, pre-hurricane, was not doing a good job of taking care of its poorer residents. For most students of urban distress, New Orleans was a problem, not an ideal. Poverty and continuing economic decline fed upon each other, delivering despair to many of the city's residents.

More Limited Rebuilding, Combined with Aid to Residents, May Be Wiser

New Orleans' decline suggests that spending huge sums betting on the future of the city makes little sense. Perhaps there are externalities or coordination failures that argue for rebuilding, but they do not immediately come to mind.

Most sensible theories about externalities suggest that giving checks to impacted residents, who then will move to Houston or Atlanta or Las Vegas, will actually reduce the negative spillovers from dysfunctional neighborhoods —not increase them.

None of this means, of course, that we shouldn't rebuild New Orleans' port or its pipelines. But rebuilding this basic infrastructure doesn't mean rebuilding the entire city, and it doesn't necessarily require federal funding.

The port and the energy sector are thriving economic entities. Their users can be charged for the costs of this infrastructure. We will all eventually pay those costs in the form of higher prices, but this is surely more efficient than funding reconstruction with tax dollars.

Rebuilding New Orleans requires a cost-benefit analysis that is far behind the scope of this essay. At this point, the only thing that I strongly endorse is having an open-minded national debate about costs and benefits. However, I suspect that for much of the proposed rebuilding, the costs will greatly outweigh the benefits.

One of the biggest problems of urban decline is how to help those residents caught in a declining city. Perhaps, if significant funds are given to New Orleans residents to help them start life anew in some more vibrant city, then there will be a silver lining to Katrina after all.

NOTES

1. Suppose that, as Glaeser suggests, residents accepted cash settlements instead of having their homes rebuilt. This would show that they prefer to live elsewhere. Would it show that relocating the population was in the interests of society? Consider the environmental and infrastructure costs of urban expansion in other places, in addition to the possibility that some of the moves would be motivated by better public services or higher welfare payments. On the other hand, if few people would really want to return to New Orleans, why bother to rebuild it?

2. One of the key questions is whether to rebuild the Ninth Ward. Consider the following divergent viewpoints:

> Originally a cypress swamp, the community of 20,000 is overwhelmingly black; more than one-third of residents live below the poverty line, according to the 2000 census. The people of the Lower Ninth are the maids, bellhops and busboys who care for New Orleans tourists. They are also the clerks and cops now helping to get the city back on its feet. The ward is home to carpenters, sculptors, musicians and retirees. Fats Domino still has a house in the Lower Ninth. Kermit Ruffins—a quintessential New Orleanian trumpeter whose band likes to grill up some barbecue between sets—attended local schools. About half the houses are rentals.
>
> "It's a scrappy place where people don't take a lot of guff, but a place where people really respect each other," said Pam

Dashiell, president of the Holy Cross Neighborhood Association. "It has heart and soul and beauty."

Dashiell is annoyed by comments by House Speaker J. Dennis Hastert (R-Ill.) and some developers suggesting there is no point in restoring the most flood-prone parts of the city—the Lower Ninth, everyone knows, even if it is not mentioned by name. She wants "an independent expert who can be trusted" to assess the condition of buildings there and a hefty investment in levees that can withstand a Category 5 hurricane.

Yet even some liberal activists, people who have worked to buoy the fortunes of the Lower Ninth, are beginning to talk favorably about clearing it away—if residents are well compensated and given suitable housing elsewhere.

"It would be negligent homicide to put people in the Lower Ninth," said Russell Henderson, a veteran community organizer who has formed the Rebuilding Louisiana Coalition. "If you put people back in there, they're going to die."

But scraping away the Lower Ninth would most certainly change the already delicate equations of racial and economic politics in one of America's poorest cities, a city that was 67 percent black but is likely to have a smaller black majority once it is resettled. LSU's Colten fears middle-class Gentilly and wealthy Lakeview—just as prone to severe flooding—will nevertheless be rebuilt, while the Lower Ninth is abandoned.

The temptation will be to "open up spaces where there has been a lot of poverty," similar to the urban renewal projects of the 1960s, he said: "Those were seen as a way of cleansing a problem. It didn't eliminate poverty; it just moved it."

Ceci Connolly, *9th Ward: History, Yes, but a Future?* WASHINGTON POST, Oct. 3, 2005, at A1.

3. Would you accept a payment to move away from your home, job, friends, and community? Can you determine a value for how much it would take? One way to think about this is to ask how much of a salary difference would be necessary to induce you to move.

4. Why do you think people originally built in low-lying areas like New Orleans? If the United States could replan all its development to avoid areas prone to natural disasters, would areas such as California and Florida have their present populations?

B. RECONSTRUCTING THE FLOOD CONTROL SYSTEM

It would be inordinately foolish to rebuild the city without providing improved flood protection. Creating a more reliable flood control system may not be an easy matter, however, and it may involve more than simply improved design for levees. Legal, political, engineering, scientific, sociological, and economic decisions are all involved.

CONGRESSIONAL RESEARCH SERVICE, COASTAL LOUISIANA ECOSYSTEM RESTORATION: THE RECOMMENDED CORPS PLAN

(April 11, 2005)

Scientists agree about the general parameters of past and future rates and patterns of land (and wetland) loss in coastal Louisiana. Since the 1930s, more then 1.2 million acres, mostly coastal wetlands, have been converted to open water. The Corps forecasts that land losses will continue, and that approximately 462,000 acres (including 328,000 wetland acres) will be converted to open water by 2050. The Corps and others who study these changes believe that future losses will continue to be caused by some combination of human activities, such as navigation improvements and development related to oil and gas, and natural causes, such as relative sea level change. These factors have contributed to losses over the past 75 years. These losses reduce the quality and productivity of this wetlands ecosystem, and are accompanied by economic and social costs. While these costs are concentrated in Louisiana, impacts on navigation, energy, and commercial fisheries could be felt much more widely. (For more information on the wetland loss problem, see CRS Report RL32673, *Coastal Louisiana: Attempting to Restore an Ecosystem.*)

Federal (and state) actions to address extensive land conversion to open water have been growing over the past 15 years. These actions include analyzing the causes and extent of the problem, and initiating projects that are designed to counter it. The most recent federal action is the release of the Corps' *Louisiana Coastal Area Ecosystem Restoration Study* (hereafter referred to as the Report) in January 2005. The Report recommends five construction projects for immediate authorization, 10 projects for additional study, and several other actions that would slow the forecast rate of land loss. The Report provided the basis for the Chief of Engineers report making recommendations to the Assistant Secretary of the Army for Civil Works on January 31, 2005. The Report will be a major source of information for Congress during consideration of legislation that would respond to past and anticipated land loss. (The Corps' Report and related documents can be found at [http://www.lca.gov]. For more information on the process by which Corps projects are developed, see CRS Report RL32064, *Army Corps of Engineers Water Resources Activities: Authorization and Appropriations.*

If the projects recommended in the Report are fully implemented, the Corps estimates that they would reduce the estimated loss from 462,000 acres by 2050 to about 170,000 acres (a reduction of 62.5%), by both reducing the number of acres that would be converted to open water, and by reestablishing wetlands at some sites where they had been lost. The Corps estimates that the five construction projects also would have significant ecosystem benefits. It estimates these benefits to be "22,000 habitat units," if the projects are fully implemented.

Recommendations in the Corps Report

The Corps Report was prepared to document how it determined which construction projects, termed "near-term critical restoration features," and other activities would be recommended, and what benefits can be anticipated from this suite of proposals. The Corps has organized these proposals into seven elements in the Report. Drafts of the Report were reviewed and commented on by others, including representatives of federal, state, and local units of government.

Recommended Elements. If authorized and fully funded, the seven elements would be implemented over a decade. The Corps estimates the total cost to complete these elements is $1,996 million, and that the federal portion of this total is $1,283 million (62.9%). The entire federal portion is funding, while the non-federal share is divided between funding ($326 million) and real estate ($387 million). The proposed recommendations include specific construction projects that could be initiated relatively quickly because the preliminary planning and design work is largely completed (element 1), research and demonstration activities (elements 2 through 5), continuing studies of construction projects that require more extensive planning and design work than those in element 1 and would have to be authorized for construction at a later date (element 6), and projects that are at a more conceptual stage (element 7). The seven elements (and estimated cost in June 2004 and percentage of the total program cost) are as follows:

- **Element 1:** Five near-term critical restoration features that "have relatively advanced investigations and could be implemented expeditiously" (in 5 to 10 years) after they are authorized by Congress and pre-construction documentation is completed. (These are shown on the map on the next page as items 1 through 5.) ($864 million, or 43.3% of the total)
- **Element 2:** Science and Technology Program to decrease scientific and engineering uncertainties about ecosystem restoration for 10 years. ($100 million, or 5.0% of the total)
- **Element 3:** Demonstration Projects recommended as a result of the Science and Technology Program over 10 years. ($100 million, or 5.0% of the total)
- **Element 4:** Programmatic authorization for beneficial uses of dredged materials to benefit coastal wetlands. ($100 million, or 5.0% of the total)
- **Element 5:** Programmatic authorization for investigating modification, rehabilitation, or management of existing water resources structures. ($10 million, or 0.5% of the total)
- **Element 6:** Further analysis and possible future congressional authorization for 10 additional listed features. (These are shown on the

map on the next page as items 6 through 15.) ($762 million, or 38.2% of the total)

- **Element 7:** Feasibility studies to evaluate six large-scale and long-term concepts to determine their potential for contributing to the restoration effort. ($60 million, or 3.0% of the total)

The Corps started the planning process leading to these recommendations by identifying 166 "restoration features." It then winnowed the list down to the five projects in element 1 and the 10 projects in element 6 using a complex sorting process described in detail in the Report. These 15 projects are located on the map below. All projects are located in the eastern and central portions of coastal Louisiana. Funding for these projects would account for almost 82% of the $1,996 million in the Corps' proposed budget. In addition, the Corps identified the six "restoration concepts" in element 7, which are much less developed and larger in scale. Two of the six concepts, for example, are a Mississippi River Delta Management Study and an Acadiana Bays Estuarine Restoration Feasibility Study.

The Chief's report recommends these elements. It distinguishes projects and programs for which it is seeking immediate authorization (elements 1 through 4, at a total cost of $1,123 million), further investigations of programs and projects that have already been authorized (elements 5 through 7, at a total cost of $145 million), and future authorization of project construction (implementing element 6, at a cost of $728 million).

In addition to recommending these elements, the Chief's report makes two related recommendations. First, it plans to develop a cross-cut budget to show annually funding from all federal and non-federal sources for each project and activity that is considered to be part of this restoration effort. Cross-cut budgets are already being used for some other ecosystem restoration programs, such as the South Florida Ecosystem Restoration Program. Second, the Corps plans to issue a status report to Congress every five years to discuss accomplishments and consider refinements to the restoration effort. The discussion of this report suggests that it may include recommendations to add or remove projects from this effort, changes to implementation procedures, and other adjustments. Many might consider this periodic reporting process to be a type of adaptive project management. The Corps has used adaptive management in other restoration efforts.

Plan Costs, Uncertainties, and Benefits.

The Corps concludes that its recommended plan is the most cost-effective of eight alternative plans when comparing average annual costs and average annual benefits. The average annual cost of this option is $66 million; the other seven options range from $171 million to $543 million. However, it provides only slightly less in "average annual benefits," which the Corps calculated as a composite of land building, habitat suitability, and nitrogen removal. It calculates a numerical value for the benefits of the recommended plan to be 2865; the other seven options range from 3094 to 3202.

The Corps points out that, even with all the research that has been performed, there would still be significant uncertainties that accompany the restoration effort. The Report identifies 19 uncertainties in four groupings: knowledge of baseline physical conditions, engineering concepts and project implementation methods, ecological processes and responses to the proposed actions, and socioeconomic and political conditions and responses. The Corps identifies actions that can be taken to minimize the uncertainty by collecting additional data or monitoring certain aspects of changing conditions. In addition, as stated above, the Corps anticipates reviewing the effort every five years, and making recommendations for adaptive changes as uncertainties are reduced or resolved.

The benefits of the five projects in element 1 that the Corps proposes for congressional authorization are stated almost entirely in terms of wetland creation and restoration data. This should not be a surprise since halting wetland deterioration (and expanding wetland acreage) has been the core concern in coastal Louisiana. Actual wetland benefits, however, will depend on other factors beyond measuring acres gained and lost, such as where those wetlands are located, what types of wetlands are reestablished, and improvements in ecological performance in reestablished wetlands.

The benefits that the Corps identifies and discusses in greater detail in the Report when it compares future conditions with and without the proposed projects (and the wetlands that will be lost or created) include hydrology, coastal habitats and productivity, and socioeconomic factors (energy activities, navigation/shipping, and commercial fishing, among others). It shows that as the amount of land and habitat decreases, the productivity (measured in amount of vegetation) will decrease as well. It concludes that land loss will continue, but be limited to about 170,000 acres, if the proposed projects are constructed. It does not compare overall losses in coastal Louisiana if no additional projects are implemented and if this proposal is fully implemented. It does identify and briefly discuss losses with no additional projects (all discussed qualitatively), to include:

- disruption of oil, gas, and pipeline infrastructure;
- deterioration of navigable waterways;
- diminished coastal fisheries production;
- losses to recreation, especially forms that depend on wetlands and habitat diversity; and greater exposure and possible destruction of cultural resources.

The proposed projects would meet the Corps' general mandate that the environmental benefits "including improvement of the environment and fish and wildlife enhancement" are assumed to exceed costs, which is standard practice for Corps environmental projects; in this case, created or reestablished wetlands are assumed to provide greater benefits than open waters, and areas of open water will increase in both number and size if no projects are constructed.

Next Steps

Federal Authorization. With the issuing of the Chief of Engineers report on January 31, 2005, the next steps in the approval process are review by the Secretary of the Army and Office of Management and Budget for compliance with Administration policy. An informal copy of the Chief's report has been sent to Congress. If Congress authorizes the entire recommended plan, the agency would construct the five projects in element 1, initiate the programs in elements 2 through 5, and continue the preliminary investigations of the projects listed in element 6 and the concepts listed in element 7. It is widely anticipated that Congress will consider this plan with the next Water Resources Development Act (WRDA) legislation, which may be taken up this year. While awaiting congressional action, the Corps states that it will continue, under existing authority, with the necessary "investigations and pre-construction engineering and design activities." (To follow the likely legislative process, see CRS Issue Brief IB10133, *Water Resources Development Act (WRDA): Army Corps of Engineers Authorization Issues in the 109th Congress.*)

The State Role. The Chief of Engineers report identifies the State of Louisiana Department of Natural Resources as the nonfederal cost-sharing sponsor for the recommended plan. According to this report, the recommended cost-sharing for each of the project elements is consistent with current law and Corps policies. Prior to implementation, the state must agree to a number of cost-sharing and other requirements that are listed in the Chief's report. The nonfederal portion of the funding is 37.1% of the total, or $714 million, and a majority of this is for real estate. The split between federal and nonfederal shares varies in the Corps other large-scale restoration programs; the south Florida program is a 50-50 split, while a proposal for the upper Mississippi would be 91% federal and 9% nonfederal.

Future Planning and Authorizations. The Corps will continue to investigate projects identified in elements 6 and 7 for study. It then may submit them for congressional authorization. Although the Corps can continue these investigations under existing authority, it requests additional funding authorization in its Report to help accelerate this work. Each of the projects in elements 6 and 7 appears to require substantial additional study before the Corps would be ready to submit them to Congress to authorize construction, although exactly what additional work is required is not stated.

NOTES

1. The Corps seems to be moving with what could be called rather deliberate speed. Should more resources be poured into restoration of wetlands? Or would this be premature?
2. How should we determine the appropriate level of investment in wetland restoration? Would a cost-benefit analysis be appropriate?

3. Development alone did not destroy the wetlands. The environmental organization Save Our Wetlands estimates that the oil and gas industry
causes $2 to $4 billion in damage to Louisiana's wetlands each year
through draining and dredging. http://www.saveourwetlands.org/news-
paper.htm. A task force of federal, state, and private groups promulgated
a plan called Coastal 2050 to restore the Louisiana wetlands. Prior to
Katrina, the plan had received only a small amount of funding. The following excerpt considers the future of the wetlands.

OLIVER HOUCK, CAN WE SAVE NEW ORLEANS?

19 Tul. Envtl. L.J. 1 (2006)

[T]here is a more fundamental problem with Coast 2050, its mission,
stated as "to sustain coastal resources and provide an integrated multiple use
approach to ecosystem management." Who could object to that? Only someone familiar with the practice of multiple use management in the United
States. The term first appeared in federal legislation attempting to insert
environmental protection into rangeland and forest decisions, and it was
shortly chewed to pieces by its very vagueness. Landscapes as vast as southern Alaska could commit 99% of the Tongass National Forest to clearcutting
and still be "multiple use"; large and biologically unique areas of the California Desert could be turned over to off-road vehicle races. The concept of "multiple use" failed so utterly to protect the environment that more recent laws
have imposed specific environmental baselines (e.g., regeneration within 5
years) instead. In short, multiple use has become a code word for let'er rip
and Katy-bar-the-door.

The same inherent conflict can be seen in the Louisiana coastal management statute, which seeks both to "protect" and to "develop" the coastal zone.
So what comes first? According to one of its first administrators, it is a "resource management" program that "practically precludes the Secretary from
stopping any activity per se in the coastal zone." At which point we know very
well what comes first, and it will not be coastal protection. So when Coast
2050 also states its intention to provide a "clear vision" for the coast, it is calling for something that it can't deliver.

A second problem with Coast 2050 is its inability to deal with projects
that run counter to its objectives. The Breaux Act directs the Corps and other
federal agencies to ensure that all of the activities are "consistent" with the
"purposes of the restoration plan." Some activities are clearly not. But rather
than calling for closure of the Mississippi Gulf Outlet, for example, the current 2050 work plan calls for—with an alarmingly straight face—the placement of rocks along its eroding banks. They are called "environmental
improvements." Nor has 2050 insisted on accessing oil and gas deposits by
means other than dredging, or raised a peep over government permitting for
new wetland development. Indeed, 2050 has yet even to develop a process to
determine the consistency of any of this stuff with coastal restoration. It is
still, like the rest of the state, in the mitigation-based, we-can-have-our-cake-

and-eat-it-too mode that has presided over the destruction of the coastal zone for more than three decades. Are we serious yet?

The most obvious shortcoming of 2050, however, is that, even under the best of circumstances—its projects fully funded and the adverse consequences of new levees, canals and urban development magically wished away —it would not restore the coast. It would reduce the rate of loss. Not by all that much. About 500,000 acres would be lost without 2050's restoration projects, and about 400,000 acres with them. Under 2050, three of the four coastal regions would continue to experience a seriously disappearing landscape. The one that gains is next to the Mississippi and the subject of a new diversion project. This is before Katrina and Rita came along and took out 100 square miles in a single blow. Post-Katrina, a goal of reducing loss is no longer sufficient.

These shortcomings noted, Coast 2050 was still a credible game plan until it had a terrible accident, and barely emerged alive. In the summer of 2005, it ran into a highly skeptical Office of Management and Budget in Washington, D.C., and, after much haggling, its $14 billion asking price was whittled down to $250 million. Worse, the monies would be restricted to projects that could be implemented in the near term, the next 5 to 10 years, and to studies of "long-range feature concepts." Rome is burning. They sent a fiddle.

Katrina and Rita, in turn, had several impacts of their own on Coast 2050. On the positive side, they highlighted the relationship between coastal restoration and hurricane protection for all the country to see. Case in point: One evening this November, I was walking my dog down on the levee and met a group of workers from Minnesota (it was already cold up there). One of them began telling me about the river and how it was carrying all this silt and the coast was collapsing at three football fields an hour—seven football fields, said another—and so they argued about it. A bunch of twenty-somethings from 1,000 miles away had the message.

Second, Katrina and Rita opened the money faucet. Unimaginable sums will now be pouring into South Louisiana, much of it for the coast. For good or ill. By the same token, the two hurricanes exploded the rate of loss. The Lake Pontchartrain basin lost 50 square miles (they'd been averaging 4 square miles a year). Southeast Louisiana, below New Orleans, may have lost 100 square miles, 40 years worth by current rates. Two months after the storm more than half a million acres of the coast were still under water. These were tremendous hits. More hurricanes are coming. So what do we do?
* * *

What comes next is the hardest step for any American community to take, and all but heresy in South Louisiana. A plan. The mere mention of planning raises blood pressures and brings on cries of Godless Communism. The property rights movement is nowhere stronger than on the American coastline, stoked by folks who are either constructing, selling or occupying condos on places like Hilton Head, Pensacola and Padre Island, and it loves insurance payouts and second home mortgage deductions and it hates planning. Now we add the prevailing attitude of a state like Louisiana where most towns do not even have zoning, and a city like New Orleans whose tout ensemble is absolutely critical to its economy but which has spent the last 10 years avoiding the preparation of a master plan. To this we add the very human fact that everybody wants to live everywhere, most of all where they always have. And as close to water as possible.

What we have had in the city of New Orleans and along the entire Gulf Coast is planning by default (local attorney Bill Borah calls it "planning by surprise"). Planning takes place. It's just that we haven't taken part in it. Where water resources are concerned, it starts with real estate developers, port authorities, levee boards and other outside-the-ballot-box enterprises, their projects facilitated and funded by the Army Corps of Engineers. In their minds, the only question is a technical one: what kind of engineering do we need to get our project done? The system has produced the expected results: more rip-rap here, more drainage there, and levees to the horizon. The goal is —although it is never stated anywhere—to develop as much of the coast as possible. When you add the projects up, they determine the destiny of the city and South Louisiana.

Case in point: There are three, mind-blowing maps in South Louisiana right now. One shows how Katrina and Rita came into New Orleans (wide arrows pointing in at the city, it looks like the Blitzkrieg). A second shows what these same storms did to the coastal zone south of New Orleans (it goes from a green carpet of grass to a hole in the ground). The third map hasn't gotten much play. It shows a levee stretching from the Mississippi border to Texas, cutting across the belly of South Louisiana like a tourniquet. About half the wetlands of coastal Louisiana are above it, the other half below. The first piece of this levee to move forward is called Morganza to the Gulf.

The Morganza project loops down from Larose to within a mile or so of the open Gulf, and then back up to Houma. It is a considerable undertaking, with 72 miles of levees, gates and other structures, at a cost of $40.5 million (probably twice that, if history is any guide). It will destroy 3,743 acres of wetlands outright in construction and enclose the greater part of another 270,000-plus wetland acres in its study area, along with three good-sized lakes. Gates will be provided in an attempt to maintain the hydrological connection between the wetlands within the system and those to the south—but you have to perform a kind of auto-lobotomy not to see the consequences over time.

Natural History: widespread natural flows do not do well through culverts and passes. Neither do fish and plankton. Neither do sediments, large volumes of which are provided to the interior marshes from the south, by the very coastal storms that will close the gates and keep them out. And that's just the surface water. Water is moving underground as well, and the levees press down on that circulation like a boot on a rabbit. The rabbit doesn't fare so well.

* * *

Suppose, now, we were to start from a different point of departure. We aim to maximize the sustainability of the natural systems of the Louisiana coastal zone. We accept that hurricanes and major floods are going to come, and that attempts to confine them are as self-defeating as those of Persian King Xerxes, sending his sailors down to the beach with whips to beat down a stormy sea. Better to cede the waves some space. The goal here is not maximum human development but a coastal zone that will maintain itself and its inhabitants for generations to come. The mechanism is to use the coast as a first line of defense. And to cede it, including the violence of floods and storms, the space it needs to protect us, and thrive.

Fact is, there are many lines of defense out there, starting with the barrier islands and moving inland to ridges, natural land bridges, estuaries, interior roads and railroads, locks and floodgates, then levees, and then things we always did and then forgot how, like elevating houses. The point is that no one defense has to do the whole job. New Orleans might live quite safely surrounded by valid Category three levees, if over time its buildings were raised a few feet, as they historically were, and far barriers, both natural and man-made, served to knock down wave heights before they arrived. If the danger points for maximum storm surge are the Rigolets and the Chef passes, they might be gated in ways that do not require a continuous levee from the Pearl River to the Mississippi. The same incremental protections would be gained from closing the MRGO. We have a mix of options in which structures do not come first, they come last.

Here is a problem. With all the attention of coastal scientists, engineers and federal and state agencies to this question over the years, we still have no idea how much of the coast we can save, and where. Instead we have Coast 2050 which, despite its price tag, is a losing game plan, nearly half a million acres in the next few decades. We are entitled to know more. If a sustainable coast is the goal, we need a map of what we can sustain. That map, in turn, should drive what we do for restoration and for human development, and for its protections.

Here is the second problem. If we are not going to try to protect everything with large structural works, then we are going to have to give water its space, as the Dutch themselves have concluded. The idea is not revolutionary. We routinely take space for highways and other public works, with compensation, but with no greater rationale than the public good. The Supreme Court has recently approved takings for such dubiously public ventures as shopping malls, which makes taking private property to protect the general public, and the private owners themselves, from hurricanes seem like a no-brainer. Truth is we rarely buy space for natural processes, but there is no reason not to. In fact, always in response to disasters and never without pain, we have actually gone in this direction several times.

* * *

The point of this Essay is that we have a choice. Rather than start with the premise that we are going to protect as much of the Louisiana coast as we can from hurricanes and then graft on some restoration measures, we can start with the premise that we are going to restore as much of the Louisiana coast as we can and then see what we need to do, within that context, to protect people from hurricanes. The approaches are not the same, and they will lead to two very different futures. We are entitled to see the second one, before we are handed the first as a fait accompli. The first one is being prepared, by the Corps, on an unrealistically hasty schedule, as we speak.

There is another engineering outfit on the scene, however. Mother Nature. The best way to restore coastal Louisiana and to provide long-term safety for New Orleans and other coastal residents is to help nature get back in the game, and then stand back. Not very far back. Just far enough for it to work for us: a natural, self-sustaining, horizontal, first and major line of defense spinning off renewable resource dividends for generations to come. We can have our coast and live and work in it safely for a very long time. Just not everywhere, and doing every damn thing we want.

Can we save New Orleans? It'll be a journey. Will we? Depends on no rain in the morning, and the path we choose.

NOTES

1. Whether the cost of restoring the Gulf Coast is justified by flood control benefits depends on a number of factors, including how much of the area is eventually rebuilt and how much alternative methods of flood control would cost. Of course, there would be other advantages of coastal wetlands. How should we decide if the costs are worthwhile? Should we use cost-benefit analysis or some other approach?

2. It is not clear how effective current restoration plans would be:

> Over the years, scores of scientists have struggled to determine the best way to approach Louisiana's vanishing wetlands. Last week, experts convened by the National Academy of Sciences reported their recommendations in an evaluation of the state's major marsh-restoration proposal.
>
> Though they praised most of the plan's major components as scientifically sound, they said it would reduce annual wetland loss by only 20 percent and that it was time to consider what areas could be preserved and what areas could not.

Cornelia Dean, *Louisiana's Marshes Fight for Their Lives*, NEW YORK TIMES, Nov. 15, 2005, at D2, D4 (national edition). For further discussion of wetlands issues, see GWEN ARNOLD (ED.), AFTER THE STORM: RESTORING AMERICA'S GULF COAST WETLANDS (2006).

C. LAND ACQUISITION

After a disaster like Katrina, it may be necessary for the city to acquire land for redevelopment. Presumably, voluntary transactions will play a central role. However, voluntary transactions may not always be possible, either because of "holdout" problems or because owners cannot be located. Is it appropriate for the city to use eminent domain to acquire property from current landowners and then turn it over to developers for reuse? Consider the opinions in the following case.

KELO V. CITY OF NEW LONDON

___ U.S. ___,125 S. Ct. 2655, 162 L. Ed.2d 439 (2005)

JUSTICE STEVENS delivered the opinion of the Court.

In 2000, the city of New London approved a development plan that, in the words of the Supreme Court of Connecticut, was "projected to create in excess of 1,000 jobs, to increase tax and other revenues, and to revitalize an economically distressed city, including its downtown and waterfront areas." In assembling the land needed for this project, the city's development agent has purchased property from willing sellers and proposes to use the power of eminent domain to acquire the remainder of the property from unwilling owners in exchange for just compensation. The question presented is whether the city's proposed disposition of this property qualifies as a "public use" within the meaning of the Takings Clause of the Fifth Amendment to the Constitution.

* * *

Two polar propositions are perfectly clear. On the one hand, it has long been accepted that the sovereign may not take the property of A for the sole purpose of transferring it to another private party B, even though A is paid just compensation. On the other hand, it is equally clear that a State may transfer property from one private party to another if future "use by the public" is the purpose of the taking; the condemnation of land for a railroad with common-carrier duties is a familiar example. Neither of these propositions, however, determines the disposition of this case.

As for the first proposition, the City would no doubt be forbidden from taking petitioners' land for the purpose of conferring a private benefit on a particular private party. Nor would the City be allowed to take property under the mere pretext of a public purpose, when its actual purpose was to bestow a private benefit. The takings before us, however, would be executed pursuant to a "carefully considered" development plan. The trial judge and all the members of the Supreme Court of Connecticut agreed that there was no evidence of an illegitimate purpose in this case.

On the other hand, this is not a case in which the City is planning to open the condemned land—at least not in its entirety—to use by the general public. Nor will the private lessees of the land in any sense be required to operate like common carriers, making their services available to all comers. But although such a projected use would be sufficient to satisfy the public use requirement, this "Court long ago rejected any literal requirement that condemned property be put into use for the general public." Indeed, while many state courts in the mid-19th century endorsed "use by the public" as the proper definition of public use, that narrow view steadily eroded over time. Not only was the "use by the public" test difficult to administer (e.g., what proportion of the public need have access to the property? at what price?), but it proved to be impractical given the diverse and always evolving needs of society. Accordingly, when this Court began applying the Fifth Amendment to the States at the close of the 19th century, it embraced the broader and more natural interpretation of public use as "public purpose." Thus, in a case upholding a mining company's use of an aerial bucket line to transport ore over property it did not own, Justice Holmes' opinion for the Court stressed "the inadequacy of use by the general public as a universal test." We have repeatedly and consistently rejected that narrow test ever since.

The disposition of this case therefore turns on the question whether the City's development plan serves a "public purpose." Without exception, our cases have defined that concept broadly, reflecting our longstanding policy of deference to legislative judgments in this field.

In Berman v. Parker, 348 U.S. 26 (1954), this Court upheld a redevelopment plan targeting a blighted area of Washington, D.C., in which most of the housing for the area's 5,000 inhabitants was beyond repair. Under the plan, the area would be condemned and part of it utilized for the construction of streets, schools, and other public facilities. The remainder of the land would be leased or sold to private parties for the purpose of redevelopment, including the construction of low-cost housing.

The owner of a department store located in the area challenged the condemnation, pointing out that his store was not itself blighted and arguing that the creation of a "better balanced, more attractive community" was not a valid public use. Writing for a unanimous Court, Justice Douglas refused to evaluate this claim in isolation, deferring instead to the legislative and agency judgment that the area "must be planned as a whole" for the plan to be successful. The Court explained that "community redevelopment programs need not, by force of the Constitution, be on a piecemeal basis—lot by lot, building by building." The public use underlying the taking was unequivocally affirmed:

> We do not sit to determine whether a particular housing project is or is not desirable. The concept of the public welfare is broad and inclusive . . . . The values it represents are spiritual as well as physical, aesthetic as well as monetary. It is within the power of the legislature to determine that the community should be beautiful as well as healthy, spacious as well as clean, well-balanced as well as carefully patrolled. In the present case, the Congress and its authorized agencies have made determinations that take into account a wide variety of values. It is not for us to reappraise them. If those who govern the District of Columbia decide that the Nation's Capital should be beautiful as well as sanitary, there is nothing in the Fifth Amendment that stands in the way.

In Hawaii Housing Authority v. Midkiff, 467 U.S. 229 (1984), the Court considered a Hawaii statute whereby fee title was taken from lessors and transferred to lessees (for just compensation) in order to reduce the concentration of land ownership. We unanimously upheld the statute and rejected the Ninth Circuit's view that it was "a naked attempt on the part of the state of Hawaii to take the property of A and transfer it to B solely for B's private use and benefit." Reaffirming Berman's deferential approach to legislative judgments in this field, we concluded that the State's purpose of eliminating the "social and economic evils of a land oligopoly" qualified as a valid public use. Our opinion also rejected the contention that the mere fact that the State immediately transferred the properties to private individuals upon condemnation somehow diminished the public character of the taking. "[I]t is only the taking's purpose, and not its mechanics," we explained, that matters in determining public use.

* * *

Viewed as a whole, our jurisprudence has recognized that the needs of society have varied between different parts of the Nation, just as they have evolved over time in response to changed circumstances. Our earliest cases in particular embodied a strong theme of federalism, emphasizing the "great respect" that we owe to state legislatures and state courts in discerning local public needs. For more than a century, our public use jurisprudence has wisely eschewed rigid formulas and intrusive scrutiny in favor of affording legislatures broad latitude in determining what public needs justify the use of the takings power.

Those who govern the City were not confronted with the need to remove blight in the Fort Trumbull area, but their determination that the area was sufficiently distressed to justify a program of economic rejuvenation is entitled to our deference. The City has carefully formulated an economic development plan that it believes will provide appreciable benefits to the community, including—but by no means limited to—new jobs and increased tax revenue. As with other exercises in urban planning and development, the City is endeavoring to coordinate a variety of commercial, residential, and recreational uses of land, with the hope that they will form a whole greater than the sum of its parts. To effectuate this plan, the City has invoked a state statute that specifically authorizes the use of eminent domain to promote economic development. Given the comprehensive character of the plan, the thorough deliberation that preceded its adoption, and the limited scope of our review, it is appropriate for us, as it was in *Berman*, to resolve the challenges of the individual owners, not on a piecemeal basis, but rather in light of the entire plan. Because that plan unquestionably serves a public purpose, the takings challenged here satisfy the public use requirement of the Fifth Amendment.

To avoid this result, petitioners urge us to adopt a new bright-line rule that economic development does not qualify as a public use. Putting aside the unpersuasive suggestion that the City's plan will provide only purely economic benefits, neither precedent nor logic supports petitioners' proposal. Promoting economic development is a traditional and long accepted function of government. There is, moreover, no principled way of distinguishing economic development from the other public purposes that we have recognized. * * * It would be incongruous to hold that the City's interest in the economic benefits to be derived from the development of the Fort Trumbull area has less of a public character than any of those other interests. Clearly, there is no basis for exempting economic development from our traditionally broad understanding of public purpose.

It is further argued that without a bright-line rule nothing would stop a city from transferring citizen *A*'s property to citizen *B* for the sole reason that citizen *B* will put the property to a more productive use and thus pay more taxes. Such a one-to-one transfer of property, executed outside the confines of an integrated development plan, is not presented in this case. While such an unusual exercise of government power would certainly raise a suspicion that a private purpose was afoot, the hypothetical cases posited by petitioners can be confronted if and when they arise. They do not warrant the crafting of an artificial restriction on the concept of public use.

Alternatively, petitioners maintain that for takings of this kind we should require a "reasonable certainty" that the expected public benefits will actually accrue. Such a rule, however, would represent an even greater departure from our precedent. "When the legislature's purpose is legitimate and its means are not irrational, our cases make clear that empirical debates over the wisdom of takings—no less than debates over the wisdom of other kinds of socioeconomic legislation—are not to be carried out in the federal courts." *Midkiff.* * * * The disadvantages of a heightened form of review are especially pronounced in this type of case. Orderly implementation of a comprehensive redevelopment plan obviously requires that the legal rights of all interested parties be established before new construction can be commenced. A constitutional rule that required postponement of the judicial approval of every condemnation until the likelihood of success of the plan had been assured would unquestionably impose a significant impediment to the successful consummation of many such plans.

JUSTICE KENNEDY, concurring.

A court applying rational-basis review under the Public Use Clause should strike down a taking that, by a clear showing, is intended to favor a particular private party, with only incidental or pretextual public benefits, just as a court applying rational-basis review under the Equal Protection Clause must strike down a government classification that is clearly intended to injure a particular class of private parties, with only incidental or pretextual public justifications.

A court confronted with a plausible accusation of impermissible favoritism to private parties should treat the objection as a serious one and review the record to see if it has merit, though with the presumption that the government's actions were reasonable and intended to serve a public purpose. Here, the trial court conducted a careful and extensive inquiry into "whether, in fact, the development plan is of primary benefit to . . . the developer [i.e., Corcoran Jennison], and private businesses which may eventually locate in the plan area [e.g., Pfizer], and in that regard, only of incidental benefit to the city." * * * Even the dissenting justices on the Connecticut Supreme Court agreed that respondents' development plan was intended to revitalize the local economy, not to serve the interests of Pfizer, Corcoran Jennison, or any other private party. This case, then, survives the meaningful rational basis review that in my view is required under the Public Use Clause.

Petitioners and their *amici* argue that any taking justified by the promotion of economic development must be treated by the courts as *per se* invalid, or at least presumptively invalid. Petitioners overstate the need for such a rule, however, by making the incorrect assumption that review under *Ber-*

man and *Midkiff* imposes no meaningful judicial limits on the government's power to condemn any property it likes. A broad *per se* rule or a strong presumption of invalidity, furthermore, would prohibit a large number of government takings that have the purpose and expected effect of conferring substantial benefits on the public at large and so do not offend the Public Use Clause.

My agreement with the Court that a presumption of invalidity is not warranted for economic development takings in general, or for the particular takings at issue in this case, does not foreclose the possibility that a more stringent standard of review than that announced in [earlier cases] might be appropriate for a more narrowly drawn category of takings. There may be private transfers in which the risk of undetected impermissible favoritism of private parties is so acute that a presumption (rebuttable or otherwise) of invalidity is warranted under the Public Use Clause. This demanding level of scrutiny, however, is not required simply because the purpose of the taking is economic development.

This is not the occasion for conjecture as to what sort of cases might justify a more demanding standard, but it is appropriate to underscore aspects of the instant case that convince me no departure from [precedent] is appropriate here. This taking occurred in the context of a comprehensive development plan meant to address a serious city-wide depression, and the projected economic benefits of the project cannot be characterized as *de minimus*. The identity of most of the private beneficiaries were unknown at the time the city formulated its plans. The city complied with elaborate procedural requirements that facilitate review of the record and inquiry into the city's purposes. In sum, while there may be categories of cases in which the transfers are so suspicious, or the procedures employed so prone to abuse, or the purported benefits are so trivial or implausible, that courts should presume an impermissible private purpose, no such circumstances are present in this case.

JUSTICE O'CONNOR, with whom CHIEF JUSTICE REHNQUIST, JUSTICE SCALIA, and JUSTICE THOMAS join, dissenting.

This case returns us for the first time in over 20 years to the hard question of when a purportedly "public purpose" taking meets the public use requirement. It presents an issue of first impression: Are economic development takings constitutional? I would hold that they are not. We are guided by two precedents about the taking of real property by eminent domain.

* * *

The Court's holdings in *Berman* and *Midkiff* were true to the principle underlying the Public Use Clause. In both those cases, the extraordinary, precondemnation use of the targeted property inflicted affirmative harm on society—in *Berman* through blight resulting from extreme poverty and in *Midkiff* through oligopoly resulting from extreme wealth. And in both cases, the relevant legislative body had found that eliminating the existing property use was necessary to remedy the harm. Thus a public purpose was realized when the harmful use was eliminated. Because each taking *directly* achieved a public benefit, it did not matter that the property was turned over to private use. Here, in contrast, New London does not claim that Susette Kelo's and Wilhelmina Dery's well-maintained homes are the source of any social harm. Indeed, it could not so claim without adopting the absurd argument that any single-family home that might be razed to make way for an apartment building, or any church that might be replaced with a retail store, or any small business that might be more lucrative if it were instead part of a national franchise, is inherently harmful to society and thus within the government's power to condemn.

In moving away from our decisions sanctioning the condemnation of harmful property use, the Court today significantly expands the meaning of public use. It holds that the sovereign may take private property currently put to ordinary private use, and give it over for new, ordinary private use, so long as the new use is predicted to generate some secondary benefit for the public—such as increased tax revenue, more jobs, maybe even aesthetic pleasure. But nearly any lawful use of real private property can be said to generate some incidental benefit to the public. Thus, if predicted (or even guaranteed) positive side-effects are enough to render transfer from one private party to another constitutional, then the words "for public use" do not realistically exclude *any* takings, and thus do not exert any constraint on the eminent domain power. * * *

Any property may now be taken for the benefit of another private party, but the fallout from this decision will not be random. The beneficiaries are likely to be those citizens with disproportionate influence and power in the political process, including large corporations and development firms. As for the victims, the government now has license to transfer property from those with fewer resources to those with more. The Founders cannot have intended this perverse result. "[T]hat alone is a *just* government," wrote James Madison, "which *impartially* secures to every man, whatever is his *own.*"

JUSTICE THOMAS, dissenting.

The most natural reading of the [Takings] Clause is that it allows the government to take property only if the government owns, or the public has a legal right to use, the property, as opposed to taking it for any public purpose or necessity whatsoever. At the time of the founding, dictionaries primarily defined the noun "use" as "[t]he act of employing any thing to any purpose." 2 S. Johnson, A Dictionary of the English Language 2194 (4th ed. 1773) (hereinafter Johnson). The term "use," moreover, "is from the Latin *utor,* which means "to use, make use of, avail one's self of, employ, apply, enjoy, etc." J. Lewis, Law of Eminent Domain § 165, p. 224, n.4 (1888) (hereinafter Lewis). When the government takes property and gives it to a private individual, and the public has no right to use the property, it strains language to say that the public is "employing" the property, regardless of the incidental benefits that might accrue to the public from the private use. The term "public use," then, means that either the government or its citizens as a whole must actually "employ" the taken property. * * *

Our current Public Use Clause jurisprudence, as the Court notes, has rejected this natural reading of the Clause. The Court adopted its modern reading blindly, with little discussion of the Clause's history and original meaning, in two distinct lines of cases: first, in cases adopting the "public purpose" interpretation of the Clause, and second, in cases deferring to legislatures' judgments regarding what constitutes a valid public purpose. Those questionable cases converged in the boundlessly broad and deferential conception of "public use" adopted by this Court in *Berman* and *Midkiff*, cases that take center stage in the Court's opinion. The weakness of those two lines of cases, and consequently *Berman* and *Midkiff*, fatally undermines the doctrinal foundations of the Court's decision. Today's questionable application of these cases is further proof that the "public purpose" standard is not susceptible of principled application. This Court's reliance by rote on this standard is ill advised and should be reconsidered. * * *

The Court relies almost exclusively on this Court's prior cases to derive today's far-reaching, and dangerous, result. * * * When faced with a clash of constitutional principle and a line of unreasoned cases wholly divorced from the text, history, and structure of our founding document, we should not hesitate to resolve the tension in favor of the Constitution's original meaning.

NOTES

1. Justice Thomas noted in his dissent that "[o]ver 97 percent of the individuals forcibly removed from their homes by the 'slum-clearance' project upheld by this Court in *Berman* were black." Of course, if economic development programs are successful, the beneficiaries from increased employment and better-funded government services might also be poor and minority. How, if at all, should the Court take into account potential racial and class dimensions of the problem?
2. Are you persuaded by Justice O'Connor's effort to distinguish prior cases (including the Hawaiian decision, which she wrote)? Under her proposed approach, how would efforts to assemble land for new development in low-lying portions of New Orleans fare? What would it take to satisfy the test suggested by Justice Kennedy in his concurrence?
3. There is serious political opposition to the use of eminent domain for private development. For example, shortly after Katrina, a member of Congress warned against this approach:

> Rep. Maxine Waters, a Los Angeles Democrat, warned Tuesday against using government's power of eminent domain to redevelop New Orleans after Hurricane Katrina concentrated its devastation on largely poor African American neighborhoods.
>
> "We have to watch the redevelopment of New Orleans for a lot or reasons, and one of them is to make sure that the shadow government of the rich and powerful does not end up abusing eminent domain to take property that belongs to poor people in order to get them out of the city," Waters said.

Carolyn Lochhead, *Lawmaker Cautions Against Eminent Domain in Rebuilding*, S.F. CHRONICLE, Sept. 21, 2005, If eminent domain is not used, how can the government assemble parcels of land for redevelopment? We will consider some possible approaches below.

4. One possibility is obviously to try to rebuild the city just the way it was. But a more comprehensive planning effort may be preferable, as discussed in the following excerpts.

**BRING NEW ORLEANS BACK COMMISSION
URBAN PLANNING COMMITTEE, ACTION PLAN FOR NEW
ORLEANS, FINAL REPORT, JANUARY 11, 2006**

http://www.bringneworleansback.org/Portals/BringNewOrleansBack/
Resources/Urban%20Planning%20Action%20Plan%20Final%20Report.pdf

The Committee gave much thought to developing a long-term vision of the new New Orleans, one based on the best of its legacy. The vision captures the spirit and aspirations of the committee members and participants:

> *New Orleans will be a sustainable, environmentally safe, socially equitable community with a vibrant economy. Its neighborhoods will be planned with its citizens and connect to jobs and the region. Each will preserve and celebrate its heritage of culture, landscape, and architecture.*

Therefore, the Committee did not consider rebuilding as a way to replace what was damaged, but as an opportunity to create the best city New Orleans could be—not just for people to return, but also to attract people from around the world to visit and live. This will be a city that is bigger and better than before, a city with:

- Downtown: vibrant and bustling with people who want to live, work, eat, shop, experience culture and art, bring their children, and stay. A downtown that remains the economic and cultural center of the region and, in fact, of much of the south.
- Neighborhoods: the heart of activity and services, celebrating their unique heritage and welcoming the new.
- Parks and open space: bringing sustainable nature into every neighborhood, linking every part of the city.
- Educational, technical, and medical institutions: employment powerhouses, supporting their neighborhoods and energizing the economy of the region.
- Connections: beautifully landscaped connections throughout the city and region for pedestrians, bicycles, cars, and transit.

* * *

As we plan to rebuild New Orleans with these aspirations in mind, we have to remember that in the short term population and City revenue will be greatly reduced. We must use these resources wisely. Most important to accomplish now is the immediate provision of temporary housing to enable citizens to return; it is the lack of usable housing that is keeping citizens away. As we are doing that, we immediately need to turn our attention to establish neighborhood-planning teams to complete plans for the neighborhoods by May 20, 2006—in a little over four months from today. This is fast, but achievable. Remember that providing houses quickly is the overriding concern now. It must be done in a manner that builds a better city in the long term as well. We must face the fact that there will have to be some consolidation of neighborhoods that have insufficient population to support the equitable and efficient delivery of services. In the short term, there will be half the population of July 2005. We have no choice but to be responsible with use of limited City resources. We must provide public facilities and services where population is concentrated so these resources can be used in the most equitable and efficient manner possible. We also need to keep in mind that publicly subsidized housing is an asset, and work with HUD where appropriate to make the most of that asset.

Everything we do now must be considered for its long-term impact on city-wide recovery and growth. How can every short-term action help to make New Orleans a great city–one that is sustainable over the long term? We have developed guidelines to assist the neighborhood planning teams as they address the specifics of their unique situations.

- Many years of experience support a neighborhood population of between approximately 5,000 and 10,000 people as ideal.
- We should know that most residents are committed to return, at least half.
- There should be enough people living close together (density) to permit the delivery of public infrastructure, services, and utilities in an efficient manner.
- Many studies, and the experience and common sense of parents, support the model of small schools: two K-8 public schools and a shared high school to serve a population of approximately 11,000 people.
- Other aspects of a full and satisfying daily life include places of worship, access to convenience retail, health, community, and cultural facilities, parks and open space, accessibility to the rest of the city and region by transit, and contiguous relationship to other neighborhoods.

After it becomes clear who will return and where, there is likely to be an amount of land not required for the short-term population. Neighborhood planning teams will make recommendations on the best use of these urban preserves. These are areas, of all sizes, that will not be immediately reoccupied. They should be treated physically and legally in a manner that will contribute to the long-term recovery and health of the city. The neighborhood and the city-wide planning teams should keep in mind the long-term use of

the land as the city [grows] again. Rather than leave buildings and land fallow, the city must prepare plans for their management. Many practices can be used to help, including planting of species capable of phyto-remediation of contaminants, tree planting for the "environmental services" they provide and as a way to create suitable environments in which new residents may wish to live, park and open space, and others.
* * *

What Will It Cost?

What will all this cost? We have early estimates for some elements, while others need to be determined. Likewise, we have made initial determinations of specific potential sources of funding.

- Acquisition of heavily flooded and damaged houses: estimated cost is $4 billion (funding source: CDBG, FEMA HMGP).
- Demolition and site remediation: estimated cost is $700 million (funding source: FEMA Public Assistance–Category A Debris Removal, CDBG).
- Public transit (including the airport line, but excluding Baton Rouge and Gulf coast lines): estimated cost is $4.8 billion (funding source: US DOT-FHWA and FTA, FEMA Public Assistance, CDBG). Of this total, $1 billion is for the immediate construction of the airport to downtown New Orleans East line.
- Damaged public buildings: estimated cost is $413 million (funding source: FEMA Public Assistance).
- NORC operation over its ten year life: estimated cost at $1 million per year is $10 million (funding source: other).
- Reconstruction and long-term recovery planning: estimated cost is $7.5 million (funding source: FEMA, US Economic Development Administration).
- Parks and open space costs will be calculated as part of the planning process. (Funding source: FEMA HMGP and Individual Assistance, US DOT-FHWA Transportation Enhancement Program).

This is evolving on a daily basis. We expect the estimates and funding sources to continue to be refined as work on the detailed city-wide and neighborhood plans progresses.
* * *

Key Recommendations

This executive summary covers a great deal of material; yet it only touches superficially on the Committee's work. Much of that is contained in the collected working papers and memoranda of the Urban Planning Committee's six sub-committees. It is clear that we must move quickly and decisively, focusing on short term needs while working toward a sustainable future. Therefore, we summarize our key recommendations.

- Complete the structure necessary and CDBG funding to accomplish the buyout of heavily flooded and damaged homes and provide for the repair and reconstruction of those who wish to return.
- We must aggressively pursue the neighborhood planning process and implement the recommendations of those efforts within a coordinated city-wide plan.
- We should not issue building permits in the heavily flooded and damaged areas until the neighborhood planning process is complete this summer. Investment decisions in these areas must be based on facts that are not yet available.
- We must create the Crescent City Recovery Corporation which is necessary to manage and direct the recovery process.
- We must start major housing construction in the target development areas to provide the houses people need as quickly as possible.
- We must design, fund and construct the high-speed transit system which will strengthen and support the city.

There will [be] more work and sacrifice ahead. Therefore, we should remind ourselves of the vision that calls us to action. New Orleans will be a city that is environmentally, socially, and economically sustainable. A city built on the best of its legacy. The best city in the world.

NOTES

1. It remains to be seen whether these ambitious plans will be realized. Presumably, federal support will be needed, as well as a clear federal plan for flood control in order to encourage private investors.
2. The most controversial proposal by the commission was to limit the issuance of building permits in certain neighborhoods to freeze rebuilding. This recommendation was rejected by the mayor:

> Nagin said he appreciated the committee's desire to protect residents from spending money on houses or stores that could be vulnerable to flooding again and might not be eligible for flood insurance. But, he said, "I have confidence that our citizens can decide intelligently for themselves where they want to rebuild, once presented with the facts."
>
> He also rejected the committee's suggestion that hard-hit neighborhoods should have to prove themselves viable, probably by showing that at least 50 percent of residents intend to return, before the city would agree to provide services to them.
>
> "I believe government investment should follow our citizens' investment," Nagin said, without setting up what critics considered arbitrary criteria.

But even as he refused to deny any neighborhood the right to rebuild, Nagin warned residents of the Lower 9th Ward and "the lowest-lying areas of New Orleans East" that the Army Corps of Engineers has told him those areas are likely to flood again if a Katrina-style hurricane hits New Orleans this year or in 2007.

"That's why it's important that you as citizens have the option of rebuilding on your own, or taking advantage of the buyout option in the Failed Levee Homeowners Recovery Program I pioneered," Nagin said. That option, if it wins state and federal approval and financing, would offer homeowners up to $150,000.

Bruce Eggler, *Mayor Accepts BNOB Blueprint*, TIMES PICAYUNE, March 21, 2006.

3. Developing a governance structure to make rebuilding decisions is a challenge because of the need for state, federal, and local cooperation, and also because so many of the affected residents are not currently living in New Orleans. For thoughts about those challenges, see *Recovering From Katrina and Rita: Environmental Governance Lessons Learned and Applied*, 36 ENV. L. REP. 10139 (2006).

D. HOUSING

Property of all kinds was destroyed by Hurricane Katrina: government buildings, infrastructure such as utilities, private businesses, and public spaces such as parks. But when we think of the damage, we tend to think first of the housing that was destroyed. Restoring the city's housing involves some difficult issues, which will determine to some extent the future of the city as a community—for who lives in the city in the future will be partly a function of housing decisions made today.

FROM THE LAKE TO THE RIVER: THE NEW ORLEANS COALITION FOR LEGAL AID & DISASTER RELIEF, REPORT TO MAYOR NAGIN'S BRING NEW ORLEANS BACK COMMISSION

http://www.fromthelaketotheriver.org/files/final_report_11.29.pdf
(Nov. 29, 2001)

As many have observed, Hurricane Katrina has provided an unprecedented opportunity to address entrenched inequities that have plagued the City of New Orleans and hindered its growth and prosperity. The pervasive poverty that had shamefully become an accepted part of our reality and culture was suddenly exposed worldwide as a brutal determinant of who would be winners and losers in the hurricane survival "game." This poverty, with which we had grown so accustomed, was spacially and racially concentrated. It did not result from purely private and random decisionmaking, but was borne of historic inequality and government-sponsored segregation. This may sound like civil rights rhetoric, but Katrina shone such a spotlight on the economically crippling effects of historic racial segregation that even the President felt compelled to acknowledge and atone for them.

Fair housing advocates and scholars frequently make the link between housing opportunity and access to education, jobs, and other goods and services. They have perhaps not yet thought to make the link between housing mobility and, quite literally, survival. Tragically, Hurricane Katrina has now helped us to make that link. We will never know for sure whether more poor people would have been able to evacuate if they had not been so racially and economically segregated. It is certainly true that families of all incomes and races were affected by this storm, with homes in many parts of the city being flooded. But when one lives in a housing development, a block, or neighborhood where very few—if any—people have cars, then it is not likely that anyone will leave. Segregation breeds poverty and poverty breeds isolation. And in New Orleans in August 2005, isolation was a misery.

Now, almost three months later, we are challenged to confront a similar isolation. This time, we wonder how many of the people who were without the resources to leave will find the resources to come back. Some have remarked that perhaps the City would be better off without its poorest residents. Others have remarked that perhaps the City's poorest residents would be better off without their City. Either way, the policy choices we make now will affect the choices our residents make. And the choices our former residents make will certainly affect the make-up of 21st century New Orleans.

The economic viability of the City of New Orleans cannot be assured unless its residents have a home to which to return. The recommendations that follow will address six aspects of the housing challenges affecting our City and State: Scarcity and Segregation; Inclusionary Zoning; Public and Federally Assisted Housing; Landlords, Tenants, and Evictions; Special Needs Housing; and Property Rights.

Scarcity and Segregation

Many, if not all, neighborhoods in the metropolitan area have felt the effects of Katrina. Some neighborhoods are turning the corner on their recovery. Others have barely begun. Some houses were left unscathed while many are totally destroyed. FEMA contractors and others assisting in the recovery process have increased the demand for housing. The net result is a severe housing shortage.

Historically, when disadvantaged groups have faced severe housing shortages, the impulse is always there to take whatever housing can be gotten despite the effects on segregation, i.e., better to get some housing on a segregated basis than none at all. This is a false choice and should be avoided. If New Orleans is to address historic inequities and plan for a more inclusive community that does not perpetuate poverty by building subsidized enclaves, it will look for creative approaches to embedding affordable housing options into every neighborhood, every block, and every building. Affordability and inclusiveness should be the ideal and the vision that govern all residential development.

- Design and facilitate a right of residents to return to their homes and neighborhoods and contribute to the rebuilding process, consistent with the United Nations Guiding Principles on Internal Displacement.
- Create an immediate supply of workforce housing. Consider how technology may be used to facilitate a centralized means of posting available housing opportunities.
- Support federal funding of emergency and long-term housing needs consistent with the recommendations of the National Policy and Advocacy Council on Homelessness.
- Both temporary and permanent housing should be sited in a way so as to avoid concentration of [trailers] and/or other affordable units in few, isolated neighborhoods. This recommendation is almost universal among civil rights groups and planners.
- Work immediately with FEMA to create an anti-displacement policy ensuring that FEMA's efforts to create short-term housing do not result in evictions of other residents, resulting in the creation of new homeless populations.
- Support survivors in their efforts to require FEMA to make it easier to apply for temporary housing assistance and to provide immediately more transitional housing in the place of shelters, tents, and other makeshift arrangements.
- Residents who rent their homes should be able to return to those homes and resume their rental payments in accordance with their leases.
- Residents without leases, or those who are renewing their leases, should be protected from rental increases that exceed 15 percent of their previous rental amount. This is particularly critical also for those whose FEMA rental payments are insufficient to cover the prevailing rental rates in the post-Katrina housing market.
- Housing opportunity must be equal for all, and patterns of discrimination and segregation that pre-existed Katrina will only exacerbate the scarcity of housing for working-class New Orleanians if left unaddressed. There must be zero tolerance for discrimination and strong support for aggressive fair housing enforcement to ensure a level housing playing field.
- Fair housing laws protect people from discrimination on the basis of national origin. Oppose any efforts or actions that restrict or deny the housing opportunities of temporary workers on the basis of national origin.

- Make use of existing housing units in the private market before relying on mobile homes.
- Create an inventory of blighted properties located in neighborhoods that were not affected by flooding. Considering that non-flooded neighborhoods already have utilities and other infrastructure not yet available in flooded areas, plan and implement incentives for currently blighted properties to be placed in commerce.
- Look at strategies for acquisition of blighted properties to be renovated for workforce housing, affordable rental housing, and home ownership.
- Use the rebuilding effort as a means of creating wealth and building the assets of New Orleans residents through home ownership opportunities, training in the building trades, and small business development.

Inclusionary Zoning

Consider the pre-Katrina landscape when making post-Katrina housing policy decisions. Prior to the hurricane, several moratoria were in place that limited the construction of multi-family housing in certain councilmanic districts. These moratoria also limited the operation of group homes in certain districts. Although some of the resistance may have originated in communities with a higher concentration of federally assisted housing and housing for people with disabilities as compared with other areas of the city, these pockets of resistance may re-emerge in the post-Katrina housing development environment.

Adopt an inclusionary zoning ordinance that requires any development of over 5 units to restrict occupancy in 20% of the total units to low or very low-income households. In developments between 6 and 20 units, require that 20% of the total units be set aside for households under 60% of the median income for metropolitan New Orleans. For developments of over 20 units, require that 5% of the total units be set aside for households under 30% of the median income, and 15% of the total units be set aside for households under 60% of the median income.

Public and Federally Assisted Housing: "Where will Public Housing Residents Call Home?"

Now, three months after the storm, few public housing residents have been allowed to return to their subsidized apartments, regardless of whether their individual unit has been made less habitable by the storm. Some residents fear that public housing units that had been "acceptable" prior to the storm will now be declared uninhabitable, not because of flooding or serious storm-related damage, but because HANO has decided to use Hurricane Katrina as an opportunity to make sweeping changes to its inventory and programs. No one will question the need for HANO to make sweeping changes. Indeed, residents are least served by maintaining the status quo. But low-income residents with few housing options are concerned that their inability to return to their federally assisted units will prevent their return to New Orleans. HUD's Secretary has been quoted as follows: "There should be no doubt that we are committed to making certain that New Orleans' public housing residents will have a place to call home." This begs the question whether they will be calling New Orleans home or some other place.

Certainly, relocation of public housing residents is a major hurdle in any redevelopment process. Hurricane Katrina has eliminated that hurdle. The fact that HANO's public housing stock is now vacant gives it the opportunity to consider "ambitious" plans. * * * Iberville is, of course, adjacent to the French Quarter and could arguably attract market rate tenants. Some public housing residents and advocates fear that Katrina might open the door to an abusive land grab, in which private interests use Katrina to carry out an economic development agenda that pre-existed the storm. If history is any judge, it takes years to engage in the planning processes and put together the financing packages necessary to implement a public housing redevelopment plan. Where will residents live during this extreme makeover of public housing?

And will former residents ever be able to occupy it once it is redeveloped? Efforts to redevelop public housing are frequently controversial because they typically involve a reduction in density, which necessarily entails a reduction in the overall number of units developed on site. Also, because the majority of the redeveloped units would likely be market rate under the prevailing "mixed income" public housing development model, less than half of the already reduced number of redeveloped units would be considered "affordable." Add to that the wide latitude developers have in setting criteria for the "affordable" units, and you could wind up with new, federally subsidized public housing developments that house mostly middle-class people and few to no former public housing residents.

So what are our options? The status quo is unacceptable. The next generation of New Orleans public housing residents should have housing choices beyond the segregated and substandard units that were considered "habitable" before Katrina, but look scarcely different now. The following recommendations seek to balance the various concerns:

- HANO should immediately establish the right of every former HANO-assisted public housing or voucher resident to return to New Orleans to a unit that is affordable, and inform every displaced HANO-assisted tenant of this right.
- Displaced tenants should be provided with any necessary transportation assistance to enable their return.
- The physical condition of all public housing units should be determined: habitable, needs minor rehabilitation, needs more substantial rehabilitation, or must be demolished. * * *
- Honor existing leases held by tenants on any units that were not totally destroyed. Tenants should be permitted to have temporary

guests and to temporarily overcrowd without penalty, especially for those guests without affordable housing who are disabled or seeking work.

- Every tenant holding a lease to a unit that is currently habitable must be allowed to return to that unit within 30 days. This includes the former St. Thomas residents who were about to be leased units at River Gardens. River Gardens, a model of mixed income housing development, has reportedly rented a number of its affordable units to HANO employees in place of former public housing residents. Do not demolish any structurally sound buildings in any publicly subsidized developments just for the purpose of facilitating redevelopment.

- If units were partially destroyed, allow tenants to decide whether to terminate the lease or to accept a transfer to another HANO property while the unit is being repaired. Make all repairs to public housing units that were only partially destroyed within 90 days.

- Assist public housing residents in locating alternative temporary housing during the interim period while their units are being repaired.

- Implement a tracking system to ensure that HANO continues to communicate with public housing and voucher residents about the housing and moving resources available to them both in the short term and after any redevelopment activities are completed. Few residents will be able to take advantage of redevelopment if HANO has no way to contact them. This could include providing a means for HANO residents to ask questions of an ombudsperson, as well as to update their contact information and check their waiting list status, etc.

- Once buildings or developments are identified as uninhabitable, make nonnegotiable the participation of former public housing residents in the planning and implementation of any redevelopment plans. Make training and employment of former public housing residents in redevelopment activities a condition of funding and contracting.

- Support the increase of voucher payments up to 150% of fair market rents or higher when necessary to assist lower income households to compete for scarce, more expensive housing. Residents on fixed incomes would have to spend nearly all of their income on rent to pay the difference between their voucher payments and the actual rental costs in the post-Katrina rental environment. Currently residents participating in the Katrina housing voucher program (KDHAP) are reportedly capped at 100% of the fair market rents set prior to Katrina. Even residents using vouchers prior to Katrina were able to request payments of 110% of fair market rents.

- Provide housing counseling assistance for families with vouchers who need help finding affordable housing near jobs, schools, and services.

- Oppose efforts to siphon off existing voucher funds to pay for redevelopment of public housing. Vouchers may be one of the few means to provide housing to public housing residents waiting for public housing units to be redeveloped.

- Provide incentives to suburban jurisdictions that accept former New Orleans public housing residents using vouchers. Support the portability of voucher use between parishes.

- Prevent the exodus of landlords from the Section 8 programs by paying fair rental amounts to landlords whose properties are currently habitable.

- Create an inventory of low income tax credit properties, which are unable to deny housing to families on the basis of their use of a housing voucher.

- Facilitate the right to return of New Orleans residents by prohibiting discrimination on the basis of the use of a housing subsidy or voucher. Many families seeking to return may be forced to rely on housing vouchers to be able to afford housing in the private market. Policies that excluded renters with housing subsidies were pervasive in the New Orleans housing market before Katrina and will inhibit the return of residents if allowed to continue.

Landlords, Tenants, and Evictions

In the wake of Katrina, both landlords and tenants faced tremendous uncertainties about their futures. Evacuated tenants were unable to determine whether their leased apartments or houses were in habitable condition, whether their personal property was salvageable, what their obligations were with respect to the payment of rent, and in some cases how to reach their landlords. Landlords were unsure whether some of their tenants would return and in some cases were unable to reach their tenants. Communication in the weeks following the storm was severely impaired.

Some landlords had included provisions in their written leases reserving the right to enter their rental property for the purpose of making repairs. Other landlords without this lease provision entered their tenants' property anyway, with some even throwing tenants' property away without providing notice to tenants or giving them the opportunity to remove their personal property on their own. The legislature during their extraordinary session attempted to deal with the removal of personal property through House Bill 88, by Reps. Gallot, Ansardi, and Lentini. This bill initially sought to retroactively provide immunity from suit for landlords who removed property without permission. Ultimately, the bill was amended to apply only prospectively, until June 2006, and to require landlords who needed to remove tenants' personal property in order to make repairs to undergo a number of protective measures designed to inventory the property and ensure that salvageable property was preserved. Furthermore, tenants would have to be notified ten days in advance of such property removal by means other than tacking notice, if the tenant's whereabouts could be determined. At the time of this writing, the bill passed as amended in both the Senate and House and is awaiting the Governor's signature.

With respect to the payment of rent, some landlords did not demand rent for September and any other months during which their properties were undergoing repairs. Other landlords demanded full rent for September onward, regardless of the property's condition. Even if rental properties were in perfect condition, the lack of utilities rendered units in Orleans Parish uninhabitable until at least early October 2005. The Governor had issued an Executive Order that had the effect of suspending evictions until October 25, 2005. Because Louisiana law had allowed for notice of eviction by tacking only, many tenants who were still evacuated after the Governor's order expired had eviction judgments entered against them without their knowledge. A recent lawsuit, Sylvester v. Boissiere, alleging that such notice by tacking violated the due process rights of evacuated tenants has been resolved. Now, landlords will be required to provide notice by mail (with FEMA's assistance) and give residents 45 days to return and defend themselves in eviction proceedings.

* * *

Special Needs Housing

Katrina presents enormous opportunities to address the lack of affordable housing that is accessible for persons with disabilities. Before Katrina housing that was both affordable and accessible was in short supply. HANO had not historically inventoried the need for accessible housing among its residents, and funds have not always been made available for New Orleans residents with disabilities to make necessary modifications for disability access.

On November 7, 2005, HUD issued two Notices to remind jurisdictions receiving HOME and CDBG funds of their obligation to refrain from discriminating against persons with disabilities and to make housing and facilities accessible. Section 504 requires newly constructed multifamily projects with five or more units to have at least 5% of the units accessible to people with mobility impairments, and an additional 2% of the units accessible to people with hearing or vision impairments. The Fair Housing Act has design and construction requirements that apply to all newly constructed units in buildings with at least four units and an elevator, or all ground floor units in non-elevator buildings with at least four units. Section 504 also requires that HOME and CDBG programs be made accessible, which includes providing notice of the existence of accessible units.

It is imperative that all rebuilding efforts maximize this opportunity to provide for greater levels of accessibility in both private and publicly assisted housing.

Property Rights & Final Recommendations

Some final recommendations to ensure protection and security of property rights include the following:

- Consider the creation of a landowners' compensation fund, which has been proposed by a number of sources. Tulane Law School Professor M. David Gelfand, in an article he wrote shortly before he died, suggested that such a fund would involve the setting of "fair (that is, pre-Hurricane) levels of compensation that landowners in the redevelopment area could receive quickly without expensive, time-consuming litigation. . . . Funds for tenants to relocate within New Orleans should also be part of the overall package." This may be similar to the Crescent City Rebuilding Corporation recently proposed by the Urban Land Institute.
- Adopt the Urban Land Institute's suggestions regarding extension of the mortgage forbearance period, provision of design and technical assistance to homeowners, and provision of financial assistance to homeowners to facilitate their right to return.

* * *

The Urban Environment

New Orleans is one of the most enviable urban environments in the nation: mixed income, mixed race, and mixed small-scale commercial and residential neighborhoods, corner bars and restaurants, a unique housing stock, a viable trolley system, accessible terrain, parks and green spaces, and a climate that supports outdoor activity through much of the year. No one needs to build a new New Orleans. Models of redevelopment that predominate in other American cities would overwhelm and destroy this one. The governing principle of recovery should be the rehabilitation of existing neighborhoods and the improvement of services to them.

Recommendations:

1. Don't tear it down. The great majority of city housing can be restored. We need to begin with a strong presumption against demolition, overcome on a case-by-case basis only through a showing of irreparable damage, continuing flood risk, contamination or the absence of architectural or social value.
2. The New Orleans Reconstruction Corps. All restoration contracting should require the employment of local residents. Centers should be created to train New Orleanians in restoration work, and to recruit and place skilled New Orleans workers with private employers. Task forces of a New Orleans Reconstruction Corps should be available to low-income, uninsured and other city residents on a reduced fee or

no-fee basis to elevate and rehabilitate homes. The objective is to bring back our people and our houses at the same time.

3. A master plan. New Orleans planning and zoning decisions have been made on an ad-hoc basis short on standards and long on political influence. A sustainable city requires a detailed and binding master plan that informs developers of their rights and rules, levels the playing field, and is enforceable by the city and by neighborhood organizations which are the ultimate guarantors of sound planning decisions.

4. Elevate. Levees fail, pumps fail, and ordinary rainstorms overwhelm the drainage systems. All new and existing structures should be elevated, as once they were. Slab development should be prohibited.

5, Natural flood storage. New Orleans has lost much of its flood storage capacity to concrete and asphalt. More sewer hookups are not the answer. The existing system is hard pressed to keep up with existing tie-ins, and its discharges constitute the largest source of pollution to Lake Pontchartrain as well. Low-lying areas should be set aside for passive uses, including natural water retention and drainage. New construction should be required to use pervious materials and other measures to offset the loss of land area.

6. Rail and trolley systems. New Orleans once held the most convenient public transit system in America. The restoration of these systems will enhance property values, attract tourist revenues, and protect human health and air and environmental quality. New and expanded roads will do the opposite. We are informed that Skoda, the largest manufacturer in the Czech republic, has offered to build a new trolley car plant in New Orleans. Such offers should be pursued.

7. Pedestrian and bicycle transit. A city of neighborhoods does not need automobiles for every expedition. The flat terrain and neighborhood layout of New Orleans is conducive to walking and to commuter bicycling. The economic and public health benefits of these activities are consequential, as well. Safe and convenient pedestrian and bike ways are the key.

8. Trees and green space. The affluence of New Orleans neighborhoods can be correlated directly to their amount of trees and green space. These amenities should be commonplace, not luxuries. Trees, urban gardens and green space cost very little, reduce the heat index of the city considerably in the summer, and make important contributions to life quality. They encourage people outdoors. They help bind the neighborhood.

9. Recycling. New Orleans had initiated a modest program of recycling. The potential for expanded recycling is high. The costs of not recycling will increase with the decrease of available landfill space, already stressed by the volume of Katrina and Rita debris.

10. The river. The longest and most historic river in America is largely hidden behind walls and warehouses. The port is important, but it can share. We should open the river to mixed public and private use through low-rise commercial and public space. The success of similar

renovations in other cities and countries is impressive. The river should not be committed to high-rise and other development that excludes others. It is the defining public asset of New Orleans.

Architecture and Energy

Most of New Orleans does not need to be built anew. But some of it will. The incorporation of sustainable building and energy standards in the rehabilitation and new construction will create a new economy, reduce the impacts of pollution and waste, and create a more livable environment.

Special opportunities are available in the adoption of sustainable energy strategies. Louisiana is one of the most energy wasteful states in America, ranking third in energy consumption per capita. While much of this consumption is industrial (which presents its own conservation opportunities), a significant percentage is attributed to–and paid by–individual residents. The US Department of Energy estimates that local governments can save $3.4 billion with more efficient practices, some of which are quite simple. These same efficiencies reduce air pollution and global warming precursors by several hundred million tons per year.

Many of the strategies for sustainable building and energy efficiency are the subject of detailed standards such as the Environmental Protection Agency Energy Star Program, the Department of Housing and Urban Affairs guidelines for Indoor Air Quality, and the 2000 International Conservation and Energy Code. The Energy Policy Act of 2005 imposes additional efficiency standards on all projects built or assisted by the Department of Housing and Urban Affairs. Several states such as California and Wisconsin have developed detailed energy conservation programs as well. There is no want of standards and models. The challenge is to adopt and institutionalize them.

Recommendations:

1. The State should adopt building codes and other standards for sustainable architecture and energy efficiency, based on the highest achievable standards of other states and the federal government.
2. All rehabilitated housing and commercial buildings should be encouraged to conform to these standards to the fullest extent possible. New construction should be required to apply them.
3. New construction should be integrated with public transportation, schools, and neighborhood food stores and other services to increase the sense of community and reduce the demands for private transportation (the second highest monthly cost for low-income families).
4. Audit teams of experts in sustainable building and energy efficiency should be formed to assist in specific recommendations and the drafting of implementing instruments.
5. Pilot projects of advanced technologies should be located throughout the city, with relevant information and technical assistance made available to builders and private owners.

Process

No change in human behavior happens on its own. The status quo is not evil, but it resists new ways. What is needed, then, are mechanisms to advance sustainability forward, against the odds.
Recommendations:

1. A State Sustainability Policy Act. Paralleling the National Environmental Policy Act, this statute should declare the sustainable policy goals of the state with sufficient specificity so that their fulfillment, or non-fulfillment, can be monitored and, if necessary corrected. Its basic elements include:
     a. An Office of Sustainability with the responsibility to consult with other agencies on compliance with statutory and regulatory policies.
     b. A Sustainability Audit, by state and national experts for each primary activity sector, e.g. energy, transportation, construction, recycling. The audits will identify opportunities and mechanisms to carry them out. Audit reports will be made available to the Governor and the legislature.
     c. A Sustainability Incentives Study, to include demonstration projects, education, market and other incentives to advance sustainability goals.
     d. A Citizen Advisory Committee, to the State Office, with the authority to investigate and recommend.
     e. A Sustainability Trust Fund composed of monies from developers and others seeking city and state approvals.
2. Revitalization of the Mayor of New Orleans Environmental Office with a broader, sustainability mission. This Office should be assisted by a citizen advisory board with the authority to review and recommend.
3. Codification of policy and law, to include both regulatory and incentive measures. Without this step, all plans die.
4. Partnerships and volunteers. Much of New Orleans' existing sustainability agenda is carried out by non-profit organizations such as the Preservation Resource Center and the Lake Pontchartrain Basin Foundation, often assisted by Entergy and other corporate partners. These and other partnerships should be fostered and assisted for presently unattended needs, including the creation of urban gardens, bikeways and tree planting. Most of us can plant a tree. Many of us would like to. We need to put this good will to work.

NOTES

1. In terms of tax base and minimizing the cost of services, a city is better off without a low-income population. So called "fiscal zoning" is a common

issue for local governments. For the constitutional questions raised by land use planning to exclude the poor, see Morales v. Haines, 349 F. Supp. 684 (N.D. Ill. 1972) *modified* 486 F.2d 880 (7th Cir. 1973); Ybarra v. Town of Los Altos Hills, 503 F.2d 250 (9th Cir. 1974). Are there countervailing political incentives in the case of New Orleans? If not, should the state or federal government encourage redevelopment to attract affluent new residents or to restore housing for less affluent former residents?

2. As we have seen, outside groups see some exciting opportunities to make the "new" New Orleans a model city. But it is also easy to imagine redevelopment taking the easier path of least resistance, or perhaps even worse, becoming so mired in political and legal obstacles that the city remains scarred for decades. How can the process be structured so as to favor the more desirable outcomes?

3. One advantage of a creative rebuilding strategy is that it allows the use of New Orleans as a "test bed" for new ideas. Doing so could benefit the rest of the country by providing insights about improved building and development techniques. That seems only fair, since it seems likely that the rest of the country will foot part of the bill.

4. Reconstruction after national disasters is a problem that many cities around the world have faced. For some important lessons to be learned from cities as diverse as Los Angeles, Mexico City, and Kobe, Japan, see MARY C. COMERIO, DISASTER HITS HOME: NEW POLICY FOR URBAN HOUSING RECOVERY (1998).

5. Notice how all aspects of reconstruction are interrelated. People cannot be expected to rebuild until they are assured of flood protection. But a flood protection system cannot be properly designed unless we know just what it will be protecting. Thus, comprehensive planning seems to be required. Such planning, however, does not come naturally to our system of government.

6. For additional ideas about reconstruction, see NATURAL RESOURCE DEFENSE COUNCIL, AFTER KATRINA: NEW SOLUTIONS FOR SAFE COMMUNITIES AND A SECURE ENERGY FUTURE (2005), and BROOKINGS INSTITUTION, NEW ORLEANS AFTER THE STORM: LESSONS FROM THE PAST, A PLAN FOR THE FUTURE (2005). An important recent development involves the Louisiana Recovery Authority (LRA) "Road Home" Housing Plan, which has been approved both by the state legislature and HUD. The program has secured more than $10 billion in federal funding. Under the terms, homeowners are eligible for rebuilding grants or buy-outs up to $150,000. More than 120,000 homeowners are eligible for assistance. See http://www.doa.la.gov/cdbg/dr/Housing%20Action%20Plan%20No%202%20FINAL.pdf; http://www.doa.louisiana.gov/cdbg/DRHousing.htm.

8

BEYOND KATRINA

As bad as it was, Hurricane Katrina was not the last word in disasters on American soil. Unfortunately, Americans face a number of other serious risks today that present unsettled legal issues. Other disaster scenarios may make us confront from a different perspective the questions of where we live and work, how we choose to develop our communities, and how our economy depends on the globalization of business and communication. While no society can live in constant fear of impending catastrophe, we can prepare for a variety of situations. Potential threats include terrorism, major flooding (the Gulf region will face another hurricane season each fall, and many other cities are at risk from inadequate flood protection), earthquakes, and pandemics like avian flu. Global climate change has the potential to create dramatic shifts in weather that could cause disaster on a widespread scale not previously seen. Thinking *now* about the questions these events might raise will allow us to have better answers and avoid much of the confusion and tragedy seen in the aftermath of Katrina.

Space precludes us from covering all of the major potential disaster threats here. Emergency response, compensation, and reconstruction issues regarding terrorism are similar to those for natural disasters, but we will not address them directly. Also because of space limitations, we will have little to say about seismic risks. We certainly do not mean to minimize those risks, and they present some interesting and distinctive issues. (For example, at least in parts of the United States, building codes seem to have been more rigorously applied to earthquake risks than is the norm for flood risks.) The risks that we do cover, however, should give the reader plenty of food for thought.

A. OTHER FLOOD RISKS

California's San Joaquin Delta and the land to the north and east of it is a rich ecosystem for water fowl and marine species. The area is also home to many agricultural uses. At the same time, it is under intense pressure from housing and commercial developers. The Delta and the rivers that feed it are an important source of fresh water for the Bay Area and Southern California.

Similar to New Orleans, much of the land in the Delta and the surrounding areas requires an elaborate system of levees and dams to prevent flooding. The problem, though, is that the levee system is broken. Breaches are common and when they do occur, salt water devastates farms, private property, and ecosystems; even the state capitol is threatened. Supplies of fresh water are also compromised when the system fails.

Even though the cost to rebuild and reinforce the levee system will be significant, in a rare show of bipartisanship California's governor, senators, and representatives are uniformly committed to maintaining and reinforcing the levee system. Most, but not all, also support the construction of another dam at a time when scientists are questioning the wisdom of dams in general. In addition, the governor has declared the levees to be in a "state of emergency," allowing exemptions from some state environmental laws, in order to allow repairs to proceed more quickly.

Other stakeholders argue that (1) reinforcing the levee system is not a long-term solution and is doomed to failure anyway, (2) parts of the Delta should be restored for the benefit of marine ecosystems, and (3) government should not permit development in floodplains in any event. At this point, however, developers are continuing to move forward with new housing in areas that are well below sea level. *See* Patrick Hoge, *Homes in Flood Catastrophe Zones: A Booming Demand for Housing Has Developers Building New Earthen Levees Inside the Old Ones in the Delta Floodplain,* S.F. CHRONICLE, Jan. 30, 2006.. These issues are explored in the following excerpts.

CALIFORNIA DEPARTMENT OF RESOURCES, FLOOD WARNINGS:
RESPONDING TO CALIFORNIA'S FLOOD CRISIS

(Jan. 2005)

Over the years, major storms and flooding have taken many California lives, caused significant property losses and resulted in extensive damage to public infrastructure. However, a combination of recent factors has put public safety and the State's financial stability at risk for even greater calamity in the future:

- Escalating development in floodplains increases the potential for flood damage to homes, businesses and communities.

- California's flood protection system, comprised of aging infrastructure with major design deficiencies, has been further weakened by deferred maintenance.
- State and local funding for effective flood prevention and management programs has been reduced.
- Court decisions have resulted in greater State flood damage liability.

Unless California implements a strategic plan, the next major flood could easily overwhelm the state's deteriorating 50-year-old flood protection system and have catastrophic consequences for our people, property and environment. The State will continue to pay out millions, and potentially billions, of dollars every time a levee break occurs in the flood control system. An aggressive investment in the flood management system and a new flood management philosophy is vitally important to public safety and our economic well-being.

California's Central Valley flood control system of levees, channels and weirs is old. Many levee reaches were built more than a century ago on foundations that are subject to seepage and movement. Over time, the levee system has significantly deteriorated, partly due to deficiencies in the original design and partly due to deferred maintenance. Observed deterioration includes levee reaches with internal and external erosion, degradation/removal of natural berms, animal burrows, and settlement. In addition, the uncontrolled growth of vegetation and build up of sediment deposits [have] greatly reduced the amount of water that flows smoothly through critical channels and rivers. Riverbank and levee erosion has been a particularly devastating part of the overall deterioration. In many levee reaches, the flood control channels were designed to flush out sediments that accumulated in the Sacramento River system from hydraulic mining activities in the late 1800s. These designs were quite successful in flushing out the mining debris. However, with the debris removed, the powerful flows are now eroding the natural channel banks and the flood protection levees placed on them. This ongoing erosion causes more damage than can be repaired by the State or local reclamation districts using normal maintenance programs. A significant strategic plan element must include a proactive short-term maintenance approach and a long-term project solution.

Many places within the levee system have developed problems caused by under seepage and other internal weaknesses. While studies to uncover these weaknesses have been completed and extensive remedial work has been performed on some parts of the system, much work remains. In addition, it is extremely difficult to detect all hidden deficiencies. As a result, failures occur unpredictably and with little warning.

In addition to the challenges of maintaining a viable flood control system in the Central Valley, there are also great challenges in the Sacramento-San Joaquin Delta. The Delta includes nearly 60 islands and tracts lying below sea level that are kept dry by more than 600 miles of marginal levees, many founded on peat soils.

Most of these levees have problems associated with long term levee settlement and island subsidence. During the last century there have been more than 140 levee failures and island inundations, most of which occurred during flood seasons. More recently, on June 3, 2004, a huge dry weather levee failure occurred without warning on Upper Jones Tract. The cause remains unknown but the effect was the inundation of 12,000 acres of farmland with approximately 160,000 acre-feet of water.

Higher Flood Flows

Traditionally, levee heights and channel capacities have been designed using historical data related to precipitation and runoff. However, due to either limited historical data or climate change, the general trend is for flood flows to be higher than anticipated. Consequently, flood inundations by 100-year flood events now cover much greater areas than those used for design and floodplain mapping just a few years ago. Thus, many existing floodplain maps are woefully out of date.

Costs and Consequences

The potential impacts on people and communities of a single failure or multiple failures are catastrophic. These risks tend to be disproportionately higher in rural and economically disadvantaged communities that are often unable to invest in flood control improvements. The 1997 floods forced more than 120,000 people from their homes. More than 55,000 were housed in 107 shelters, the largest sheltering operation in California's history. An estimated 30,000 residential and 2,000 business properties were damaged or destroyed.

The recent levee break on Upper Jones tract in the South Delta will cost nearly $100 million for emergency response, damage to private property, lost crops, levee repair, and pumping water from the island. There were also significant costs associated with losses in water supply and conveyance. Following the break, Delta pumping was curtailed for several days to prevent seawater intrusion at the State and Federal pumping plants, and water shipments to Southern California were continued only through unscheduled releases from San Luis Reservoir, a large offstream reservoir where water is held after it is pumped from the Delta. Releases were also increased at Shasta and Oroville reservoirs, sending more fresh water to the Delta for salinity control.

In general, the flood control system does not provide the necessary protection for public safety, property and economic values.

* * *

The potential impacts on people and communities of a single failure or multiple failures are catastrophic. These risks tend to be disproportionately higher in rural and economically disadvantaged communities that are often unable to invest in flood control improvements.

Growing Risks for Flood Damage and Loss of Life

California's population growth presents a major challenge to the State's flood management system. In the Central Valley alone, much of the new development is occurring in areas that are susceptible to flooding. In some cases, land use decisions are based on poor or outdated information regarding the seriousness of the flood threat. For example, many flood maps used by public agencies and the general public are decades old and do not reflect the most accurate information regarding potential flooding. Even worse, many maps were made by simply assuming that federal project levees provided protection from 100-year flood events. Unfortunately, recent experience has shown that this assumption is not necessarily valid.

Land use decisions at the local level that allow developments in floodplains protected by the State-federal levee system in the Central Valley greatly increase the risk of State liability for loss of life and property damage. Better coordination is needed between agencies making land use decisions and the parties, often the State, which must bear the burdens and liabilities of those decisions. The State must develop a process that guides regional development with the goal of protecting people and property at risk in floodplains, while connecting the legal liability of ill-advised land use decisions to those making the decisions to approve development in these areas.

Another challenge is that people who live and work behind levees have a false sense of protection. Many believe that the levees will protect them against any level of flooding. Even if a levee was capable of successfully holding back a 100-year flood, a target flood event used by many insurance and public agencies when providing flood protection, it doesn't mean that a larger flood, such as a 110-year or a 150-year flood event, won't flood their property. During a typical 30-year mortgage period, there is a 26 percent chance that a homeowner living behind a levee will experience a flood larger than the 100-year flood. This risk is many times greater than the risk of a major home fire during the same period.

NOTES

1. A key question in the Delta is whether it will be possible to prevent increased development in high-risk areas. Unfortunately, this may be difficult both for political reasons and for legal reasons. Environmental Planning expert Dr. Robert Twiss has said that once an area has been developed for housing, it is impossible to reclaim the area for flood control. The tax pressures on local governments further encourage them to prioritize development over open space for flood protection. Imagine you are on the board of a local government. How would you manage these issues and answer your constituent's questions and concerns?
2. Although Hurricane Katrina helped focus public attention on the long-standing threat to the California Delta, it remains unclear whether the

state's somewhat dysfunctional political system will be capable of mounting an effective response to the problem. Representative John Doolittle has pushed for construction of the Auburn Dam for decades, while Representative Doris Matsui has focused on greater levee protection. The expense of any solution means that there will be a long time before federal, state, and local governments can fund a completed project. While the political actors agree that something must be done, agreement on a particular resolution is far from certain. Think about the role that politics and political actors play as a driving force for policy and legal choices. If a solution is legally possible and pragmatic, but politically unpopular, what can be done to enact change?

3. Although levees have generally been thought of as low-risk structures, the potential for dams to cause damage has long been recognized. Unfortunately, as discussed in the following excerpt, recognition of this risk has not necessarily been matched with an equally focused response.

CONGRESSIONAL RESEARCH SERVICE, AGING
INFRASTRUCTURE: DAM SAFETY

(Sept. 2005)

While dams have multiple benefits, they also represent a risk to public safety and economic infrastructure. This risk stems from two sources: the likelihood of a dam failure and the damage it would cause. While dam failures are infrequent, age, construction deficiencies, inadequate maintenance, and seismic or weather events contribute to the likelihood. To reduce the risk, regular inspections are necessary to identify deficiencies and then corrective action must be taken.

To identify deficiencies that could cause dam failures, the federal government established inspection requirements for the nation's federal dams. Once deficiencies are identified, most agencies finance repairs through their operation and maintenance accounts. Funding mechanisms vary for larger rehabilitation activities. At the Bureau of Reclamation, for example, most larger repairs are conducted with annual appropriations to its dam safety program. At some other agencies, dam rehabilitation must compete with other construction projects for funding.

At non-federal dams, safety is generally a state responsibility, though some federal assistance has been provided. Funding through the National Dam Safety Program, which is authorized through FY 2006, helps states improve their dam safety programs and train inspectors. In addition, the Federal Energy Regulatory Commission and the Department of Labor, Mine Safety and Health Administration require regular inspections at the non-federal dams within their jurisdiction. Even so, there are concerns that most state dam safety programs have inadequate staff and funds to effectively inspect or monitor all of the dams for which they are responsible. Further, there are concerns that states, local governments, and other non-federal dam owners may not have the financial resources to maintain and rehabilitate their dams.

Following the failure of the levee at Lake Pontchartrain in 2005, it is likely that there will be increased scrutiny of flood control infrastructure and the structural stability of high hazard-potential dams. Further, there has been periodic pressure for Congress to pass legislation authorizing federal support for rehabilitation work at non-federal dams. Demand for such assistance is likely to increase, but there is currently no federal policy that describes the conditions under which federal funding is appropriate, nor has Congress established criteria for prioritizing funding among non-federal projects.

* * *

Prior to the events of September 11, 2001, Congress had expressed an increasing interest over several decades in dam safety. In recent years, congressional interest focused largely on securing and protecting U.S. dams and water storage facilities from terror attacks. Following Hurricane Katrina and the disastrous failure of levees that once protected New Orleans, however, there may be renewed interest in the structural integrity of other major water infrastructure.

The modern period of congressional concern began in the 1970s with dam failures that resulted in loss of life and billions of dollars in property losses. Congress and private groups interested in dam safety noted that, while states and localities are responsible for the maintenance and safety of 95% of the nation's dams, large numbers of older dams lacked the maintenance needed to guarantee operational integrity and prevent failure. These aging dams presented then—and continue to present—a potential hazard to downstream populations.

Following the first of these dam failures, an essential first task was to develop accurate data on the nation's dams: their number, type, structural condition, and other information useful for making decisions about dam safety policy and priorities. This was achieved through creation in 1972 of the National Inventory of Dams (NID)—a computerized, periodically updated catalogue of U.S. dams, maintained by the U.S. Army Corps of Engineers—that presently lists 79,777 public and private "dams."[1] For the purposes of the NID, a dam is defined as "any artificial barrier that has the ability to impound water . . . for the purpose of storage or control of water" that (1) is greater than 25 feet in height with a storage capacity of more than 15 acre-feet[2] (af), (2) is greater than 6 feet in height with a storage capacity of more than 50 af, or (3) poses a significant threat to human life or property should it fail.

Federal and non-federal dams in the NID were constructed for a variety of purposes. By far, the greatest number of dams—approximately a third— were constructed primarily for recreational purposes. About 21.4% were built primarily for fire protection. The others, in descending order of their primary

---

1. Other sources cite different figures; the online NID data is used throughout this report unless otherwise specified. When appropriate, this data will be referred to as *NID Data*, 2005.

2. One acre-foot of water is the amount of water that will cover an acre of land to a depth of one foot, approximately 326,000 gallons.

purpose, are: flood control (16.4%); irrigation (10.1%); water supply (7.4%); hydroelectric (2.7%); fish and wildlife (1.3%); mining (tailings dams) (1.2%); debris control (0.8%); and navigation (0.1%). Approximately 8.7% of the dams in the NID have other primary purposes, or those purposes are unspecified. While these are the primary purposes, many dams have multiple uses.

Nearly 56% of dams in the NID are privately owned. (See Figure 1.) Slightly more than 20% are owned and operated by local—county or municipal—governments. About 4.8% of dams are owned by states and 2.4% by public utility companies. The federal government owns only 4.7% of all NID dams, but this small number (somewhat more than 3,700) includes the dams many Americans view as iconic: the great hydroelectric dams of the West, like Grand Coulee and Hoover. The ownership of some NID dams is not indicated in the database because that information was not reported to the Corps.

While the federal government owns less than 5% of NID dams, more than 30% of all dams in the NID inventory were funded, designed, or constructed with federal resources, most of them through the Department of Agriculture's Natural Resources Conservation Service (NRCS). NRCS' involvement in dam construction stems primarily from the Watershed Protection and Flood Prevention Act of 1954, which authorized it to cooperate with states and local agencies to undertake works of improvement for flood prevention and other purposes. Under this act and an earlier law to build projects in 11 designated watersheds, NRCS helped build more than 10,000 upstream flood control dams beginning in 1948. These are generally relatively small dams owned by public or private entities other than the federal government. These non-federal entities are principally responsible for the dams' operation, maintenance, and security.

Figure 1.   Dam Ownership

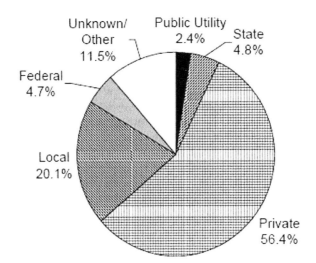

Excluding the NRCS, which does not own any dams, nine federal agencies own, operate, or regulate dam safety at approximately 8,500 sites (including non-NID dams). Six federal agencies own NID dams. These are: the Department of Defense (862), Department of the Interior (750), Department of Agriculture (326), Tennessee Valley Authority (83), Department of Energy (16), and the State Department (7). In addition, 3 agencies regulate, but do not own NID dams: the Federal Energy Regulatory Commission (FERC) regulates 1,775 hydropower dams; the Department of Labor, Mine Safety and Health Administration regulates 745 dams; and the Nuclear Regulatory Commission regulates 11 dams. While dams owned by one agency are not generally regulated by another agency, there are cases where private hydroelectric projects, regulated by FERC, are located at federal dams.

Congressional interest in dam safety generally falls into three areas: (1) dam security and the potential for acts of terrorism at major U.S. dam sites; (2) prevention of potential dam failures due to structural deficiencies; and (3) recovery from dam failures. This report focuses on the second category because it is a topic that will likely become more important as the nation's dams age; further it is likely to gain additional attention in the aftermath of Hurricane Katrina.

Dam Failure Risk

While dams have multiple benefits, their failure or misoperation could threaten public safety, local and regional economies, and the environment. Risk has two primary components: (1) the damage and deaths associated with dam failure or misoperation, and (2) the likelihood of such a failure.

Damage

To quantify the potential harm associated with a dam's failure, the Interagency Committee On Dam Safety prepared a hazard potential classification system.[3] As described in **Table 1**, the three hazard ratings (low, significant, and high) do not indicate the likelihood of failure, but reflect the *amount and type of damage* that a failure would cause. Hazard ratings for each dam are included in the NID. From 2000 to 2005 the number of high hazard dams increased from 9,921 to 11,811. According to FEMA, development below dams is the primary factor increasing dams hazard potential.[4]

---

3. Interagency Committee on Dam Safety, *FEMA 333. Federal Guidelines on Dam Safety: Hazard Potential Classification System for Dams* (Oct. 1998, reprinted Jan. 2004).

4. Federal Emergency Management Agency, *FEMA 466: Dam Safety and Security in the United States: A Progress Report on the National Dam Safety Program in FY 2002 and 2003*.

Table 1.   Hazard Level: Description and Number

Hazard Classification	Result of Failure or Misoperation	Number of Dams
High Hazard	— Loss of life is probable. — Other economic or environmental loss possible, but not necessary for this classification.	11,811
Significant Hazard	— No probable loss of human life. — Could result in economic loss, environmental damage, and disruption of lifeline facilities, etc.	13,407
Low Hazard	— No probable loss of human life.— Few economic or environmental losses; losses are generally limited to the owner.	54,349

Likelihood of Failure

While catastrophic dam failures are fairly infrequent, states reported 1,090 dam safety incidents—including 125 failures—between 1999 and 2004.[5] A number of factors, including age, construction deficiencies, inadequate maintenance, and seismic or weather events, contribute to the likelihood of dam failure. For example, some failures are the direct result of flows larger than the dams were built to withstand. With the exception of seismic or weather events, age is a leading indicator of dam failure. In particular, the structural integrity and operational effectiveness of dams may deteriorate with age and some older dams do not comply with current dam safety standards established in the 1970s. Overall, more than 30% of all dams in the National Inventory are at least 50 years old, the design life of many dams, and more than 17,000 will cross this threshold over the next 10 years. (See Figure 2.) According to the Association of State Dam Safety Officials, in 2003, approximately 3,243 U.S. dams had deficiencies that left them more susceptible to failure. In 2000, another report estimate that more than $30 billion will be needed to repair and rehabilitate the nation's aging dams.[6]

---

5. National Performance of Dams, Dam Incidents, Statistics Calculator. Available Sept. 14, 2005, at [http://npdp.stanford.edu/index.html]. This database provides a low estimate of dam safety incidents, since reporting is voluntary; few private or local dams are included.

6. Raul F. Silva, "A Methodology and Estimate of the National Cost for Dam Safety Rehabilitation," presented at a conference of the Association of State Dam Safety Officials, Providence, RI (Sept. 27, 2000).

Figure 2. Construction of Federal and Non-Federal Dams

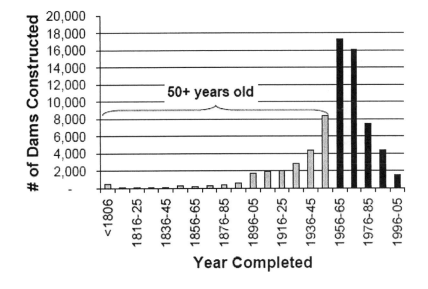

***

Managing Dam Safety

Following dam failures at Buffalo Creek (WV, 1972), Teton Dam (ID, 1976), and Kelly Barnes Dam (GA, 1977), legislative and executive actions established a program for monitoring the nation's dams and set guidelines for dam safety at federal facilities. Subsequent legislation promotes state dam safety programs and facilitates rehabilitation activities at federal and some non-federal dams.

Federal Management

Through legislative and executive actions, the federal government has become involved in multiple areas of dam safety. First, in 1972, Congress passed the National Dam Inspection Act (P.L. 92-367) which authorized the Corps to undertake a program of national dam inspections and to establish the National Inventory of Dams. Activities under this law provided the impetus for broad scale monitoring and a centralized location for information on many of the nation's dams.

In 1977, following the failure of Teton Dam and Kelly Barnes Dam, President Jimmy Carter ordered a review of federal dam safety activities and subsequently the *ad hoc* Interagency Committee on Dam Safety released safety guidelines for dams regulated by federal agencies. The *Federal Guidelines for Dam Safety* establish a basic structure for agencies' dam safety programs. In general, the guidelines encourage federal agencies, and dam-owners regulated by federal agencies, to abide by strict safety standards.

They direct that each agency with dam safety responsibilities[7] have a dam safety officer and that the agencies coordinate with other agencies. It also establishes guidelines for staff training, periodic evaluations, documenting dam safety activities, and operation and maintenance.

In addition to the Federal Guidelines for Dam Safety, Congress enacted the Reclamation Safety of Dams Act (P.L. 95-578, 43 U.S.C. § 508) in 1978 to set more detailed guidelines for the Bureau of Reclamation. This act authorizes Reclamation to preserve the structural stability of its dams and related facilities by performing modifications.

State Dam Safety Programs

States have primary responsibility for the safety of 95% of the nation's dams. According to the Association of State Dam Safety Officials, every state but Alabama and Delaware has a dam safety regulatory program. Typically these programs include "(1) safety evaluations of existing dams, (2) review of plans and specifications for dam construction and major repair work, (3) periodic inspections of construction work on new and existing dams, and (4) review and approval of emergency action plans." Many states dam safety programs are often poorly funded. In 2004, state budgets for dam safety—which averaged $742,000—ranged from less than $50 per state regulated dam (IA, IN, KS, MS, OK and TX) to more than $16,000 per dam regulated by Puerto Rico.

Federal Support for State Dam Safety Programs.

While federal activities in the 1970s generally focused on increasing dam safety information and strengthening requirements at the nation's federal dams, subsequent legislation began to address the safety of non-federal dams. In 1996, Congress created the National Dam Safety Program (NDSP) and assigned responsibility for administering it to FEMA. The NDSP is the nation's principal dam safety program; prior to creation of the program, there was no comprehensive national effort devoted to dam safety and the safety of downstream populations.

Management of the NDSP. The NDSP is a mechanism for federal and state cooperation that includes an Interagency Committee on Dam Safety (ICODS) with the Director of FEMA as its chair. ICODS, which was initially formed in 1980, is comprised of representatives from the FERC, the International Boundary Water Commission, the Nuclear Regulatory Commission, the Tennessee Valley Authority and the Departments of Agriculture, Defense, Energy, the Interior, Labor, and Homeland Security (FEMA). ICODS is responsible for coordinating information exchange among federal dam safety agencies.

---

7. Agencies with dam safety responsibilities include the Tennessee Valley Authority, Federal Energy Regulation Commission, and the Departments of Agriculture, Defense, Energy, the Interior, Labor, and State.

The act also established a National Dam Safety Review Board (NDSRB) consisting of: five representatives appointed from federal agencies, five state dam safety officials, and one representative from the U.S. Society on Dams. All the representatives are appointed by the director of FEMA. This board advises the FEMA director on dam safety issues, including the allocation of grants.
* * *

Reducing Dam Failures

As the nation's dams age, they are likely to develop various deficiencies. For example, dam's foundations can show signs of seepage, cracking, and movement. To prevent failure or misoperation, these deficiencies must be identified and corrected.

Identifying Unsafe Dams

The first step toward rectifying dam-safety issues is to identify safety deficiencies. Such deficiencies are often identified by engineers during informal inspections, or during formal inspections conducted by senior engineers. Formal inspections are generally conducted after major seismic or weather events, and on a periodic basis. As described below, the frequency and type of periodic inspections varies across agencies.

Inspections of Federal Dams.

Each of the six federal agencies that owns dams is responsible for maintaining dam safety by performing maintenance, inspections, and rehabilitation work. The *Federal Guidelines for Dam Safety*, established in 1979 by President Carter, provides basic guidance for agencies' dam safety programs. Specifically, this document recommends that agencies formally inspect each dam at least once every five years. * * * These inspections are typically funded through the agencies' operations and maintenance (O&M) budgets.

Inspection of Non-Federal Dams.

Inspecting non-federal dams is generally a state responsibility, but the states are often poorly funded. According to the Association of State Dam Safety Officials, 10 state regulators are needed for every 250 dams to do the best job of carrying out their responsibilities. However, the average number of dams per FTE is 395 and only two states (CA and FL) and one territory (PR) have the recommended number of staff.

Federal Involvement. While regulating non-federal dams is generally a state responsibility, the federal government has assumed regulatory authority over certain non-federal dams. As described below, two federal agencies—the Federal Energy Regulatory Commission (FERC) and the

Department of Labor's Mine Safety and Health Administration (MSHA)—participate in inspections of certain private dams. In addition, the NRCS may become involved with inspections at the dams it constructed.

Private Hydropower Dams. Under the 1920 Federal Power Act, the FERC (formerly the Federal Power Commission) regulates more than 2,500 non-federal hydropower dams. Pursuant to the *Federal Guidelines on Dam Safety* and FERC Order 122, FERC's regional engineers inspect each high-hazard dam annually and outside consultants inspect these dams every 5 years. Low-hazard dams are inspected every 3 years. The federal government recovers the costs of these and FERC's other activities from the hydropower industry. In general, FERC's dam safety program has received positive recognition.

Private Mining Dams. Under the Mine Safety and Health Act (1977),[8] the Department of Labor's Mine Safety and Health Administration, regulates 745 private dams. Under these regulations, dams used for surface mining are normally inspected every 2 years and those used for underground coal mines are inspected every 4 years.

NRCS Constructed Flood Control Dams. Since 1948, the NRCS constructed more than 10,500 flood control dams. These dams were turned over to local entities under contracts that stipulate their responsibility for operation and maintenance of the dams. Therefore, the dam owners are responsible for conducting inspections pursuant to state regulations. As resources permit, however, NRCS may use funding appropriated under the Small Watershed Rehabilitation Act to help dam owners assess specific structural or operational problems. In certain situations, NRCS will conduct an inspection as part of this assessment process.

Dam Rehabilitation

After dam safety deficiencies have been identified, rehabilitation activities should be undertaken. However, most federal agencies do not have funding available to immediately undertake all non-urgent repairs. Rather, they generally prioritize their rehabilitation needs—based on various forms of risk assessment—and schedule these activities in conjunction with the budget process. At some agencies, dam rehabilitation needs must compete for funding with other construction projects. Rehabilitation activities at a major dam-owning agenc[y] are described below.

Department of Defense, U.S. Army Corps of Engineers. At the Corps, most dam deficiencies are addressed through the normal operation and maintenance (O&M) procedures. However, "rehabilitation or modification of Corps' dams for safety purposes is accomplished through the Major Rehabilitation Program and the Dam Safety Assurance Program." The purpose of the Major Rehabilitation Program "is to allow accomplishment of significant,

---

8. Mine Safety and Health Act, P.L. 91-173, as amended by P.L. 95-164 (30 U.S.C. § 801). Available Sept. 14, 2005 at [http://www.msha.gov/REGS/ACT/ACTTC.HTM].

costly, one-time structural rehabilitation or major replacement work (other repairs related to dam safety are accomplished under the normal O&M program)." This program does not apply to facilities that were turned over to local interests for operation, maintenance, and major replacements after they were constructed by the Corps. The Dam Safety Assurance Program, however, applies to all dams built by the Corps regardless of current ownership. Specifically, this program "provides for modification of completed Corps dam projects which are potential safety hazards in light of current engineering standards and criteria. . . . This program is intended to facilitate upgrading of those project features which have design or construction deficiencies."[9] The Corps schedules rehabilitation under all of these programs based on funding availability.

* * *

Conclusions

As the nation's dams age and development continues in floodplains, the structural integrity of this infrastructure will become a more significant public safety issue. In the aftermath of Hurricane Katrina, it is likely that dams' planned capacity to withstand floods and other natural disasters will come under increased scrutiny. However, it is unclear to what extent there will be a widespread re-evaluation of flood and earthquake ratings at high-hazard dams. Such an evaluation could raise additional policy questions. For example, (1) what criteria should be used to determine whether current risks are acceptable; (2) if risks are not acceptable, should the dam be improved, or should other activities (e.g., changes to the design and or placement of downstream development) be undertaken; and (3) who will pay?

Regardless of whether dams were constructed to withstand an earthquake or flood of appropriate magnitude, they may have age-related deficiencies that need to be corrected to maintain current levels of safety. Therefore, it is likely that appropriations requests for safety inspections and rehabilitation activities will continue. It should be noted, however, that there currently are no clear criteria for prioritizing dam rehabilitation funding across agencies.

It is also unclear to what extent the federal government will fund inspection and rehabilitation activities at non-federal dams. Through the National Dam Safety Program, the federal government provides training and assistance to state dam safety programs; authorization of appropriations for this program expires in FY2006. Further, Congress has authorized appropriations for rehabilitation activities at several non-federal dams. While there is likely to be an increasing demand for such assistance, there is currently no federal policy that describes the conditions under which federal funding is appropriate, nor has Congress established criteria for prioritizing funding among non-federal projects.

---

9. Army Corps of Engineers, *Dam Safety Preparedness*, EP1110-2-13 (June 1996), p. 5-1.

NOTES

1. Have we learned any useful lessons from the failure of the New Orleans levees that could help us in planning for dam safety? Do we need a more systematic response than the current chaotic pattern of ownership and regulation is likely to supply?
2. Tsunamis present another major flood risk. Almost a quarter of a million people died in the December 26, 2004, tsunami, and efforts have begun to prevent similar casualty levels in the future. See Richard Stone and Richard A. Kerr, *Girding for the Next Big Wave*, 310 SCIENCE 1602 (2005).
3. Unlike the other catastrophic risks discussed in this book, disease does not pose a direct threat to physical infrastructure. However, it may have a devastating effect on social infrastructure, as discussed below.

B. PANDEMICS

In terms of threat to human life, pandemics dwarf more localized natural events such as earthquakes and floods. Events like the influenza pandemic at the beginning of the twentieth century[10] or the ongoing worldwide AIDS pandemic cause untold human, economic, and societal costs. We can only hope that future pandemics will turn out to be on the mild end of the spectrum. However, it behooves us to prepare for some of the graver possibilities.

CONGRESSIONAL RESEARCH SERVICE, PANDEMIC INFLUENZA:
DOMESTIC PREPAREDNESS EFFORTS

(November 10, 2005)

In 1997 a new strain of influenza (flu) jumped from poultry directly to humans in Hong Kong, causing several human deaths. This was the first documented occurrence of direct transmission of an avian flu virus from birds to people. Despite efforts to contain the virus through mass culling of poultry flocks, the virus (also called H5N1 for specific proteins on its surface) re-emerged in 2003. It has since been reported in domestic poultry and/or migratory birds in more than a dozen Asian countries, and in Europe. Also since 2003, it has infected more than 120 people in Cambodia, Indonesia, Thailand, and Vietnam, resulting in more than 60 deaths. As of yet the virus has not developed the ability to transmit efficiently from person to person. Were that to occur, a global influenza pandemic would be likely.

---

10. For a very readable historical account, see JOHN M. BARRY, THE GREAT INFLUENZA: THE EPIC STORY OF THE DEADLIEST PLAGUE IN HISTORY (2004).

The high lethality of the H5N1 strain and its tendency to affect healthy young people remind health authorities of the deadly 1918 Spanish flu, which is estimated to have killed up to 2% of the world's population, and was a substantial cause of mortality in U.S. military personnel in World War I. The World Health Organization (WHO) says, "If an influenza pandemic virus were to appear again similar to the one that struck in 1918, even taking into account the advances in medicine since then, unparalleled tolls of illness and death could be expected."

U.S. and world health authorities believe that while periodic influenza pandemics are inevitable, their progress may be slowed, and their impacts blunted, by rapid detection and local control efforts. The added time would allow affected countries to better manage the situation, and countries not yet affected to better prepare. To realize these benefits, countries affected by avian flu must be able to track the spread of the virus in birds, and quickly detect and investigate suspected human cases. Hence, a country's capabilities in epidemiology, laboratory detection and other public health services affect the welfare of the global community as well as the country itself. This fact presents developed nations with novel policy challenges, such as whether to reserve scarce health resources such as antiviral drugs for themselves, or to deploy them to other countries at the center of an emerging pandemic.

* * *

Historical records suggest that influenza pandemics have occurred periodically for at least four centuries. In the 20th century there were three influenza pandemics, and three "pandemic scares."

- **The 1918 Spanish Flu** pandemic is estimated to have killed between 20 and 100 million people worldwide and at least 500,000 in the United States. Illness and death rates were highest among adults 20-50 years old. HHS notes that "the severity of that virus has not been seen again." Similarities between the 1918 pandemic and the current H5N1 avian flu situation have the global public health community on edge.
- **The 1957 Asian Flu** was first identified in Asia in February 1957 and spread to the United States during the summer. Health officials responded quickly and vaccine was available in limited supply by August. This pandemic killed about 69,800 people in the United States.
- **The 1968 Hong Kong Flu** became widespread in the United States in December of that year. It is estimated that 33,800 people died from this pandemic in the United States, (affecting those over the age of 65 disproportionately), making it the mildest pandemic of the 20th century.
- **The 1976 Swine Flu Scare** began when a novel virus, identified in New Jersey, was thought to be related to the Spanish flu virus of 1918 and to have pandemic potential. Federal officials mounted a vaccination campaign, and Congress provided liability protection for the manufacturer and federal injury compensation for those harmed by the vaccine. Ultimately, the virus did not spread, but the vaccine

was linked with a rare neurological condition that affected more than 500 people and killed 32. The episode damaged confidence in public health officials.

- **The 1977 Russian Flu Scare** involved a virus strain that had been in circulation prior to 1957. As a result, severe illness was generally limited to those without prior immunity (i.e., children and young adults). The epidemic is not, therefore, considered a true pandemic.

* * *

The H5N1 strain now circulating has been especially virulent in both human and avian hosts. Laboratory studies suggest that the virus prompts an over-reaction of the inflammatory response in humans, causing rapid and severe damage to the lungs. This primary damage cannot be remedied with antibiotics or antiviral drugs. Victims may require mechanical ventilation, and may succumb despite swift and capable care. In 2004, scientists published the results of research in which they sequenced several genes from the 1918 pandemic strains. These genes, when inserted into flu viruses and used to infect mice, were found to have a similar property. Recently, scientists re-created and published the entire genome of the 1918 strain, reinforcing this finding. This property may explain the high lethality of both the 1918 and H5N1 strains in apparently healthy young people.

The H5N1 avian flu may never slip its moorings as a bird pathogen and become a serious human threat. But that possibility is a worst-case scenario for the world's public health experts. Should H5N1 become a pandemic strain, scientists are concerned that it may retain much of its virulence as it changes to a more transmissible form. In the face of such a deadly pathogen, miracles of modern medicine, unavailable in much of the developing world, may not be of much help in developed countries either. Such a scenario would challenge governments around the globe.

* * *

Potential Impacts of an Influenza Pandemic

Deaths and Hospitalizations

A WHO influenza expert has said that estimates of the global death toll from a future pandemic are "all over the place." The WHO estimates that, in the best case, there would be 2 million deaths worldwide from a possible influenza pandemic, and, in the worst case, more than 50 million. In its final pandemic flu plan, HHS estimates that about 209,000 U.S. deaths could result from a moderate pandemic, similar to those in 1957 and 1968, while 1.9 million deaths could result from a severe pandemic like that in 1918. (CDC estimates that on average, about 36,000 die of influenza during an annual flu season.)

Estimates of impacts of a future pandemic are generally based on experience from past pandemics, which varied considerably in their severity. Trust for America's Health (TFAH), a non-profit public health advocacy group, published a report estimating deaths and hospitalizations in the United States based on mild, moderate and severe pandemic scenarios. The report presents death estimates that range from 180,000 to more than 1 million. The report also contains estimated state-by-state health impacts.

Predicted hospitalization rates provide an idea of the potential burden on the U.S. healthcare system, but they are prone to the same degree of uncertainty. In its final pandemic plan, HHS estimates of hospitalizations range from 865,000 to 9.9 million. TFAH estimates that U.S. hospitalizations would range from almost 800,000 to more than 4.7 million, and cites a statistic from the American Hospital Association that in 2003 there were 965,256 staffed hospital beds in registered hospitals. These projected impacts would occur over a compressed time frame of several weeks or a few months, rather than spread over a full year.

Simple extrapolations of health effects from events in 1918 do not account for advances in medical care that have occurred since then. Antibiotics are now available to treat bacterial pneumonia that often results from influenza infection, and sophisticated respiratory care is now available to treat those with severe pneumonia. Experts caution, though, that the H5N1 avian flu virus can cause severe primary damage to the lungs. If this strain were to launch a pandemic and retain this trait, large numbers of victims may require intensive care and ventilatory support, likely exceeding national capacity to provide this level of care. In any event, such specialized care is not available in most developing countries, and access to it is uneven within the United States.

An influenza pandemic of even limited magnitude has the potential to disrupt the normal workings of the healthcare system in a variety of ways. These may include deferral of elective medical procedures; diversion of patients away from overwhelmed hospital emergency departments and tertiary care facilities; protective quarantines of susceptible populations such as residents of long-term care facilities; and hoarding, theft or black-marketeering of scarce resources such as vaccines or antiviral drugs.

Several additional factors complicate the healthcare burden posed by pandemic flu. First, it is thought that a pandemic would spread across the United States in a compressed timeframe similar to seasonal flu, that is, over a six to eight week period. Second, while it is desirable that affected patients be kept in isolation, domestic isolation capacity is limited. Third, the healthcare workforce is likely to be affected by pandemic flu. Even if they are protected directly by limited vaccines or antiviral drugs, their family members may be affected and require additional care at home. Fourth, supplies of healthcare consumables such as gloves, masks and antibiotics would be stressed by a surge in global demand. Even a mild flu pandemic would likely place a significant and near-simultaneous strain on the nation's healthcare system.

Economic Impacts

There are few estimates of the potential economic impact of a flu pandemic. An analysis published by CDC in 1999, based on the relatively mild 1968 pandemic, estimated the cost of a pandemic in the United States at between $71.3 and $166.5 billion. The study modeled direct healthcare costs, lost productivity for those affected, and lost expected future lifetime earnings for those who died. Loss of life accounted for the majority of economic impact. The model did not include the potential effect of disruptions in commerce. In a recent analysis, the World Bank estimated the overall U.S. economic impacts of a potential pandemic of moderate severity at $100 to $200 billion, and global impacts at around $800 billion, if certain impacts were to last for a full year.

Several economists studied the economic impacts of Severe Acute Respiratory Syndrome (SARS) in 2003. One analysis showed significant short- and long-term decreases in Gross Domestic Product (GDP) in China and Hong Kong, attributing most of the losses to "the behavior of consumers and investors" rather than to actual medical costs. In May 2003, the Conference Board of Canada estimated that the SARS outbreak in Toronto would lower real GDP in Canada by approximately $1.5 billion, or 0.15 percent, in 2003, projecting that the largest effect would be seen in the travel and tourism industries. Consumer behavior and its economic consequences may be affected by official actions and the response of the news media. Some Canadian officials were critical of a WHO advisory warning against travel to Toronto at the height of the outbreak. The World Bank economic analysis of avian flu discusses the likely interplay between government statements and actions, public behavior, and economic effects.

* * *

Could an Influenza Pandemic Be Stopped?

Public health experts note that vaccine, the primary measure for influenza prevention, will be available in very limited supply at the start of any pandemic, and is unlikely ever to be available to everyone. Antiviral drugs are also likely to be available in a limited supply. For both, there is limited global surge capacity for production during a pandemic. Conventional wisdom once held that there was an inevitability to the global wave of disease that a pandemic would bring, but lately this notion has been challenged. WHO and many national experts believe that scientific advances in studying and detecting flu viruses may make it possible to detect the spread of the virus early and rein in localized clusters of infection. While not suggesting that a pandemic could necessarily be averted, they posit that if progression were slowed enough, a vaccine could be available by the time worldwide infection ensued. While there still might not be enough vaccine for everyone, if countries had at least enough for essential personnel, it would soften the impact somewhat.

Realizing this hope rests on two conditions: first, exceptional "pandemic intelligence" in countries at the epicenter of a developing pandemic; and second, priority use of control measures in these epicenter countries. In hopes of having the best possible information in real time, WHO, CDC, and health officials from many other nations are building epidemiology and lab capacity in Southeast Asian countries affected by H5N1 avian flu, when those countries have requested assistance. This aid is layered onto an uneven patchwork of existing capacities. In supplemental appropriations for FY2005 (P.L. 109-13), Congress provided $15 million (through the foreign assistance account at the State Department) to supplement CDC's existing activities to expand epidemiology and laboratory capacity in that region.

The second requirement for successful pre-pandemic containment, namely priority use of control measures in affected countries, is politically difficult. It would require that countries contribute vaccine and antiviral drugs to a global stockpile to be used in epicenter countries to slow a pandemic. Costs notwithstanding, given that countries would face severe shortages of these precious assets if a pandemic reaches them, would they share their national stockpiles with other countries? Many U.S. analysts believe that doing so is not merely altruistic. They argue that providing antiviral drugs to an affected country in the early going would save American lives in the long run. While plausible, this thesis is untested, and WHO has had limited success to date in getting nations to commit assets to the global stockpile.

Who's in Charge?

The National Response Plan (NRP) published by DHS, is a blueprint for the coordinated efforts of federal agencies during disasters. In the event of a significant influenza pandemic, the NRP may be activated to coordinate federal agency activities. Responsibilities for specified activities (e.g., transportation, energy, and public works) are set out in 15 *Emergency Support Functions* (ESF). When asked who would be in the lead for the federal response during a pandemic, Dr. Jeffrey Runge, Chief Medical Officer for DHS, replied:

> When critical infrastructures are threatened, the secretary of DHS is responsible for the preservation of critical infrastructures. HHS will continue to have the lead in prevention, containment and treatment of avian flu. But if the government surges, and if the ESFs (Emergency Support Functions) stand up and so forth, the secretary of DHS will be responsible for each of those emergency support functions discharging their duty. One of the duties of HHS is containment, prevention and treatment of avian flu.

When the NRP is activated, the Secretary of Homeland Security serves as the overall lead for a coordinated federal response, while the Secretary of HHS serves as the lead for ESF#8, Public Health and Medical Services. While public health and medical activities may comprise the bulk of the federal response to a pandemic, other ESF authorities may be involved to sustain infrastructure affected by absenteeism or supply chain disruptions, requiring the coordination of other federal departments.

Overarching federal leadership in DHS may be called upon to address problems such as the prioritization of federal non-medical resources, if these resources were exhausted by demands from many states simultaneously. State disaster planning commonly relies on state-to-state mutual aid, in addition to federal assistance. In a severe pandemic, assistance from other states may be limited, and federal assistance may be thinly stretched.

The NRP is intended to identify federal roles and leadership for a *response* to an emergency, and resolve coordination difficulties. Experience gained from the implementation of the NRP after Hurricane Katrina indicates that there may be a gap in leadership for *preparedness*.

WHO urges that countries plan for a pandemic as a multi-sector threat, not merely a health challenge. Planning in HHS and state health agencies is ongoing, but some assert that a clear point of leadership is needed at the federal level to engage state, local and municipal officials in multi-sector planning. The National Strategy notes that lead departments have been identified for the medical response (HHS), veterinary response (Department of Agriculture), international activities (Department of State) and overall domestic incident management (DHS). Each of these departments would serve as the federal liaison to assist its respective sectors in planning. In addition, DHS is responsible for coordinating the preparedness of privately owned critical infrastructures such as banking or telecommunications.

However, federal relationships that support state and local jurisdictions traditionally operate sector-by-sector (e.g., HHS with health services, and the Department of Transportation with transit agencies). At this time, a mayor would have difficulty identifying one point of contact concerning the spectrum of planning activities that would be needed to keep water running, lights on, food stocked, and gasoline flowing during a serious flu pandemic. Further, while pandemic influenza scenarios have been used to exercise specific elements of response, such as distribution of stockpiled medications, there has been no large-scale exercise to study a coordinated, multi-sector response to this potential nationwide threat.

Emergency Declarations and Federal Assistance

In the United States, public health authority rests principally with the states as an exercise of their *police powers*. States play a leading role in preparing for and responding to public health threats, with HHS (primarily CDC) providing support through funding, training, technical assistance, advanced laboratory support, data analysis and other activities. The Public Health Service Act grants the Secretary of HHS the authority to declare a situation a public health emergency, which triggers an expansion of certain federal authorities. Though states already have considerable power in responding to public health events, most can also declare public health emergencies and expand their powers further. In an influenza pandemic, response measures such as quarantine or prohibitions against administration of vaccine to non-priority individuals would likely be carried out, at least initially, by state rather than federal authorities.

An influenza pandemic may disrupt services beyond the health sector. A multi-sector federal response to a pandemic could be directed by provisions in the NRP. Both the HHS pandemic plan and the DOD pandemic guidance are written with the premise that the NRP would be triggered by a severe influenza pandemic, thereby guiding a coordinated federal response to problems within the health sector and other sectors that may be affected, through routine (non-emergency) federal assistance mechanisms. The Biological Incident Annex in the NRP notes that "Actions described in this annex take place with or without a Presidential Stafford Act declaration or a public health emergency declaration by the Secretary of (HHS)." While the annex addresses intentional bioterrorism events, it also addresses naturally occurring biological threats such as pandemic influenza.

States may require additional federal assistance to maintain essential services during an influenza pandemic. Typically, such assistance is triggered by Presidential emergency or disaster declarations under the Stafford Act. Disaster assistance authorized by the Stafford Act includes the provision of emergency funds and supplies to stricken households as well as aid in clearing and rebuilding damaged infrastructure. While a virus would not cause such damage directly, certain sectors may nonetheless be affected as a result of widespread absenteeism or supply chain disruptions. For example, water treatment facilities may be damaged, or may have to be shut down, if they are not adequately maintained, or if replacement parts are unavailable. Sectors which depend heavily on continuous computer support (e.g., banking) may be disrupted by absenteeism.

Some may question whether the Stafford Act is an appropriate legislative base for action in the event of a flu pandemic. In a recent terrorism preparedness exercise, TOPOFF III, concerns were raised that because the Stafford Act explicitly defines a "major disaster" as a *natural* catastrophe, states facing a terrorism incident would not be eligible for the full range of federal disaster assistance authorized by the act. Such concerns may be met, however, with the recognition that the definition of the term "emergency" in the statute provides greater discretion to the President in issuing an emergency declaration. However, pursuant to the Stafford Act, considerably less financial assistance may be provided under an emergency declaration, compared to that authorized under a major disaster declaration.

An influenza pandemic may pose a challenge in national disaster response that is without recent precedent. A pandemic could affect all or almost all areas of the United States with multi-sector impacts within a six to eight week period, involving the entire country nearly at once. A severe pandemic could cause "extraordinary levels of mass casualties" and substantial disruptions in services, and thereby meet the definition of a *Catastrophic Incident* according to the NRP. Questions might be raised about the adequacy of the Catastrophic Incident Annex in the NRP. The Annex was not activated during the response to Hurricane Katrina. DHS officials have said that the Annex and related planning documents are not yet complete.

Limited Surveillance and Detection Capability

The CDC coordinates domestic surveillance for seasonal flu. Monitoring for pandemic flu is integrated into these existing systems. Key challenges in the rapid detection of novel flu viruses are the vagueness of flu symptoms, which can be seen with many other diseases, and the difficulty in distinguishing specific strains of interest from the background of other flu strains commonly in circulation.

The routine CDC system for domestic flu surveillance has seven reporting components: (1) more than 120 laboratories; (2) more than 1,000 sentinel healthcare providers; (3) death records from 122 cities; (4) reports from health departments in the states, territories, New York City and the District of Columbia; (5) influenza-associated deaths in children; (6) Emerging Infections Program sites in 10 states; and (7) laboratory-confirmed hospitalizations of young children in three sentinel counties. Reporting to these systems by state and local health departments and healthcare providers is voluntary. Information is gathered and analyzed weekly during the winter flu season. The final HHS pandemic plan proposes that BioSense, a new system to gather, in real time, information such as emergency department admissions, be incorporated along with other flu detection systems.

Through the Health Alert Network, CDC has issued recommendations to public health and medical professionals, addressing domestic surveillance and laboratory investigation of possible cases of avian or pandemic influenza. CDC recommends that health professionals use screening tests for influenza on individuals who have a history of recent travel to an affected region and exhibit symptoms of severe respiratory disease. Specimens that test positive on screening for influenza should be followed up with samples sent to CDC to determine which flu strain is involved. CDC is working with states to develop state-based lab capability for testing flu viruses for the H5 antigen, but this capability is not yet in place.

Isolation and Quarantine

Isolation and quarantine have been used for hundreds of years to prevent the spread of communicable diseases. Both methods restrict the movement of those affected, but they differ depending on whether an individual has been exposed to a disease (*quarantine*), or is actually infected (*isolation*). Persons in isolation may be significantly ill, so isolation often occurs in a healthcare setting. Persons under quarantine are, by definition, not ill from the disease in question, though they may have other health conditions that complicate the quarantine process.

In the United States, quarantine authority is generally based in state rather than federal law. The federal government has the responsibility to prevent the introduction, transmission, and spread of communicable diseases from foreign countries, and the authority to impose quarantine on incoming travelers suspected to be infected with or exposed to certain diseases on a list of quarantinable communicable diseases. Diseases are listed by an executive order of the President, in consultation with the Secretary of HHS. On April 1, 2005, President Bush added to the list "influenza caused by novel or re-emergent influenza viruses that are causing, or have the potential to cause, a pandemic." Federal quarantine is carried out by CDC's Division of Global Migration and Quarantine, which operates quarantine stations at major ports, and also works closely with states to carry out quarantine activities. CDC has noted that having pandemic influenza on the list assures the agency of this option for disease control, should it be felt to be worthwhile.

On October 4, 2005, in response to a question at a press conference, President Bush suggested the use of the military to enforce quarantines during a flu pandemic. The comment prompted responses on two issues: the role of the military in domestic disasters, and the role of quarantine in controlling pandemic flu.

Following the terror attacks of 2001, in October of 2002, DOD activated a new combatant command, Northern Command or NORTHCOM, to, among other functions, provide military assistance to civil authorities in response to terrorist attacks. The NRP also articulates this role for the military in response to terrorist attacks, major disasters, and other emergencies. There has, however, long been a prohibition against the use of federal military personnel for domestic law enforcement, except in extraordinary circumstances. There are no instances in the 20th century in which federal troops were used to enforce a domestic quarantine for any disease, though there are earlier examples. Secretary of Defense for Homeland Defense Paul McHale commented that the threshold for use of troops during a domestic disaster would be high, but that " . . . an outbreak of avian flu could be so severe that active-duty forces might need to help the National Guard enforce quarantines," and that " . . . Congress and federal agencies must establish clear guidelines on what would trigger a broad U.S. military response to restore law and order."

While isolation and quarantine were crucial in the worldwide response to SARS, these methods are less likely to be successful in controlling influenza. Influenza is more highly contagious than SARS, has a shorter incubation period, and is often contagious in the absence of symptoms or before symptoms appear, making it difficult to identify persons who should be quarantined. Public health officials have suggested the use of quarantines in certain circumstances (e.g., incoming passenger flights) to delay the emergence of pandemic influenza in an area, but have generally steered away from suggesting the more traditional use of quarantine of individuals as a containment measure for pandemic flu, recommending instead the use of voluntary, population-based approaches (e.g., canceling sporting events).

NOTES

1. The probability of an avian flu pandemic remains unclear. Person-to-person transmission would require that the virus mutate in terms of what kinds of lung cells it binds to and enter. *See* Nicholas Wade, *Studies Suggest Pandemic Isn't Imminent*, NEW YORK TIMES, March 23, 2006, at A16. For this reason, experts disagree about the likelihood of human-to-

human transmission, though there seems to be widespread agreement that the virulence of the virus would make it very dangerous if it does learn to spread directly between humans. *See* Denise Grady and Gina Kolata, *How Serious is the Risk?*, N.Y. TIMES, March 26, 2006, at D1.

2. Civil liberties concerns are more significant in terms of disease response than with most other disasters, because of the loss of freedom associated with isolation and quarantine. What should be the trade-off between civil liberties and disease control? What findings should an administrator have to make before isolating an individual? Should there have to be any kind of hearing, either before or after the decision is made? For discussion of these and other legal issues, see LAWRENCE O. GOSTIN & PETER D. JACOBSON, LAW AND THE HEALTH CARE SYSTEM 128-185 (2006).

3. What should be the federal role in disease response? Should the ground rules for federal intervention be different than for other types of disasters? And within the federal government, who should be in charge: the Defense Department, the Department of Homeland Security (including FEMA), or the Centers for Disease Control? For further discussion, see Michael Greenberger, *The Role of the Federal Government in Response to Catastrophic Health Emergencies: Lessons Learned from Hurricane Katrina,* www.papers.ssrn.com/sol3/ papers.cfm?abstract_id=824184.

C. CLIMATE CHANGE

Is the world becoming more dangerous? It is well-known that the number of catastrophic weather events with extremely high costs (in the billions of dollars) has been increasing. But this is partly due to increased social wealth and a higher number of people who live in vulnerable areas such as seacoasts. However, as we shall see, there is good reason to suspect that we are seeing the early stages of what could turn out to be a long-term trend, unless preventative measures are taken.

CENTER FOR HEALTH AND THE GLOBAL ENVIRONMENT,
HARVARD MEDICAL SCHOOL, CLIMATE CHANGE FUTURES:
HEALTH, ECOLOGICAL, AND ECONOMIC DIMENSIONS

---

http://www.climatechangefutures.org/pdf/CCF_Report_Final_10.27.pdf

(Nov. 2005)

Climate is the context for life on earth. Global climate change and the ripples of that change will affect every aspect of life, from municipal budgets for snowplowing to the spread of disease. Climate is already changing, and quite rapidly. With rare unanimity, the scientific community warns of more abrupt and greater change in the future.

Many in the business community have begun to understand the risks that lie ahead. Insurers and reinsurers find themselves on the front lines of this challenge since the very viability of their industry rests on the proper appreciation of risk. In the case of climate, however, the bewildering complexity of the changes and feedbacks set in motion by a changing climate defy a narrow focus on sectors. For example, the effects of hurricanes can extend far beyond coastal properties to the heartland through their impact on offshore drilling and oil prices. Imagining the cascade of effects of climate change calls for a new approach to assessing risk.

The worst-case scenarios would portray events so disruptive to human enterprise as to be meaningless if viewed in simple economic terms. On the other hand, some scenarios are far more positive (depending on how society reacts to the threat of change). In addition to examining current trends in events and costs, and exploring case studies of some of the crucial health problems facing society and the natural systems around us, "Climate Change Futures: Health, Ecological and Economic Dimensions" uses scenarios to organize the vast, fluid possibilities of a planetary-scale threat in a manner intended to be useful to policymakers, business leaders and individuals.

Most discussions of climate impacts and scenarios stay close to the natural sciences, with scant notice of the potential economic consequences. In addition, the technical literature often "stovepipes" issues, zeroing in on specific types of events in isolation from the real-world mosaic of interrelated vulnerabilities, events and impacts. The impacts of climate change cross national borders and disciplinary lines, and can cascade through many sectors. For this reason we all have a stake in adapting to and slowing the rate of climate change. Thus, sound policymaking demands the attention and commitment of all.

While stipulating the ubiquity of the threat of climate change, understanding the problem still requires a lens through which the problem might be approached. "Climate Change Futures" focuses on health. The underlying premise of this report is that climate change will affect the health of humans as well as the ecosystems and species on which we depend, and that these health impacts will have economic consequences. The insurance industry will be at the center of this nexus, both absorbing risk and, through its pricing and recommendations, helping business and society adapt to and reduce these new risks. Our hope is that Climate Change Futures (CCF) will not only help businesses avoid risks, but also identify opportunities and solutions. An integrated assessment of how climate change is now adversely affecting and will continue to affect health and economies can help mobilize the attention of ordinary citizens around the world and help generate the development of climate-friendly products, projects and policies. With early action and innovative policies, business can enhance the world's ability to adapt to change and help restabilize the climate.

* * *

The first impact scenario, or CCF-I, portrays a world with an increased correlation and geographical simultaneity of extreme events, generating an overwhelming strain for some stakeholders. CCF-I envisions a growing frequency and intensity of weather extremes accompanied by disease outbreaks and infestations that harm humans, wildlife, forests, crops and coastal marine systems. The events and their aftermaths would strain coping capacities in developing and developed nations and threaten resources and industries, such as timber, tourism, travel and the energy sector. The ripples from the damage to the energy sector would be felt throughout the economy.

In CCF-I, an accelerated water cycle and retreat of most glaciers undermine water supplies in some regions and land integrity in others. Melting of permafrost (permanently frozen land) in the Arctic becomes more pronounced, threatening native peoples and northern ecosystems. And gradually rising seas, compounded by more destructive storms cascading over deteriorating barrier reefs, threaten all low-lying regions.

Taken in aggregate, these and other effects of a warming and more variable climate could threaten economies worldwide. In CCF-I, some parts of the developed world may be capable of responding to the disruptions, but the events would be particularly punishing for developing countries. For the world over, historical weather patterns would diminish in value as guides to forecasting the future.

The second impact scenario, CCF-II, envisions a world in which the warming and enhanced variability produce surprisingly destructive consequences. It explores a future rife with the potential for sudden, wide-scale health, environmental and economic impacts as climate change pushes ecosystems past tipping points. As such, it is a future inherently more chaotic and unpredictable than CCF-I.

Some of the impacts envisioned by the second scenario are very severe and would involve catastrophic, widespread damages, with a world economy beset by increased costs and chronic, unmanageable risks. Climate-related disruptions would no longer be contained or confined.

Threshold-crossing events in both terrestrial and marine systems would severely compromise resources and ecological functions, with multiple consequences for the species that depend upon them. For example:

- Repeated heat waves on the order of the 2003 and 2005 summers could severely harm populations, kill livestock, wilt crops, melt glaciers and spread wildfires.
- The probability of such extreme heat has already increased between two and four times over the past century and, based on an IPCC climate scenario, more than half the years by the 2040s will have summers warmer than that of 2003.
- Chronic water shortages would become more prevalent, especially in semi-arid regions, such as the US West.
- With current usage levels, more environmentally displaced persons and a changing water cycle, the number of people suffering water stress and scarcity today will triple in two decades.

* * *

Still, CCF-II is not a worst-case scenario.

A worst-case scenario would include large-scale, nonlinear disruptions in the climate system itself—slippage of ice sheets from Antarctica or Greenland, raising sea levels inches to feet; accelerated thawing of permafrost, with release of large quantities of methane; and shifts in ocean thermohaline circulation (the stabilizing ocean "conveyor belt").

Finally, there are scenarios of climate stabilization. Restabilizing the climate will depend on the global-scale implementation of measures to reduce greenhouse gas emissions. Aggressively embarking on the path of non-fossil fuel energy systems will take planning and substantive financial incentives—not merely a handful of temporizing, corrective measures.

This assessment examines signs and symptoms suggesting growing climate instability and explores some of the expanding opportunities presented by this historic challenge.

* * *

Global warming is not occurring uniformly. The three warmest "hotspots" are Alaska, Northern Siberia and the Antarctic Peninsula. Since 1950, summer temperatures in these regions have increased 4-6°F (2-3°C) while winter temperatures have risen 8-10°F (4-5°C). Nights and winters—crucial in heat waves and important for crops—are also warming twice as fast as globally averaged temperatures (Easterling et al. 1997). Clouds contribute to warmer nights, while atmospheric circulation of winds and heat create disproportionate heating during winters. All of these changes—warmer nights and winters, and wider swings in weather—affect people, disease vectors and ecological systems.

One of the earliest and most noticeable changes detected as a result of recent warming has been an increase in extreme weather events. Over the last half-century, weather patterns have become more variable, with more frequent and more intense rainfall events. As Earth adjusts to our rewriting of the climate script, there have been changes in the timing and location of precipitation, as well as more intense heat waves and prolonged droughts.

* * *

While the amount of rain over the US has increased 7% over the past century, that increase camouflages more dramatic changes in the way this increased precipitation has been delivered. Heavy events (over 2 inches/day) have increased 14% and very heavy events (over 4 inches/day) have increased 20%. The increased rate of heavy precipitation events is explained in great part by the tropical ocean surfaces along with a heated atmosphere. The frequency and intensity of extremes are projected to increase in the coming decades.

Recent analysis of tropical cyclones found that their destructive power (a function of storm duration and peak winds) had more than doubled since the 1970s, and the frequency of large and powerful storms had increased, and that these changes correlated with ocean warming. Changes in the variance and strength of weather patterns accompanying global warming will most likely have far greater health and ecological consequences than will the warming itself.

Examples abound of the costs of weather anomalies. The most recent series of extremes occurred in the summer of 2005. In July, a heat wave, anomalous in its intensity, duration and geographic extent, enveloped the US and southern Europe. In the US particularly, records were exceeded in numerous cities. Phoenix, AZ experienced temperatures over 100°F for 39 consecutive days, while the mercury reached 129°F in Death Valley, CA. Drought turned a large swath of southern Europe into a tinderbox and when it ended with torrential rains, flooding besieged central and southern parts of the continent and killed scores.

Outliers and Novel Events

Beyond extremes, there are outliers, events greater than two or three standard deviations from the average that are literally off the charts. A symptom of an intensified climate system is that the extraordinary becomes more ordinary. We have already experienced major outlier events: the 2003 summer European heat wave was one such event—with temperatures a full six standard deviations from the norm. This event is addressed in depth in this report.

For developing nations, such truly exceptional events leave scars that retard development for years. It took years for Honduras to rebuild infrastructure damaged in the 1998 Hurricane Mitch, for example.

Wholly new types of events are also occurring, such as the twin Christmas windstorms of 1999 that swept through Central Europe in rapid succession (with losses totaling over US $5 billion), and the first-ever hurricane recorded in the southern Atlantic that made landfall in Brazil in early 2004.
* * *

Climate change may be altering oscillatory modes nested within the global climate system. The El Niño/Southern Oscillation (ENSO) phenomenon is one of Earth's coupled ocean-atmospheric systems, helping to stabilize climate through its oscillations and by "letting off steam" every three to seven years. Warm ENSO events (El Niño) have in the past created warmer and wetter conditions overall, along with intense droughts in some regions. ENSO events are associated with weather anomalies that can precipitate "clusters" of illnesses carried by mosquitoes, water and rodents and property losses from extremes tend to spike during these anomalous years as well. Climate change may have already altered the ENSO phenomenon, with current weather patterns reflecting the combination of natural variability and a changing baseline.

In Asia, the monsoons may be growing more extreme and less tied with ENSO (Kumar et al. 1999), as warming of Asia and melting of the Himalayas create low pressures, which draw in monsoons that have picked up water vapor from the heated Indian Ocean.

* * *

The overturning deep water in the North Atlantic Ocean is the flywheel that pulls the Gulf Stream north and drives the "ocean conveyor belt" or thermohaline circulation. Melting ice and more rain falling at high latitudes are layering fresh water near Greenland. Meanwhile, the tropical Atlantic has been warming and getting saltier from enhanced evaporation. This sets up an increased contrast in temperatures and pressures. The composite changes may be altering weather systems moving west and east across the Atlantic. These changes could be related to the following:

- Swifter windstorms moving east across to Europe.
- Heat waves in Europe from decreased evaporation off the North Atlantic.
- Ocean contrasts helping to propel African dust clouds across to the Caribbean and US.
- It is possible that more hurricanes will traverse the Atlantic east to west as pressures change (and as the fall season is extended).
- The layering of freshwater in the North Atlantic in contrast to warmer tropics and mid-latitudes may be contributing to nor'easters and cold winters in the Northeast US.

During the 1980s and 1990s, the two air systems (North and South) tended on average to be locked in a "positive phase" each winter. Modeling this interplay, Hurrell and colleagues (2001) found that Earth's rising temperature—especially the energy released into the atmosphere by the overheated Indian Ocean—is affecting the behavior of this massive atmospheric system known as the NAO. CLIVAR, Climate Variability and Predictability World Climate Research Programme, a collaborative effort that looks at long- as well as short-term variability, studies discontinuities. Several step-wise shifts in climate may already have occurred in the past three decades.

One step-wise climate shift may have occurred around 1976 (CLIVAR 1992). The eastern Pacific Ocean became warmer, as surface pressures and winds shifted across the Pacific. Between 1976 and 1998, El Niños became larger, more frequent and persisted longer than at any time according to records kept since 1887. The period included the two largest El Niños of the century, the return times decreased and the longest persisting El Niño conditions (five years and nine months; Trenberth 1997) eliminated pest-killing frosts in the southern and middle sections of the US. Termites proliferated in New Orleans.

Then, in 1998, another step-wise adjustment may have occurred, as the eastern Pacific turned cold (burying heat), becoming "The perfect ocean for drought" (Hoerling and Kumar 2003), as cool waters evaporate slowly. After this "correction," the energized climate system has ushered in an anomalous series of years with unusually intense heat waves and highly destructive storms.

Finally, there is the question of the ocean circulation system that delivers significant heat to the North Atlantic region. Most models project slowing or collapse of the ocean conveyor belt—the pulley-like system of sinking water in the Arctic that drags warm water north and has helped to stabilize climate over millennia. The cold, dense, saline water that sinks as part of the conveyor belt in the North Atlantic has been getting fresher, as melting ice flows into the ocean, and more rain falls at high latitudes and flows into the Arctic Sea. This freshening may be reducing the vigor of the global circulation.

The dangers of disruption of ocean circulation involve the counterintuitive but real possibility that global warming might precipitate a sudden cooling in economically strategic parts of the globe as well as the prospect of an economically disastrous "flickering climate," as climate lurches between cold and warm, and potentially tries to settle into a new state.

Trend Analyses: Extreme Weather Events and Costs

The Chicago Mercantile Exchange estimates that about 25% of the US economy is affected by the weather. Vulnerability to disasters varies with location and socioeconomic development. Vulnerabilities to damages also increase as the return times of disasters become shorter. More frequent, intense storms hitting the same region in sequence leave little time for recovery and resilience in developed as well as developing nations. The rapid sequences themselves increase vulnerability to subsequent events, and disasters occurring concurrently in multiple geographic locations increase the exposure of insurers, reinsurers, and others who must manage and spread risks.

The cost of climate events quickly spreads beyond the immediate area of impact, as was shown by studies of the consequences of the US $10 billion European windstorms and Hurricane Floyd in the US in 1999. To further develop the context for the scenarios, we first consider the trends in extreme weather events and associated costs, which set the stage for assessing the likelihood of more health, ecological and economic consequences of an unstable climate regime.

The number of weather-related disasters has already risen over the past century (EM-DAT 2005). The nature of the associated losses, however, varies considerably around the globe. In the past decade, more such events are occurring in the Northern Hemisphere (EMDAT 2005), and the losses are beginning to be felt by all. The composition of event types has also been undergoing change, with a particularly notable increase in events with material consequences for health and nutrition in the developing world (extreme temperature episodes, epidemics and famine).

Figure 1.5 Global Weather-Related Losses from "Great" Events: 1950-2004

Billions (in 2004 US dollars)

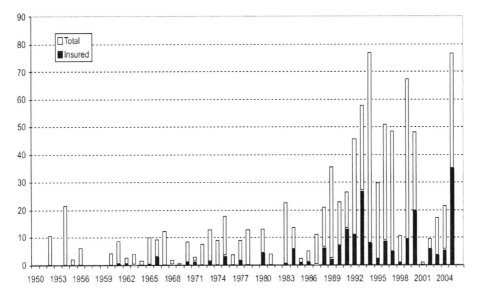

Events are considered "great" if the affected region's resilience is clearly overstretched and su-
praregional or international assistance is required. As a rule, this is the case when there are
thousands of fatalities, when hundreds of thousands of people are made homeless, or when economic losses—depending on the economic circumstances of the country concerned—and/or insured losses reach exceptional levels.   *Source: Munich Re, NatCatSERVICE.*

From 1980 through 2004, the economic costs of "all" weather-related
natural disasters totaled US $1.4 trillion (in 2004 US dollars) apportioned
approximately 40/60 between wealthy and poor countries, respectively. To
put the burden of these costs on insurers in contemporary perspective, the
recent annual average is on a par with that experienced in the aftermath of
9/11 in the US.

The insured portion of losses from weather-related catastrophes is on the
rise, increasing from a small fraction of the global total economic losses in the
1950s to 19% in the 1990s and 35% in 2004. The ratio has been rising twice
as quickly in the US, with over 40% of the total disaster losses being insured
in the 1990s.

Where the burden of losses falls depends on geography, the type of risk
and the political clout of those in harm's way. The developed world has sophisticated ways of spreading risk. While insurance covers 4% of total costs
in low-income countries, the figure rises to 40% in high-income countries. A
disproportionate amount of insurance payouts in high-income countries arise
from storm events, largely because governments, rather than the private sector, tend to insure flood rather than storm risk. In both rich and poor nations,

economic costs (especially insured costs) fall predominantly on wealthier populations, whereas the loss of life falls predominantly on the poor.

With weather-related losses on the rise and extreme events more frequent, can we look back on historical data and draw conclusions about the likely impact of climate change on future losses? Can we tease out the role of climate from other factors when looking at specific events? The consequences are due to the combination of inflation, rising real estate values, the growth in coastal settlements and the increasing frequency and intensity of weather extremes. As the return times for extremes grow shorter, the coping and recovery capacities are stretched thin, creating increasing vulnerability to further extremes even in the wealthiest nations.

Climate signals in rising costs from "natural" disasters are evident in many aspects of the data. Insurers observe a notable increase in losses during periods of elevated temperatures and lightning strikes (predicted to rise with warming) . Other factors, not captured by an overall examination of losses, point to an inherent bias toward underreporting the economic impact of climate extremes. The total losses are underestimates, since record-keeping systematically ignores relatively small events. For example, smaller, often uncounted losses include those from soil subsidence or permafrost melt.

In the summer of 2005, for example, there were numerous areas of drought, flashfloods and wildfires that were barely accounted for.

While attention naturally focuses on headline-grabbing catastrophes, the majority (60%) of economic losses comes from smaller events. In one recent example, a month of extremely cold weather in the northeastern US in 2004 resulted in US $0.725 billion in insured losses (American Re 2005). The average annual insured loss from winter storms and thunderstorms is about US $6 billion in the US, comparable to the loss from a significant hurricane.

In addition, while the absolute magnitude of losses has been rising, the variability of losses has also been increasing in tandem with more variability in weather.

Losses are Systematically Underestimated

The magnitude of losses presented in published data systematically underestimates the actual costs. For example:

Statistical bodies commonly create definitions that exclude from tabulation those events falling below a given threshold. For example, power outages in the United States alone are estimated to result in a cost of US $80 billion per year (LaCommare and Eto 2004), and weather-related events account for 60% of the customers affected by grid disturbances in the bulk power markets (see figure 1.8). Lightning strikes collectively result in billions of dollars of losses, as do damages to human infrastructure from soil subsidence. Yet, such small-scale events are rarely if ever included in US insurance statistics due to the minimum event cost threshold of US $5 million up to 1996, and US $25 million thereafter. The published insurance figures reflect property losses and largely exclude the loss of life, and health costs (which are diffuse and rarely tabulated), business interruptions, restrictions on trade, travel and tourism, and potential market instability resulting from the health and ecological consequences of warming temperatures and severe weather.

The published data are not necessarily directly comparable with past data. For instance, in recent years, there has been a trend toward both increasing deductibles and decreasing limits, resulting in lower insurance payouts than had the rules been unchanged. Following Hurricane Andrew, insurers instituted special "wind" deductibles, in addition to the standard property deductible now in use in 18 US states plus Washington, DC. Moreover, hurricane deductibles have moved toward a percentage of the total loss rather than the traditionally fixed formulation. The effect of such changes is substantial: for example, in Florida, 15 to 20% of the losses from the 2004 hurricanes were borne by consumers.

These data also, of course, exclude the costs for disaster preparedness or adaptation to the rise in extreme weather events (flood preparedness, changes in construction practices and codes, improved fire suppression technology, cloud seeding, lightning protection, etc.). Insurance industry representatives reported that improved building codes helped reduce the losses of hurricanes in 2004.

Other countervailing factors also mask part of the actual upward pressure on costs. Improved building codes, early warning systems, river channelization, cloud seeding and fire suppression all offset losses that might otherwise have occurred. Financial factors, such as insurer withdrawal from risky areas, higher deductibles and lower limits, also have a dampening effect on losses. All this means that the data do not necessarily reflect the increased costs to society of a changing climate.

NOTES

1. Climate change potentially carries a number of different risks, but one of them is the increased likelihood of extreme weather events and the corresponding potential for disaster, particularly in the form of flooding. Research published shortly after Katrina indicates that the proportion of tropical storms reaching categories 4 and 5 has increased substantially over the past 35 years. *See* P. J. Webster et al., *Changes in Tropical Cyclone Number, Duration, and Intensity in a Warming* Environment, 309 Science 1844 (2005). New Orleans may be something of a harbinger of the future. For these reasons, the issues discussed in this book are likely to loom even larger in the future.

2. One question is whether we can limit climate change sufficiently to mitigate these climatic impacts. The next excerpt and the notes afterwards provide a quick survey of the current status of these efforts.

DONALD A. BROWN, THE U.S. PERFORMANCE IN ACHIEVING ITS 1992 EARTH SUMMIT GLOBAL WARMING COMMITMENTS

32 Environmental Law Reporter 10, 741 (2002).

Many participants in the global warming debate recounted in this Article appear either to have been unaware of or have chosen to ignore numerous commitments made by the United States pursuant to the 1992 United Nations Framework Convention on Climate Change (UNFCCC or Convention). For instance, on numerous occasions members of the U.S. Congress have opposed various global warming program proposals on the basis of alleged scientific uncertainty or the lack of commitment by developing countries to reduce emissions—positions that are arguably inconsistent with the UNFCCC. This unacknowledged relevance of the UNFCCC to U.S. policy on global warming is curious because the United States is a party to it notwithstanding the recent withdrawal from the Kyoto Protocol.

Commitments made by the United States under the UNFCCC included agreements to cooperate with other signatories in a number of specific ways, and promises to reduce U.S. greenhouse gas (GHG) emissions. In addition, the Convention itself includes various provisions which limit the excuses that a signatory might use in ignoring its commitment to address global warming.
* * *

By 1995, it was becoming quite clear that the weak nonbinding approaches to global warming contained in the UNFCCC were failing to make much progress on the growing global warming problem. As a result, at the first COP in Berlin in 1995, the Parties agreed to begin negotiations on a binding protocol on emissions limitations.

In 1995, the IPCC released its Second Assessment Report. For the first time, the IPCC scientists concluded that "the balance of the evidence shows a discernable human influence on climate."[11] In other words, in 1995, the IPCC, an organization created with the strong support of the United States to examine the science of global warming, concluded that not only was human-induced climate change a real issue with likely adverse impacts to human health and the environment, a conclusion they had reached in 1990, but that it was possible to observe actual effects of human activities on climate that could be distinguished from natural climate variability. * * *

The IPCC's Second Assessment Report also identified likely global warming impacts to human health and the environment. These included rising temperatures and oceans, adverse impacts to ecosystems, biodiversity, forests, water supplies, and human health, increased droughts, floods, and tropical storms for parts of the world, and negative impacts on farming for some parts of the world. Of great concern to many, the poorest people on the

---

11. IPCC, *Summary for Policy Makers*, THE SCIENCE OF CLIMATE CHANGE: CONTRIBUTION OF WORKING GROUP I TO THE THIRD ASSESSMENT OF THE INTERGOVERNMENTAL PANEL ON CLIMATE CHANGE, (1995), *available at* http://www.ipcc.ch/pub/sarsum2.htm (last visited Jan. 30, 2006).

planet are most vulnerable to global warming, according to the IPCC, because likely impacts will be greatest in parts of the world that are home to many of the poorest people and because the poor have the fewest financial resources to adapt to climate change.

In 1996, the United States reversed its previous position on its unwillingness to accept enforceable targets by announcing its support for negotiations of binding national emissions limitations. This announcement set the stage for international negotiations on binding national emissions targets that would be negotiated in Kyoto, Japan, in 1997.

* * *

At the last moment [at the Kyoto talks], a final deal was struck when the United States agreed to commit to a 7% reduction below 1990 emission levels in return for acceptance of much of its position on "flexibility mechanisms," particularly those relating to trading. The Kyoto flexibility mechanisms included: (1) an international trading mechanism that would allow nations or companies to purchase less expensive emissions permits from countries that have more permits than they needed, (2) a joint implementation program that allows developed nations with emissions targets to obtain credit toward the target by doing emission reduction projects in other nations that have targets, and (3) a clean development mechanism that would allow nations with targets to obtain credit by paying for projects in developing nations. The Kyoto flexibility mechanisms also allowed nations with targets to sequester carbon rather than reducing emissions as a method of achieving a target.

These flexibility mechanisms would allow the United States to achieve the majority of its greenhouse reduction target, not through actual emission reductions in the United States, but through paying for greenhouse reduction projects in other countries or by obtaining credit for carbon being stored by American forests. The EU agreed to an 8% reduction, Japan a 6% reduction, while 20 other countries agreed to be bound to emissions reductions that would in total reduce emissions from the developed nations by 5.2%.

* * *

Two negotiating meetings after Kyoto, COP–4 and COP–5, failed to make much progress on working out the details of the Kyoto Protocol. The Sixth COP was held in November, 2000. There, the United States continued to press for maximum use of the trading mechanisms and for the right to use its existing forests' ability to remove carbon from the atmosphere as a credit against the 7% reduction target that it had agreed in Kyoto. The EU and many other countries opposed the U.S. desire to have unrestricted use of the Kyoto flexibility mechanisms. The Hague conference failed to make progress on implementing the Kyoto agreements, with most nations blaming what they called the unreasonable position of the United States on forest sinks. Largely due to the U.S. position, the Sixth COP ended in impasse, forcing negotiators to reconvene for COP "Six and a Half" in July, 2001, in Bonn.

During the 2000 negotiations, advances in scientific understanding of the immense threat of global warming were being reported. At the beginning of 2001, the IPCC released summaries of its third scientific assessment. The report concluded that the earth's average surface temperature could rise by

2.5 to 10.4° Fahrenheit (F°) from 1990 to 2100—much higher than IPCC's estimate five years before, when it predicted a rise of 1.8 to 6.3° F. Should the higher estimates prove accurate, they would spell potential catastrophe for our planet. IPCC's predictions of future climate change constitute evidence of "dangerous interference with the climate system" even at the lower end of the temperature increase forecast, an outcome that the United States agreed to cooperate in avoiding in ratifying the UNFCCC. The third IPCC report also strengthened its prior conclusions that human-caused global warming was already happening.

* * *

Many scientists and policy makers believe that a doubling of CO_2 from pre-industrial levels to 560 ppm may be unavoidable in the 21st century. This is so because the world's political and economic system cannot respond rapidly enough to make faster changes in some major polluting sources such as gasoline-powered automobiles or coal-fired power plants. Some environmentalists, however, believe it is still possible to stabilize GHG at 450 ppm, a level that would limit the temperature increase (in addition to that which has already been caused by human activities) to 1.5 to 2 degrees F° during the next 100 years. Virtually nobody believes that it is possible to stabilize atmospheric concentrations below 450 ppm and concentrations could continue growing after that if third world countries do not implement aggressive reduction strategies, even if the most ambitious proposal currently under consideration were adopted. Even if all nations could have stabilized emissions in the year 2002, the concentrations of GHGs would continue to rise and would approach 500 ppm by the year 2100. After that, GHG concentrations in the atmosphere would continue to rise for several hundred years before stabilization would be achieved. Even to stabilize CO_2 at 1,000 ppm will require reductions of emissions below current levels.

For all of these reasons, it appears that many of the climate impacts identified by the IPCC are likely to occur regardless of the nature of the international policy response. In fact, the IPCC has recently concluded that regional changes in climate, particularly increases in temperature, have already affected a diverse set of physical and biological systems in many parts of the world. Examples of observed changes caused by human releases of GHG include shrinkage of glaciers, thawing of permafrost, later freezing and earlier break-up of ice on rivers and lakes, lengthening of mid-to high-latitude growing seasons, poleward and altitudinal shifts of plants and animal ranges, declines of some plant and animal populations, and earlier flowering of trees, emerging of insects, and egg-laying in birds.

* * *

On March 13, 2001, President Bush announced that he would abandon his campaign promise to regulate CO_2 emissions from electrical generation facilities. In making this announcement, President Bush pointed to the same three reasons that had become an American refrain of reasons for refusing to take serious action to reduce domestic emissions, namely scientific uncertainty, cost to the U.S. economy, and the failure of the developing world to make commitments. A week later, the Bush Administration announced that it was repudiating the Kyoto Protocol. The Bush Administration's decision to reject the Protocol so painfully agreed to in Kyoto provoked a stunned and angry reaction among America's allies in Europe and Japan. Many allies loudly urged the United States to reconsider its decision.

* * *

On June 7, 2001, the National Academy of Sciences (NAS) issued a report that had earlier been requested by the Bush Administration. This report confirmed that global warming was a real problem and getting much worse. On June 11, 2001, President Bush gave a policy address on global warming in the Rose Garden of the White House. Although he acknowledged that the NAS had concluded that recent heating of the earth had been caused in part by human activities, Bush also emphasized scientific uncertainty about consequences of global warming as a continuing basis for rejection of the Kyoto Protocol. He also attacked the Protocol for exempting developing countries and for not basing the emission reduction targets on sound science. He asserted that a negative economic impact would occur if the Protocol were implemented in its present form.

* * *

On February 14, 2002, President Bush announced his Administration's approach to global warming. This approach to reduce the threat of global warming relies primarily on reducing the ratio of GHG to economic output. The Bush policy seeks to reduce emissions intensity by 18% in 10 years through voluntary measures and some tax incentives. Yet because the United States has been achieving almost 1.8% per year increases in efficiency, the proposal will achieve exactly the same results that have been seen recently in the absence of a new policy. For this reason, the policy's only significance is that it is at least some official recognition that global warming is a problem. Yet because it is only directed to increases in efficiency, as long as economic growth continues to outstrip efficiency gains, a phenomenon experienced throughout the 1990s, U.S. GHG emissions will continue to soar. For this reason, Members of the EU have charged that the Bush plan violates the UNFCCC, both because of its failure to stabilize GHG emissions at 1990 levels and due to the fact that it will not reverse trends that will lead to "dangerous interference" with the climate system.

NOTES

1. The Kyoto Protocol went into effect in February 2005, without U.S. participation. The Kyoto commitments run only from 2008 to 2012. Conference of Parties ("COP") 11, held in Montreal in December 2005, produced some incremental progress toward a post-Kyoto regime, but it remains to be seen how the post-Kyoto regime will evolve.

2. The Bush administration emphasizes technological development and voluntary efforts, with particular attention to the use of hydrogen as an energy source and carbon sequestration as a method of reducing carbon dioxide emissions. *See Administration to Focus on Voluntary Efforts as More States Move to Regulate Emissions*, 37 ENV. REP. S-11 (Jan. 20,

2006). At the Montreal meeting in December 2005, the United States did agree to join a "dialogue" on climate change issues, the first step toward American participation in negotiations since President George W. Bush took office. *See Agreement to Join "Dialogue" Does Little to Bring U.S. Toward Mandatory Reductions*, INT'L ENV. REP. 994 (2005).

3. Legal efforts to force federal regulation of global warming have so far been unsuccessful. In Massachusetts v. EPA, 415 F.3d 50 (D.C. Cir. 2005), the court upheld EPA's refusal to regulate greenhouse gas emissions from new motor vehicles. On the other hand, some conservatives have taken up the issue of climate change. *See* Laurie Goodstein, *Evangelical Leaders Swing Influence Behind Effort to Combat Global Warming*, N.Y. TIMES, March 10, 2004, at A14. Judge Posner, alarmed about the potential for low-probability but highly harmful outcomes, suggests the adoption of a carbon emissions tax. *See* RICHARD A. POSNER, CATASTROPHE: RISK AND RESPONSE 156-157 (2004).

4. The climate change issue has attracted considerable interest from insurance companies because of its potential effect on the industry:

> The prospects of forced reductions in coverage, loss of market share, periodic bankruptcies, eroded reputations, and regulator rejection of requests to withdraw from markets are material business risks that merit concern. Moreover, insurers hold major investments that may be vulnerable to climate change. A few insurers will no doubt be inappropriately opportunistic— and should be called to task for doing so—but those who have expressed concern are actively supporting climate change adaptation and mitigation, which will ultimately curb price increases.
>
> The future role of insurance in helping society cope with climate change is uncertain. Insurers may rise to the occasion and become more proactive players in improving the science and crafting responses. Or, they may retreat from incoming risks, thereby shifting a greater burden to governments and individuals.

Evan Mills, *Insurance in a Climate of Change*, 309 SCIENCE 1040, 1043 (2005).

4. Interestingly, while the federal government has continued to remain aloof, a number of state and local governments have seized the initiative to address climate change. The following excerpt discusses the state efforts.

DAVID R. HODAS, STATE LAW RESPONSES TO GLOBAL WARMING: IS IT CONSTITUTIONAL TO THINK GLOBALLY AND ACT LOCALLY?

21 Pace Environmental Law Review 53 (2003)

Over the past few years, the public policy news in America on global warming has generally fallen into two categories. Either the reports relate

Bush Administration opposition to all international and national legal action addressing global warming, or the reports relate that yet another state or local government is adopting new laws or regulations to reduce or mitigate greenhouse gas (GHG) emissions. It is as though we live in two different countries. At the federal level, all policy makers oppose all efforts to control GHG emissions—from the Bush Administration's rejection of the Kyoto Protocol, to policies as subtle as the recent U.S. Department of Energy rule proposal that quietly removed language about tracking potential future credits industry might be entitled to for their voluntary, private GHG reduction projects. Thus, despite occasional public protestations that it favors voluntary actions, the Bush Administration's actions send the message that the federal government will let all good climate change deeds be punished, for otherwise the public verification of private sector voluntary actions might give the private sector a stake in promoting a global warming legal regime.

In contrast, policy initiatives at the state level generally take the opposite approach, encouraging GHG mitigation actions, whether big or small, at every turn. Beginning over a decade ago, there has been a steady drumbeat of announcements of state and local initiatives to mitigate global warming from the emission of greenhouse gases (GHG). There are various motivations for these developments, but it is fair to say that in one way or another, each initiative has been motivated by a combination of worry about the economic and environmental risks of global warming and future regulations of GHG emissions. These state initiatives promote policy innovation, provide implementation experience and learning, promote diversity of approaches, and "provide a forum for moving forward on climate change mitigation that is largely unavailable at the national level. . . ." These activities are part of a long history of "bold experiment[ation] in cooperative federalism" so central to environmental law, and especially air pollution law, in the United States. Some form of cooperative federalism will be necessary for an effective GHG policy because the U.S.'s variety of GHG emitters and sinks is so numerous and varied that any purely national-level response will have minimal chances for success.

In the past two years, as states have become frustrated with the failure of the Bush Administration to develop national and international global warming mitigation policies, and with President George W. Bush's rejection of the Kyoto Protocol, that drumbeat from the states has become louder and more insistent. For example, Governor Pataki of New York and the governors of nine other states in the northeast recently agreed "to develop a flexible, multi-state cap and trade . . . program from power plants . . . [that would be] the first multi-state greenhouse gas control program in the United States." Maine passed a law in late June 2003 that requires Maine to reduce carbon dioxide (CO_2) emissions to 1990 levels by 2010, and then to 90% of 1990 levels by 2020; Maine's "long-term object is to cut emissions by as much as 80%." "Three Western States Announce Plan to Slash GHG Emissions" was the September 23, 2003 headline for the article describing the plan between Washington, Oregon, and California to reduce transportation sector GHG emissions, to provide renewable energy and energy efficiency standards, and to "coordinate their GHG emissions inventories." In May 2003, "six Northeast States announced a voluntary greenhouse gas registry." Regionally, the governors of New England states and the premiers of the provinces in eastern Canada (in total, eleven jurisdictions are involved) are collaborating to develop a regional approach to the reduction of GHGs. In July 2002, California enacted Assembly Bill 1493 to "require the [State Air Resources Board] to develop and adopt, by January 1, 2005, regulations that achieve the maximum feasible reduction of greenhouse gases emitted by passenger vehicles and light-duty trucks" which would go into effect for 2009 model-year vehicles.

States have also been actively pressing the federal government to address global warming. In 2002, the Attorneys General of eleven States (Alaska, California, Connecticut, Massachusetts, New Hampshire, New Jersey, New York, Rhode Island, and Vermont) asked President Bush to reconsider his voluntary climate policies and to move instead toward "a 'strong national approach' to the 'most pressing environmental challenge of the 21st century." The Administration did not change its policy. These states also petitioned the EPA to list carbon dioxide (CO_2) as a criteria pollutant under the Clean Air Act. However, in the summer of 2003, EPA denied the various petitions to list carbon dioxide as a pollutant under the Clean Air Act. These states, with others, are now seeking judicial review of the denial. These state legislative, policy, and litigation initiatives are but the tip of the iceberg of state and local legal proposals to reduce GHG emissions.

* * *

The list of state and local laws addressing global warming is very long and growing rapidly. Some are comprehensive while others are sector-driven. Some are regulatory, others voluntary or market based; some seek to control GHG emissions, others seek to promote carbon sinks. Some are regional, even international in scope, while others are local. Even within particular approaches, there is much variety. For instance, some economics-based approaches anticipate emissions credits and market trading, others look to taxes and pricing mechanisms to change consumer behavior, and others look to supplant electricity regulation with market oriented performance standards such as renewable portfolio standards, environmentally costed integrated resource planning, and environmental system benefits charges. Obviously, this article is not the place to evaluate the particulars of these approaches. Rather, this article will consider on a more general level whether these, or other, efforts by states to act locally on the global warming problem offend federalism conceptions of the constitution, particularly the foreign affairs power of the national government.

* * *

This leads us to the question of whether state and local legislative initiatives to address global warming are valid within our constitutional system. The question can be analyzed at several levels. The first is whether any of the specific state laws are preempted by federal statutes. Clearly, if a state statute conflicts with federal statute, the state statute is preempted. So, for instance, a Massachusetts law (the so-called Burma Law) enacted to support human rights and democracy in Burma by barring state agencies from purchasing goods and services from Burma was unconstitutional because it conflicted with a subsequent federal statute which imposed sanctions on Burma, and authorized the President to impose further sanctions. The Massachusetts law, more stringent and rigid than Congress' enactment, was "an obstacle to the accomplishment of Congress's [sic] full objectives under the federal Act."

At present there is no federal statute that directly regulates greenhouse gas emissions, so, statutorily, there can be no express preemption. Moreover, the Environmental Protection Agency (EPA) recently announced that it does not have authority under the Clean Air Act to regulate carbon dioxide as a criteria pollutant for which it would be obligated to establish a national ambient air quality standard. Thus, in terms of ambient air quality, it appears that the federal government has abandoned the field to the states. Moreover, even if EPA were to designate carbon dioxide to be a criteria pollutant, and were to promulgate national ambient air quality standards for carbon dioxide, that would not preclude a state from adopting and implementing a more stringent standard for that pollutant.

Although EPA does not appear interested in regulating carbon dioxide as a pollutant from motor vehicle emissions, the Clean Air Act generally prohibits states from setting mobile source emission limitations under the Clean Air Act, except for the California car. The Clean Air Act allows only two varieties of motor vehicle emission limitations, the so-called national car, and the California car. Thus, to the extent that a particular state GHG statute is deemed to regulate motor vehicle emissions in a manner inconsistent with the California car preemption waiver it might conflict with the Clean Air Act's two car mandate. For instance, California has recently enacted a statute limiting future greenhouse gas emissions, which might be deemed an effort to regulate motor vehicle emissions beyond what EPA currently allows under its approved version of the California car. However, should California petition EPA to approve a new version of the California car, which incorporates reduced carbon dioxide emissions, EPA might be obligated to approve the application, thereby waiving any Clean Air Act preemption.
* * *

The states are policy development laboratories. They are innovators, and they are taking direct political responsibility for their innovations. According to Washington State Governor Gary Locke, "The states are taking action for one simple reason: because the federal government is not." State initiatives represent local political actions designed, in part, to push global warming onto the national agenda, even though it is universally recognized that uncoordinated state and local efforts can only be a weak stand-in for federal leadership and action in the realm of climate change.

NOTES

1. Other state initiatives have emerged since the preceding article was written. Seven northeastern states adopted a regional trading system to reduce power plant emissions of carbon dioxide. Massachusetts withdrew

near the end of the negotiations, perhaps because of its Republican governor's presidential aspirations. *See Governor Romney Bails Out,* N.Y. TIMES, Dec. 18, 2005, at A18. In the meantime, California is seeking to cut its greenhouse emissions by 11 percent over the next five years. *See Schwarzenegger Issues Executive Order to Cut Greenhouse Gas Emissions in State,* 36 ENVT. REP. 1145 (Jun. 3, 2005).

2. Northeastern and Pacific Coast states are traditionally leaders in environmental regulation. However, other states are now increasingly concerned about climate change. *See Southern States Call for U.S. Action, Note Increased Vulnerability of Coasts,* 36 ENVT. REP. 2539 (2005). Hurricanes Katrina and Rita undoubtedly helped spark such concerns among the Gulf Coast states.

3. Given the global scale of climate change, are such localized efforts worthwhile? Can these state efforts succeed without federal coordination and support? Or do they have the potential to nudge the federal government into action?

TABLE OF CASES

TABLE OF AUTHORITIES

Books and Treatises

Abbott Ernest B., Hetzel, Otto J. & Cohn, Alan D., State, Local, and First Responder Issues, American Bar Association, Hurricane Katrina Task Force Subcommittee Report (Feb. 2006), 79-82

Arnold, Gwen, ed., After the Storm: Restoring America's Gulf Coast Wetlands (2006), 248

Barrett, Justin L., Why Would Anyone Believe in God? (2004), 71

Barry, John M., Rising Tide: The Great Mississippi Flood of 1927 and How It Changed America (1998), 99

Beck, Ulrich, Risk Society: Toward a New Modernity (1986), 109-110

Blaikie, Piers, Cannon, Terry, Davis, Ian & Wisner, Ben, At Risk: Natural Hazards, People's Vulnerability and Disasters (1994), 123

Brookings Institution, New Orleans After the Storm: Lessons From the Past, A Plan for the Future (2005), 272

Bullard, Robert D., Dumping in Dixie: Race, Class and Environmental Quality (3d ed. 2000), 123

Cawardine, William, The Pullman Strike (1973), 45

Center for Law and the Public's Health, The Model State Emergency Health Powers Act (2001), 47

Center for Progressive Reform, An Unnatural Disaster: The Aftermath of Hurricane Katrina (2005), 110, 126-127, 128

Chomsky, Noam, Language and Mind (enlarged ed. 1972), 72

Cohen, Joel, How Many People Can the Earth Support? (1995), 114

Cole, Luke W. & Foster, Sheila, Environmental Racism and the Rise of the Environmental Justice Movement (2000), 128

Comerio, Mary C., Disaster Hits Home: New Policy for Urban Housing Recovery (1998), 272

Cross, Terry L. et al., Towards a Culturally Competent System of Care, Volume I: A Monograph of Effective Services for Minority Children Who Are Severely Emotionally Disturbed (1989), 131

Department of Homeland Security, Interim National Infrastructure Protection Plan (2005), 101

Department of Homeland Security, National Response Plan (2004), 63, 73

Department of Justice, Bureau of Justice Assistance, Mutual Aid: Multijurisdictional Partnerships for Meeting Regional Threats (September 2005), 84

Ehrlich, Paul & Ehrlich, Anne, The Population Explosion (1990), 114

Gabe, Thomas, Falk, Gene & McCarty, Maggie, Hurricane Katrina: Social-Demographic Characteristics of Impacted Areas 14 (Nov. 4, 2005) (CRS Order Code RL33141), 127-128, 138-140

Godschalk, David R. et al., Natural Hazard Mitigation: Recasting Disaster Policy and Planning 545 (1999), 229-230

Gostin, Lawrence O. & Jacobson, Peter D., Law and the Health Care System 128-185 (2006), 298.

Hensler, D., et al., RAND Inst. Civ. Just., Compensation for Accidental Injuries in the United States (1991), 169

Holland, John H., Emergence: From Chaos to Order (1998), 78

Hollander, Jack M., The Real Environmental Crisis: Why Poverty, Not Affluence, Is the Environment's Number One Enemy (2003), 119

Homeland Security Council, National Strategy for Pandemic Influenza (2005), 99

Human Rights Center, University of California, Berkeley, After the Tsunami: Human Rights of Vulnerable Populations (October 2005), 116-117

Intergovernmental Panel on Climate Change, Climate Change 2001: Working Group II, Impacts, Adaptation and Vulnerability (2001), 113

Johnson, Steven, Emergence: The Connected Lives of Ants, Brains, Cities, and Software (2001), 78

Kakalik, J. & Pace, N., RAND Inst. Civ. Just., Costs and Compensation Paid in Tort Litigation (1985), 169

King, Elizabeth M. & Mason, Andrew D., Engendering Development— Through Gender Equality in Rights, Resources, and Voice (2001), 138

Kosar, Kevin R., Disaster Response and Appointment of a Recovery Czar: The Executive Branch's Response to the Flood of 1927 (Oct. 25, 2005) (CRS Order Code RL33126), 93-99

Kunreuther, Howard and Roth, Richard J., Jr, Paying the Price: The Status and Role of Insurance Against Natural Disasters in the United States (1998), 200

Lemann, Nicholas, The Promised Land: The Great Black Migration and How It Changed America (1991), 99

Lipsey, Richard G. & Steiner, Peter O., Economics (5th ed. 1978), 148

McCarthy, John A., Jackson, Randall & Dion, Maeve, Posse Comitatus and the Military's Role in Disaster Relief, American Bar Association, Hurricane Katrina Task Force Subcommittee Report (Feb. 2006), 50-52

National Academy of Public Administration, Coping With Catastrophe: Building an Emergency Management System to Meet People's Needs in Natural and Man-made Disasters (1993), 102

Natural Resources Defense Council, After Katrina: New Solution for Safe Communities and a Secure Energy Future (2005), 272

Posner, Richard A., Catastrophe: Risk and Response 156-157 (2004), 312

Sphere Project Handbook: Humanitarian Charter and Minimum Standards in Disaster Response (2004), 118-119

United Nations, Human Development Indicators (2005), 117-118

U.S. Department of Health and Human Services, Developing Cultural Competence in Disaster Mental Health Programs: Guiding Principles and Recommendations (2003) (DHHS Pub. No. SMA 3828), 131-134

U.S. Department of Health & Human Services, HHS Pandemic Influenza Plan (2005), 99

U.S. House of Representatives, A Failure of Initiative: Final Report of the Select Bipartisan Committee to Investigate the Preparation for and Response to Hurricane Katrina (2006), 53, 69-70, 74-77, 90-91, 101-102, 119-120

United States Senate Committee on Homeland Security and Governmental Affairs, Hurricane Katrina: A Nation Still Unprepared (2006), 6-17, 72, 74, 82, 104-107

Warren, Robert Penn, All the King's Men (Harvest 1996; 1st ed. 1946), 2

Weart, Spencer, The Discovery of Global Warming (2003), 113

The White House, The Federal Response to Hurricane Katrina: Lessons Learned (2006), 2-5, 24, 59-63, 63-64, 103-104

Yonder, Ayse, Akcar, Sengul & Gopalan, Prema, Women's Participation in Disaster Relief and Recovery (2005), 137

Articles

AAA Offers New Disaster Recovery Services, 60-JAN Dispute Res. J. 4 (2005), 193

Abbott, Ernest B., Representing Local Governments in Catastrophic Events: DHS/FEMA Response and Recovery Issues, 37 Urb. Law. 467 (2005), 33

Administration to Focus on Voluntary Efforts as More States Move to Regulate Emissions, 37 Env. Rep. S-11 (Jan. 20, 2006), 311-312

Agreement to Join "Dialogue" Does Little to Bring U.S. Toward Mandatory Reductions, Int' Env. Rep. 994 (2005), 312

Ainsworth, Jack & Doss, Troy Alan, California Coastal Commission, Presentation To The Post-Fire Hazard Assessment Planning and Mitigation Workshop: Natural History of Fire & Flood Cycles Post Fire Mitigation Efforts. University of California, Santa Barbara (August 18, 1995), 206-210

Army Corps of Engineers, Dam Safety Preparedness, EP1110-2-13 (June 1996), p. 5-1, 287

Arzt, Donna E., Sound and Fury: Katrina and the "Refugees" Debate, Jurist Legal News & Research, http://jurist.law.pitt.edu/forumy/2005/10/sound-and-fury-katrina-and-refugees.php (Oct. 3, 2005), 151-152

ASFPM, White Paper, Hurricanes Katrina & Rita: Using Mitigation to Rebuild a Safer Gulf Coast, Sept. 9, 2005, available at http://www. floods.org, 202-206

Bankoff, Greg, The Tale of the Three Pigs: Taking Another Look at Vulnerability in the Light of the Indian Ocean Tsunami and Hurricane Katrina, http://understandingkatrina.ssrc.org/bankoff (Dec. 12, 2005), 118

Bea, Keith, Disaster Evacuation and Displacement Policy: Issues for Congress 5 (Sept. 2, 2005) (CRS Order Code RS22235), 71

Belmont, Elisabeth et al., Emergency Preparedness, Response, and Recovery Checklist: Beyond the Emergency Management Plan, 37 J. Health L. 503 (2004), 47

Bolin, Robert & Stanford, Lois, The Northridge Earthquake: Community-Based Approaches to Unmet Recovery Needs, 22 Disasters 21 (1998), 134

Braine, Theresa, Was 2005 the Year of Natural Disasters? 84:1 Bull. World Health Org. 4 (Jan. 2006), 110-113

Brown, Donald A., The U.S. Performance in Achieving its 1992 Earth Summit Global Warming Commitments, 32 Env. L. Rep. 10, 741 (2002), 308-311

Brumbaugh, David L., & King, Rawle O., Congressional Research Service, Tax Deductions for Catastrophic Risk Insurance Reserves: Explanation and Economic Analysis, (Sept. 2, 2005), 193-195

Bullard, Robert D. & Wright, Beverly, The *Real* Looting: Katrina Exposes a Legacy of Discrimination and Opens the Door for 'Disaster Capitalism', http://www.seeingblack.com/2005/x101105/411_oct05.shtml (Apr. 4, 2006), 162

Byrnes, P. D., Lowry, W. J. & Bondurant, E. J. II, Product Shortages, Allocation and the Antitrust Laws, 20 Antitrust Bull. 713 (1975), 148

California Department of Resources, Flood Warnings: Responding to California's Flood Crisis, http://www.publicaffairs.water.ca.gov/newsreleases/2005/01-10-05flood_warnings.pdf (Jan. 2005), 274-277

Center for Health and the Global Environment, Harvard Medical School, ·Climate Change Futures: Health, Ecological, and Economic Dimensions, http://www.climatechangefutures.org/pdf/CCF_Report_Final_10.27.pdf (November 2005), 298-307

Center For Progressive Regulation, An Unnatural Disaster: The Aftermath of Hurricane Katrina (Sept. 2005), available at http://www.progressiveregulation.org/articles/Unnatural_Disaster_512.pdf, 210-212

Chen, Jim, Of Agriculture's First Disobedience and Its Fruit, 48 Vand. L. Rev. 1261 (1995), 99

Chen, Jim, The Nature of the Public Utility: Infrastructure, the Market, and the Law, 98 Nw. U. L. Rev. 1617 (2004), 99

Cohen, Roberta, Time for the United States to Honor International Standards in Emergencies, The Brookings-Bern Project on Internal Displacement, http://www.brookings.edu/views/op-ed/cohenr/20050909.htm (Sept. 9, 2005), 152-153

Congressional Research Service, Aging Infrastructure: Dam Safety, http://www.ewrinstitute.org/files/pdf/aidamsafetyreport.pdf (Sept. 29, 2005), 278-288

President's National Security Telecommunications Advisory Committee, Legislative and Regulatory Task Force, Federal Support to Telecommunications Infrastructure Providers in National Emergencies: Designation as "Emergency Responders (Private Sector)", http://www.ncs.gov/nstac/reports/2006/NSTAC%20LRTF%20Stafford%20Act%20Report_Final.pdf (Jan. 31, 2006), 100-101

Rabin, Robert L., The Quest for Fairness in Compensating Victims of September 11, 49 Clev. St. L. Rev. 573 (1991), 163

Rabin, Robert L. & Bratis, Suzanne A., Financial Compensation for Catastrophic Loss in the United States, in Financial Compensation for Victims after Catastrophe, ed. M. Faure, T. Honlief, Springer Verlag 2005, available at http://ssrn.com, 162-170, 195-198

Recovering From Katrina and Rita: Environmental Governance Lessons Learned and Applied, 36 Env, L. Rep. 10139 (2006), 260

Romano, Jay, Protecting Pets in a Disaster, N.Y. Times, Sept. 25, 2005, at 14, 83

Rose, Carol M., The Story of Lucas: Environmental Land Use Regulation Between Developers and the Deep Blue Sea, in Richard J. Lazarus & Oliver A. Houck, Environmental Law Stories 268-269 (2005), 226

Rubin, Edward L. & Feeley, Malcolm, Federalism: Some Notes on a National Neurosis, 41 UCLA L. Rev. 903 (1994), 20

Schwarzenegger Issues Executive Order to Cut Greenhouse Gas Emissions in State, 36 Envt. Rep. 1145 (Jun. 3, 2005), 316

Serota, James I., Monopoly Pricing in a Time of Shortage, 33 Loy. U. Chi. L.J. 791 (2002), 148

Shays, Christopher, Animal Law: Its Place in Legislation, 12 Animal L. 1 (2005), 83-84

Silva, Raul F., A Methodology and Estimate of the National Cost for Dam Safety Rehabilitation, presented at a conference of the Association of State Dam Safety Officials, Providence, RI (Sept. 27, 2000), 282

Slovic, Paul, Perception of Risk, 236 Science 280 (1987), 71

Smith, Neil, There's No Such Thing as a Natural Disaster, http://understandingkatrina.ssrc.org/Smith (Sept. 26, 2005), 113

Southern States Call for U.S. Action, Note Increased Vulnerability of Coasts, 36 Envt. Rep.. 2539 (2005), 316.

Stone, Richard and Kerr, Richard A., Girding for the Next Big Wave, 310 Science 1602 (2005), 288

Sunstein, Cass, Terrorism and Probability Neglect, 26 J. Risk & Uncertainty 121 (2003), 71

Taylor, J. Edward, Differential Migration, Networks, Information and Risk, in Migration Theory, Human Capital and Development 147 (Oded Stark, ed., 1986), 144

Thompson, Martha & Gaviria, Izaskun, OxfamAmerica, Weathering the Storm: Lessons in Risk Reduction From Cuba (Apr. 2004), available at http://www.oxfamamerica.org/newsandpublications/publications/research _reports/pdfs/cuba_hur_eng.pdf, 214-219

Trebilcock, Craig T., The Myth of Posse Comitatus, J. Homeland Security (October 2000) (available at http://www. homelandsecurity.org/journal/ articles/Trebilcock.htm), 42, 43

Urban Planning Committee, Bring New Orleans Back Commission, Action Plan for New Orleans, FINAL REPORT, http://www.bringneworleansback. org/Portals/BringNewOrleansBack/Resources/Urban%20Planning%20Acti on%20Plan%20Final%20Report.pdf, (January 11, 2006), 256-259

Vandall, Frank J. & Vandall, Joshua F., A Call for an Accurate Restatement (Third) of Torts: Design Defect, 33 U. Mem. L. Rev. 909 (2003), 72

VandeHei, Jim and Geyelin, Milo, Economic Impact: Bush Seeks to Limit Liability of Companies Sued as Result of Attacks, Wall St. J., Oct. 25, 2001, at A6, 164

Wade, Nicholas, Studies Suggest Pandemic Isn't Imminent, N. Y. Times, March 23, 2006, at A16, 297

Wasem, Ruth Ellen, Katrina-Related Immigration Issues and Legislation (Sept. 19, 2005) (CRS Order Code RL33091), 142-144

Webster, P. J. et al., Changes in Tropical Cyclone Number, Duration, and Intensity in a Warming Environment, 309 Science 1844 (2005), 307

Welborn, Angie A. & Flynn, Aaron M., Price Increases in the Aftermath of Hurricane Katrina: Authority to Limit Price Gouging (Sept. 2, 2005) (CRS Order Code RS22236), 145-146, 147

Winthrop, Jim, The Oklahoma City Bombing: Immediate Response Authority and Other Military Assistance to Civil Authority (MAC), Army Law, July 1997, at 3, 49, 102

Wood, Hugh L., Jr., The Insurance Fallout Following Hurricane Andrew: Whether Insurance Companies Are Legally Obligated to Pay For Building Code Upgrades Despite The "Ordinance Or Law" Exclusion Contained In Most Homeowners Policies, 48 U. Miami L. Rev. 949 (1994) (student comment), 192

Zeichner, Lee M., Private Sector Integration, in American Bar Association, Hurricane Katrina Task Force Subcommittee Report 33 (Feb. 2006), 99

Congressional Reports

H.R. Rep. No. 97-71, Part II, 97th Cong., 1st Sess. 4 (1981) (citing 1 William Blackstone, Commentaries *343-44), reprinted in 1981 U.S.C.C.A.N. 1781, 37

Legislative Proceedings

Federal Emergency Management Agency: Oversight and Management of the National Flood Insurance Program: Hearing before the Subcommittee on Housing and Community Opportunity of the House Committee on Financial Services (Oct. 20, 2005) (statement of William O. Jenkins, Jr.,

GLOSSARY OF ACRONYMS

ASFPM	Association of State Floodplain Managers
ASPHEP	Assistant Secretary for Public Health Emergency Preparedness
BCEGS	Building Code Effectiveness Grading Schedule
BNOB	Bring New Orleans Back Committee
CCF	Climate Change Futures
CDBG	Community Development Block Grant
CDC	Centers for Disease Control
CEA	California Earthquake Authority
CI/KR	Critical Infrastructure and Key Resources
CLIVAR	Climate Variability and Predictability World Climate Research Programme
COP	Conference of Parties (Montreal, post-Kyoto)
DCN	Cuban National Civil Defense
DED	Deferred Enforced Departure
DHS	Department of Homeland Security
DoD	Department of Defense
EMAC	Emergency Management Assistance Compact
ENSO	El Niño/Southern Oscillation
ESF	Emergency Support Functions
EVD	Extended Voluntary Departure
FCA	Flood Control Act
FCO	Federal Coordinating Officer
FEMA	Federal Emergency Management Agency
FERC	Federal Energy Regulatory Commission
FHWA	Federal Highway Administration
FTA	Federal Transit Administration
GAO	Government Accountability Office
GDP	Gross Domestic Product
GHG	Greenhouse Gas
HANO	Housing Authority of New Orleans
HHS	Health and Human Services

HMGP	Hazard Mitigation Grant Program
HSC	Homeland Security Council
HSOC	Homeland Security Operations Center
HUD	Housing and Urban Development
ICODS	Interagency Committee on Dam Safety
ICS	Incident Command System
IDP	Internally Displaced Persons
IHP	Individual Housing Program
IIMG	Interagency Incident Management Group
IIPL	Insurance Institute for Property Loss Reduction
ILS	Insurance-Linked Securities
INA	Immigration and Nationality Act
INS	Incidents of National Significance
INV	Cuban National Housing Institute
IPCC	Intergovernmental Panel on Climate Change
IPF	Cuban Institute of Physical Planning
JFO	Joint Field Office
MRE	Meals Ready to Eat
MSHA	Mine Safety and Health Administration (Dept. of Labor)
NAO	North Atlantic Oscillation
NAS	National Academy of Sciences
NDSP	National Dam Safety Program
NDSRB	National Dam Safety Review Board
NFIP	National Flood Insurance Program
NHC	National Hurricane Center
NID	National Inventory of Dams
NIMS	National Incident Management System
NPRA	National Preparedness and Response Authority
NRCS	Natural Resources Conservation Service (Dept. of Agriculture)
NRP	National Response Plan
NRP-CIA	National Response Plan's Catastrophic Incident Annex
O&M	Operation and Maintenance Procedures (Army Corps of Engineers)
PAHO	Pan American Health Organization
PETS	Pet Evacuation and Transportation Standards Act
PFO	Principal Federal Official
PML	Probable Maximum Losses
RRCC	Regional Response Coordination Center
SAD	State Active Duty
SARS	Severe Acute Respiratory Syndrome
SNS	Strategic National Stockpile
SPR	Strategic Petroleum Reserve
SREMAC	Southern Regional Emergency Management Assistance Compact
SRFCP	Sacramento River Flood Control Project
SSA	Social Security Act

TFAH	Trust for America's Health
TPA	Temporary Protected Status
TRIA	Terrorism Risk Insurance Act of 2002
UNFCCC	United Nations Framework Convention on Climate Change
WHO	World Health Organization
WRDA	Water Resources Development Act

INDEX

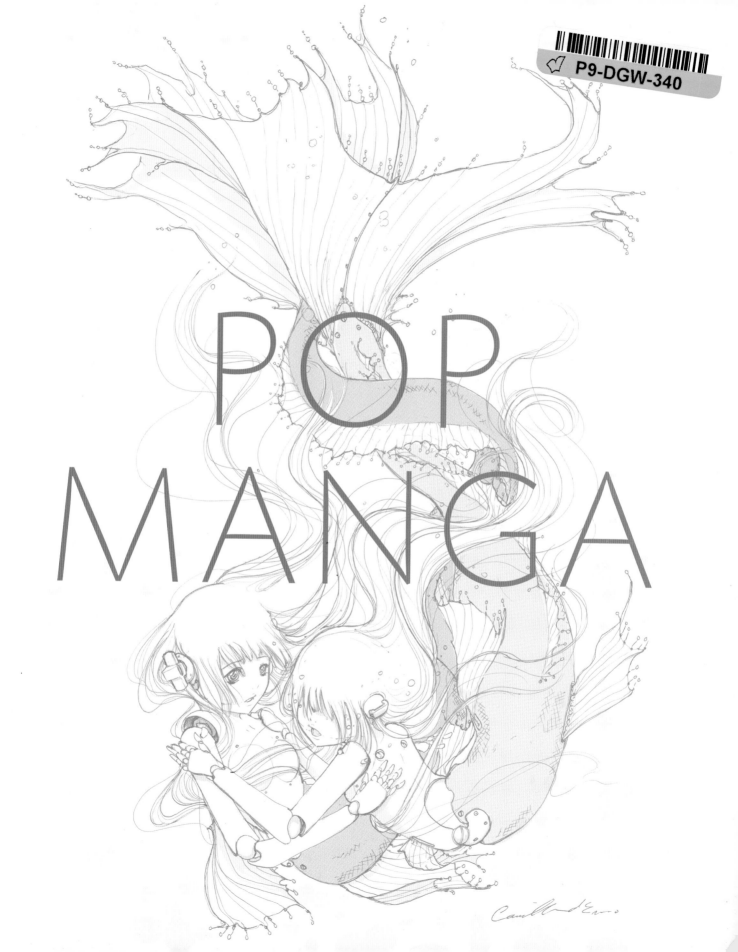

POP
MANGA

POP
MANGA

How to Draw the Coolest, Cutest Characters,
Animals, Mascots, and More

CAMILLA D'ERRICO AND STEPHEN W. MARTIN

Watson-Guptill Publications · New York

Published in the United States by Watson-Guptill Publications,
an imprint of the Crown Publishing Group, a division of
Random House, Inc., New York.
www.crownpublishing.com
www.watsonguptill.com

WATSON-GUPTILL and the WG and Horse designs are registered
trademarks of Random House, Inc.

Library of Congress Cataloging-in-Publication Data
d'Errico, Camilla
Pop manga: how to draw the coolest, cutest characters,
animals, mascots, and more/Camilla d'Errico and
Stephen W. Martin.
Pages cm
1. Comic books, strips, etc. Japan—Technique. 2. Cartoon
characters—Japan. 3. Figure drawing—Technique.
NC1764.5.J3 D47 2013
741.60952   2012042393

ISBN 978-0-307-98550-7
eISBN 978-0-307-98551-4

Printed in China

Illustration credits appear on page 191
Cover design by Jim Massey
Cover illustrations by Camilla d'Errico

10 9 8 7

First Edition

CAMILLA'S DEDICATION

To the tallest man with a plan: Without your watchful eye I wouldn't be the artist I am today. And to my true love, you are this girl's best friend and dragon slayer.

STEPHEN'S DEDICATION

For Lola, my true love. Without you're watchful eye, sentences would remain like this one.

CONTENTS

INTRODUCTION

When I was a kid, I loved Saturday-morning cartoons! Every Saturday, my sister and I would wake up at the crack of dawn, grab a bowl of Lucky Charms, and bask in the wonders of eighties cartoons. Whether we were defending Eternia and the secrets of Grayskull or the streets of Manhattan with Spider-Man, we could not get enough! But that was nothing compared to when we discovered *Tekkaman Blade*, a Japanese anime series. It had everything—amazing action, steamy romance, cute boys, and giant robots! We were obsessed! This show sparked my love of Japanese animation, and then, in the mid-nineties, the show *Sailor Moon* aired; this cemented my passion forever. To this day, I still have a small crush on Tuxedo Mask. (But who doesn't!)

When I hit my teens, I discovered manga. Don't get me wrong—I love Peter Parker, but American comics just didn't set off my spider-sense like manga did. The characters in the stories were just like me: They had everyday struggles with friends and parents. They laughed, loved, and even cried. It wasn't just about fighting or saving the world (although there was some of that); it was about internal struggles and personal tragedies. Plus, the girls were prettier and the boys were way cuter! Manga stories like *Sailor Moon* and those from Clamp, the all-female artist group, inspired me to start drawing comics.

A handful of my paintings, drawings, and panels are sprinkled throughout this book. I included these not only because I love to share my work with others, but also because I'm hoping they might inspire you to keep creating and encourage you to find your own artistic style!

Getting Ideas

I'm often asked in interviews where I find inspiration for my art. The answer is rather simple: all around me! Sometimes I like to wander the streets armed with my iPhone so that I can snap pictures of anything that catches my eye. It could be a broken toaster in the garbage or a bent pipe on the street— you'd be surprised where some of my helmet designs come from! What I'm getting at is, don't wait for inspiration to come knocking on your door. Get up and go find it. Finding inspiration is about being active, constantly challenging yourself, and opening your mind to new creative wonders, be they music, movies, books, art, or even random things on the street. Trust me, you never know what will spark your imagination and lead you to your next great creation.

CHOOSING YOUR "WEAPONS"

This is my studio—a.k.a. my Batcave—where I do all my drawing, painting, and plotting.

Just like a samurai has his sword, every manga artist has an arsenal of supplies. Pens, paper, and Photoshop are my tools of the trade. With these mighty weapons, I do battle every day with the evil blank page, creating characters and backgrounds. Before we get started, I'm going to tell you a little bit about some of the tools I can't live without, starting with my favorite pens, which are, in fact, mightier than most manga swords.

The Bic Pen

My first weapon of choice is a run-of-the-mill, find-it-on-the-floor, top-probably-chewed-off classic black Bic ballpoint pen. These are cheap and amazing! Every time I go to Staples, I buy a box, and I have literally thousands of them. Why do I love these pens so much? Well, they produce a smooth line and are comfortable to hold while drawing. They have the feel of a pencil in your hands, but unlike pencils, they never smudge. Another fantastic feature of this pen is that it lets me alter my lines from thick to thin, from subtle to hard, just by adjusting my grip or by putting extra pressure on the tip. I can't live without them.

Faber-Castell Pitt Artist Pens

When I want to make my lines superthick or superthin, I use the Faber-Castell Pitt Black 199. I find that the tips on these pens are very delicate but sturdy. The "B" brush tip is especially good for drawing hair because it allows me to draw a thicker or thinner line, depending on the character's hairstyle. This is also what I use to fill in any solid black areas I want on my drawings.

Pilot Color Eno Mechanical Lead Pencil

I do all my initial, or base, drawings with a Pilot Color Eno mechanical lead pencil before moving on to my final black ink. The color I use is called "soft blue." (It's actually a teal, or light turquoise, shade.) The soft-blue pencil is amazing because when you scan your image in grayscale, the scanner will not pick up the blue lines. It's like an invisible ink. All the step-by-step drawings in this book were done with this lead.

Staedtler Mars Plastic Eraser

The Staedtler Mars eraser—an eraser made of white plastic—is the only one I use. It is accurate and easy to hold, making it the perfect weapon for destroying all evidence of my mistakes. So throw those big pink erasers in the garbage and replace them with a white Staedtler Mars eraser.

I'm giving you a list of some of my favorite "weapons," but you should feel free to experiment. Try out an assortment of tools and find the ones that work for you. Remember, the artist doesn't choose the pen—the pen chooses the artist.

Cougar Paper

I have tried hundreds of paper types over the years, and the one that beats all the others is the 11 x 17, 100-pound Cougar Opaque White Digital Choice Super Smooth paper. This paper has a little bit of weight but almost no surface texture, which allows you to use an assortment of pens without smudging or ripping the paper. You can get it at any print or copy shop, and it's much cheaper than buying prelined manga boards or sketch paper. I buy it in bulk and draw a border around each sheet myself.

Scanner and Photoshop

I scan everything I draw and import it into Photoshop, where I can scale it down to manga-size boards or panels. Working with a scanner and Photoshop, I can draw my images at a larger scale and then shrink them down while keeping all the detail.

BECOMING A MANGA ARTIST

Whether you got this book as a gift or picked it up yourself, I want to say I'm honored to show you everything I know to help you become a manga artist. Trust me, it's not easy, but I know you have what it takes. Together we're going to tackle all the techniques you'll need to bring your characters to life, and along the way we're going to get some help from a little creation of mine—Inku!

Hi! My name is Inku. Throughout this book, I'm going to offer you little tips—and stuff that Camilla doesn't even know. And, of course, a joke or two, since we all know Camilla isn't that funny! With my help—and, yeah, a little from Camilla—you'll be drawing your own creations in no time.

Sorry about Inku's attitude! You'll find that when you start drawing your own manga, some characters take on lives of their own.

Before we begin, I want to take a moment to explain how to use this book. First, I don't want you to think you have to master each and every step before you continue on to the next chapter. If you find a particular step a little challenging, try tracing it—that's what I did when I was learning—or skip it and come back to it later. And don't worry if your drawings don't look exactly like mine. This book's purpose is to help you discover your own voice, so feel free to experiment. Remember, there's just one rule when comes to learning manga: Have fun!

Now, just one last thing before we get started drawing. It's a word of wisdom from one of my all-time favorite comic artists, John Buscema. John, who drew everything from *The Avengers* to *Conan the Barbarian* to *Silver Surfer*, once said, "People who draw comics don't do it for the money. They don't do it for the fame. If you want to be rich and famous, you're better off being an actor. We draw and write comics for the love and passion of it, and we don't give up if it's something that we really love to do!" So ask yourself why you want to draw manga. If it's for love, then you'll be successful no matter what.

Okay, let's draw manga!

FROM THE TOP

DRAWING THE HEAD

The face showcases a character's emotions and creates a connection with the reader. That's why all manga artists should begin their study with the face. In this chapter, we are going to learn how to draw the eyes, the nose, and the mouth. I'll also give you pointers on facial expressions and tips on drawing hair. Once you've mastered each element, you'll practice putting them together.

DRAWING EYES

Whenever I'm creating a new character, I always start with the eyes. You get all the emotion from the eyes; they are the gateway to the character's soul. Eyes are the manga artist's catchphrase or calling card. The next time you're reading *Naruto*, *Chobits*, or even *Vampire Knight*—some of my personal favorites—take a look at the characters' eyes, and notice the differences in the style and execution. Each manga artist has a signature way of drawing eyes. My eyes are "circle eyes," and that's the style you're about to learn. But I want you to take the steps I teach you and run with them, altering them to match your own style and your own characters' personalities. Remember, it's *your* signature, so have fun!

GIRL EYES

Girls' eyes are really fun to draw. They are big, round, and beautiful. Girls' eyes are the biggest set of eyes you will draw, next to toddler eyes. Okay, let's begin!

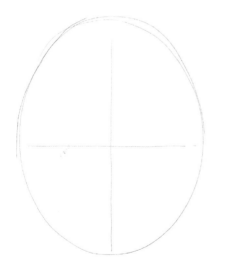

STEP 1 Using your blue pencil, draw an oval shape for the head and then crosshairs going from top to bottom and side to side. The crosshairs will give you the position of the eyes on the face and also determine which way the head is turned. In this case, the view is full frontal, so the lines of the crosshairs run straight down the middle of the face and horizontally across.

STEP 2 Add the eyebrow and the upper eye line. Here we are drawing a classic bright-eyed girl, so the eyebrows are arched. The upper eye lines should curve in the same direction as the eyebrows.

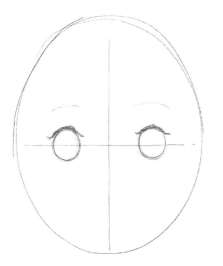

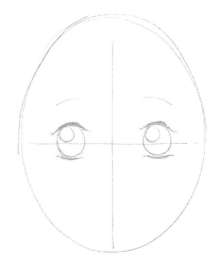

STEP 3 Each eye is a simple circle centered on the horizontal line halfway between the side of the face and the central line. Make sure you draw the circle touching the upper eye lines you previously drew.

STEP 4 It's time for the highlights. For each, draw a little circle inside the larger eye circle—it should be about a quarter of the larger circle's size. I place the highlight at the top left, which is my standard look. (Some artists put three or four of these little circles in each eye.)

Then draw the lower eye line. It's basically a mirror of the upper line. I don't like to draw the lower line as full as the upper. Why? Because every artist has her secrets . . .

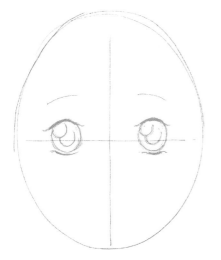

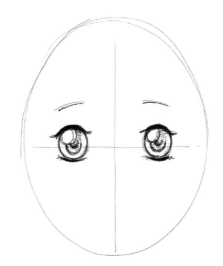

STEP 5 Okay, now for the iris, which is the colored part of the eye. Draw a half-circle, starting at the bottom middle of the highlight and going around to the other side. I don't go all the way to the top of the eye, but you certainly can, if you like. Remember, it's all about finding your own personal style.

STEP 6 It's time to get out your black pen and go over the drawing to add a little depth and character. Draw the pupil right in the middle of the iris, and fill it in. Then lightly shade in the area between the edge of the iris and the pupil, being careful to avoid the highlight. You can also fill in more of the upper and lower eye lines with a few black pen strokes to give things a little more depth.

GUY EYES

When you're drawing female eyes in manga, everything is soft and round. But guys' eyes have to look more masculine, so you don't want to make them quite as circular as female eyes.

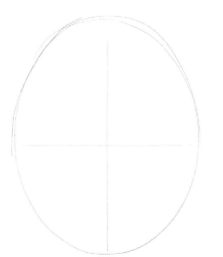

STEP 1 Once again, begin with a circle and crosshairs. Remember, we're using our blue pencil here—no black ink yet.

STEP 2 Now draw the circles for the eyes and the eyebrows above them. Guys' eyebrows are less arched and extend farther toward the outer edges of the face.

STEP 3 Now let's do the top eye lines. For guys' eyes, we're not going to follow the contour of the eye circle like we did when drawing girls' eyes. Instead, the top eye line should overlap the circle slightly, like a little hat. Next, draw the bottom eye lines, which are gentle, continuous curves.

STEP 4 Draw the highlight circles and the half-circles for the irises, just like you did for the girl eyes. Feel free to flip back for a reminder.

STEP 5 Using your black pen, go over all the lines you've drawn so far to give them a little more depth and strength.

STEP 6 Time to shade! I do the initial shading with a steady, straight-line motion. This gives the eyes more depth and a fuller, finished look.

STEP 7 Now intensify the darkness by adding more shading at the top. Also, here I've waited until the last minute to add the pupil, drawing in a small U shape and making it the very darkest part of the eye. *Bang!* Just like that, the eyes are complete!

Don't add any lashes to the male eyes. Those are just for females. Then again, who knows? Maybe your guy likes to wear mascara!

TODDLER EYES

The younger the manga character, the bigger the eyes should be. In proportion to the face, toddler eyes are huge—which makes them supercute! In fact,
you can use that as a general rule: The younger the character, the larger the
eyes. (By contrast, grandparents' eyes are barely visible.) Also, a toddler's
eyes are closer together than an older boy's or girl's eyes.

Here, we follow the same steps for drawing the girl and guy eyes, but
everything is exaggerated. When it comes to eyelashes, gender is not an
issue; you can add them to both male and female toddler eyes.

ADULT EYES

The main difference between adult eyes and younger manga characters' eyes is that adult eyes are smaller. In fact, they should be half the size of teenagers' or kids' eyes. Everything, including the pupil and the highlight, is smaller. You can also see more of the whites of the eyes in older adult characters. Adult eye lines are longer than those of young people, and they are positioned slightly farther apart. Otherwise, the steps for drawing adult eyes are basically the same as those you've already learned—though there are a few differences between women's and men's eyes.

Women

When drawing female adult eyes, give them heavy eye lines to show that they're wearing makeup—and add some extra eyelashes at the ends of the eye lines to indicate mascara and a single line above the eye for the eyelid. (Younger manga characters tend not to wear any makeup.)

Men

Men's eyes are similar to those of women, except that—like young guys' eyes—they're less rounded. Also, I tend to draw men's pupils a little smaller, but that's just a style thing. (Remember what I said about finding your own signature.)

Wait, Camilla! What about the stink eye? How do you draw that?!

GRANDPARENT EYES

In manga, the classic way of drawing old-people eyes is to draw no eyes at all, because they appear to have their eyes closed all the time. But I thought it might be fun to draw an old grandmother's eyes. Why? Because I love old ladies—they're so much fun to draw. And, well, I love my grandmother!

STEP 1 Draw eye circles and thick eyebrows with your blue pencil. Lay in the eye lines so that they cut across the top and bottom of each circle—which makes it look like the old person's eyes are half open (or half closed). Also, most grannies stop wearing mascara at a certain age!

STEP 2 Now add in the highlights and pupils, remembering that highlights are always smaller in older people. If you've forgotten how to do this, flip back a few pages. (Just make sure Inku doesn't catch you!) Now, with your blue pencil, start adding in the details that make people look old—wrinkles! Draw two little strokes under the lower eye line and above the eye. Finish by adding a few little lines indicating crow's-feet at the corner of each eye and some wrinkle lines near the eyebrows.

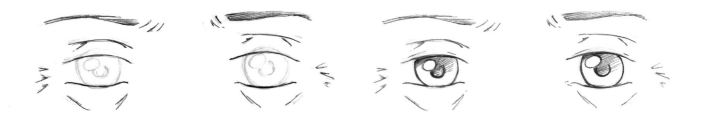

STEP 3 Use your black pen to go over the lines. I usually start with the eye lines, because they should cover the tops and bottoms of the eyes. Drawing them first lets you know where to draw the eye. From there, draw the eyelids, eyebrows, and wrinkles. The more wrinkles, the older the character.

STEP 4 Finally, shade the eyes. Remember to avoid the highlight as you shade the iris and pupil. The highlights in older characters' eyes are smaller than those of any other character.

VILLAIN EYES

Now it's time to create the all-important villain eyes. The steps are basically the same, with just a few twists. Every element should be slightly smaller than that of a regular adult eye. And you'll want to give villains' eyes some dramatic angles to make them look extra-evil.

STEP 1 Draw the eye circles with your blue pencil. Then draw the upper eye lines so that they point downward and inward. The upper eye lines curve downward. Add slanting eyebrows to match, showing that these characters are always angry.

STEP 2 Trace over your initial drawing with your black pen, making sure to smooth out your line work around the eyebrows.

STEP 3 Add the pupils, making them slightly smaller than you would in a normal adult eye. Also note that you are not going to draw highlights in these eyes—just the pupils. Without the highlights, the eyes take on a more devious look.

STEP 4 Now shade in the irises above the pupil. This makes the character appear sinister. You may want to give female villains extra eyelashes. Think of the Evil Queen in *Snow White*—the meaner a female villain is, the more makeup she wears!

DRAWING NOSES

Fresh lilacs, cotton candy, and freshly cut grass—those are my favorite smells. If I could bottle them, I would. My least favorite? Well, my French bulldog Loki's superfarts.

You've probably guessed we are about to learn how to draw noses. In manga the nose is often overlooked or simplified, but I like to give my characters button noses. I guess it's another one of my signatures.

I always start with the nostrils, then draw the line of the nose to show the direction the face is pointing. If the character is facing straight ahead, there's no need to draw the nose line. All the noses shown here belong to younger characters, but it's important to note that older characters' noses are longer and pointier. Note, too, that there's no difference between female and male noses in manga.

Here the nose line extends past the cheek because of the face's position.

In manga, a nose can be as simple as two small points indicating the nostrils.

With noses, don't be afraid to experiment with shading and line work. As you can see, I do!

A small button nose gives the character a cuter, younger look.

When drawing a nose line in three-quarter view, I begin the incline at the point where the crosshairs meet. Keep in mind that the nostril should be positioned about midway between the horizontal crosshair and the mouth.

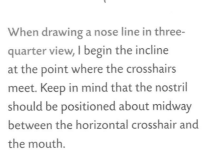

I hate noses! Mostly because I look like I came from inside of one. Anyway, did you know that the direction the nose points is the direction the eyes are looking?

This painting drove me crazy! It wasn't working
until my editor, Sean, came over and said,
"You forgot her shoulder." He was right!
Sometimes we artists miss the obvious.

DRAWING MOUTHS

The way you draw the mouth gives you another opportunity to subtly put your own personal stamp on a character. One characteristic of my mouths—unique among manga artists—is that I draw lips. Traditionally, manga characters are highly simplified, which usually means no lips. But I like to add lips to my female characters because lips are sexy. I also like to give my characters teeth, which a lot of manga artists don't do. The next time you're reading your favorite manga, pay attention to the mouths. I started drawing my characters' teeth when I was young—probably subconsciously, because I had braces and envied other people's perfectly formed pearly whites.

When drawing mouths, I always start with the opening and then draw the bottom lip, followed by the top lip, and finally, the sides. It is important to start with the opening because it's the overall shape of the mouth that defines a character's expression. Here, I'm showing you an assortment of mouths to give you a lot of examples of how to craft some superexpressive pieholes. Before you start practicing, take the time to study these mouths and look for the tiny details that differentiate them. For example, in the Vampire Mouth—a villain's mouth—I've stretched the grin to almost double the size of a normal grin.

I tend to make men's mouths larger while keeping women's mouths smaller and more pouty—but again, you should make whatever changes you like.

What can I say? I love a boy with fangs!

When a character is speaking—or, in this case, shouting—I like to color in the interior of the mouth. It gives more punch to the image.

Here the character is speaking softly, so we see only a hint of teeth.

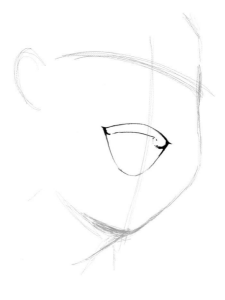

When drawing sexy, pouty lips, keep the mouth opening small to accentuate the lips.

Here is your classic "Genki" girl mouth, laughing.

I call this the "Ticked-Off Girlfriend Mouth."

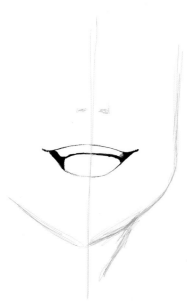

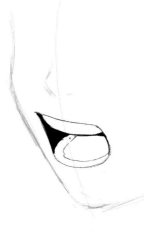

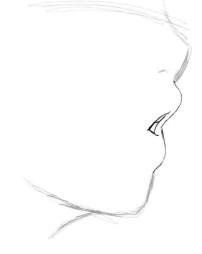

You can tell by the wide opening and the lines of his smile extending up and out that this character is laughing.

This character is shouting. There is always shouting in manga, especially if there is a *Yu-Gi-Oh!* battle happening.

Here's a side view of a guy speaking.

DRAWING HAIR

I think everyone wishes they had manga hair. Short or long, curly or straight, it always looks fantastic! One thing to remember is that in manga, the hair is often a literal extension of the character's personality. Greasy, slicked-back hair usually means a gruesome greasy villain, and bountiful bouncing curls usually mean a bouncy bubbly blonde. But remember, rules can be broken, so have fun with it. Here, I'm giving you an assortment of different hairstyles for both female and male characters.

Girls' Hairstyles

I love drawing girls' hair and making it look soft and flowy—creating a sense of whimsy in the female characters. Honestly, it's pretty easy to do—just never draw a straight line.

For me, a girl's hairstyle should always have an overall direction, with most of the strands moving in that direction. When drawing a girl's hair, I always start with the bangs and curve them up to the crown of the head. Then I draw the outer edges of the hairstyle, finishing it off with the strands of hair that are closest to the face.

Manga girls' hair often looks like it is blowing in the breeze. It's kind of a charismatic look, and it makes all the manga boys stop and stare.

MEDIUM-LENGTH HAIR

Farrah's Flow

Bold Bangs

Cute and Tidy

The Snow White

LONG HAIR

Treasure Hunter

Sultry Smooth

Behind Wave

Sleek and Straight

Innocent Wave

Banged Beauty

SHORT HAIR

The Sixties Schoolgirl

Sleek and Sexy Bob

Long and Bouncy Bob

Puffy Princess

UPDOS

The Pull-Back

The Tie-Back

Pigtails

Ponytail

Space Buns

Boys' Hairstyles

What's really fun about guys' hair in manga is that if a real-life boy wore a hairstyle like that, you'd probably tell him to get a haircut. In manga, though, the boys always look superhot! Note that the invisible-wind effect applies to manga boys as well as to manga girls. Remember, combed or gelled hair is for villains only.

The Rebel

The Rock Star

The Seventies Shag

Messy Magnificent

Sleek and Serious

The Rascal

The Beaver

The Beatle

The Villain

The Cloud

Short Spikes

Bed Head

THE FACE—PUTTING IT ALL TOGETHER

Now it's time to put together everything we've learned so far and make some faces. We'll start with the front view and then move on to three-quarter and profile views. We'll be alternating between girls' and boys' faces—but always with some tips on how to draw a character of the other sex. Always remember that girls have rounder faces, and the lines for their features are always softer and curvier, whereas those for guys are more angular. Also, in manga, details such as dimples or lines around the eyes, nose, and mouth don't exist—at least not in young characters.

FRONT VIEW—GIRL'S FACE

The front view is the facial angle you'll draw most often—I think I draw it about a hundred times a week. It's also probably the easiest of the facial angles to draw. The front view is commonly used when characters are speaking, looking in the mirror, driving, or sitting in class. For this lesson, we'll focus on drawing a girl's face—but don't forget to study the tips on drawing boys' faces in the front view on page 37.

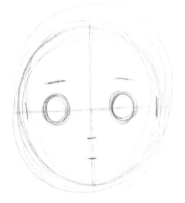

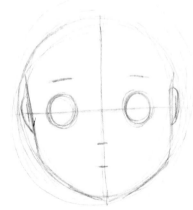

STEP 1 Start with an oval and crosshairs, drawing the eyes on the horizontal line and then the eyebrows just above the eyes. Next, draw a little line to indicate the nostrils, halfway between the place where the crosshairs meet and the chin. Then add the mouth halfway between the nostrils and the chin. To complete this step, draw little vertical lines for the ears, which are on the same horizontal line as the eyes.

STEP 2 Shape the head a bit by making the sides of the face straighter and by creating the jawline, which begins at either side of the face midway between the nose and mouth. Now make little half-ovals for the ears. The ears should barely be noticeable in a front view of a manga character's face.

STEP 3 Define the nose with just two small dots for nostrils. Define the mouth with a very small line that bumps up slightly in the middle. Also, draw the neck. A female character's neck is slimmer than a guy's, so curve the neck lines inward. Now is also the time to begin defining the chin. I use a point similar to the bottom of a heart shape, but feel free to use another shape for your characters.

STEP 4 Define the eyes and eyebrows further. (Flip back to the section on drawing eyes (page 16) if you don't remember all the steps.) You might also begin sketching in the hairline at this stage.

STEP 5 Begin defining the basic shape and texture of the hair. Don't worry if you don't get it quite right when working with your blue pencil—you'll be able to refine it later on.

STEP 6 Now it's time for the black ink. Start with the eyes, further defining their shape; then move on to the nose, mouth, and eyebrows. You don't have to follow your blue lines exactly, so don't be afraid to make adjustments.

STEP 7 Fill in the rest of the face, shading the eyes and adding details to the hair.

STEP 8 Finally, erase your blue lines, and—presto!—you have a supercute girl's face. Easy as store-bought cake!

FRONT VIEW—GUY'S FACE

Like I mentioned earlier, the basic approach to drawing a guy's face is the same as for a girl's—it's the details that make all the difference. Guys' faces are more angular, and their necks are thicker. As you probably remember from the section on eyes, guys' eyes are slightly smaller and less rounded than those of girls, and male eyebrows are straighter and thicker. Their mouths aren't quite so puckered—and I like to extend the line for a guy's mouth just a little wider than I would a girl's. Finally, the chin is squarer and more masculine.

THREE-QUARTER VIEW—GUY'S FACE

The three-quarter view is the most common view in manga. When characters are looking at something or talking to someone, their faces are often shown in this position. The three-quarter view is a slight turn of the head, so we have to do a little foreshortening to make it look like one side of the face is slightly closer to us than the other. We'll practice this view with a guy's face, but don't forget to read the tips on drawing girls' faces in three-quarter view on page 41.

STEP 1 As always, we begin with an oval for the head and a pair of crosshairs. Note that the vertical crosshair curves toward one side of the face. Whichever direction the curve goes in will be the direction in which the head is turned. In this case, it's toward the left. For the eye on the far side of the face, it's just the opposite: Place it slightly closer to the left edge of the oval than to the vertical crosshair. Also, the far eye should be a bit smaller than the near eye, since nearer things appear bigger and more distant things appear smaller.

The nose and mouth—here indicated by little lines—appear at the same height as in the front view, but you want to position them on the vertical crosshair. Then add in little lines for eyebrows and also indicate the ear's position. In the three-quarter view, you see only the ear on the near side of the head.

STEP 2 Now you're going to give the head some shape. On the far side of the face, make a slight indent, starting at about the level of the eyebrow and ending at about the same level as the nose. From there, continue the line, curving it around the bottom of the vertical crosshair. Now that you've established the chin, continue the line up and over to define the jawline on the near side of the face. This side of the face should be a little fuller than the lower far side. Complete this step by adding a half-oval for the ear and sketching in the neck lines.

STEP 3 Define the eyes and eyebrows a bit, remember-ing that guys' eyebrows are longer and not so curved as girls'. Also, begin defining the nose, making a tiny arrow, like this: <, for the nostril on the far side of the face. Define the neck lines as well: The line defining the front of the neck extends down directly from the point of the chin; the line for the back of the neck should align with the near jawline.

STEP 4 Sketch in the hair—and don't be afraid to make the hairstyle one of your own creation!

STEP 5 It's time for the black ink. Begin with the eyes, defining their shape, and then move to the nose, the mouth, and finally the eyebrows. Remember, if you don't love your blue lines, you don't have to follow them exactly.

STEP 6 Fill in the rest of the face using the black ink, shading the eyes and adding details to the hair and ears.

STEP 7 Erase your blue lines. Isn't he dreamy?

THREE-QUARTER VIEW—GIRL'S FACE

With the three-quarter view of the female face, you are going to notice more of the female facial characteristics. The chin is pointier, and the cheeks are fuller and rounder, making the face appear heart shaped.

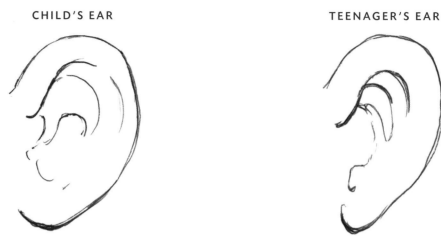

CHILD'S EAR

TEENAGER'S EAR

EARS

Ears are my least favorite part of the human body. They are stinky, wax-filled caverns of funk. When drawing ears, along with other parts of the body that I find particularly hard or gross, I sometimes look for references. In this case it's oysters. Seriously, next time you see an oyster on the half shell, check it out—or find a picture on the Web! The oyster's shape resembles that of an ear, with the meaty, delicious part closely resembling the inner part of the ear. I like to start at the middle and work my way out, like a ripple in the water. Remember that females tend to have rounder, cuter ears than males. And the older a person gets, the longer and more pronounced their ears become.

ADULT'S EAR

OLD PERSON'S EAR

PROFILE—GIRL'S FACE

In the profile view, the head is turned completely to the side, so we're seeing just one side of the face. I find this view the trickiest to draw. But don't worry—we'll rock it together.

STEP 1 Begin with your oval. Bisect it with a horizontal line. In the middle of the line, indicate the ear with a little straight line. In profile, the eye is a very narrow oval that sits near the edge of the larger oval of the head—but not *on* the edge, because that area will become the bridge of the nose. Just outside the oval, draw a little line to indicate where the nose will end and another little line to indicate the mouth.

STEP 2 Make an indent for the bridge of the nose. This line curves inward just above the eye and then curves outward just below the eye. For the chin, draw a small diagonal line outside the lower left-hand edge of the oval and then a longer, slightly curved diagonal line that moves back into the oval to indicate the jawline. The end of the jawline aligns with the ear, stopping at about the same level as the mouth.

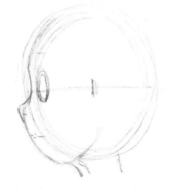

STEP 3 Define the nose. From the bottom of the bridge of the nose, extend the line out in a little downward swoop. Hitting the guideline you drew for the nose in the last step, create a little button nose and add a small line for a nostril at the base. Draw the line of the mouth. Finally, add lines for the neck, which will tilt forward toward the face.

STEP 4 Beginning at the tip of the nose, draw a line that extends down to the point of the chin—with three little indents along the way: one for the space between the nose and the upper lip; one for the divot where the lips meet; and one for the space between the lower lip and the chin.

Straighten out the eye's curves at the top and bottom, so that they meet at the outer corner of the eye. Then, where those two diagonal lines are farthest apart, draw a straight vertical line between them. This line defines the front of the eye.

STEP 5 Add a small vertical line in the center of the eye to represent the iris. At this point, you can also start to sketch in the girl's hair.

STEP 6 For the ear, make a half-oval that's a little taller than the eye, and draw a few little lines inside to indicate the whorls in the ear. Using the black pen, finish defining the hairstyle and the individual strands of hair.

STEP 7 Erase your blue pencil lines—and *finito*!

PROFILE—GUY'S FACE

As is always the case with guys' faces, the lines are going to be less curvy and all the shapes are going to be more angular than when you're drawing a girl's face. In the profile especially, there's much less definition in the lips. Guys' noses are a little more pointed, with straighter lines.

I'll tell you a secret: This painting is about heartbreak! I was totally heartbroken but was getting ready for a show and I had one more painting to finish. This painting is the result of, no joke, a thousand tears. I was literally crying while I was painting it. However, when I finished it, I felt better! Painting and drawing can be a way to get out all those emotions that you can't express any other way. Well, besides *burning* pictures!

EXTREME HEAD TURNS

It's time to turn up those expressions to 11 on the Richter scale. I wanted to include some extreme head turns for you to see. In manga anything goes, so feel free to experiment with some extreme angles of your own!

DRAWING EXPRESSIONS

I could draw an entire book of expressions! One of the reasons that I love manga is that the characters are just so expressive. Manga books are roughly thirty to forty pages longer than a typical American comic book, giving artists more panels to express the many subtle emotional changes a character experiences in a story. One of the things that bugs me about American comics is the really long text balloons that sometimes appear alongside an image. In one long text balloon there might be three or four different things that a character would react to, but the shorter page count limits the artist to giving the character just one expression. In manga you can hit each one of those emotional beats with a separate image, which elevates the character and the story to another level.

Here, I'm giving you a whole bunch of different examples of expressions. I've tried to make sure they run the gamut. I've also tried to make them gender neutral, so when you are drawing your characters, alter the expressions with subtle differences in the eyes and body to match each character's gender. Remember, when it comes to eyes: rounder for girls, half-moon shaped for guys, and smaller for older people.

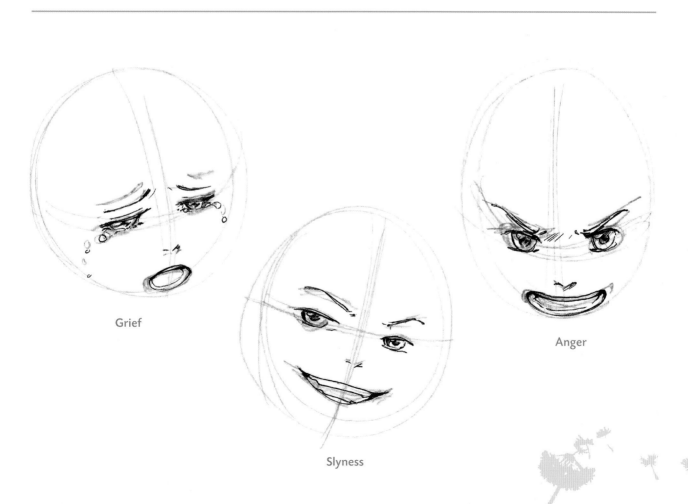

Grief

Slyness

Anger

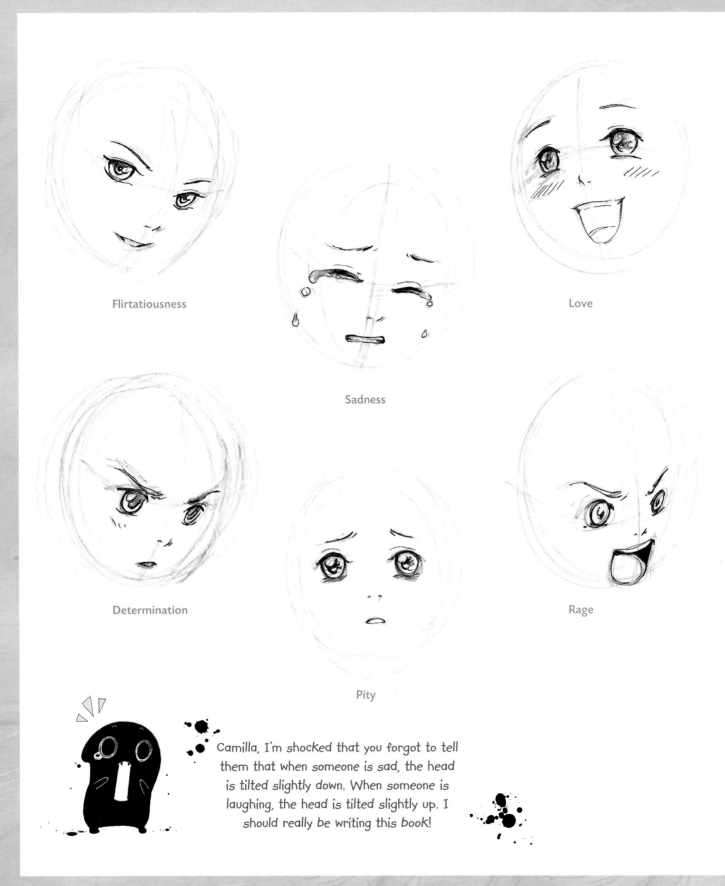

Flirtatiousness

Sadness

Love

Determination

Pity

Rage

Camilla, I'm shocked that you forgot to tell them that when someone is sad, the head is tilted slightly down. When someone is laughing, the head is tilted slightly up. I should really be writing this book!

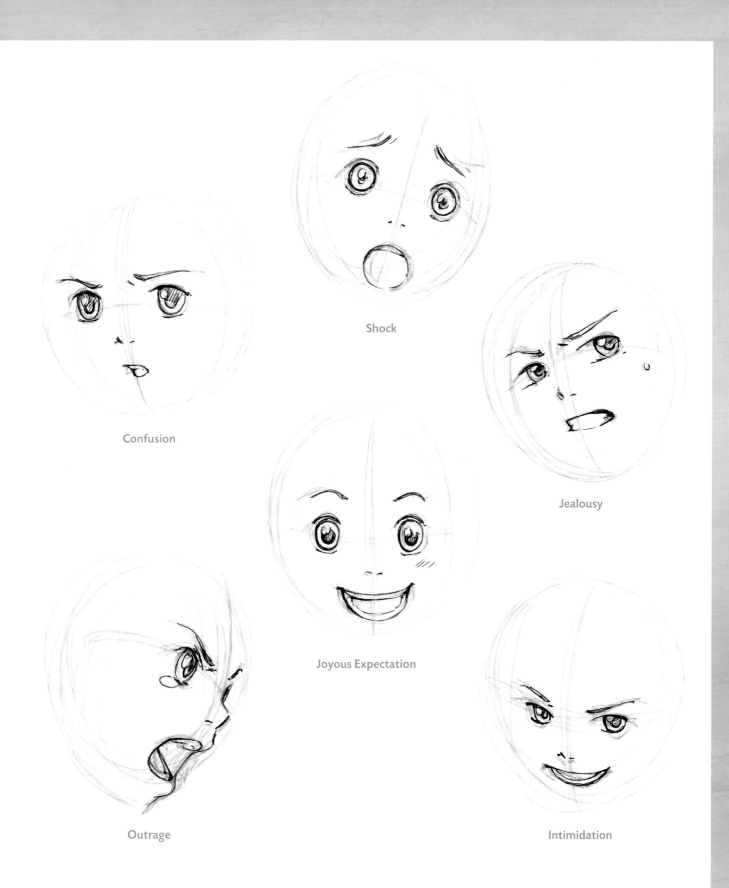

Confusion

Shock

Jealousy

Joyous Expectation

Outrage

Intimidation

THE
BIRTHDAY
SUIT

DRAWING THE BODY

Now that you've mastered the head, it's time to place it on a body—unless your character is a floating head, but that's another story! Drawing a body can be a little intimidating for new artists, because there are so many parts and everything should be proportional. The best advice I can give you is to love your mirror! I myself sometimes have trouble drawing various body parts, so a little trick I've learned is to draw in front of a mirror—or, if you aren't too shy, you could ask your friends, siblings, cousins, or even the cute boy next door to model for you. Remember, when tackling anything, it's important to go step by step—starting with one part of the body and then moving to the next. In this chapter, we are going to start with my favorite part: the hand.

DRAWING HANDS

I grew up in an Italian-Canadian family where everyone could speak without saying a word. We are masters of the hand gesture. Honestly, if you were to press mute while I was talking, I bet you'd still understand what I was saying! Hands dance and communicate, so remember when drawing characters that their hands are extensions of their hearts and minds. Drawing a hand can be a little tricky—in fact, a lot of artists say hands are the hardest things to draw—but I'm going to show you some classic tricks that make drawing hands as easy as pie.

Girl's Hand—Palm Down

Before we begin, take a look at one of your hands. Turn it palm up. Really—do it! I can wait . . . Did you do it? Good! Now turn your hand over and look at the back. Do you know the expression "I know it like the back of my hand"? Well, I want you to actually know what the back of your hand looks like. Now that you've become better acquainted with your hand, we are going to break it down into basic shapes. Everything is much easier to draw once you've broken it down into shapes.

STEP 1 Okay, grab your blue pencil and draw a square. The square shouldn't quite be perfect—it should be a little wider at the top. This will serve as the back of the hand—in this case, a right hand.

STEP 2 Now let's start on the fingers. Draw four circles above your square, then add four vertical rectangles extending from the tops of those circles. Since we're drawing the right hand as seen from the back, each of these rectangles, except for the one at the far right, will be slightly angled to the left. (If this doesn't make sense to you, take a quick look at the back of your right hand.) Note that the two rectangles in the middle are slightly longer than the ones on the far left and right.

STEP 3 Above these rectangles, draw a second set of circles for the knuckles. They should be slightly smaller than the ones at the bases of the rectangles.

STEP 4 Draw another set of four slightly narrower vertical rectangles above the knuckles.

STEP 5 Draw one more set of slightly smaller circles, which are the final joints at the ends of the fingers, as well as the fingertips. Now take a step back and assess. Does every finger have two rectangles and three circles? Is the middle finger the longest? If not, now is the time to go back and adjust.

STEP 6 Moving on to the thumb: Draw a circle a little larger than those at the top of the square. Draw another, smaller circle about forty-five degrees slightly above and to the left of the bigger circle. The distance between these circles should be about the same as the length of the bottom rectangle in the pointer finger.

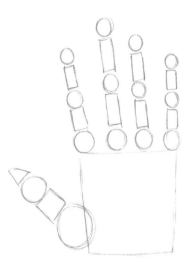

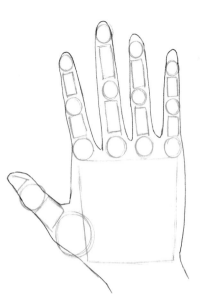

STEP 7 Between the two circles, draw a square that just touches both of them. Then add a small triangle—kind of like a little bird beak—with its base at the upper left-hand side of the small circle.

STEP 8 Now it's time to flesh things out—literally! Grab your black pen and draw one big outline around all the shapes that you have just created, extending the lines at the base of the hand to form the wrist.

Girl's Hand—Palm Up

To draw the hand palm up, you follow exactly the same steps as you did to draw the hand palm down, until you get to the end. Instead of adding fingernails, draw the lifelines in your palm, and make sure you don't forget all the indents.

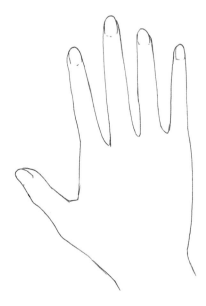

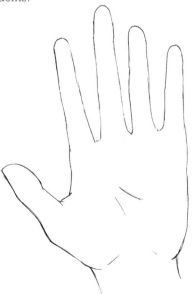

STEP 9 Erase your blue lines. To draw the fingernails, make a half-moon near the top of each finger, and then draw two straight lines down the sides to complete the nail. The thumbnail is different, since you're not looking at it head-on.

DRAWING GUYS' HANDS

There a few things to remember when drawing guys' hands. Male fingers are drawn a little more square than female fingers. Male fingers also have bigger knuckles and are drawn with heavier lines than female fingers. Most manga artists don't draw fingernails on guys' hands. Some artists believe fingernails make male hands look feminine. Other artists just draw a straight line going across the finger near the fingertip to represent the base of the nail, making it appear very square. But, honestly, it's up to you.

Guy's Hand—Palm Down
Leave a tiny bit of space between the rectangles and circles inside the fingers.

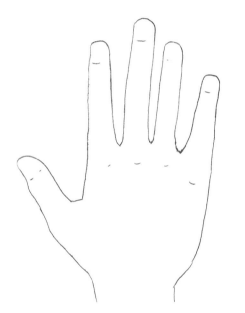

Remember: no fingernails on guys. Just draw a straight line to indicate the base of the nail. Also draw some little lines to indicate the knuckles.

Guy's Hand—Palm Up
It's important to make a guy's hands bigger than a female's, so take this into account when outlining the form of the hand.

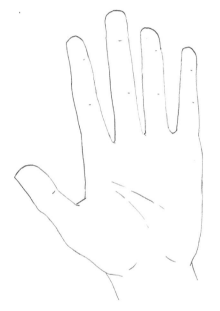

Don't forget to add some small marks showing the creases on the palm and at the finger joints.

THE FIST

Okay, same as before, I want you to form a fist with your hand, palm facing up, and study it before beginning to draw. Remember, you're looking for the basic shapes.

STEP 1 The overall shape of the fist is a big square, so go ahead and outline that in blue pencil.

STEP 2 Next come the knuckles, which are once again drawn as circles, the bottoms of which should overlap slightly with the top of the square. Note that the second circle in from the left (for the middle finger) is the biggest and the one on the far right (for the pinky finger) is the smallest. Now add circles for the joints below the knuckles. Note that in this drawing of a left hand, the two joints on the right side are lower than the ones on the left side, and they crowd in toward the middle of the palm.

It's time to get tough!
Are you ready to rumble?
Let's go! Inku smash!

STEP 3 Add rectangles connecting the joints. Then add the thumb by first drawing a circle just below and slightly to the left of the circle for the joint of the pointer finger. Left of the circle you have just drawn, make another circle, just slightly lower. All three of these circles should be touching one another. Now add a square to the right of the first circle you drew, and a funny little triangle (or bird-beak shape) to the right of the square. These shapes should form a line that slants down slightly across the palm.

STEP 4 Once again, it's time to flesh things out. Grab your black pen and outline the shapes you've just drawn. Stop the outlines between the fingers just inside the top line of the square. At the outside of the pinky, make the outline a little shorter—only about a third of the length of the finger. Add parallel lines for the wrist at the base of the palm as well as a few lines to define the shape of the palm. Finally, add the thumbnail and some faint lines for the creases on the palm.

STEP 5 Erase those pencil lines, and you're ready to go!

Hand Gestures and Positions

Here are a few examples of some common hand gestures and positions.

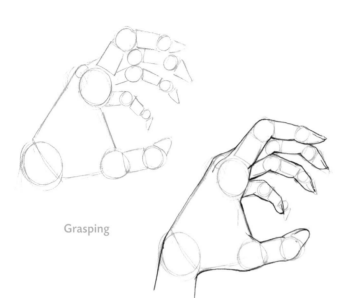

Grasping

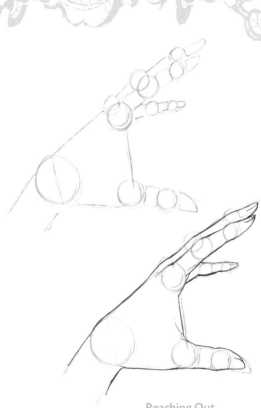

Reaching Out

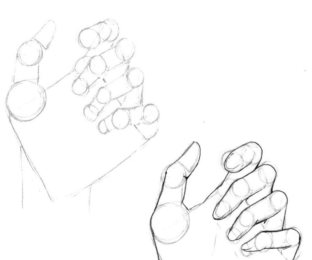

Holding a Phone

Touching Someone's Face

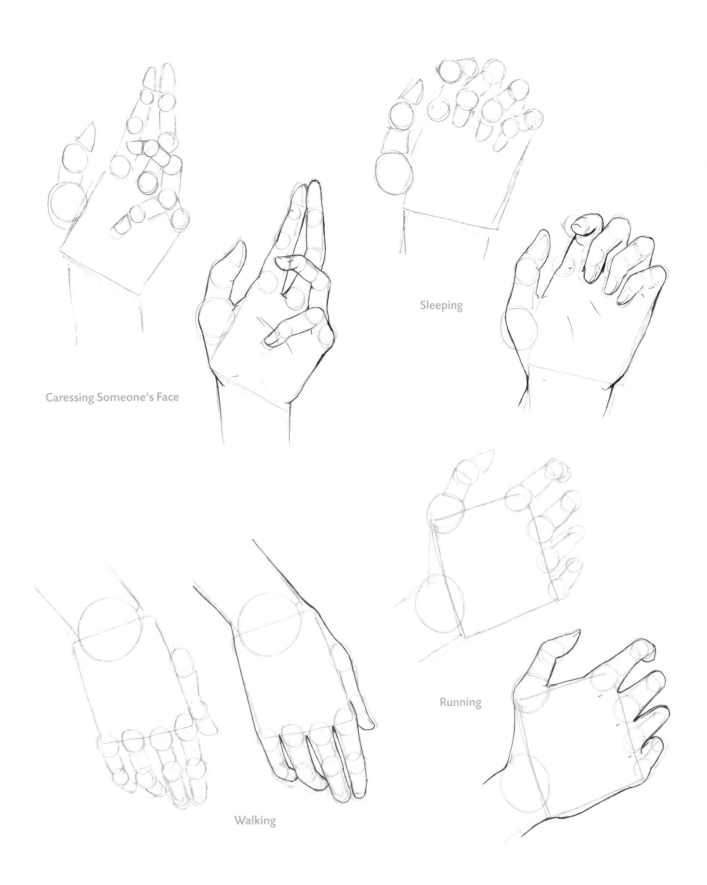

Caressing Someone's Face

Sleeping

Walking

Running

Hands and Age

In manga, there is a *huge* difference between a six-year-old hand and a sixty-year-old hand. Younger hands are rounder and simpler, while older hands are bonier and have more detail.

CHILD'S HAND

For a younger character, don't define the knuckles as much—children's hands are rounder, chubbier, and thicker. They're kind of like Inku's hands! Don't use too many straight lines; keep the hand round-looking. Also, for kid characters, boys' and girls' hands look the same.

OLD LADY'S HAND

Show age in the hands by making them look frail, or even skeletal. This means you have to do the exact opposite from what you do when drawing children's hands. Make your lines thinner, curving them inward slightly. The lines around the palm and the fingers give the appearance of frailty. To make the hands look even older, add some liver spots!

Well, I've got to HAND it to you—you made it through our lessons on hands in one piece! We think you'll find this knowledge HANDY as you start to draw characters! Hahahaha, I'm hilarious!!!!

DRAWING FEET

They are stinky, sweaty, ugly, and a little bit intimidating for new artists, but once you break them down into basic shapes, feet can be a snap to draw. One reason for the misconception that feet are hard to draw may be that we don't see our feet as often as we do our hands—they're often wrapped up in socks or concealed by shoes. So before you read even one more word, take off your shoes and socks—if you're wearing them—and look at your feet. I myself have lovely feet—I just have ugly toes!—but when I was first learning to draw feet, I would often stare at mine as I was drawing. I want you guys to do the same thing, and as you look at your feet, I want you to see whether you can spot the basic shapes into which they can be broken down. These shapes will change depending on the foot's position, the angle from which it's viewed, and whether the character is standing, walking, or running.

THE FLAT FOOT

Let's start with a foot in the standing position, flat on the ground. We'll begin with the left foot as seen from the side.

STEP 1 I always start with an isosceles triangle for the base; then use circles to define where the ankle is going to be, which in this view is at the top of the isosceles triangle. Then I draw an open-ended rectangle at the top of the circle for the calf.

STEP 2 Now I want you to draw the toes. These will be little ovals, which get smaller as you move from left to right. This is just your blue-line sketch, and we will define the toes further in the next step. Once you've drawn the toes, define the curves of the foot, giving it shape. Follow the curvature of the ankle circle with your blue pencil, connecting it to the line of the triangle to form the top of the foot. The lines here should be smooth and rounded. For the heel, follow a similar pattern, curving the corner of the triangle at the heel.

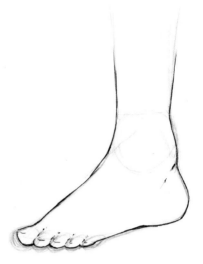

STEP 3 Define the curves and lines a little bit more, outlining the foot and smoothing the lines of the ankle. We are also defining and deepening the lines between the toes, thus giving them more shape and showing the separations more clearly.

STEP 4 Grab that black pen and start defining the toes. Draw in the toenails, and don't forget to add some small marks for the spaces between the toes. Remember, if your toes aren't perfect, don't stress. In real life, no one's are perfect—trust me, I know! Now go over the rest of your blue lines.

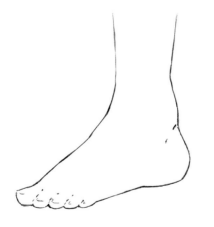

STEP 5 Erase your pencil lines, and off you go!

There is also a little dimple between the ankle and the heel, so don't forget to draw it. Sometimes I have to remind Camilla!

The Stepping Foot

In the stepping foot, the heel becomes more prominent. To draw the foot in the act of stepping, you'll begin with four basic shapes: two rectangles and two circles.

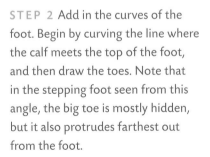

STEP 1 Begin with two upright rectangles set at an angle, as shown in the drawing. The top rectangle, representing the calf, is open at the top. In the upper portion of the lower rectangle, draw a large circle that's about halfway inside and halfway outside the rectangle. This will be the heel. Then draw a smaller circle next to it, inside the rectangle, for the ankle.

STEP 2 Add in the curves of the foot. Begin by curving the line where the calf meets the top of the foot, and then draw the toes. Note that in the stepping foot seen from this angle, the big toe is mostly hidden, but it also protrudes farthest out from the foot.

STEP 3 Add more roundness to the ankle and toes by going over the lines and smoothing them out. Also, in this position, there will be two dimples: one for the ankle and one for the heel. These are the little lines and creases where the arch of the foot meets the heel. Don't forget to add them.

STEP 4 Time for your black line. When drawing the foot in this position, emphasize the curved points at the ankle and calf, which help show movement or action. This can be done simply by making the line a little bit thicker along the curves. Also, I don't draw toenails on feet in this position, but that's just a personal choice. Feel free to add some toenails if you choose.

STEP 5 Erase the blue lines, and get steppin'!

STEPPING FOOT—FRONT VIEW

TOP OF THE FOOT

FOOT POSITIONS

Here are a few examples showing the foot in some other positions.

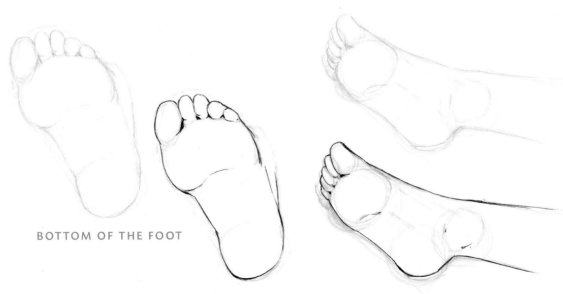

BOTTOM OF THE FOOT

BOTTOM OF A KICKING FOOT

This drawing is a secret portrait of my sister! I have never told her this, so if you're reading this, Ada Pia, I hope you like it!

DRAWING THE FULL BODY

Congratulations on all your hard work on drawing hands and feet. Now it's time to bring all the parts together to create a full body. I liken this section to *Power Rangers*, in which each Zord, or element, comes together to form an even bigger Zord. I myself sometimes have trouble bringing it all together, but that's why we have an eraser—or, in my case, a box of erasers!

In this section, you'll learn some basics for drawing the body. But if you're serious about drawing, you may also want to consider taking a life-drawing class. Seeing the many different shapes the body takes in various positions can be extremely advantageous for an artist. If you can't take a class, I recommend taking some pictures of yourself to work from or getting friends to pose for you. (I find that cupcakes really work as bribes!)

FRONT VIEW—GIRL

We are going to begin with a female form in a very basic front-on pose. As you look at these steps, notice that I'm giving you a very natural pose—as opposed to some drawing books, which show a really rigid form. To make the girl's stance look more natural, I'll draw her spine with a slight curve.

STEP 1 Start by drawing a stick man—or in our case, a stick woman. I always start with the head, which is a simple circle, and then connect it to the spine. The way the spine falls and the shape it takes will define how the character is standing and where she is placing her weight.

From the spine, draw a line connecting the shoulders. Note that in manga, a girl's shoulders are exactly the same width as her hips—but the circles you draw for the hips should be larger than the circles for the shoulders here. Then draw a set of lines to represent the arms and legs, with small circles for the hands, elbows, knees, and feet.

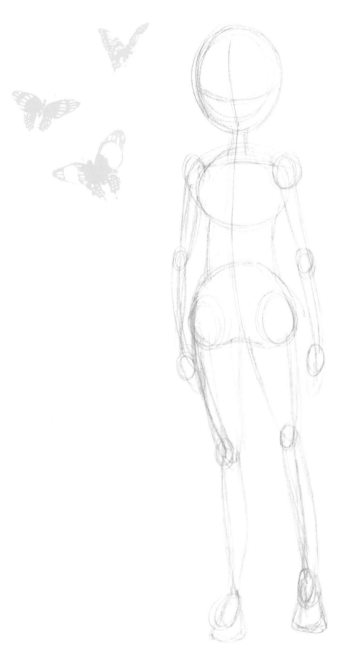

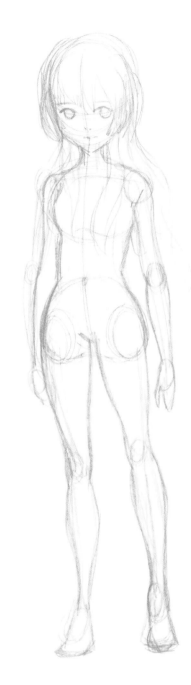

STEP 2 For the chest area, draw an oval connecting the shoulders. Then, following the curvature of the spine and hips, outline the shape of the bottom half of the torso or pelvic area. This should resemble a delicious lima bean. When you outline the thighs and calves, make sure the lines are curvy—give your girl some meat! In this stance, she is putting more weight on the right leg—thus the thicker line on the right leg.

STEP 3 Now sketch in her face and give her some hair. In this step, you should also emphasize her waist and her hips more. Also, make the curves of her thighs wider— slightly thicker in the middle but then curving back in toward the knees. Do the same thing with the calves, thickening them in the middle but then narrowing them at the ankles. Remember, wherever there's a joint, the form curves in toward it.

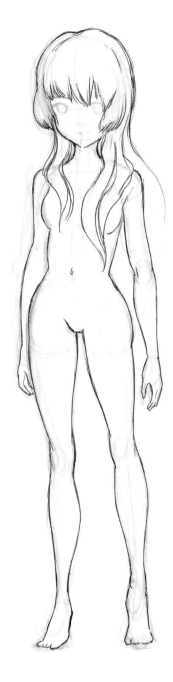

STEP 4 Here, I'm showing you how I begin my black line, rather than just filling everything in at once. I always start at the top of the character, with her hair, and work my way down. For this girl's hair, I decided to go with a seventies Farrah Fawcett–meets–*Macross* look.

STEP 5 Now, using your black pen, start drawing in the arms, torso, thighs, and feet. Again: Be sure to keep your lines curvy when working on female bodies.

STEP 6 Fill in the face and give some extra shading to the eyes.

STEP 7 Erase your blue lines, and you're done! You have created your first full-body female character!

FRONT VIEW—GUY

Drawing guys is always fun—and painless. They are easier to draw than girls because the male body is relatively straight, unlike its curvy female counterpart. Okay, let's get going!

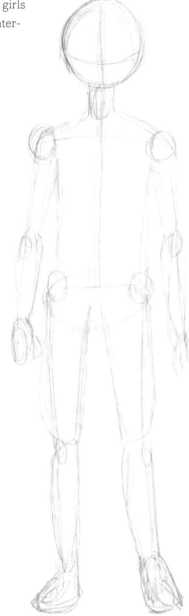

STEP 1 Just like when you drew the girl character, you're going to start with a stick figure, but here you want the shoulders to be wider than the hips. Make sure the hands fall midway down the thighs. The position we are drawing is a natural, casual pose, with our guy putting his weight on his right leg. The right foot should therefore be flatter, and the left foot should appear slightly raised.

STEP 2 Outline the basic body masses, making sure not to add too much muscle definition. When drawing the legs, take note that guys' legs are actually quite thin. The knees should be pointing outward, and the feet should always be pointing in the same direction as the knees—unless a character is doing something strange with his feet.

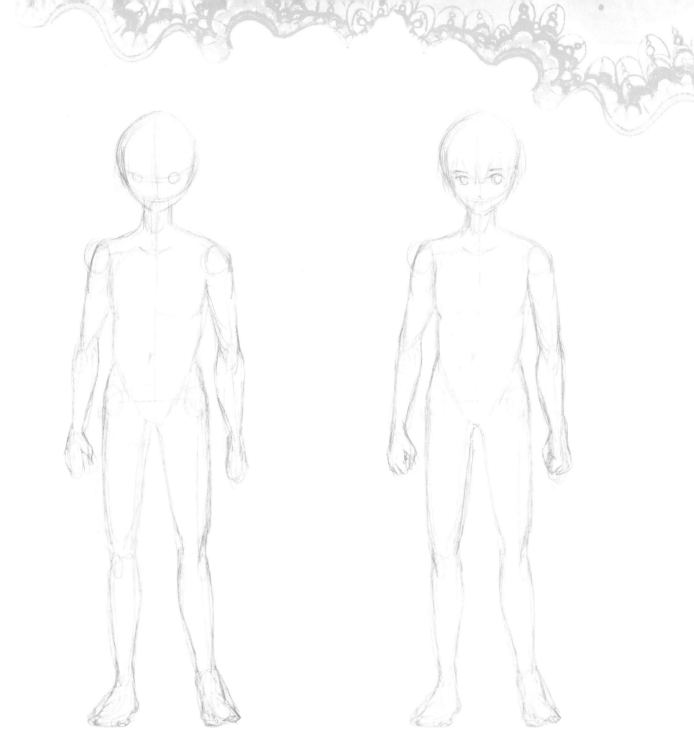

STEP 3 Give the neck and collarbone some definition. For his pecs, just draw two simple lines—remember, in manga, less is always more. Next, give him a belly button, and add in his pelvic line. Give some definition to the hands and feet.

STEP 4 Sketch in the hair and facial features.

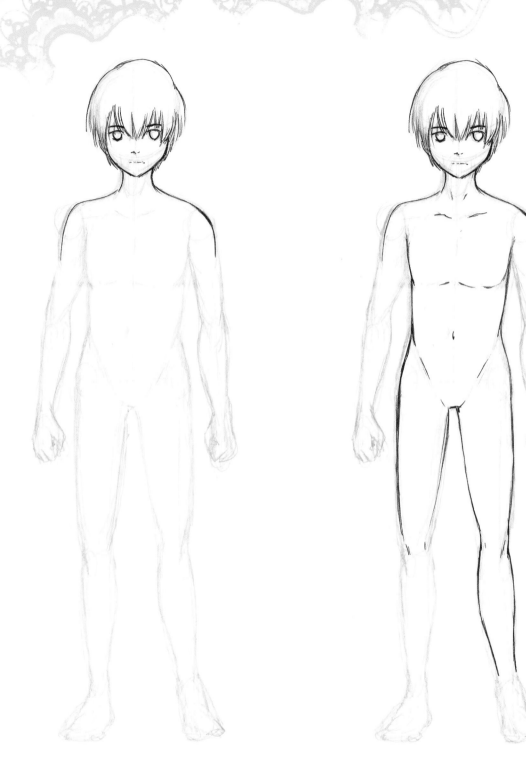

STEP 5 Now you're ready to move to your black line. Starting at the top, define the face; then work your way down, defining the shoulders. Guys have broad shoulders, so make sure your lines move outward before curving down.

STEP 6 Define the rest of the body with your black pen.

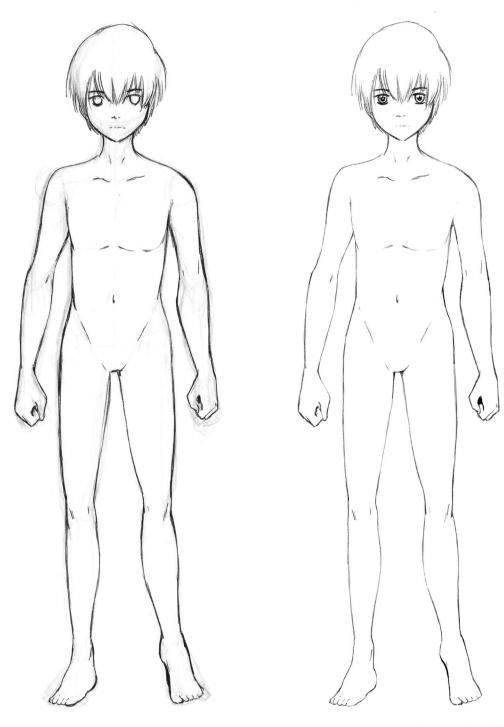

STEP 7 Now, lose those blue lines. If only finding a good boyfriend was this easy!

THREE-QUARTER FRONT VIEW—GIRL

In manga, the three-quarter view is used in dialogue scenes. The character
in this position is the one speaking, and gives the conversation a natural look.
The three-quarter view is also used to show depth within an environment.
Here, we'll draw a girl in the three-quarter front view, and then I'll give you a
few tips on adapting the basic rules when drawing guys in the same position.

STEP 1 As always, start with the head, followed by a
horizontal line for the shoulders. Draw a curved line for
the spine, an oval for the hips, and a smaller oval for the
chest. Go ahead and outline the legs and arms, again
taking note that the hands fall midway down the thighs.

STEP 2 Fill in the face, belly button, and hair. Also, add
some definition to the breasts by drawing small marks at
the top and bottom of each breast, partly outlining their
circular forms.

STEP 3 With your black pen, begin drawing the hair; then work your way down the body, making sure to curve inward at the waist and outward at the buttocks.

STEP 4 Still using your black pen, fill in the eyes and add little marks at the joints in the arms and knees. I also like to add three tiny lines to define a girl's collarbones.

STEP 5 Erase those blue lines, and—*whammo!*—you're
finished.

Be-
fore we begin drawing our three-quarter guy, here are
some tips: Our character will have a bent knee and his
arms should be positioned at his sides, relaxed. Finally,
his feet should be pointed out . . . kind of like a duck's.

THREE-QUARTER BACK VIEW—GUY

The three-quarter back view, like the three-quarter front view, is often used during heavy dialogue scenes. The character drawn from this angle is often the listener. This view also can be used in a wide shot where a character is looking at an important object or location in the background.

STEP 1 This stance looks and feels stiffer than other poses. Thus the line work is going to be mostly straight, with very slight curves at the spine and legs. The ankles should be positioned behind the shoulders. Finally, the lines for the legs are broken with circles at the knees.

STEP 2 Add some definition to the body, taking care to partly hide the left foot, the left arm, and the left hand, which aren't fully visible in this stance. Also, because of the perspective, the right hand should be drawn a fraction larger than the left.

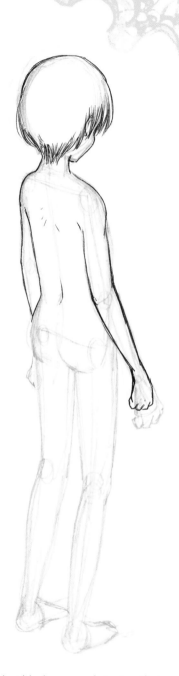

STEP 3 In this step, add some small curves at the shoulders, pointing them downward. Then you're ready for your black line.

STEP 4 Grab that black pen, and start outlining and filling in from the top of the head down. You can see that at this stage of the drawing, I realized that the right hand shouldn't be positioned at the midway point of the thigh. Because the arm is bent, the hand should be drawn slightly above that position—so I changed it. We all make mistakes, so don't worry about messing up with your blue line. You can always fix it with the black line.

STEP 5 Continue with your black lines.

STEP 6 Erase those blue lines, and you're all set!

THREE-QUARTER BACK VIEW—GIRL

Just like the male three-quarter back view, the female three-quarter back view is often used in dialogue-heavy scenes or to give depth and perspective to your panel—not to mention giving the reader a better view of the character's booty!

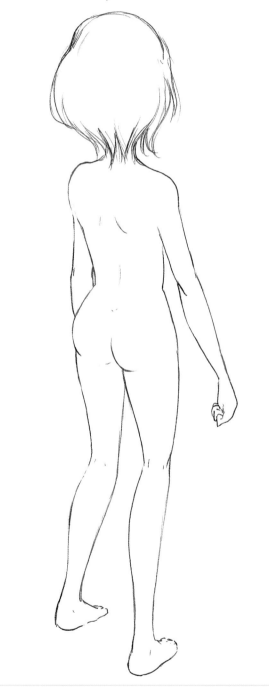

When you are drawing arms and legs, getting the proportions correct can be difficult. But I picked up a little trick watching Camilla: The hands fall about midway down the thighs. And remember, of course, that legs are longer than arms! Except in the case of amazingly awesome bodies . . . like mine!

CASUAL BACK POSE—GIRL

I also want to show you an approach to drawing a character from the back that's different from the standard, rigid, statuelike pose. Once again, this is not going to be your standard anatomy pose, because, honestly, people never stand like statues—I know I don't. For this drawing, our girl is just about to step into the shower.

STEP 1 Start by drawing the head, and give the spine a slight upward curve for the natural look we are going for here. Then give her a nice booty. It should be roughly the same width as her shoulders, creating an hourglass figure. Then add two narrow ovals for the thighs, two ovals for the calves, and two rectangular shapes for the ankles. Take note that in this drawing one of the girl's feet is slightly raised.

STEP 2 Define her hair and shoulders. Add in the details of the elbows and hands, and start giving the booty some shape. You want to take that big circle and crack it in half to get the right shape, bearing in mind that the lines for the cheeks should go halfway across the thighs. Finish this step by giving the ankles a little more definition.

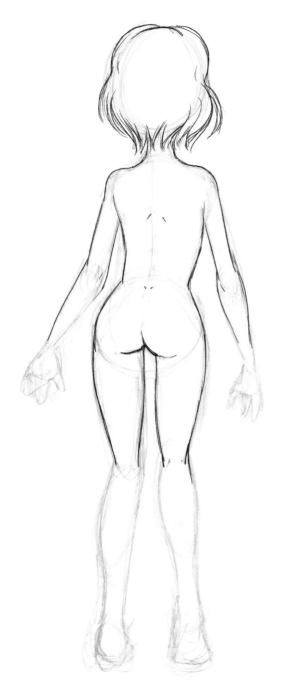

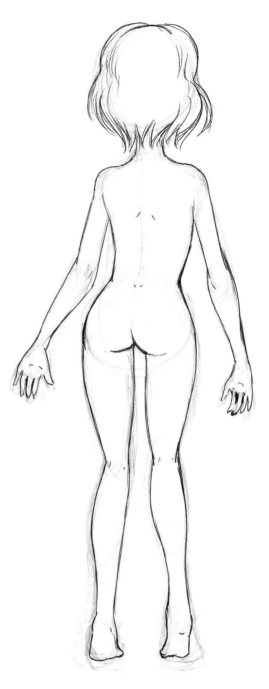

STEP 3 Begin your black line with her hair. Where the shoulders approach the neck, indent your lines slightly. Add two very small lines for the shoulder blades, on either side of the spine. Next, draw two dimples near the tailbone and the elbows. Give the legs a slight curve in toward the knee joint and out toward the ankle. Apply this same curve to the arms.

STEP 4 Define the fingers, add dimples behind each knee, and finally, make a slight mark at her right heel to show that the foot is raised.

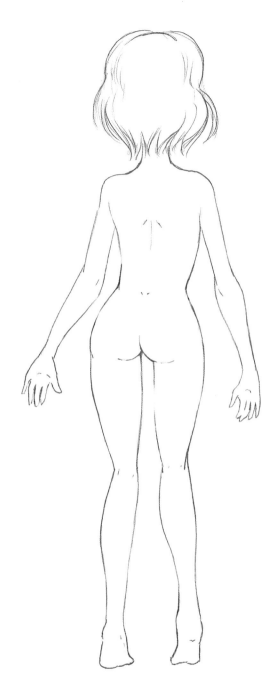

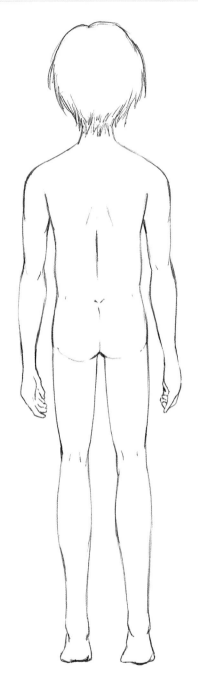

STEP 5 Lose those pencil lines. Easy peasy lemon squeezy!

CASUAL BACK POSE—GUY When drawing a guy from the back in a similar casual pose, make sure that his butt is a lot smaller than it would be for a girl. Guys do not have big booties in manga! For the legs, keep in mind that the thighs should be the same thickness as the calves.

AGING A CHARACTER

Often in manga, especially in a long series or epic, a character will age from a boy or girl into a man or woman. Even in a shorter series, you may need to use flashbacks to show what your character looked like as a child, or flash-forwards to show the character as an elderly man or woman.

Aging Males

To age a male character, we'll make an age chart—start with the toddler. He should be round and candy-apple–like with a large head, big hands, and huge feet. Moving to the right, we come to the kindergartner. We are going to elongate that initial shape, thus his head will appear slightly large for his body. Finally, keep the legs bow shaped, which will make him appear mischievous but adorable.

For the young teenager, keep elongating your initial design, accounting for a big growth spurt. A teenage boy stands with his legs farther apart, conveying the sense of self-awareness and awkwardness that comes with being a teenager. Moving on to the young adult, your drawing should reflect the last growth spurt in your character's life. Here, his age and maturity can be seen in his shoulders, which should be drawn broader. His

Manga characters are often distinguished by their hairstyles, so a character's hair should remain similar as he ages, with small variations at each stage in his life cycle, until he gets to that certain age—when you lose all your hair, grow a huge beard, and shrink like a raisin!!!

legs should be drawn closer together, with his hips tilted slightly forward, conveying casual confidence. Finally, when the character reaches his senior years, his body shrinks tremendously; he is shorter than his teenage self, with his legs just a mere fraction apart. The character becomes hunched, and his shoulders, neck, and eyes disappear.

In the black-line drawing, I've added clothing: The school uniform the character wears as a kid morphs into a suit as he reaches young-adult age. As an elderly gentleman, he wears a sashed cardigan. Have fun drawing your character's clothing, and try to establish a few elements that repeat through the years.

Aging Females

Aging a female is quite similar to aging a male. The major variations arise in the teen years, when the girl's body becomes curvier. As a teen, the manga female often stands with bent knees in a pigeon-toed position. (This pose does not reappear in her adult years.) When she reaches young adulthood, her breasts and thighs become more prominent, so the lines become even curvier. Also, the cute, flirty poses are gone, and now she is a confident, sexy young woman. Finally, as an elderly woman, the female shrinks even more than her male counterpart. She should be only a little bit taller than a female kindergartner. As with the elderly male character, she should be drawn without a neck or shoulders.

Like the male character, she wears a school uniform in her childhood and teenage years. Especially with females, the clothing should reflect the character's personality and age. Have some fun drawing all the cool details. Notice that I gave the toddler some tiny frills on her socks and the young adult some high, sexy boots. Like they say, "The clothes make the man"—or, in this case, the woman! Finally, make sure the hairstyle remains somewhat consistent over the years. The clothes should remain similar, too, but should become more sophisticated as the character ages.

VOGUE AND STRIKE A POSE

DRAWING ACTION AND MOVEMENT

Manga characters seldom just stand around—unless they've been paralyzed by some poisonous rhinoceros venom! Usually, their bodies are in action. Movement brings your drawings to life, transforming them from one-dimensional illustrations or portraits into living, breathing depictions of your characters. In this chapter, we look at a few different kinds of action, but remember, let your character tell *you* how he or she will move. Trust me—no two characters ever move in the same way.

DRAWING CLOTHING

You'll notice that all of the characters in this chapter have outfits. Drawing clothing is one of those fun things that we get to do when we are drawing characters. So before we jump into drawing action and movement, I want to take a second to give you a few fashion tips.

The trick when drawing clothing is that you really have to know your fabric. Depending on the type you use—the way it folds, bunches, and moves—it will look very different. For example, silk is very smooth but creases and folds easily at every bend. Jeans, on the other hand, are much more stiff, wrinkling only at the knees and crotch. The most important thing to remember is that this is manga, so have fun with your clothing, and think outside the box. Okay, designers, let's get to work!

PANTS

Take note that the fabric bunches at the crotch, at the knees, and at the hem.

GLOVES

Drawing a glove is like drawing a hand, except that the shape is much more squared and the fingers will be bigger and blockier. Finally, the fabric in gloves will bunch at the wrist and the knuckles.

JACKET

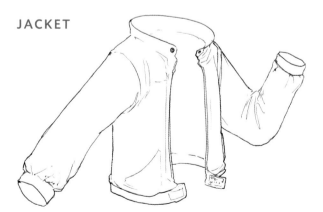

This is like a guy's letterman jacket. Once again, notice where the fabric will fold—the elbow, the armpit, and also the wristband. Here I'm using leather for the sleeves and wool for the body; the wool will have more texture. Finally, don't forget to draw the collar nice and stiff.

JAPANESE SCHOOL UNIFORM SKIRT

When drawing skirts, start with the waistband at the top, and then tackle the pleats one by one. Sometimes with difficult clothing, I like to use reference material. In the case of this Japanese skirt, I used a cupcake wrapper.

CAPE

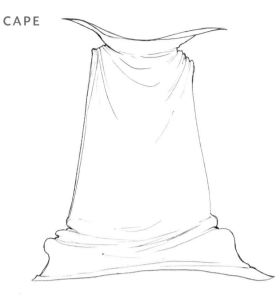

Capes are usually made of satin, which will bunch at the shoulders, creating folds that extend to the bottom. The bottom of the cape will roll and bunch on the ground.

DRESS

This dress is made of a soft material, so it bunches at the front, near the princess-cut neckline and at the waist, where the belt is cinched.

CLASSIC BOW

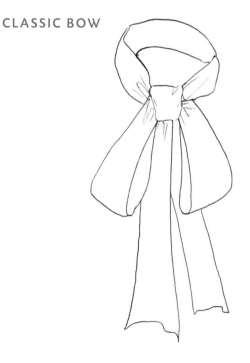

I love using bows instead of ties for schoolgirls. This is a satin ribbon. Notice the wrinkles where it is tied together and the lack of wrinkles where it hangs.

GIRL WALKING

Showing a character walking is very common in manga. I must draw hundreds of people walking every month. As frequently as walking action is depicted, it's actually a bit complicated to make the character appear to be walking naturally. A girl's walk is quite different from a guy's: The female walk is more dainty and streamlined, while the male's is more of a strut or swagger (as we'll see on page 99).

STEP 1 To make your characters walk naturally, pay attention to the arms. When she steps forward with the right leg, the right arm swings back. If she steps with the left leg, the left arm moves back. One leg is in front of the other and for girls the space between them is minimal. One leg bends as it brings the foot up to take a step. The free arm angles away from the body.

STEP 2 Begin outlining the female form, making sure you give your lines a lot of curve, creating that feminine figure and suggesting a sense of motion. At the calves, emphasize the feeling of movement by making your lines straighter on the inside of the legs and more curved on the outside. In addition, the left shoulder should appear more defined and farther forward than the right shoulder, because the right leg is moving forward.

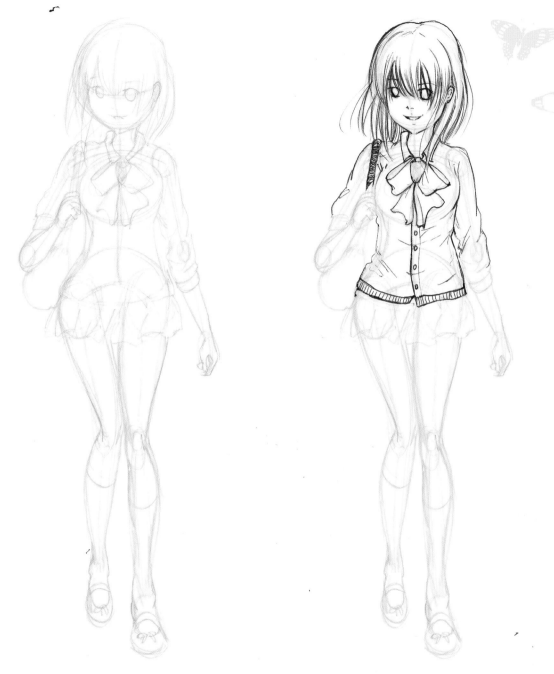

STEP 3 Now we can add the clothing and facial details. When I am activating a character, I always want to show some wind, so I've drawn the skirt being ruffled by the wind along with some movement in the hair. Make sure the hand is in a casual, half-open position and not a fist.

STEP 4 When you move to your black line, make sure that the hair and skirt are moving/blowing in the same direction. You can also add some wrinkles in the blouse at the elbows to heighten the feeling of action.

STEP 5 As you go over the legs with your black pen, you're going to obscure part of her right leg. We finish our lovely lady by filling in tiny details on the clothing and the body. Make sure the hand holding the purse strap is relaxed and that one finger is a little more loose, not wrapped around the strap, as this adds to the natural look we are going for.

STEP 6 Presto—a walking girl!

GUY WALKING

Guys walk with more of a strut; they appear very nonchalant and laid-back, especially if they are cool, which our guy is.

STEP 1 To animate our character, we are going to turn his head—he's either talking to one of his friends or, even better, scoping out a hot girl. We are also going to draw him with one hand inside his pocket to give him an even more casual, Ian Somerhalder look. Notice that the arm that's farther forward appears slightly longer; the other arm swings farther back. Also notice that his knees are farther apart than the girl's and pointed in the same direction as his feet.

STEP 2 Outline the shape, making sure to keep the legs angular. The leg in front should appear larger than the one behind. Furthermore, you want to show that, in this position, the character's weight is on the forward foot. To do this, the foot that has the weight should be drawn slightly thicker and flatter. Next, outline the arms, making sure that the hidden hand is in the position where the pocket will be.

STEP 3 Begin filling in the hair, but don't give it too much movement, as that would create a more feminine look. In this drawing, you can indicate movement by drawing wrinkles on the jacket and pants. In designing his clothes, I decided to make them look futuristic, but you could give him any style you want. A manga artist is also a fashion designer, so have some fun with it.

STEP 4 Continue defining the facial features, and decide how much detail you want to work into the clothing. As you can see, I didn't want to go overboard. When beginning with the black pen, I usually work from the top down, but here I'm kind of loving his clothing, so I'm going to jump to his hair and coat before finishing the face. Be sure to add some wrinkles to the elbows and the coat.

STEP 5 Continue defining our guy. Note that I decided to make his shirt solid black and gave him a checkered belt. Why not?

STEP 6 Erase those blue lines, and watch your guy spring to life!

While I was painting this piece,
Resurrected Bone Collective,
I was listening to J-pop. It's funny, but
sometimes when I work with
oils, I like to shut off one
part of my brain and listen to
music and let the brush do all
the work. What do you think? It's crazy
what the subconscious can come up with!

GUY SITTING

Manga artists love putting their characters in the classroom. I'm not sure if it's the sexy uniforms, the teenage emotional dramas, or a subliminal message strategically placed by necktie companies! But whatever the reason, every manga artist must learn how to draw characters sitting at desks. Of course, this pose could be transferred to any number of environments in which characters are shown sitting, but because I love a cute guy in a school uniform, I thought we would learn this pose as it occurs in the classroom.

A girl usually sits with her legs crossed, but a guy usually sits with his legs open—unless he is wearing a kilt! The look is relaxed and slouched, which gives the character a cool, nonchalant vibe.

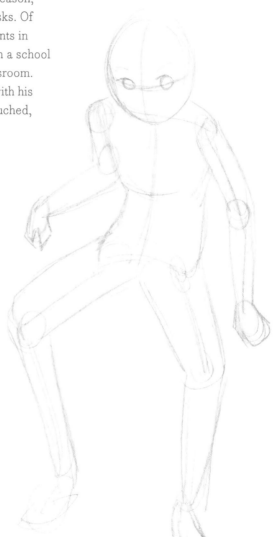

STEP 1 Start by drawing a circle for the head. Because the viewpoint is slightly above the character, the neck is not visible. Bend the spine so that it curves slightly toward the hips. This character's arms are bent, because he has one arm on the desk and the other on the chair. Spread the legs so that the knees face away from each other; remember, the feet point in the same direction as the knees.

STEP 2 As in our other action poses, we draw the anatomy before we draw the clothing. Draw the crosshairs on the head, and position the eyes on the face. Draw the arms and the torso, letting it obscure the left elbow slightly. Next, add a little detail to the hips and the abdomen, which will be curved inward because of the way he is slouching. And finally, sketch in the hands and feet.

STEP 3 Now we are ready to give our guy a long-sleeved shirt, worn untucked, and slacks. Make sure the shirttails fan out at the bottom. (Sometimes I look at myself in the mirror to see how a shirt falls.) It's also important to note that the creases in clothing occur at points where the body bends, so be sure to add creases at the elbows and knees. Remember that when drawing a male character you should keep the line work sharp and angular.

STEP 4 Define the guy's expression, his hands, and his feet. Move on to his clothing, adding a necktie as well as some detail to the fabric. Start by adding a pocket, and then go over your drawing, adding little details, such as some lines indicating where the fabric is bunching, as at the crotch.

STEP 5 Pick up your black pen and start defining from the top down. As you can see, I realized here that the left shoulder was poking out too far, so I brought it in and straightened the tie for a cleaner look. Always remember that your blue line is just your base; it can easily be changed and erased.

STEP 6 Finish off your guy, using your black pen.

STEP 7 And there you have him— a cute, school-uniform-clad, sitting schoolboy.

GIRL KNEELING

Whether your girl is kneeling in a meadow, on her bed gossiping with her girlfriends, or eating Pop-Tarts with her boyfriend, this pose will—I promise you—appear more than once in every manga you draw. At first glance, the pose may appear easy, but because some body parts are hidden in the kneeling position, it can be a little tricky.

STEP 1 Begin, as usual, with a stick figure. Her legs are bent at the knee, and because we're looking at her from the side, her legs appear to be stacked one on top of the other. As you draw her upper torso, curve the spine. Also, because this character is female, all the lines, even for the stick woman, should be curvy—never completely straight. Do not draw the right hand or foot in this pose, because they will be hidden behind the rest of the body. Draw circles where the joints are.

STEP 2 Start outlining the body, but don't add any lines for clothing yet. You need to understand how the body is positioned before putting clothing on it. Define her chest, torso, hands, back, and face. Finally, further define the thighs by adding the single line that divides the thigh from the calf.

STEP 3 Now add details such as hair, fingers, facial expression, and, finally, clothing. When drawing fabric, you should usually keep your lines wavy and curved, except for coats and suits that are tailored and fitted. With this particular dress, however, the fabric is so soft that it dips between the legs and follows the curve of the thigh.

STEP 4 Continue adding detail to her eyes, hair, feet (by adding the toes), and clothing. Have some fun by adding filigree to the clothing.

STEP 5 Grab that black pen. Here, I realized that her left hand wasn't positioned quite where I wanted it to be, so I adjusted it with my black line.

STEP 6 Erase the blue pencil and let your kneeling girl shine!

GIRL WITH ARMS CROSSED

This is, without a doubt, the most difficult of all the poses in this chapter. It is, however, quite versatile and can be used to express a variety of emotions. Your character could be waiting for her boyfriend, thinking about taking over the world, or just getting really angry at her robot butler for not ironing her jumpsuit. Here, we're drawing a sexy detective who is upset about a case. First, cross your arms and look in the mirror to get an idea of how the body looks in this pose. Don't be embarrassed—I do it all the time!

STEP 1 When you cross your arms, your body will always tilt up on one side, depending on which forearm is on top. If your character has her right forearm over her left, the right shoulder will rise up and the left shoulder will drop down. The hips are affected in the same way: In this example, the right hip is positioned higher than the left. Note that the hand of the arm on top will tuck into the crook of the arm that's on the bottom.

STEP 2 Outline the form, making sure to keep your lines curvy. You want the detective to be voluptuous and sexy. Notice that her right shoulder is partly hidden by the chin. Note, too, that the right hand should be above the left arm, and the fingers of the left arm should be grasping her right bicep.

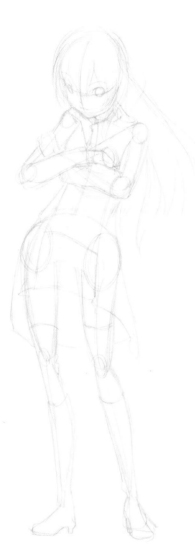 

STEP 3 Draw the clothing, and begin sketching in the hair. I decided to give her long hair and a futuristic outfit—a trench coat and boots with a little heel. Be sure to add creases to the clothes at the joints, as well as at points of movement.

STEP 4 Now comes the detail. Feel free to add as much or as little detail as you want to the clothing. At this stage, you can also choose to style the clothing in a way different from what I have done. Finish this stage by drawing the details of her fingers and facial expression before moving on to the black line.

STEP 5 Black line time! Make sure you add in those little wrinkles and stress marks on the clothing.

STEP 6 Go over the rest of your lines, and fill in her hair, shorts, knee-highs, and cuffs.

STEP 7 Now make those blue lines vanish without a trace!

I love to paint in the morning, so I make sure I'm up around 8:00 to cook myself breakfast and watch one episode of an '80s cartoon. Then, exactly at 9:00, I start painting!

GUY RUNNING

Before I draw a character running, I always like to decide why he is running. Is he late for the bus? Chasing down a villain? Or does he really just have to go to the bathroom? This decision will influence the character's expression and body position. The more intensely and forcefully the character is running, the farther forward the shoulders will be. If the character is jogging casually, the shoulders will be positioned farther back. Let's imagine that the character in our drawing is chasing a ninja purse-snatcher. He's going to be determined in his pursuit, so his shoulders will be pretty far forward. As when a character is walking, the leg that's stepping forward is matched, on the other side of the body, by an arm swinging forward.

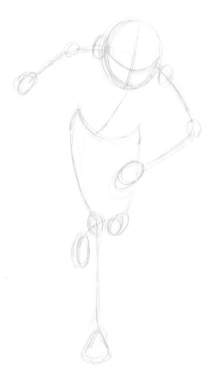

STEP 1 When drawing running characters, I always begin with the head. I draw the crosshairs, which show which way the character is looking and thus in which direction he is running. As you can see, I have not drawn his hips—that's because the torso is positioned in front of them. It's also important to note that the shoulder that swings backward is going to be partly obscured by the head. The head will also block the view of the neck in this view of a runner seen from the front.

STEP 2 Following the curve of the spine, outline the rest of the torso. Outline the front leg using the previously drawn line for reference. Then outline the arms, making sure that the arm in front of the body is larger than the one swinging behind.

STEP 3 Begin sketching in the hair. As you do so, choose from which direction the wind is coming. The wind's direction will be reflected in other elements of the drawing—in this case, the character's clothing will be flattened against the left side of his body and will flare out, blown by the wind on his right side.

STEP 4 Now we move into further detail by giving our character a tie, adding the cuffs on his jacket, and drawing his shoes.

STEP 5 Black line time! I'm giving his tie a checked pattern, adding ribbing to the sleeves peeking out from his jacket, and adding wrinkles at his right ankle.

STEP 6 Finish going over all of your lines with the black pen.

STEP 7 Erase your blue lines, and there you go! Your very own running man.

GIRL STANDING PIGEON-TOED

The pigeon-toed stance is the defining pose for manga females. Every time you see a girl fixing her tie, touching her hair, or looking left, she's standing pigeon-toed. It's everywhere! Honestly, I could not claim that this book teaches you how to draw manga without giving instructions on drawing this position.

STEP 1 Start with your basic stick figure, but be sure to point both knees inward. This is critical to obtaining the look we're going for. Pivot both feet out at the heels, with one resting on the ball of the foot.

STEP 2 Outline the structure of the body, giving mass to the torso, hips, and thighs. Then define the girl's facial features, which will help define her personality—in this case, a little shy but flirty.

STEP 3 Let's outfit our character in a schoolgirl's uniform with a frilly skirt, knee-high socks, and Mary Jane shoes. Remember, clothing must follow the contour of the body. A little trick with skirts is to start close in at the top of the hips and then flare the line out at the sides, with a ruffled edge at the bottom caused by the skirt's pleats.

STEP 4 Move on to your black line, starting at the top and working your way down.

STEP 5 Keep going with your black line, going over all your lines and filling in any areas that you want to be patterned or solid black.

STEP 6 And there you have her—the classic pigeon-toed manga girl.

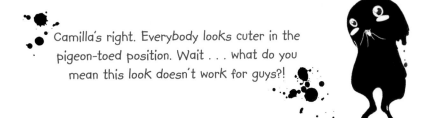

Camilla's right. Everybody looks cuter in the pigeon-toed position. Wait . . . what do you mean this look doesn't work for guys?!

TURN UP THE CUTENESS!

DRAWING MASCOTS AND CHIBIS

It's time to squeal!!! Before you turn the page, you need to prepare yourself for the urge to squirm and shake with utter excitement! If you suffer from a weak bladder brought on by laughter or sudden bursts of uncontrollable smiles, you may want to skip this chapter.

I myself could draw mascots and chibis all day, every day, for the rest of my life . . . and never get bored. They are just *that* fun to draw. And here's some more good news: They're simple to master. Okay, if you're ready, take a deep breath and turn the page. It's about to get crazy-cute up in here!

DRAWING MASCOTS

Mascots are the Jiminy Crickets of the manga world. They serve as guides for our heroes and little devils for our villains. Sometimes heroes and villains can change form themselves, becoming small mascot characters. For example, in my manga *Tanpopo*, the villainous Kuro character transforms himself into the mascot Poodle in order to spy on Tanpopo. In one of my favorite Japanese manga, Tite Kubo's *Bleach*, the soul of one character is transferred to a stuffed lion, and he is forced to continue the rest of his life as a stuffed animal. It's fantastic! Honestly, who wouldn't want one of her stuffed animals to come alive and hang out with her every day?

Mascots are among the simplest manga characters to draw because their construction is based on very simple shapes. So remember this mantra for drawing mascots: The simpler, the cuter! Okay, let's create some superadorable sidekicks.

POODLE KURO

Let's start by learning how to draw one of my favorite personal mascot creations—Poodle Kuro. The mask-wearing mascot version of Kuro from *Tanpopo*, Poodle Kuro is supercute and superevil. He's the devil in disguise—kind of like my real-life dog, Loki! If you're wondering where I got the name Kuro, it actually means "black" in Japanese, which also explains the color of this cute little demon.

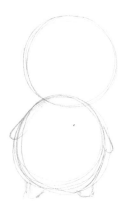

STEP 1 Begin by drawing two circles, one for Poodle Kuro's body and one for his head. Then add in two small feet at the bottom of the lower circle. Mascots are never anatomically correct. Because they are made out of a mystery material, you can place their hands, arms, and legs in any crazy position you want.

STEP 2 Add Poodle Kuro's ears, making a big half-circle on either side of his head. They should extend wider than his body. Finally, add his eyes and mouth. Poodle Kuro's expression is often blank because he is wearing a mask; however, there is a hint of a smile here.

STEP 3 Finally, draw his rectangular mask, which falls inside the first circle you drew, and add the string that holds on his mask. Then modify his body, reshaping the big circle into more of a teardrop shape.

STEP 4 Using your black pen, outline his shape. When going over the mask, add lines at the bottom of the mask and at the tops of the eye and mouth holes. That little bit of perspective shows that his head is tilted upward. Fill in the rest of the eyes and mouth with black.

STEP 5 Erase your blue lines and fill in the figure with black. Note that I've left narrow white areas between his arms and his body, to show where they begin and end.

Here's a colorized version of Poodle Kuro so you can see what this mascot character looks like in his final form.

THE IMP OF DARKNESS

The Imp of Darkness is a literary figure who appears in Pu Songling's supernatural story collection *Strange Stories from a Chinese Studio*. A couple of hundred years later, I decided to include him in volume 3 of my manga *Tanpopo*. Like Batman, the Imp is a creature of the night, but supremely evil and nasty. In Pu Songling's story "The Magic Sword," he is described as having "glaring eyes and a bloody mouth." But, of course, I turned up the cuteness in my version. I love the juxtaposition of creepy and cute that you find in evil manga mascots. For me, the Imp is the perfect hybrid.

STEP 1 Start by drawing two circles, which represent his head and his body; then add two small circles for his feet. Be aware that his body will sort of slide into the background when we draw his two large arms in the next step.

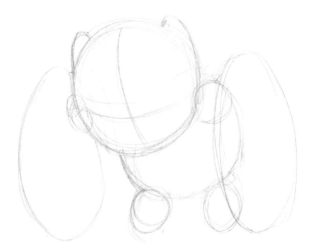

STEP 2 Draw your trusty crosshairs. Then draw two large ovals, one on either side of his body, to represent his gigantic forearms. Also add some tiny horns on top of his head and some little circles for his shoulders.

STEP 3 For the Imp's claws, make a few indents at the bottom of each of his arms. Note that the claws on his right arm are flattened, because he is putting his weight on that arm. Add his eyes and his mouth, which is going to be huge and elongated, since he is a villain. I guess he kind of resembles the *South Park* version of a Canadian at this stage. (Love that show!)

STEP 4 Now we are going to further define his facial features, as well as his shoulders, horns, and claws. Add some jagged teeth to his mouth before going to your black line.

STEP 5 Using your black pen, give him some crazy-looking eyes by drawing spirals, and add some droplets of spit coming from his mouth. Little details like these add movement to a character and make him come alive.

STEP 6 And voilà! I don't know if I want to hug our Imp or run away!

I thought you might like to see a colorized version of the Imp. Making his eyes and mouth blood red really intensifies the feeling of impish evil!

I love Hello Kitty! Love, love, love!
I went to Japan by myself and I
went crazy in the Hello Kitty store!
Honestly, if they sold Hello
Kitty toilet paper I would buy
it. So you can imagine how amazed
and touched I was when Sanrio bought
this painting from me!

INKU

It's about time you got here. I was getting *bored* waiting for you! I hope you have practiced and perfected all the drawing techniques Camilla has taught you, because you are about to embark on the awesome task of capturing the beauty, the grandeur, and the stinkaliciousness that is me, Inku! Now, *before* we get started, I want to give you some words of encouragement—just like Camilla does. If you mess this up, I WILL JUMP OFF THIS PAGE AND INK YOU UP! I will haunt your pets! I will steal all your left socks and possibly your favorite pens. JUST KIDDING! Now that we've gotten that out of the way, LET'S DO THIS.

STEP 1 Start with an oval. Try to make it as *hot* as possible.

STEP 2 By following the contour of the oval, you are going to define the top of my beautiful, knowledge-filled noggin, which resembles a drop of ink. Then outline my little round bum and, finally, my two dandy but distinguished feet.

STEP 3 Here we are going to define my shape a little more. Starting from the back of my perfect head, make your line curve in to further define my booty. My right paw is poking out. Note that in this drawing you're seeing me from behind—but I can turn my head nearly all the way around! So don't forget to draw in my little eyes so that I can watch what you are doing!

STEP 4 Next, draw my two most distinctive features: my marvelous mouth and my two tiny, pointed front teeth. Hey! My butt is not THAT big! What are you doing?! Erase this right now! That's right—I'm mad! You can tell by my swooshed eyebrows.

STEP 5 Okay, fine. I guess that's just your interpretation of me and my bum. But just so you can finish learning to draw me really supermad, pick up your black pen, go over your lines, and draw a little diamond shape above my right eye. And because I spout ink when I'm steamed, add some little ink spots in back of me and in front of my face and paws. Now add some little puddles of ink at my feet.

STEP 6 Finally, fill in everything in black except for my mouth and eyes. And there you have it!

Here I am in color!
I'm beautiful, I know.

DRAWING CHIBIS

Chibis are a cuteness nuclear explosion! Their only purpose is to make you laugh, squeal, and hug the paper they are drawn on. *I love them!* The word *chibi* comes from the Japanese word meaning "small." The first chibi I ever saw was Sailor Moon's daughter, Rini (Chibiusa in Japan); she was like an ambassador for the nation of chibis—the first chibi to premiere in the West. My sisters and I went crazy when we first saw her.

There are hundreds of ways to draw chibis: Some have huge bodies and tiny heads, some have tiny bodies and huge heads. Most chibis have massive eyes that almost cover their entire faces. My chibis are kind of pear-shaped, with huge heads, medium-size bodies, and almost no legs or feet. I describe them as extremely squishy! The kind of characters you just want to pick up and squeeze until their heads explode. As always, after you learn the basic rules you can break them by drawing your own chibis any way you like.

DRAWING TANPOPO AS A CHIBI

In this next step-by-step we are going to take my character Tanpopo and turn her into a chibi. Before we begin, though, I want you guys to take a deep breath and prepare yourself for the extreme bonanza of adorableness you are about to encounter!

Tanpopo

Chibi
Tanpopo

STEP 1 Start by drawing a large round circle and then a smaller teardrop shape under that circle. Add your crosshairs, which, again, will show in which direction the chibi is looking. Then, add two tiny swooshes, one at each side of the teardrop, which will become her arms. Finally, draw a little swoosh at the bottom, which indicates the end of her torso.

STEP 2 For her eyes, draw two circles on the horizontal crosshair. Begin defining her legs by drawing two little triangles at the bottom of the teardrop shape. For this chibi, each little triangle represents the whole leg—thigh to ankle! Define the arms by making the swooshes from the previous step into little isosceles triangles.

STEP 3 Here we add the feet and narrow the teardrop shape to make the chibi's body a little less round. We then add the ears and define the bone structure of the face. My chibis don't have chins, so just follow the contour of the circle for a very rounded face.

STEP 4 Chibis are all about extremes, including their hair, so the Tanpopo chibi has extremely long hair—long enough to touch the ground. Remember to avoid angles when drawing hair. Her mouth is drawn quite small—just a very tiny circle.

STEP 5 Start to define the clothing. In this case, she is wearing a tube top and shorts. Follow this by drawing in the wings.

STEP 6 What's Tanpopo without Chibi Kuro? He has this nasty habit of resting on her head. His shape should be very circular, in keeping with the chibi style. Draw in his eyes, mouth, and legs.

Define Tanpopo's eyes by drawing in her eyebrows and thickening the lines around her eyes.

STEP 7 Okay, take your black pen, and starting with the hair, begin tracing over your blue line.

STEP 8 Now use your pen to go over the chibi's facial structure, including the jawline and eyebrows. Add some detail to her torso, legs, and arms, as well as to her dress and pants. I added cute little stars to her top and gave her little blush marks on her cheeks. Lastly, I outlined Kuro's mask. Fill in the rest of the body with your black line, and don't forget her wings.

STEP 9 Erase your blue lines, and you're done! Nothing to it!

Here's what the Tanpopo chibi looks like in three-quarter and profile views. To make drawings like these, all you have to do is adapt the lessons you learned when drawing full-size characters in these views to the smaller—and more exaggerated—chibi form.

CHIBI EXPRESSIONS

One thing I love about chibis is their expressiveness. For example, when chibi characters are afraid, their faces melt into fear! When they are embarrassed, their faces go red and smoke comes out of their ears. And when they're sad, water pours out of their eyes like waterfalls. They are essentially the Looney Tunes of the manga world—Looney Tunes on Red Bull!

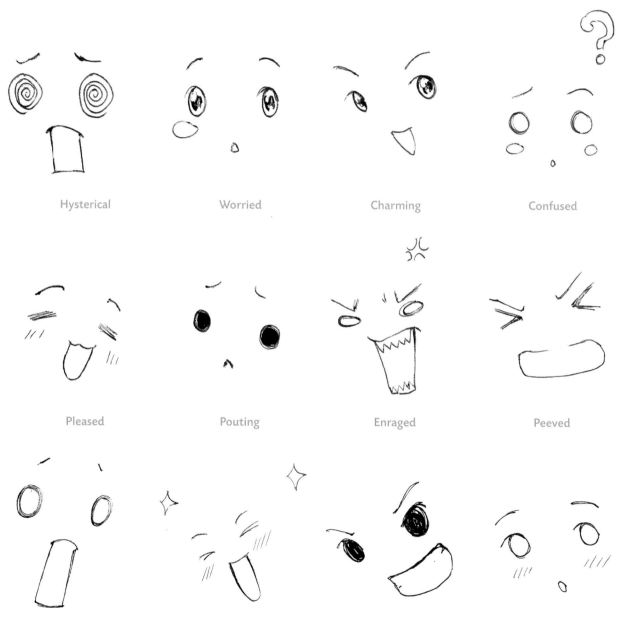

Sleepy

Hysterical

Worried

Charming

Confused

Pleased

Pouting

Enraged

Peeved

"Holy crap!"

"OMG! OMG!"

Evilly Determined

Embarrassed

"Listen to me!"

Happy Happy Joy

Grieving

Shocked

Cynical

"NO!!!!!!"

Pleading

Crying

Cute Laughter

Scared to Death!

The Crazy Eye

Yawning

137

A
DIFFERENT
KETTLE
OF FISH

DRAWING ANIMALS

I'm known for my Helmetgirls and for their animal friends.
Animals illustrate the inner feelings of my characters. A caged
bird can symbolize entrapment or a longing for freedom. A snake
around a girl's head shows her devious side. In manga, characters
often have an animal companion with them. The same goes for
villains; being bad is always more fun if you have an animal companion along for the ride, be it an evil cat or fire-breathing dragon.

In this chapter you are going to learn to create your own animal characters. The steps for animals are similar to those for creating human characters, so this should be a snap. Okay, let's jump
into the animal kingdom!

KITTEN

When you are drawing kittens, it's all about the squish factor. You want them to look as cute as possible, so we are going to be using lots of balloon shapes in this drawing. At the beginning stages, it might even help to think of the kitten as a balloon animal.

STEP 1 Start by drawing a giant circle for the head and an even bigger circle for the body. For the front legs, draw a pair of cylinders with squarish shapes at the bases for paws. The near front leg will extend farther down. For the near hind leg, make two egg shapes, overlapping at an angle. And since all we can see of the far hind leg is the paw, draw another, smaller egg shape right underneath the kitten's tummy. Now make little circles for the eyes and triangles for the ears—both the eye and the ear on the far side of the head should be a little smaller. Finally, draw a skinny triangle with a slight curve to it for the tail.

STEP 2 Give the little guy a small circle for the nose at about five o'clock (if the kitten's head were a clock). Draw a bigger circle to the left of it and then another, even bigger circle to the left that just barely touches the left eye and extends almost up to the left ear. Now add little circles for the kitten's claws on each of his paws.

STEP 3 Now it's time to add the fluff that makes kittens so snuggly. Using jagged, almost scribbly lines, retrace the outline of his form, making the scruff especially exaggerated on the top of his head, back, chest, and tummy. Soften the angles of the points of his tail and his ears. Now draw a little arch on the inside of his ear on the near side. I decided to make his ear on the far side bigger, so I drew another, bigger triangle. Connect the eyes to the nose with two small lines. Finally, make a little eyelid across the top of the near eye and two little vertical lines above and between the two eyes.

STEP 4 For your black line, start with the face by filling in the eyes and adding definition and shadows to the ears. Make thin, downward-sweeping lines from each cheek for the whiskers; then make a shadow below his near cheek to indicate his neck. Now go over the rest of your jagged lines for the fur around the body, and make even more little notches wherever you like—on the legs, the tail, the cheeks. There's no such thing as too much fluff!

STEP 5 Erase your blue lines, and you've got a cute, slightly mischievous kitten! Now, where's that ball of string?

STEP 6 As you can see here, I didn't stop at erasing my pencil lines. I decided to give our kitty some dark fur by filling in large patches around his head, body, and tail. If you choose to do the same, just remember to make your pen strokes go in the same direction as the fur—slightly up and to the left for the fur on his back, straight down for his near front leg, etc.

TIGER

To quote Tigger the tiger from *Winnie the Pooh*, "The wonderful thing about tiggers is tiggers are wonderful things." Whether they are hanging out with bears and eating honey or hunting jungle boys, tigers are some of the most powerful creatures in the animal kingdom, and some of the coolest to draw. Like me, you may want to use some real-life pictures of tigers for reference when drawing them.

STEP 1 Always start with a circle for the head; then draw a line that will represent the spine and the tail, as if the tail is an extension of the spine. This tiger will be lying down, so his front legs will hang down in front of him, while his hind legs will be slightly folded.

STEP 2 Connect his back hind leg to his right front leg. Define the upper hind leg by drawing a soft triangle with a skinny oval beneath it. Draw a diagonal line parallel to the upper hind leg for the lower hind leg. Make cylinders for the front legs, with ovals at their bases for paws, and make a curved line between the tops of the two legs to define the chest. At the head, draw a circle that overlaps half with the face and half with the chest for the snout. Draw in crosshairs on the face and add little circles on top of the head for ears. Finish by drawing a tiny circle at the tip of the tiger's tail; this will later show you how thick it's going to be.

STEP 3 Begin by filling in the tail; it will be thicker at the base than at the tip. Draw in the eyes and the nose, using the crosshairs as your guide. Make a line down the center of the chest, and define his legs, paws, and overall muscular shape. Then, draw in the stripes and show the edges of the fur by making the lines around the body more coarse. When you are drawing anything with fur, stay away from using straight lines; ripple the edges of your line work, especially at the jowls and the chest area, where you are going to want to make the fur longer and more fluffy.

STEP 4 Continue drawing in the tiger's stripes. Fill in the eyes, remembering that tigers' eyes are just pupils—no highlights. Further define the tiger's wide-set eyes by adding what I like to think of as Goth makeup around them.

STEP 5 Moving to your black pen, go over your pencil lines and make sure to fill in the stripes nice and dark to make them pop dramatically on the tiger's fur.

STEP 6 Lose those pencil lines, and admire your enchanting tiger king . . . Or is it a tiger queen?

I don't usually like to explain the
meanings behind my paintings, but I'm
going to let you in on one of them.
**This painting, *Utta*, is about
the sexiest part of a woman's
body: her brain!** And that's why
the snake, the sexiest creature in nature,
is resting on her head.

BABY HIPPO

In manga, you can be photorealistic with your animals, or you can go the opposite direction and make them teddy-bearish, soft and huggable. This baby hippo is the latter—he's about as roly-poly as you can get!

STEP 1 Start by drawing a circle for the head, a horizontal oval on top of it for the snout, and a rounded, triangular shape for the body (which is not directly below the head because he is leaning to his right). Place two little cylinders in the middle of his body for his front legs. For the back legs, make egg shapes on either side of the base of the body. Finally, don't forget to make little circles on top of the head for the ears.

STEP 2 Give your baby hippo some eyes right on top of his snout. Draw two circles, touching each other, just inside the oval for the snout. Give him small circles for hands. Layer little egg shapes for the lower parts of his legs and feet.

STEP 3 Square off the top of the head. Add little half-circles inside the ears. At the top of the connected circles and beneath the eyes, add two tiny, filled-in ovals for nostrils. Draw in the front legs and paws. Define his front and back legs, making little lines for rolls of chub and making toelike shapes at their bases. Finally, go back to the face and add freckles and whiskers.

STEP 4 Black line time! Go over all of your pencil lines, and add some details, like small shadows in the ears, lines for creases at the neck, teeny tiny toenails, and a belly button! A trick to making our baby hippo even cuter is to fill in the eyes almost completely, leaving one small dot of white.

STEP 5 Erase your pencil lines. Be honest—have you ever seen anything cuter than this little munchkin?!

LOVEBIRD

Call me a romantic, but I love lovebirds. They often appear in my Helmet Girl drawings, and if I could, I would love to make them appear in my apartment; however, I don't think my dog, Loki, would love them. Remember our kitty we drew back on page 140? Well, even though this lovebird has feathers, not fur, it's similarly round and fluffy, so we're going to make many of our initial shapes balloonlike here, too.

STEP 1 Draw a circle for the head, an upside-down teardrop shape for the beak, and one oval on each side of the beak. At about eight o'clock (if the bird's head were a clock), place a small circle for the eye. (Only one eye is going to be visible, since the head is turned and nestled into the body.) For the body, draw a much bigger, horizontal oval on a slight angle. For the wing, make a smaller horizontal, angled oval with a triangle extending from it. Make another triangle beneath it, pointing down, for the tail. At the base of the body, place a very small circle for the beginning of the foot.

STEP 2 Connect all the shapes with rounded lines. Define the chest by curving the line in and down toward the foot. Give the foot one sharp claw. For the wing on the far side of the bird's body, which we can barely see, add part of a small triangle behind the near wing. Add some notches to the near wing and tail, and start scribbling in some jagged lines for fluffy feathers.

STEP 3 With feathers, choose your battles; don't define every single feather. Focus on the fluffiest parts of the bird, which, here, are the chest, back, tail, and wing. You're going to want to add in some individual wing definition, especially at the tips of the wing and the tail.

STEP 4 With your black line, go over the outline of the bird, and then move into the detail work on the eye, wings, tail, and many layers of feathers. Give him a bit of shadow underneath the chin, and blacken the claw. I chose to fill in the tips of the wings, but you certainly don't have to. Birds come in a variety of colors and patterns, so just have fun!

STEP 5 Erase your pencil lines. Now that we've freed our lovebird from the pencil lines, do you think he'll sing us a love song?

OCTOPUS

Out of all the creatures under the sea, the octopus, I believe, is the most spectacular. It's graceful and deadly at the same time. Trust me, the octopus may look intimidating to draw, with all its tentacles, but I'll walk you through it.

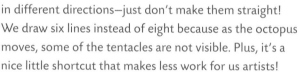

STEP 1 Start with three overlapping shapes: a football-shaped mass, a cylinder-shaped mass with an oval at the end, and an irregular trapezoid.

STEP 2 From the trapezoid, draw six curvy lines going in different directions—just don't make them straight! We draw six lines instead of eight because as the octopus moves, some of the tentacles are not visible. Plus, it's a nice little shortcut that makes less work for us artists!

STEP 3 Fill out the tentacles by drawing lines parallel to each of the original six lines you drew in the last step. At the end of each tentacle, the two lines taper to meet each other—like a lock of hair. Inside the circle that's part of the cylinder that you drew in the first step, draw a smaller circle for the eye.

STEP 4 Now come the dreaded suction cups. Depending on how the tentacle is positioned, the number of suction cups needed will vary. I make suction cups by drawing little donuts on the tentacles. For the final touch at this stage in the drawing, draw a very small little slit in the circle for the eye.

It is important to note that when the suction cups get closer to the tip of the tentacle, they get smaller. No, I am not an octopus who just happens to be missing his tentacles!

STEP 5 Once again, begin your black line at the top layer of your octopus, and work your way down to the tips of the tentacles.

STEP 6 Erase those blue lines, and check out your curly, swirly sea creature!

THE UNUSUAL SUSPECTS

CREATING CHARACTERS

You've made it to my favorite chapter! Here, I am going to give you guys a peek into my own creative process and tell the story behind some of my characters' creations. I'm also going to give you some tips on the tricks I use when developing a character.

Now, this chapter is not for the faint of heart; the drawings aren't really step-by-steps, so try not to get overwhelmed by the details. Remember, as manga artists we get to play the mad Dr. Frankenstein again and again, digging up body parts from the graveyards of our minds and connecting them to different gadgets and gizmos. If at first the creature doesn't fully come to life, that's okay! It's part of the process. So just keep digging and creating!

TANPOPO

My Tanpopo character—her name is the Japanese word for "dandelion"—is my passion project. The idea for the story and character came to me after I watched *Faust*, an opera based on a play by Goethe. In the story, Faust makes a pact with the devil. In my graphic novel *Tanpopo*, a girl without emotion trades her soul for the ability to experience feelings. I love this character and the journey she takes. As you guys know, I'm really passionate about expressing a range of different emotions with my characters. With Tanpopo, I get to illustrate what it would be like to experience these emotions for the first time.

The illustration we're drawing here is of Tanpopo right before she breaks free of the machine that has imprisoned her. She is just sitting, blank and emotionless. But not to fear, she livens up later in the story!

Notice how Tanpopo's head is looking downward, so her neck will be hidden. Also, in this seated position, her shoulders are positioned high up, next to the head. The bottom circle is going to represent the width of her thighs, so I don't make the circle too small.

I begin by outlining the chest, shoulders, and arms, as well as her eyes and her left ear. Then, following the contour of the lower circle, I define her legs, starting with the one closest to us and curving the thigh in toward the calves and feet. Finally, I place shapes for Poodle Kuro behind Tanpopo's arm and begin to shape her signature wings.

Jumping ahead to the black lines, notice how I define Tanpopo's clothing by draping the end of her long tank top across her hips and by giving her a pair of shorts underneath. I start my black line at her hair, then work down to her wings, and then to the rest of her body. I tend to leave the feet for last because, honestly, for me they are the hardest part.

Before erasing the blue lines, I color in little Poodle Kuro, leaving his mask white, and also fill in the tips of Tanpopo's wings, her shorts, and the stars on her shirt.

This is the first time that I have colored Tanpopo in a realistic color palette; usually she appears in a more abstract way. In this colorization, we can actually see that she has white hair and yellow eyes. This is in reference to her Japanese name, Tanpopo, which means "dandelion."

RED RIDING HOOD

When I was young, "Little Red Riding Hood" was one of my favorite bedtime stories. It had everything I wanted in a story: adventure, horror, and great fashion! A couple of years ago my friend Bryan Talbot was doing a comic called *Fractured Fables*. He asked me to do the art for the Little Red Riding Hood story. Of course, I jumped at the chance to redesign my favorite bedtime story. In Bryan's story, Red Riding Hood was going to be a kung fu master, and the Big Bad Wolf, well, we'll be getting to him next.

    I wanted to keep her look classic; her being a kick-butt kung fu master was already very unexpected. So I presented her as a supercute little girl, with a straw basket, cute shorts, and knee-high socks.

I begin with a stick figure and then I outline the body. Next I give Red some big peepers. Note that I draw the left arm cutting across the middle of the spine. Notice that the basket curves, following the contour of the left hip.

I sketch in the clothing little by little, starting with the hood and moving down to the shoes. I add a bow at the neck, letting the ribbons fall down over and under her left arm. I go into crazy detail here!

As always, when adding my black line, I begin at the top, tracing the hood and Red's hair. I give the basket some texture by using a crisscross pattern.

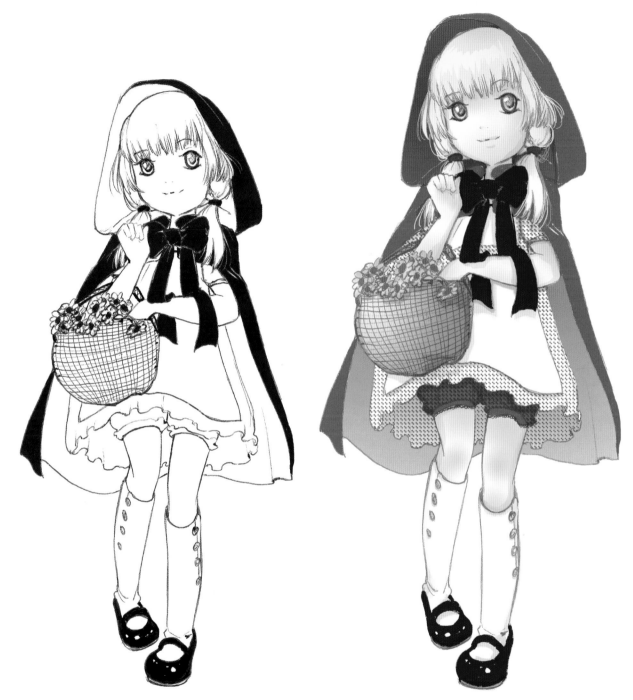

And just like that, Little Red is ready to kick some butt!

Here I'm keeping it classic with our colors: red cloak and blond hair.

BIG BAD WOLF

Bryan's description of the Big Bad Wolf was outstanding. He wanted him to be a down-on-his-luck drifter, with a belly that was distended from lack of food, and he wanted him dressed in a three-piece suit that was too small for him! I wanted to emphasize his animal characteristics by elongating his paws and giving him huge eyes. I also added some scruff and fluff to him, as well as some tears and rips to his suit, in order to rustle up some sympathy from the reader. You almost want this poor, poor wolf to gobble up Red and finally catch a break.

I start with an oval instead of a circle for the head. I draw the arms slightly longer than normal human arms so that even when they are bent, the hands rest below the waist. Note that I give him "dog-legged" hind legs to create the humanoid look I'm going for. When drawing this character, I find it helpful to look at pictures of wolves for reference.

I give our character some long ears and a long snout, which starts at the intersection of the crosshairs and curves around to end at the neck. I define the rest of the body, making sure to elongate his paws and exaggerate the size of his feet. Oh, and, of course, I add a little potbelly!

For the clothing, I start with the top layer and add the clothes piece by piece. The wolf suit is a little elaborate, but it's really just the sum of its parts, so break it down. I add a touch of class by giving him some pinstripes, and I add a couple of patches and rips to make him look downtrodden.

As I do my black lines, I fill in a little patch in the Wolf's left ear, giving it some depth. I also color in the inside portion of the jacket that is visible above his right hand.

In the Big Bad Wolf's coloring, I decided to use grays instead of whites to really emphasize his poor, pathetic look.

I'll huff, and I'll puff, and I'll spray ink all over you! When a character is a humanoid animal and is shown standing up, you'll have to adapt the animal's normal limbs to the standing human form—just like Camilla did with the Big Bad Wolf.

People often ask, **"Camilla, why don't you paint guys?"** Well, honestly, I love painting guys, but every time I start, my hand seems to take over and he ends up looking a lot like a girl. **It's like my hand has a mind of its own!**

Camilla d'Errico

HEADPHONE GIRL

I grew up during the days of the mixtape. I probably crafted more than a hundred of them during lazy Thursday afternoons, all in preparation for the weekend. This next character, the headphone girl, is not listening to a sweet mixtape on her yellow Sony Walkman. Instead, she is embracing the future and chilling in her room, listening to some J-pop on her iPhone. Also, this girl will not be wearing a schoolgirl's outfit; headphones are usually worn by the punk rock girls of manga. Remember, no tie, just attitude.

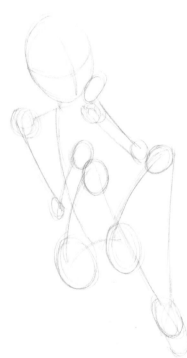

Because she is sitting, I drew this girl with bent knees, being careful not to squeeze the legs too close together; note the thickness of the shin, calf, and thigh.

After getting her framework down, I added the headphones. I wanted to keep them larger than normal: the bigger, the more fun.

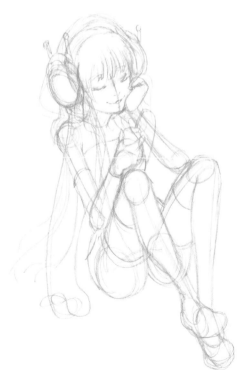

The cord to her phone moves from the bottom of the head-phones to the floor, and back up to the iPhone.

I started adding black line at the face. Moving on to the headphones, I drew in some extra details and shading. Her socks were a little tricky. Because they wrap around her legs, their pattern changes slightly, due to perspective.

Headphone girl, complete!

BURN

I love my microwave, but I don't trust it. I'm sure that given the chance, it would microwave *me* for making it pop all those bags of popcorn. My comic *Burn* is about exactly that—how the machines we humans create could turn on us. Machines revolt against us in an all-out war. Burn was a human boy until a metallic angel of death named Shoftiel fused onto him. Now Burn must fight this machine for control of his own mind and body, while the battle rages on around him.

When I designed this character, I wanted to get away from what was currently being done with robots in Japanese manga. The *Gundam* and *Robotech* series are the *Star Wars* of the manga world, and their characters and mecha are drawn with very clean, straight lines and hard edges. I did the complete opposite with *Burn*, making everything curved and jagged, so that the mecha would feel almost organic and reflect the humanity that still existed in Burn. When you are creating your own characters, try to design each one in a way that presents his or her internal conflict or conveys whatever it is that sets your character apart.

Notice that this character's robotic arm is longer than his human arm. I make sure I draw the circle representing his robotic hand larger than the circle for the other, normal hand. I continue by drawing the middle joints and the metal plating on the shoulder. To create depth in his shoulder piece, I draw a circle and then a smaller circle inside of it.

I draw in the detail work, which includes the metallic arm as well as the cyborg part of his face. I use the curve of the cheek to define the metal aspect of his face; this helps connect his human and robot sides seamlessly.

With cyborgs it is extremely important to start the black line at the top layer, with the parts that are perceived as closest to us on the page. This helps ensure that all the pieces are connected.

And here you have him—Burn. Easy as ice cream! Wait, who am I kidding? I don't even know how to make ice cream. Burn is a challenge for anyone, including myself. If you want to take a crack at creating your own Burn, I recommend you try drawing the metal parts on a separate piece of paper and then, when you're ready, fuse the metal to flesh.

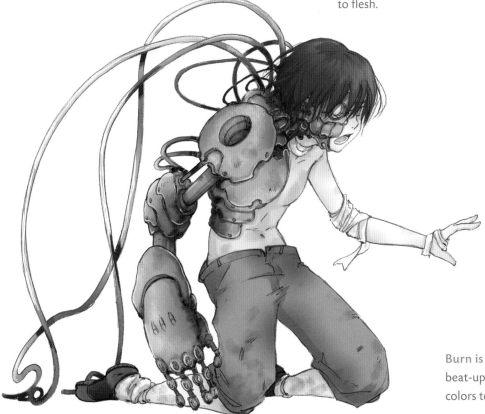

Burn is having a bad day! He is very beat-up in this pose, so I use muted colors to reflect his battle damage.

HELMETGIRL

Helmetgirls are among my signature creations. They stem from my love of steam-punk and of anything industrial or mechanical. When I was just a fledgling artist, I used to practice drawing steampunk girls, and I would always give each girl a pair of goggles. Slowly, the goggles became more detailed and larger in size, until finally the goggles changed into full machines sitting on top of my characters' heads. That juxtaposition of having an innocent-looking girl with a huge industrial machine rest-ing on her head was something I fell in love with. In the beginning, the Helmetgirls were rough, dirty, and hard, like the machines they wore. But as I grew as an artist, the girls changed into cleaner, daintier characters. To this day, Helmetgirls are my favorite characters to draw—well, aside from maybe some chibi dragons!

I start with your basic female form. The wind pushes our girl forward, almost picking her up off her feet. For the helmet, I draw two circles on each side of her face to define the helmet's size.

After drawing her outfit—keeping the lines curved and flowing naturally—I add some detail on the clothing and helmet. When draw-ing helmets, it's best to start with the front, working your way up and around to the sides. I draw in some cracks to give a bit of texture.

With my black line, I start with the face and work my way up. I add some filigree to her dress and some shad-ows to the helmet's nuts and bolts.

166

And we're done! One of my favorite things about drawing Helmetgirls is that the helmets are always different. Try creating your own helmet design—anything goes!

Any time I color a character, I like to build a cohesive palette around a main color. In this case, it's blue.

BILLY BOOM BOOM

Parrots, peg legs, and eye patches; who doesn't love pirates, especially the Sky Pirates of Neo Terra? This adventure comic is a five-issue series about a young glidewing pilot, Billy Boom Boom, and his adventures to save Neo Terra from the clutches of the Witch Queen and her minions. Billy is a young rogue and a very skilled pilot in a postapocalyptic world from the future. A good point to remember when you're designing your character is to always take heed of the story's setting and let it influence your design. Also, when you are designing your characters, make sure you have specific features that are unique to that character. Billy, for example, is covered in bandages, showing that he is always hurting himself and getting into trouble; thus his name—Billy Boom Boom.

Billy is very rambunctious, so I wanted his expression to be spirited and filled with energy. Thus, I kept the mouth open and slightly curved the eyebrows.

I started going over the lines in his face, hair, and chest in black pen. He also wears goggles and a cast on his leg. These elements illustrate his vulnerability, as well as accentuate his courage and drive.

Billy is ready for more explosive
adventures!

TINKERBELL

Tinkerbell is my all-time favorite Disney character! She has spunk, pep, and a really great pout. Now it's time I show you how I've adapted a really recognizable character like Tink. Before I begin an adaptation of any character, I first make a list of all the features that make her unique—such as her slippers, her dress, and her shape—and a list of the elements of my own style I can give the character without losing that recognizability. For example, I wanted to modernize Tinkerbell's classic hairstyle and give her my signature sexy lips.

© Disney

© Disney

© Disney

I make her a little bit flirty by slightly tilting her head toward her raised shoulder, and I put her hands together at her knees, which will be slightly bent. Notice that her proportions are slightly different from those of other characters I draw. Tinkerbell has a big booty and a little top, so her hips are going to be wider than her shoulders. I fill in her form, beginning with her hair, followed by her elfish ears, which are pointed. I make her arms quite small and dainty, and her thighs thicker than her calves.

I add in the details, starting with her face and then moving to her wings. Don't forget to add those little pom-poms to her shoes.

170

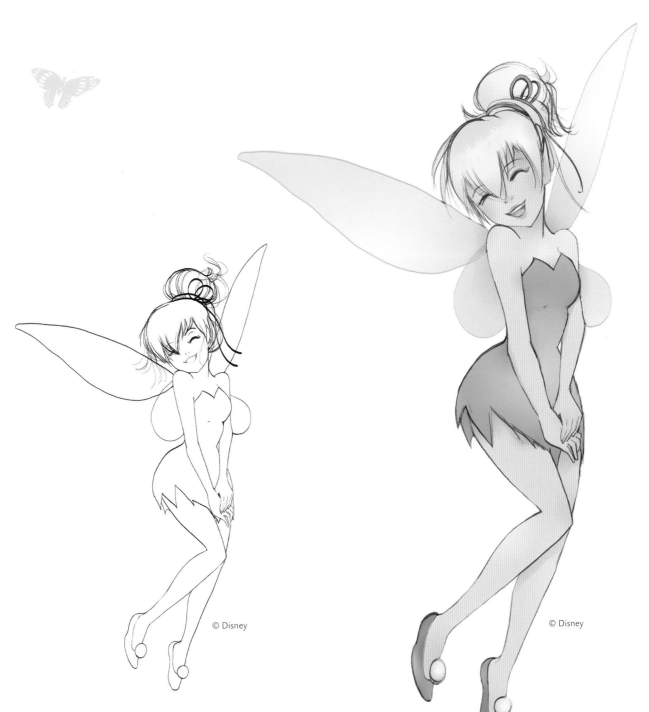

© Disney

© Disney

Skipping to my black lines, I bring in my signature style
with Tinkerbell's hair. I am known for my complex hairstyles, so I decided to give her a "Camilla updo" and then
some "Camilla eyelashes." So, as you can see, the design is
very "classic Disney" but with just a touch of me.

WHAT'S YOUR STORY?

CREATING PANELS, LAYOUTS, AND COVERS

Manga artists in Japan are a hardworking bunch. Not only do they draw their comics, but they also write them. Here in the West, artists usually work with writers when crafting the American comics we know and love. I myself work with a lot of different writers, bringing their stories to life. In this chapter, we'll look at the steps involved in paneling a manga script, from initial layout to final black line. Then it will be your turn to create a story from your own characters!

The manga we will be working on is based on the childhood of Renaissance artist Leonardo da Vinci. It was written by Stephen W. Martin, one of my colleagues in the comic world—and my coauthor for this book! Stephen's script will be the basis for our work. Just remember, Stephen and I need that final black line on my desk by eight A.M. tomorrow! Don't you love deadlines?

READING THE SCRIPT

A manga script is broken down into individual panels, and the writer describes what is happening on each panel of each page. Usually, a page is broken down into four to six panels, but in some cases, a panel can fill a whole page—we call this a splash page. I always print out a copy of the script rather than reading it on my computer screen because I like to quickly sketch my ideas in the pages' margins. After reading the written description of a panel, I draw the very first thing I see in my head. I believe it is extremely important to get these initial ideas down. You may have a flash of genius when you first read something, so make sure you draw it quickly before it vanishes into thin air.

EXT - COUNTRY SIDE - VINCI, ITALY - MID MORNING.

Page 1 Panel 1

Caption box - Vinci, Tuscany, 1456, Italy

Medium Full

A frightened young boy (9) wearing a patchwork jump suit stands on the edge of a tree. Resting on his head is a shiny steel helmet busting with gears and knobs, made out of kitchen utensils, wood and plaster. The helmet connects to a large set of poorly constructed wooden wings strapped to his arms. On the ground looking up eagerly an younger girl, Marinella (7), hands in the air, is egging the other to jump.

                    LEONARDO
        I don't know about this, maybe we
        should test it on my dog first...

                    MARINELLA
        Just jump! I'm sure it will work!

Panel 2 -

Medium Close on Leonardo.

Leonardo looks down at the ground below, his hands/wings are out bracing/balancing himself. He is quite scared but trying not to show it...

                    LEONARDO
        No, I think my design has some
        flaws, I didn't account for the
        wind today...I'd better come
        down...

Panel 3 -

Medium Close on Marinella.

Marinella looking up at Leonardo, begins to shake the oak tree.

                    MARINELLA
        Just jump, it will
        work...probably.

Panel 4 - Medium close

SMACK! A acorn hits Leonardo square in the face.

Panel 5 -Wide

                                        (CONTINUED)

DOING THUMBNAILS

The thumbnail is essentially a rough draft: It's what you'll show the writer and the editor so they can see your plan for bringing each page of script to life. The thumbnail drawings are rough sketches meant to convey what is going on in the panels, without any dialogue or narration. In this case, the page of the script that I am working on is broken down into five panels. To do my thumbnail sketches, I take the very rough doodles I made in the margins of the script and redraw them in the panels. Each panel should have a focal point, or center of interest, that grabs the reader's eye. I try not to make my pages too busy, which can distract the reader's attention away from what is important.

When Western people read comic books, they read from left to right across the panels, then cut down and start again, their eyes moving from left to right. In other words, our eyes move in a Z-shaped pattern. It is crucial that you follow this pattern when you are drawing panels, or your readers are going to get downright confused.

MAKING A STYLE SHEET

A style sheet is a collection of drawings of your characters wearing various styles of clothing. After I've read the script and done some quick sketches, the research for the style sheet begins. I search the Internet to find examples of period clothing that is relevant to the story, which, in this case, is set in Renaissance Italy. Once I have sufficient inspiration, I start my style sheet. I may draw four or five different versions of my character, in various styles of clothing, until I find one that really hits. In general, I like to give clothing a more modern look by mixing old pieces, like a rope belt, with modern ones, like short pants.

Once you have decided on your character's clothing, make sure you draw the character from a bunch of different angles so that nothing catches you by surprise as you begin to draw the story. It is a good idea to draw your characters with a few different expressions, too; that will also help as you move forward. Finally, before moving on to the next step, it is important to give your main characters some distinguishing features to separate them from your supporting cast. In this case, I decided to give our female lead, Marinella, some braids across the top of her head, and to give our protagonist, Leo, little tufts of hair moving in every direction—my take on a Renaissance-style shaggy look.

BREAKING INTO THE BIZ

Breaking into the comic industry is not easy. I started out on my own journey in 1998, when I attended my first comic book convention. Before traveling to the convention, I had taken the time to create a portfolio of drawings of various manga and American comic characters, but drawn in my own style. At that comic con, when I first sat down with an editor, I was extremely nervous and shy, but it was a tremendously valuable experience. Even though I did not get a job from that meeting, I learned a lot about what editors are looking for and about the kinds of mistakes I was making in my designs and characters. I promised myself that I would continue to improve my drawings and go back every year for more feedback, and never give up—no matter how long it was going to take.

Whether you have aspirations to be a published comic book artist or you just like to draw, think about starting to build your own portfolio and, if you have the opportunity, about attending a comic con in your area. I think you'll find it an amazing experience.

FINISHING PANELS

After everyone—the writer, the editor, and you, the artist—agrees on the layouts created in the thumbnail stage, it's time to move to the final version of the panels. At this point, I blue-line my 11 x 17–inch sheet of paper, using my thumbnails as a reference. It's important to remember to leave enough room for the dialogue balloons in the panels. I have learned that the hard way!

I always try to keep my characters active, doing something in each panel. This approach keeps up the pace and makes the art lively. Notice here that I have Leo holding on to the tree in the first panel, but in the second he has let go and is falling forward. This slight movement keeps the scene from becoming stagnant. Movement can even be achieved with background elements—birds flying in the air or little specks of dust or dirt moving beneath a character's feet. Keep in mind that when you are drawing action, be it a car chase or a space battle, you always want the action to follow the left-to-right Z-pattern eye movement that Inku described on page 175. That helps the reader's eye follow the action and move smoothly across the page.

Here are a few blank panels I've created as examples.
When doing your own manga stories, start from scratch,
designing your own style sheet and then sketching out
your thumbnails. Then take out that blue pencil and try
drawing panels for one of your story ideas.

The reason Camilla uses 11 x 17-inch paper is that all
the panels she draws will be scanned and placed in
Photoshop for coloring. After the coloring, the panels
are shrunk down to manga size. Starting in the larger
format makes it easier to draw patterns and other
details, which would be almost impossible to do if we
started out in the standard, smaller manga format.

This is a panel I created for a story that appeared in *Womanthology.*

Quiet
untroubled
soul.
awake. awake!!?

This is a splash
page from my graphic
novel *Tanpopo*.

DRAWING A MANGA COVER

I equate creating a manga cover image to going all-in at the poker table. This is where a manga artist showcases everything she's got in her drawing arsenal. When doing covers, I go for broke and hold nothing back. Just as a movie poster's job is to get people excited about seeing the movie, a manga cover's purpose is to get people to want to read the comic.

Before I start drawing a cover, I decide on the setting. I like to play with the themes of the book, placing my main characters in an environment similar to what they encounter in the story—but more elaborate, more dangerous, and more glamorous. Cover art is a special art form, and there is one illustrator, James Jean, who has taken the art to an incredible level, winning all sorts of awards and accolades for his work. If you're not familiar with Jean's work, I recommend you check out his cover work on *Fables*. I'm always amazed at the way his covers sum up the essence of each comic with just a single powerful image.

Now I'd like to invite you along with me as I design the cover image for the fifth issue of *Tanpopo*, for which I took inspiration from the HBO show *Game of Thrones*. I wanted the cover to be my take on the classic image of the iron throne in the show. Also, in the comic I use passages from Edgar Allan Poe's "The Masque of the Red Death," a creepy short story that features a prince who's trying to escape a deadly plague and hosts a masquerade ball. I'm going to give the cover a masquerade theme, with Tanpopo at the center, sitting on a throne, looking spicy-cute and surrounded by a mess of masks and multiple variations of the mascot Kuro—including Poodle Kuro, Fox Kuro, a giant Buddha Kuro, and a variation I call Bubba Kuro.

First I outline Tanpopo positioned on the throne. If I'm having trouble, I look at myself in the same pose in a mirror to understand the position of the body. In this pose, the hips are covered by the legs. Her left hand will clutch a piece of fabric to her chest and her right hand will rest on what will become the giant Buddha Kuro. Finally, I sketch in the throne.

Because this cover will have a lot of detail, I want to first establish Tanpopo, the focal point, before moving on to the smaller details. I draw her hair and then the rest of her body, before moving on to defining the fabric in her hand and the way it falls.

I now add more details to the throne, giving it texture and filigree. I draw the Poodle Kuro at the top of the throne, then the Fox Kuro at the bottom, along with our little friend Inku. Next, I add some detail to the masks that surround our characters and throne, as well as some feathers at the base of the throne. I keep adding detail to the throne, as well as to the toys and masks beneath it.

Using my black pen, I start drawing Tanpopo's hair and then move on to the fabric cascading from her hand. This fabric will cover part of the chair and some of Tanpopo herself. I continue drawing the rest of the characters with my black line, coloring in Fox Kuro, Inku, and Bubba Kuro's mask.

Now I fill in the enormous Buddha Kuro with black ink. Note that placing a large single character on the right balances the assortment of small characters on the left and keeps the image from feeling too crowded. It is important to allow the eye to rest. Finally, I continue to add detail to the throne—as you can see, I go a little crazy with the detail here!

And there you have it, the finished drawing for the cover of *Tanpopo* number 5! On the opposite page, the drawing is in color.

TWO PENS ARE BETTER THAN ONE

COLLABORATION TIME!

I love team-ups in comics. What's better than Batman fighting bad guys? Batman *and* Superman fighting bad guys! In that spirit, we are going to work together to complete two original pieces of manga art. First, I'm going to draw the Helmetgirl, and I want you to draw her helmet and mascot companion. Then, I'll draw the helmet, and you'll draw the girl. Use the skills you have obtained from other chapters in this book to create something truly yours. The sky's the limit, so use your imagination!

And once you have finished either or both of these beautiful pieces, I would love to see them! Scan them and send them to info@camilladerrico.com. I'll be refreshing my inbox every hour on the hour, so don't forget or I'll send Inku after you!

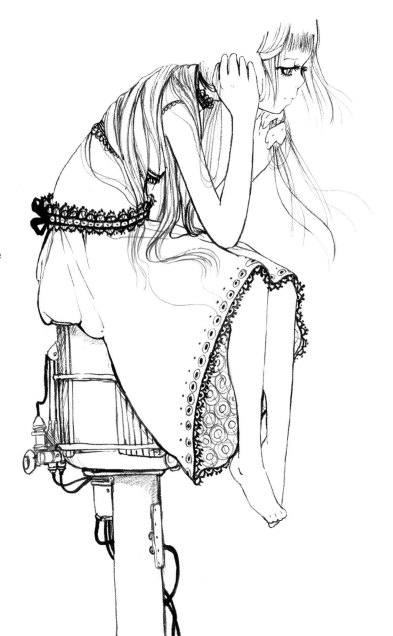

Draw the Helmet and Animal

It's time to get in touch with your wild side. Before starting to draw this girl's helmet and animal, take a moment to study the young lady. What do you think she's feeling? And what emotions do *you* feel when you look into her eyes? What kind of design will represent this character's emotion? I often use octopi to show that a character is trying to hide or bury her emotions. Lovebirds reflect a flirty playfulness, and deer often convey a tone of sadness or innocence. If drawn with a lot of hard-edged lines, the helmet can show anger or remorse. A softer style, with some playful gadgets, can be flirty or whimsical in tone. A sleek design might give the girl an even sexier look. Of course, you could always throw all that metaphor stuff out the window and just draw something kick-butt!

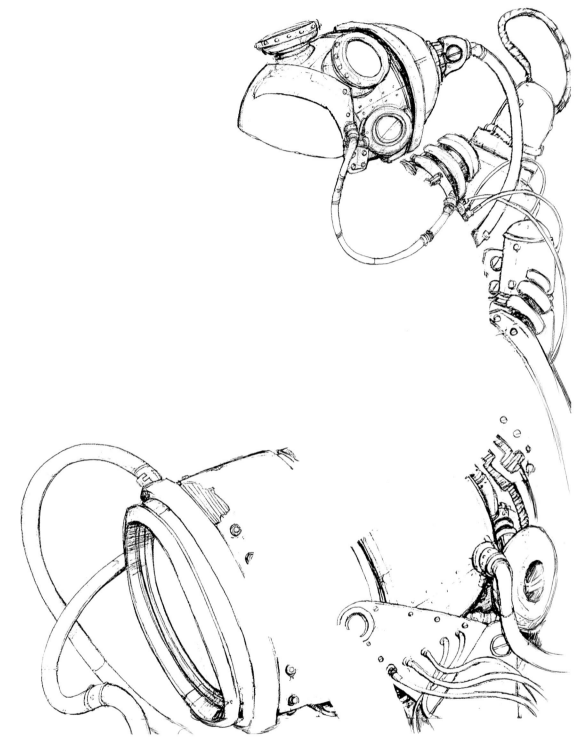

Draw the Girl

You're right on time! I just put the final touches on this helmet. Now it's up to you to finish the image by drawing the character. But before you get started, again take a moment to think about the emotion of your character and how you can show or reflect that emotion in her body language. Don't worry if you need to take a few quick looks back at some of the step-by-steps—I won't tell Inku! Just have fun and experiment.

AFTERWORD

You did it! Congratulations on making it to the end. I'm so proud and honored to have taken this journey with you. It's not easy being an artist, and some of those chapters were quite challenging, but you stuck with it and rocked it out! Now you're probably asking yourself, "Where do I go from here?" The answer is right in front of you. Flip back to your favorite chapters and do some of the drawings again! This time, try out a different style or an idea that you had, or try developing a single character through each stage of the book. The bottom line is that you should keep drawing and creating every day! For me, drawing is a lot like kung fu: By practicing every day, I slowly develop and increase my skill. After enough time, your hand will become a deadly manga-drawing weapon!

Finishing this book is just the beginning. Try taking a class at a local community college or art school. Attend a comic con and sign up for some seminars or panel discussions on drawing manga or comic book art. Start a manga club at your school, or even spend some time each day with a pencil and sketchbook, sitting on a park bench or in a coffee shop. Sketch people that you see. Then sketch them again in chibi form! Never stop learning, and never stop drawing!

Finally, I'm glad to have met another person who shares my love for the manga art form. So if you ever see me walking down the street or sitting at my table at a comic convention, stop by and say hello, give me a high five, and show me your art! I can't wait to see it!

Way to go! You made it through the entire book—or maybe you just skipped to the end. Either way, I'm proud of you. Remember, keep practicing every day, and if you ever hit a wall, just draw me! I'm easy and extremely cute. Now can you please tell Camilla to stop hugging me?!

ILLUSTRATION CREDITS

Page 5: Pirate King from *Sky Pirates of Neo Terra,* © Fathom Interactive

Page 7: "A Red Dawn" © Kuonichi Ventures

Page 26: "Peaks of Paradise," Rena of *Sky Pirates of Neo Terra,* © Fathom Interactive

Page 52: Image © LinePro Agency

Page 92: "The Depths" © Crystal Dynamics

Pages 126–127: *Hello My Kitty Land* © Sanrio and Camilla d'Errico

Page 138: *Elephantmen* cover, Issue #29, December 2010, © Richard Starkings, Image Comics

Page 152: "Glass Butterflies," cover image of *Exploded View* comics anthology, Cloudscape Comics, 2009

Pages 168–169: Billy Boom Boom of *Sky Pirates of Neo Terra,* © Fathom Interactive

Pages 170–171: Tinkerbell © Disney

Page 172: Panel from *Sky Pirates of Neo Terra,* Issue #1 page 4, November 2010, Fathom Interactive

Page 179: Panel from *Womanthology:* Heroic, d'Errico, DeLiz, and Doyle, Idea & Design Works, March 2012

Page 180: Splash page from *Tanpopo* graphic novel: d'Errico Studios, Ltd., December 2009

INDEX